LANDS AND PEOPLES

LANDS AND PEOPLES

GROLIER Danbury, Connecticut

EUROPE   Volume 4

CONTENTS

FLAGS OF EUROPE (continued)

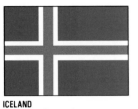

ICELAND

DENMARK

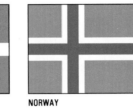

NORWAY

SWEDEN

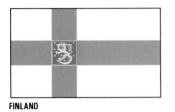

FINLAND

PORTUGAL

SPAIN

ANDORRA

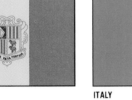

ITALY

SAN MARINO

VATICAN CITY

MALTA

GREECE

POLAND

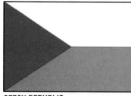

CZECH REPUBLIC

SLOVAKIA

HUNGARY

ROMANIA

BULGARIA

ALBANIA

FLAGS OF EUROPE (continued)

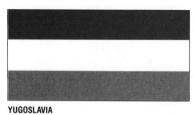

YUGOSLAVIA

SLOVENIA

CROATIA

BOSNIA AND HERZEGOVINA

MACEDONIA

ESTONIA

LATVIA

LITHUANIA

RUSSIA

UKRAINE

BELARUS

MOLDOVA

A church at Thingvellir, a plain south of Iceland's capital Reykjavik.

ICELAND

In A.D. 874 two Norwegian Vikings who had been exiled from their mother country set sail with their families, livestock, slaves, and other possessions to seek a new life. In their open Viking ships they sailed over 600 miles (1,000 kilometers) across the North Atlantic to the island of Iceland. They had come to a land where they would have to overcome great hardships in order to survive. Then, as now, with its vast areas of volcanoes and lava deserts, glaciers and ice fields, Iceland was a land of fire and ice. Today's Iceland is a land where elements of the Vikings' spirit and ingenuity have become part of the living present and where the past and the future exist side by side.

ECONOMY AND WAY OF LIFE

Iceland is located in the middle of one of the world's richest fishing grounds, and fish have always been the mainstay of the country's economy. Today, fish and fish products account for about 70 percent of Iceland's exports. The annual catch of nearly 1 million tons is made up mainly of cod, capelin, and redfish. Most of the fish is salted, canned, or quick-frozen, but some is still dried on racks in the open air—a process that dates from Viking days. The air-dried fish, or stockfish, is exported to southern Europe and in large quantities to Africa, where it supplies valuable protein for the local diet.

The Icelandic fishing fleet is one of the most modern in the world. Aircraft and radar are used to spot the best locations. Their reports, radioed back to the waiting fleet, help to ensure large catches. During the summer, hundreds of students from Iceland's universities and high schools spend their vacations working in the fishing industry. The boys usually sail with the fleet while the girls help in the salting, canning, and freezing plants.

Farming in Iceland can also be traced back to Viking origins. The Vikings were a seafaring people, so they settled on the coasts, where deep bays and inlets offered the protection of good harbors. Iceland's farms also had to be near the coastal settlements, since about 75 percent of the interior is an uninhabitable region of rocks and lava formations, volcanoes, and glaciers. The main farm crop is hay, which is used to feed cattle and the long-haired Icelandic sheep. The sheep, too, came to Iceland with the Vikings, and for hundreds of years they were the Icelanders' most dependable source of food and clothing. Because of a short summer season, only fast-growing vegetables are cultivated.

The original settlers also brought with them a special breed of small horse, somewhat larger than the Shetland pony. The hardy, surefooted ponies were the main means of transportation on the island until the beginning of the 20th century. Icelandic horses are still used for recreation and during the great sheep roundups in the fall. In many parts of Iceland today, pony trails worn into the earth by centuries of hooves are still in use and can be seen crisscrossing moors and meadows.

Since the 1990s, Iceland's economy has diversified to include production of computer software and development of biotechnology. Another promising addition is the blossoming tourist trade, especially so-called ecotourism, which includes such attractions as whale-watching.

THE LAND

On November 14, 1963, near the Westman Islands (Vestmannaeyjar) off Iceland's south coast, a towering plume of steam and water shot out of the sea, raining ashes and molten lava over a wide area. As the lava flow began to cool and harden, a volcanic island was formed. It was named Surtsey, for a giant of fire in Norse mythology. Then, on January 23, 1973, calamity struck near the Helgafell volcano on the island of Heimaey, the largest in the Westman group. The volcano erupted so violently that all of the island's inhabitants had to be evacuated.

The intense volcanic activity in and around Iceland is due to its location on a great rift, or crack, in Earth's surface. Earthquakes occur so frequently that all of Iceland's houses must be built of reinforced concrete, which has a high resistance to such tremors. Sometimes it seems as if

Geysers occur throughout Iceland. The water that erupts from the geysers has been heated by volcanic rock.

Iceland must be very close to the hot, restless core of the earth. In fact, it has been estimated that one third of the earth's lava output in the last 500 years was produced in Iceland.

Iceland has over 100 volcanoes in all. Among the best-known is Hekla, 4,892 feet (1,491 m.) high, which was once thought to conceal one of the gates of hell. Another is Laki, near the vast Vatnajokull glacier in the southeast. In 1783 Laki killed 70 percent of Iceland's livestock and ruined most of its crops, causing a famine in which 20 percent of the population died of starvation. Dust clouds from Laki's eruption drifted across Europe, darkening the skies as far away as Finland and Russia.

But not everything in Iceland's volcanic environment is destructive. There is much that has a harsh, desolate beauty, like the surface of the moon. And, in many cases, the Icelanders have learned to tame the violence of nature and even to turn it to their use, as a servant.

Because Iceland's many rivers are too fast-flowing, too rocky, or too short, not one of them is navigable. Most of them provide excellent salmon and trout fishing, as well as hydroelectricity. Iceland has waterfalls by the score. There are delicate lacy ones and large powerful ones— which are also harnessed to produce hydroelectricity. Some have fanciful names, like Gullfoss ("golden falls"); others, like Godafoss ("gods' falls"), carry echoes of ancient legends as they crash down over their lava cliffs.

There are many beautiful lakes in Iceland; perhaps the best-known is Myvatn, in the northeast. The lake contains numerous small islands, and it is set among some of Iceland's most grotesque lava formations.

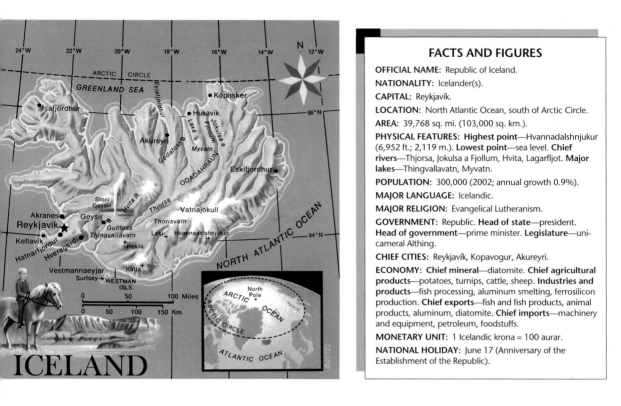

ICELAND

FACTS AND FIGURES

OFFICIAL NAME: Republic of Iceland.

NATIONALITY: Icelander(s).

CAPITAL: Reykjavík.

LOCATION: North Atlantic Ocean, south of Arctic Circle.

AREA: 39,768 sq. mi. (103,000 sq. km.).

PHYSICAL FEATURES: Highest point—Hvannadalshnjukur (6,952 ft.; 2,119 m.). **Lowest point**—sea level. **Chief rivers**—Thjorsa, Jokulsa a Fjollum, Hvita, Lagarfljot. **Major lakes**—Thingvallavatn, Myvatn.

POPULATION: 300,000 (2002; annual growth 0.9%).

MAJOR LANGUAGE: Icelandic.

MAJOR RELIGION: Evangelical Lutheranism.

GOVERNMENT: Republic. **Head of state**—president. **Head of government**—prime minister. **Legislature**—unicameral Althing.

CHIEF CITIES: Reykjavík, Kopavogur, Akureyri.

ECONOMY: Chief mineral—diatomite. **Chief agricultural products**—potatoes, turnips, cattle, sheep. **Industries and products**—fish processing, aluminum smelting, ferrosilicon production. **Chief exports**—fish and fish products, animal products, aluminum, diatomite. **Chief imports**—machinery and equipment, petroleum, foodstuffs.

MONETARY UNIT: 1 Icelandic krona = 100 aurar.

NATIONAL HOLIDAY: June 17 (Anniversary of the Establishment of the Republic).

Myvatn is also known for the large variety of birds that inhabit its shores, and for its excellent fishing. The lake has become a favorite vacation spot for Icelanders and tourists alike.

A major problem created by the environment is the island's lack of wood. The Vikings cut down the trees carelessly and at random for boats, houses, fences, and hundreds of other everyday uses. The trees were never replaced. Poor soil, glacial erosion, volcanic eruptions, climate, and grazing sheep (which eat tender tree seedlings) took care of the rest. Reforestation experiments, using Alaskan spruce and other conifers, are being carried out today in protected areas, such as Hallormsstadur in the east.

There are hot springs all over the island, which the Icelanders use in several ways. In Reykjavík, the capital, the natural hot water is piped to nearly all of the city's homes and businesses, as well as to several year-round outdoor swimming pools. Elsewhere, especially around Hveragerdi—*hver* means "hot spring" in Icelandic—the hot springs heat greenhouses, allowing the Icelanders to raise tomatoes, cucumbers, lettuce, and flowers that would otherwise have to be imported at great cost. Some oranges, pineapples, and bananas have also been grown in the greenhouses. Plans have been made to use steam from the hot springs to generate electricity, as in Italy, New Zealand, Mexico, and Japan.

Iceland is home to many geysers. The Icelandic word *geysir* means "gusher," and some 50 mi. (80 km.) east of Reykjavík, in a stone pool atop a deep natural shaft, there is Stóri Geysir, or "great gusher." Like America's Old Faithful and New Zealand's North Island geysers, Stóri Geysir erupts spectacularly. Unlike most of the others, however, it no longer erupts without help. It must be fed many shovel-loads of soap flakes to create the conditions that cause it to spout.

HISTORY

In many parts of the world, a country's history can be read in the remains that are left behind—a Gothic church here, a medieval fortress there, a baroque palace somewhere else. In Iceland there are very few such remains, and though the country is developing rapidly, the past lives on in the Icelanders themselves, because they are so intensely aware of their heritage.

The purity of their language, which is basically Old Norse, is one example of how the Icelanders keep tradition alive. If the word *geysir* was a gift from Iceland to the rest of the world, the Icelanders took almost nothing in return. This is because Icelandic does not easily borrow words from other languages, even for new and technical terms. So, today, the Icelandic word for "telephone" is *simi*, which means "thread" or "cord." The word for electricity comes from two old words that mean "amber power"; the lumbering tanks of World War II were "creeping dragons"; and today's swift jet planes are *thota,* or "darter." It is said that if the original settlers were to return to Iceland today, the country's appearance might surprise them, but they could speak to anyone and be understood.

The special history that produced today's proud, heritage-conscious Icelanders is long and filled with hardships. The Vikings came to Iceland to escape domination by the Norwegian king. Gradually a system of local *things,* or assemblies, developed, and finally, in A.D. 930, on a plain near Reykjavik, all the chieftains, with their families and retinues, met and established the Althing—an all-island assembly. Today that plain—the Thingvellir, or "plain of the thing"—is Iceland's national shrine. It is a major landmark in world history as well, for the Althing was the world's first democratic parliament.

But the Althing lacked the power to enforce the laws it made, and by 1262, struggles between rival chieftains had so divided the country that King Haakon IV of Norway found it ready to accept his royal authority. It was the end of the old republic and the end of independence. Iceland was under Norwegian domination until 1380, when the Norwegian royal house died out. Then both Norway and Iceland came under the Danish Crown. For Iceland, this marked the beginning of almost 300 years of decline. It proceeded slowly at first, but then at a faster and more dangerous pace. For Denmark did not consider Iceland a colony to be helped and supported. Iceland was given little or no protection against marauding pirates who raided the coasts. Supplies from abroad were erratic, and no new ships were built. Iceland soon lost contact with the tiny outpost it had established on Greenland in 985. The Greenland settlement died out completely. In 1602 Iceland was forbidden to trade with other countries. By the 18th century, Iceland's climate had entered its grimmest, coldest phase. In 1783 Laki erupted. In 1800 the Althing was suspended by the Danish. It seemed that nature and events had combined to make life in Iceland almost impossible.

The 19th century brought some improvement in Iceland's situation. The Althing was reconvened in 1843, and in 1854, after the Danish Government relaxed its trade ban, Iceland gradually began to rejoin the world of Western Europe. With the return of contact with other peoples came a reawakening of Iceland's arts—especially its literature—and of its old, proud nationalism.

Fishing boats in Husavik harbor. Fish products make up more than 90 percent of Iceland's exports.

This movement was led by Jón Sigurdsson, a statesman, historian, and authority on Icelandic literature. To help his fellow citizens take pride in their past, he published an edition of Iceland's ancient sagas—many of them telling of the gods of Norse mythology or of the Viking settlement. He also founded a political journal in which he called for a return to national consciousness and for practical measures such as cooperatives and training schools to speed up Iceland's development. In 1854, Denmark finally revoked the ban on foreign trade, and 20 years later Iceland was granted a constitution. Icelanders today still credit Jón Sigurdsson's efforts for both achievements.

Iceland gained independence in 1918, retaining only a formal bond with the Danish Crown. After the outbreak of World War II, Iceland's strategic location on the North Atlantic shipping routes became extremely important to the Allies. In 1940, the British placed Iceland under protective occupation, and, in 1941, Americans took their place. The Americans built an airfield at Keflavík, which remains an important North Atlantic Treaty Organization (NATO) base. On June 17, 1944, after a national referendum, Iceland broke its last tie with Denmark and declared itself a republic.

Reykjavik was the site of a two-day meeting in 1986 between U.S. President Ronald Reagan and Soviet leader Mikhail Gorbachev. There they discussed the issues that led to a 1987 agreement eliminating the medium-range missiles held by the two nations.

Reykjavik, the largest city in Iceland, is the world's northernmost capital.

GOVERNMENT

Iceland is a republic. The president, who is elected to a four-year term, is the head of state. Under the constitution, the president is vested with certain executive power. Meanwhile, the prime minister, who is selected by the president and leads the cabinet, serves as the head of the government. The legislative body, the Althing, is also elected to a four-year term. Icelanders elected Vigdís Finnbogadóttir as their first woman president in 1980, reelecting her in 1984, 1988, and 1992. Veteran left-wing politician Olafur Ragnar Grimsson won the June 1996 presidential elections. In 2000, he was the only candidate; the elections were cancelled for that year, and he remained president for a second term.

ICELAND TODAY

Iceland is an example of what a small nation with few natural resources can accomplish. In 2001, the economy was growing vigorously and there was virtually no unemployment. It is a fascinating country to visit, but its prices are the highest in Europe. Icelanders are avid readers and storytellers and one of their most popular writers continues to be Halldór Laxness, who won the Nobel Prize for Literature in 1955. In the 1990s, Einar Már Gudmundsson drew attention with his book *The Angels of the Universe*, and pop star Björk won international acclaim.

Reviewed by KARL F. ROLVAAG, Former United States Ambassador to Iceland
JOHN FISKE Cultural Affairs Officer, United States Embassy, Reykjavik

Fredriksborg Castle, completed in 1620, now serves as Denmark's National History Museum.

DENMARK

Writers have called Denmark a kingdom of reason, a close-up of democracy, a social laboratory, a land of balance, and a toyland run by adults. Although their nation is small and lacks natural resources, the Danes are praised for their contributions to culture and crafts, industry and commerce, education and science. Aided by their strategic location in the North Sea, near the great Western industrial nations, the Danes have met the problems of their country with skill and talent. These qualities have managed to provide all of the inhabitants of this smallest Scandinavian nation with a good life.

THE LAND

Denmark is made up of the peninsula of Jutland—which faces north to Norway and points toward Sweden—and 482 islands, of which only 99 are inhabited. Denmark's islands range in size from mere dots in the sea to middle-sized islands such as Zealand (Sjaelland)—on which Copenhagen, the Danish capital, is built—to the world's largest island, Greenland, off northeast North America. (Greenland is discussed in a sidebar in the NORTH AMERICA article in Volume 5.) Other islands in Denmark are Fyn (Fünen), Lolland, Falster, and Bornholm. The Kingdom of Denmark also includes the Faeroes, a group of 21 islands north of Scotland.

Almost everywhere in Denmark one breathes the sea air. Except for the 42-mile (68-kilometer) boundary with West Germany at the south of Jutland, all of Denmark is surrounded by water. This fragmented little kingdom thus has a remarkably long seacoast—over 4,600 miles (7,400 km.). To the west is the North Sea; to the north, the Skagerrak; to the east, the Kattegat and Øresund (The Sound); and on the south, the Baltic Sea. All along the shores of Jutland and the larger islands there are fiords and bays. In addition, there are numerous small rivers and lakes.

There are no mountains in Denmark. The landscape is gently rolling. In some areas low hills rise between the plains. The highest point—in southeast Jutland—is only 568 feet (173 meters). Even the 531-foot (162 m.) hill in the heart of Jutland has earned the name of "heaven mountain" (Himmelbjaerget). The west coast of Jutland along the North Sea is lined with ridges of sparkling white sand dunes. There are heaths and moors in the western part of Jutland that have been turned into needed

Ribe, on the Jutland peninsula, is said to be the oldest city in Denmark.

forests and farmland. Eastern Jutland and the islands have the best soil. About 10 percent of the total land area of Denmark is forested. Since the country is mostly plains and water, the Danes take great pride in two unusual sights. On the island of Møn are spectacular milky-white chalk cliffs, which rise more than 400 ft. (120 m.) over the blue Baltic Sea. And on the island of Bornholm, which lies in the Baltic Sea and is more like nearby Sweden than the rest of Denmark, are jagged granite cliffs, the only hard rock in the whole country.

The Danes have tied together the bits and pieces of their country and connected it to the outside world with a system of bridges, highways, buses, railroads, planes, and spotless ferries that run like clockwork. The 10-mi. (16 km.)-long Oresund Bridge, connecting Copenhagen with the Swedish town of Malmö, was inaugurated in mid-2000. During the weekend opening ceremonies, 43,000 cyclists, 93,000 marathon runners, and 150,000 pedestrians crossed the bridge prior to its dedication. The bridge can now be used by cars, buses, and trains only.

Agriculture

Although Denmark's soil is not naturally fertile, it is the nation's most important natural resource. Climate also adds to the difficulty of farming. During most of the year westerly winds blowing over waters warmed by the Gulf Stream make the weather relatively mild for so northerly a country. Rainfall ranges from 16 to 32 in. (40 to 80 cm.) per year, but the wettest months are in late summer and early autumn, when the farmer needs fair weather for the harvest. The driest months come in the spring.

In spite of these natural obstacles, the Danes today are one of the world's largest exporters of meat and meat products, of butter and eggs, and of cheeses. It was not always so.

Most farms in Denmark are small, efficiently run family operations.

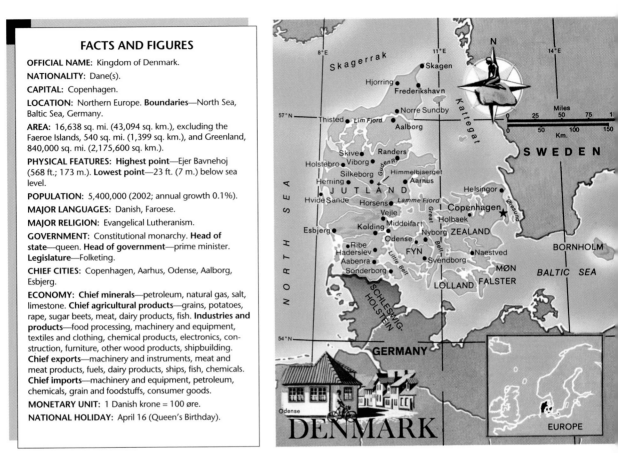

FACTS AND FIGURES

OFFICIAL NAME: Kingdom of Denmark.

NATIONALITY: Dane(s).

CAPITAL: Copenhagen.

LOCATION: Northern Europe. **Boundaries**—North Sea, Baltic Sea, Germany.

AREA: 16,638 sq. mi. (43,094 sq. km.), excluding the Faeroe Islands, 540 sq. mi. (1,399 sq. km.), and Greenland, 840,000 sq. mi. (2,175,600 sq. km.).

PHYSICAL FEATURES: **Highest point**—Ejer Bavnehoj (568 ft.; 173 m.). **Lowest point**—23 ft. (7 m.) below sea level.

POPULATION: 5,400,000 (2002; annual growth 0.1%).

MAJOR LANGUAGES: Danish, Faroese.

MAJOR RELIGION: Evangelical Lutheranism.

GOVERNMENT: Constitutional monarchy. **Head of state**—queen. **Head of government**—prime minister. **Legislature**—Folketing.

CHIEF CITIES: Copenhagen, Aarhus, Odense, Aalborg, Esbjerg.

ECONOMY: **Chief minerals**—petroleum, natural gas, salt, limestone. **Chief agricultural products**—grains, potatoes, rape, sugar beets, meat, dairy products, fish. **Industries and products**—food processing, machinery and equipment, textiles and clothing, chemical products, electronics, construction, furniture, other wood products, shipbuilding. **Chief exports**—machinery and instruments, meat and meat products, fuels, dairy products, ships, fish, chemicals. **Chief imports**—machinery and equipment, petroleum, chemicals, grain and foodstuffs, consumer goods.

MONETARY UNIT: 1 Danish krone = 100 øre.

NATIONAL HOLIDAY: April 16 (Queen's Birthday).

Until 1880, the Danes were mostly producers of grains. With the growth of railroads and improved shipping, Denmark could not compete with the giant grain-growing countries. Therefore, Danish farmers began to specialize in butter, bacon, eggs, cheese, and ham—foods that were needed by other Western European nations. Denmark soon became known as the country that was sending the ingredients of a hearty breakfast to millions of people throughout Europe.

Cooperatives. This successful and rapid transformation of Danish agriculture was made possible by the establishment of a system of cooperatives. The original Danish agricultural cooperative grew out of the simple idea of collecting the milk from a number of small farms, processing it into butter in one central place, selling the large batches of butter, and distributing the profits according to each farmer's individual contribution. From 1882 to 1890, nearly 700 dairies became cooperatives. The movement grew rapidly to include cooperative buying of machinery, fertilizers, and feed; cooperative egg collecting, pig slaughtering, and bacon and ham processing; and cooperative exporting. From buying and selling together, it was natural to go on to establish uniform standards of quality and to benefit from centralized agricultural research. The cooperative system has been more widely applied in Denmark than anywhere else in the world. Eggs are graded, sized, and packed under rigid rules for quality and uniformity. The buyer can be certain of the same uniformity and quality in the bacon, the chickens, the butter, the many types of potatoes, the more than a dozen varieties of cheeses, and all other exported food.

Folk Schools. Where did the Danish farmers learn how to organize for such economic and social change? For the answer one must go back to a remarkable man, Nikolai Frederik Severin Grundtvig (1783–1872). A theologian, historian, educator, poet, philosopher, hymn-writer, and politician, Grundtvig was interested in encouraging adults to take an intelligent interest in representative government. He thought this could be done at folk high schools (folkehøjskoler). His disciple, Kristen Kold (1816–70), a teacher, set the pattern for these adult schools, which were soon established all over the country. Teaching was largely oral, relying mainly on lectures and discussions. The idea was not only to teach facts, but to arouse intellectual curiosity and an interest in social problems. The folk high schools are credited with transforming peasants into enlightened, well-educated farmers.

THE ECONOMY

Industry, Transport, and Services

The talented and energetic Danes have turned a small country with no coal, no iron, and no hydroelectric power into a modern industrial nation. Long ago the Danes learned to use fully almost every inch of their country. The bedrock of chalk and limestone is used to make cement. The island of Bornholm, which lies in the Baltic Sea, yields the hard rock used for cobblestones that pave some of the streets of the leading cities of Denmark. Bornholm also provides kaolin, the clay used in making the porcelain figurines and fine chinaware sold all over the world.

Denmark does not have enough natural forests to produce the wood needed for building and making newsprint. But since 1805, when Denmark passed the first forest protection law in the world, the Danes have managed to convert some lowland into forests of spruce and pine to fill some of their paper and building needs.

Much of Danish industry is based on processing farm products. The factories are busy turning milk into butter and cheese; packaging bacon, sausage, and hams; and converting malt, hops, and grain into world-famous beer. Denmark also has a large fishing industry, with a fleet of more than 8,000 fishing vessels. About 90 percent of the catch comes from the seas around Denmark, where herring, plaice, mackerel, eel, and cod are found. Tiny, delicious shrimp come from the world's largest shrimp grounds in the waters off southern Greenland.

In recent years the Danes have made great strides in many new industrial fields and expanded ones for which they have been renowned. Their modern furniture, often made from teak imported from Southeast Asia, has won acclaim for its elegantly simple design and fine quality. The same craftsmanship and advanced design have made Danish silver, porcelain, textiles, and rugs greatly prized in homes all over the Western world. Denmark also produces ships, engines, chemicals, medicines, machinery (including electrical machinery and parts), toys, clothing, shoes, and prefabricated housing elements.

In 1932, a carpenter named Ole Kirk Christiansen began assembling his own wooden toys. Two years later, the toys began to be called "lego," from the Danish expression "legt godt," which means "to play well." Only later did the toy makers realize that the word also means "I learn" or "I construct" in Latin. In 1958, plastic replaced the original wood materials in the toy's design. By 2000, the Lego Company was the world's sixth-largest toy manufacturer.

To carry on foreign trade, Denmark has a large, modern merchant marine. The Danes perfected the diesel engine and launched the first oceangoing motor ship in the world in 1912. Copenhagen, the capital, is the leading industrial center and largest port. Ships come in carrying raw materials and fuel and leave carrying export products.

In 1973, Denmark joined the Common Market, the precursor of the present European Union (EU). This membership has provided the nation with vast new markets. In the early 2000s, Denmark was one of the strongest supporters of EU enlargement and approved the addition of former Communist countries, especially those bordering the Baltic Sea (Poland, Estonia, Lithuania, and Latvia).

Tourism is an important part of the economy. Among foreign visitors, Germans are the most numerous, followed by people from other Scandinavian nations.

THE PEOPLE

Almost the entire Danish labor force, skilled as well as unskilled, is organized in unions. In addition, Denmark has one of the most comprehensive social-welfare systems in the world. The Danes have simply decided that no one is to suffer any avoidable hardship.

The beaches of Holbæk on Zealand are popular in the summertime.

Children in a state-run day care center enjoy an outing.

Denmark has achieved so many firsts in social welfare that one cannot list them all. In 1792 Denmark became the first European state to abolish slave trading. In 1814 it was the first to make elementary education compulsory. The Danes were the first people in the world to organize a complete old-age pension system and one of the first to have a superb system of municipal hospitals. In medical standards, preventive medicine, and patient care, they rank among the world leaders. As far back as 1870 Denmark converted former monasteries into comfortable, attractive homes for the elderly, and today people come from all over the world to study the charming living arrangements Denmark has provided for its older citizens.

Taxes are very high, but a large amount of the revenue is used for the support of hospitals, day care centers for children, disability payments, pensions, unemployment insurance, and education. The Danish program of social legislation has been so successful that, as an old Danish song says, Denmark is truly a land where "few have too much, and fewer too little." It has been said that if there are social ills that intelligence can cure, the Danes will take care of them.

The Danes, whether they live in modern apartment houses in the cities, in timbered farmhouses, or in whitewashed country cottages with tiled roofs, are proud of their homes. As one leaves the cities one can see neat rows of gardens, for many city-dwellers have plots where they cultivate vegetables and flowers. The Danes love flowers, and in the summertime Denmark is like one big garden. Flowerbeds and green lawns are everywhere.

The typical Danish home is *hyggeligt,* a word the Danes use to express the ideas of coziness, warmth, attractiveness, and friendliness. The home may include a shining old porcelain stove, a modern abstract art poster, inherited antique tables or chairs, and books. The Danes love to eat, and whether at home or in restaurants, their food is served attractively, and there are usually fresh flowers on the table. Many Danes are good cooks, often making their own bread and baking any of the dozens of different cream cakes, tarts, and Danish pastries that delight the eye and the taste.

Few foods in Denmark are more celebrated than the famous *smørrebrød* (literally, "bread and butter"). *Smørrebrød* is a Danish invention that has become a folk art. It is an open-faced sandwich—thick, pure butter spread on a slice of delicious Danish bread and covered with tiny shrimp, liver paste, cold meats, or any of more than 100 variations of local delicacies. Other favorite foods are roast pork stuffed with prunes and apples, and *frikadeller* (meat patties). They may be followed by a dessert of delicious cheeses, fresh fruits, or a marvelous pudding of raspberry and currant juices called *rødgrød med fløde*.

Whatever the Danes choose to eat, the drink is quite often beer. The nation's two giant breweries, Carlsberg and Tuborg, are known worldwide. Denmark is among the largest beer exporters on the European continent, and the profits from beer sales have aided Danish art, culture, and education. The Carlsberg Foundation is Denmark's greatest cultural benefactor, using its money for museums,

Beer made in Denmark's giant breweries is enjoyed throughout the world.

statues, gardens, and a wide variety of educational and cultural events and institutions. Tuborg, a smaller company, has provided funds for foreign study grants for young Danes and for various commercial activities to benefit the community.

The Arts and Education in Denmark

Denmark's most famous export is, strangely enough, a collection of fairy tales. To readers all over the world, Denmark is known as the home of Hans Christian Andersen (1805–75). His stories are a part of the heritage of children everywhere. Another Danish writer well-known outside his country is the 19th-century philosopher Søren Kierkegaard. He is now recognized as the founder of the philosophy of existentialism. Baroness Karen Blixen, who wrote under the name of Isak Dinesen, achieved an international reputation for her work, especially for her brilliant storytelling in *Seven Gothic Tales* and for the autobiographical *Out of Africa*. Many Danish authors, including some Nobel Prize winners, are not read outside Denmark because they have not been widely translated. The Danes, who are great readers of books, read even more newspapers. Cities of 20,000 people usually have more than one daily newspaper, and Copenhagen has about 10.

Children in Denmark attend school from the age of 7 to 16. After the age of 16 school is voluntary, and students who desire to continue their education by attending college may apply for admission to one of Denmark's 15 universities with their many associated specialized institutes. All who qualify attend free.

Continuation schools (*efterskoler*) have been set up to meet the demand for additional education for those boys and girls who have left school. These schools are residential, and they provide general education in an informal atmosphere, with no entrance tests and no examinations unless the students wish to go into specialized fields. The adult folk high schools still flourish. They are also informal and residential. Men and women may attend a 5- or 6-month winter course or shorter ones, including even two-week summer family courses.

The Danes have made many significant contributions to research and learning as well as to education. They have produced great astronomers, such as Tycho Brahe, who discovered a new star in 1572 and whose precise observations in fixing the positions of the planets and stars were of enormous importance. There have been many world-famous Danish mathematicians, medical scientists, chemists, and physicists. Perhaps the best-known in modern times was Niels Bohr, who made historic discoveries in atomic physics. Bohr attracted scholars from all over the world to the University Institute of Theoretical Physics, which he founded in Copenhagen in 1920.

One needs neither an understanding of the language nor a knowledge of science to appreciate one of Denmark's greatest treasures, the Royal Danish Ballet. The Danes take pride in this notable company and support it generously, as they do their symphony orchestras and opera companies. The Danes also love to dance and sing. As far back as A.D. 1100, many aristocrats had their own dance festivals, and to this day folk dancing as well as social dancing is widely enjoyed. Whether dancing outdoors or sailing, the Danish people love the outdoors and are dedicated Sun-worshipers, as are many other northern people who have a

Young ballet students practice for the internationally known Royal Danish Ballet.

short summer. As soon as weather permits, they take to the beach—to swim, to sail, to row, to canoe, or just to sunbathe. They also enjoy bicycle races, badminton, and tennis; but their favorite non-water sport is soccer. For skiing the Danes travel to Norway and Sweden.

COPENHAGEN, THE CAPITAL

To many people Copenhagen's Tivoli Gardens, the world's most famous amusement park, is the key to Denmark. There, on 20 acres (8 hectares) in the heart of the capital, is something for everyone, old, young, rich, poor, serious, frivolous. There are restaurants and snack bars, concerts by symphony orchestras and performances by jazz groups and brass bands, ballet and pantomime, flea circuses and fun rides, playgrounds, paths on which to stroll under shady trees, and places to sit amid beautiful flowerbeds. From May to mid-September thousands of Danes and visitors "tivolate"—as one happy visitor explained—in an atmosphere that is a mixture of lightness, color, and gaiety combined with orderliness, good taste, and superb organization. At night Tivoli becomes a fairyland of twinkling lights and floodlit waters. Twice a week before closing time there is a display of fireworks that ends when the huge bell in the nearby City Hall tower strikes midnight.

About one fourth of the Danes live in Copenhagen and its suburbs. The city was founded in 1167 by Bishop Absalon on the east shore of Zealand across Øresund from Sweden. Its name means "merchant's harbor," and since its founding, Copenhagen has been the center of Danish life, although it did not become the capital until 1445. It is a windswept city of slender, pointed spires, copper-green roofs, and domes topped with gold balls, coronets, and clocks; of old and new buildings on narrow streets; and of a sparkling harbor alive with ships being built, being loaded and unloaded, and under sail.

Copenhagen's world-famous Tivoli Gardens feature everything from concerts and ballets to circuses and rides.

Cafés, restaurants, and shops line a canal in Nyhavn, Copenhagen's harbor district.

Amalienborg, the royal palaces in Copenhagen, dates to the 18th century.

Much of the character of Copenhagen was set by King Christian IV (1577–1648), who planned and built much of the city. Not only did he plan the unique Stock Exchange (*Børsen*) building, but while it was being erected, it is said, he himself worked on its strange spire, which is formed by the entwined tails of four copper dragons that appear to be standing on their heads. It is the world's oldest market exchange building in continuous use. Christian also built churches, the Rosenborg Castle, which is now a great museum, and the Nyboder, a group of houses for men of the Royal Navy and their families, often called the first public housing project. Four succeeding kings continued building the city. About 1750 King Frederik V permitted four noblemen to build four palaces enclosing an octagonal plaza. These buildings, Amalienborg, are now the home of the Danish royal family.

Visitors to Copenhagen flock to the National Museum; to the Glyptotek to see the collection of French art; and to the Thorvaldsen Museum to see the works of Denmark's great sculptor, Bertel Thorvaldsen (1768–1844). They also stroll through many parks, including the Langelinie, where, from a large boulder at the water's edge, a bronze statue of Andersen's fairy-tale Little Mermaid watches the ships come and go.

HISTORY

Hunters and fishermen were living in Denmark as far back as the Old Stone Age (about 10000 B.C.). Many relics of the peoples of the Stone, Bronze, and Iron ages have been found in Denmark. The oldest surviving costumes in Europe have been recovered from oak-coffin graves dating from the Bronze Age. Among the interesting relics of this period are lurs. These musical instruments—long, elegantly carved horns—are in pairs that are identical except for being curved in reverse. The lur has survived as a symbol on Danish butter.

The Danes took part in the Viking raids, which started out as pirate raids and ended as large-scale military expeditions and invasions. The Viking period—between the 9th and 11th centuries—was a time of trade and emigration and led to the settlement of thousands of Danish peasants in England, Normandy, and northern Germany. The royal line of Denmark began in the Viking period.

History tells us that the Danish monarchy, rulers of the oldest kingdom in Europe, goes back to Gorm the Old, who died in A.D. 940. Gorm and his wife, Queen Thyra Danebod, had a son Harold Bluetooth, who was the first Christian ruler of Denmark. The Danish warrior kings continued their raids until 1016, when the Danish king Canute (Knud) the Great completed the conquest of England. At his death, he was the ruler of Denmark, England, and Norway. After his death there was a period of turmoil and civil war, and the empire fell apart.

In 1397 Denmark, Norway, and Sweden were united by Queen Margrethe I, following a meeting in the Swedish town of Kalmar. This union became known as the Kalmar Union and continued officially until 1523, when it was finally dissolved. The truth is that after the death of Queen Margrethe, who had been a remarkable diplomat, the union began to disintegrate, and very little significance was attached to it. Sweden left the union in 1523, but Norway remained a part of Denmark until 1814. Norway had brought to the union the Faeroe Islands, Iceland, and Greenland. Iceland became independent in 1918. (An article on ICELAND appears in this volume.)

The Faeroe Islands remain a part of Denmark to this day. These 21 volcanic islands, whose name means "sheep islands," are in fact used for raising sheep. The Faeroe Islanders are fishermen as well as shepherds, and they make their own local laws, use their own language, and have their own flag. Greenland, which has also remained a part of Denmark, held its first elections under home rule in 1979. The Faeroe Islands and Greenland each send two representatives to the Danish parliament.

Costly Wars

From earliest times, Denmark was almost continuously engaged in some war. Many of the battles were with Sweden, and finally, in the mid-17th century, Denmark was defeated and lost the rich provinces of Skane, Halland, and Blekinge to Sweden. Norway was lost to Sweden in 1814 as a result of Denmark's involvement in the Napoleonic Wars. When war broke out in 1803 between England and France, Denmark first chose to remain neutral. The Danes rejected a demand that they turn over their fleet to the British. As a result, the British fleet bombarded Copenhagen and destroyed much of the city. The Danes were ultimately forced to surrender their fleet and angrily concluded an unhappy alliance with Napoleon. At a peace conference in Kiel, Germany, in 1814, Denmark gave up Norway.

For many years, tensions had been growing in the area known as Schleswig-Holstein, in the south of Jutland. Schleswig, an ancient Danish duchy, and Holstein, which had traditionally been German but had come

Hvide Sande on Jutland is a fishing center.

under Danish rule in the 15th century, were to create trouble with Germany that lasted through World War II. In the first war (1848–49) fought over Holstein, the Danes were victorious. But this led to a second war (1864) against Austria and the German state of Prussia. In this war many Danes were killed. The day the peace treaty of Vienna was signed—October 30, 1864—was perhaps one of the darkest days in Danish history. The Danes had to surrender not only German Holstein and southern Schleswig, but also northern Schleswig, which had always been Danish. Denmark thus lost one third of its already diminished territory and two fifths of its population.

A Danish patriot said, "What has been lost outside must be gained inside." Each time Denmark has suffered severely, the Danes have managed to turn adversity into advantage. After the Napoleonic Wars, the country was bankrupt and the people impoverished and in despair. Yet this was a time of great achievement in art, literature, and government. The beginning of compulsory education for all, important economic reforms, a movement to limit the absolute monarchy, and demands for a new constitution all followed the losses in 1814. The losses of 1864 were followed by a drive for land reclamation that created tens of thousands of new acres of farmland out of the heathlands of Jutland. It was also the time of the great agricultural revolution.

Denmark, neutral during World War I, got back part of Schleswig in 1920. The Danes insisted on a plebiscite since they wanted only the part of the country where the people voted overwhelmingly to return to Danish rule. At the outbreak of World War II, Denmark again hoped to remain neutral, but on April 9, 1940, German troops occupied the country. For 3 years the Germans tried to make Denmark a model Nazi protectorate, but as they failed to win over the Danes, more and more restraints were imposed and a strong resistance movement developed. The Germans were beset with constant sabotage and with subtle defiance and outright ridicule. The press went underground so effectively that in the last year of the war almost 180 illegal papers were published, with a total daily edition of 1 million copies. People began public songfests, singing the national anthem, which begins, "There is a lovely land," until the Nazis forbade public singing. Suddenly it seemed the whole country took to wearing little woolen beanie hats, knitted with the design of the British Royal Air Force insignia, and the Nazis passed a law forbidding Danes to wear the beanies. When a bookstore displayed English books, the Nazis complained, and the Danish owner substituted German books with a sign saying, "Learn German while there is still time."

But no other Danish war story shows the cohesion of the people and their bravery as does the story of Denmark's rescue of almost its entire Jewish population. When word was received in September 1943 that the Nazis planned to round up all the Jews, the Danes acted within 24 hours. Almost every citizen participated in the rescue, in which Jews were found; warned; hidden in homes, woods, hospitals, inns, and churches; and taken by fishing boats across the sound to Sweden. Of almost 8,000 Danish Jews, all but a few hundred—too ill to be moved or unwilling to cooperate—were saved. This almost unbelievable feat of courage and organization was arranged in one day and night in a wholly occupied country.

The war left Denmark with a severely crippled economy, although it had suffered little physical damage. With the aid of the U.S. Marshall Plan, it became possible to put the country back on a prosperous basis in a relatively short time. Denmark became a member of the United Nations and also of the North Atlantic Treaty Organization (NATO).

GOVERNMENT

Denmark is a constitutional monarchy with a single-chamber parliament (the Folketing). The nation's head of government, the prime minister, is responsible to the 179-member Folketing. Social Democrat Poul Nyrup Rasmussen served as prime minister from 1993 to 2001, when he was replaced by liberal Anders Fogh Rasmussen. Denmark's current monarch, Queen Margrethe II, ascended to the throne in 1972 after the death of her father, King Frederik IX. The queen is highly educated (she studied at Danish universities, at the London School of Economics, and at the Sorbonne), speaks several languages, and is dearly beloved by the whole nation. In her regular New Year's speeches, which she writes herself, she addresses moral and ethical issues of the contemporary world. In 1967, she married a French count and together they have two sons; the older, Frederik, is the heir apparent.

The Danes approach difficulties with logic and imagination. In a time when many countries in the world are in turmoil, Denmark is often cited as a unique example of a land where the people have learned to cope successfully with the challenges of their time and their environment. In 1992, Danish voters first rejected the proposal to join the European Union (EU), but after negotiations that granted Denmark increased independence within the EU, the second referendum in May 1993 reversed the earlier decision. Although it is among the smaller EU countries, Denmark has a very pragmatic attitude toward the organization. As of 2002, it continues to be one of three EU nations, (along with Great Britain and Sweden) that has not replaced its currency with the euro.

CASPAR H. W. HASSELRIIS, Former Director, Danish Information Service, New York

NORWAY

A thousand years ago Vikings from Norway roamed the coasts of Europe in their dragon-headed longboats, plundering and raiding wherever they touched land. They penetrated inland by river, even sacking cities like London and Paris. The Vikings were fierce, merciless warriors. People all over Europe feared their cruelty and prayed for protection from "the wrath of the Norsemen." Today the Norwegians live in what has been called the peaceful corner of Europe, at peace not only with their fellow Europeans but with themselves. The descendant of the Vikings is a soft-spoken individual with a highly developed sense of responsibility for his neighbor.

About 100 years ago many Norwegians left their country to build a new life on the continent across the Atlantic. Altogether about 800,000 Norwegians left for the United States between 1855 and 1920 because they could not make a living in their homeland. Today, however, Norway is a prosperous member of the Western European family of nations, with one of the highest standards of living in the world.

Geiranger Fjord, one of the many fiords that indent Norway's west coast.

Norway above the Arctic Circle, part of the "land of the midnight sun."

What changed Norway over these 1,000 years, and especially during the last century? The most important answers lie in the country itself and in the people who live there.

THE LAND

Roughly speaking, Norway is one long and massive chain of mountains facing the North Atlantic. It forms the western part of the Scandinavian peninsula, which it shares with Sweden. Norway also includes Spitsbergen (Svalbard), some 400 mi. (640 km.) to the north; Jan Mayen Island, about 640 mi. (1,030 km.) to the west; and Bouvet and Peter I islands, near Antarctica.

Norway's mainland area of about 125,000 sq. mi. (324,000 sq. km.) makes it one of the larger European nations. Its long coastline is cut by deep fiords, narrow arms of seawater sometimes reaching 100 mi. (160 km.) inland, with towering mountains rising on each side. Fertile green valleys stretch inland along the rivers that flow from the high mountains towards the coast. The actual distance from the southernmost tip of Norway to its North Cape is over 1,000 mi. (1,600 km.), but if the fiords could be straightened out, the Norwegian coastline would reach halfway around the equator. Along this coast are scattered more than 150,000 islands and skerries—reefs of tiny uninhabited rock islands. These islands serve as barriers that protect the coast from Atlantic storms.

About one third of Norway lies north of the Arctic Circle. At the North Cape, some 71 degrees north of the equator, the sun shines day and night from mid-May through the end of July and is completely absent for about 2½ months in winter. But in spite of its high latitude,

Norway does not have an Arctic climate. The warm waters of the Norway Current of the Gulf Stream system give the coastal areas of the country a temperate climate, with ice-free harbors even in the extreme north. Deep inland and in the mountains winter temperatures are more severe, but that is not where most Norwegians live. Actually only about 3 percent of the country can be farmed, while 25 percent is covered by forests. Mountains, lakes, rivers, forests, and bare wasteland—including the 340-square-mile (880 sq. km.) Jostedalsbre—take up nearly all of the land. It is not surprising that Norway is the second most sparsely populated country in Europe (after Iceland), or that most of its population lives along the coasts, close to the sea.

HISTORY

The sea was always a challenge to the Norwegians. In the early days of settlement, land communications were virtually impossible and farmland was even scarcer than it is today. The sea naturally became both the principal artery of transport and, because of its abundance of fish, a major source of food. The Norwegians soon learned to dominate the sea —the most important factor in their environment. It was the superior skill of the Norwegian Viking shipbuilders and sailors that made possible their impact on the rest of Europe, starting about A.D. 800. However, in spite of the fear the Vikings caused wherever they went, they were more than raiders. They were also discoverers and colonizers, and Viking kingdoms existed outside Scandinavia for hundreds of years. During the 9th and 10th centuries, Norwegians discovered and settled far-off Iceland, and from Iceland, Greenland was later settled. Around the year 1000 Leif Ericson and his men set sail from Greenland for the shores of North America. There they established a colony they called Vinland. Remnants of a Viking-Age settlement dating from that time were discovered in Newfoundland in the 1960's. Norwegian Vikings also invaded and settled much of Ireland, northern England, and Scotland and its surrounding islands.

About 885–890 the scattered chiefdoms and provinces that had made up the country were gathered into one kingdom by Harold the Fairhaired, who became the first king of Norway. Harold tried to replace the system of local *things,* or assemblies, with one central assembly, and he collected taxes from the lesser chiefs. (Some who were unwilling to live under his rule emigrated to Iceland.) Viking raids and conquests in the rest of Europe continued, but the conversion to Christianity in the early 11th century was an important factor in calming the wrath of the Norsemen. Gradually, instead of plundering, Norwegians went abroad to trade. Cultural influences from Europe swept through Norway and blended with the Viking heritage. During the late Middle Ages, Norway entered a period of great expansion and prosperity. Some of Norway's cities, including Oslo and Bergen, were founded or grew into important trade centers during this time.

But prosperity was not to last. Conflicts between local rulers broke out, leading to civil war. The population was growing too fast to be supported by the land, and Norway had to import all of its grain. In the 14th century the great plague known as the Black Death swept across Europe. Almost half the Norwegian population died. Agriculture, crafts, and trade came to a standstill. The powerful Hanseatic League, a group of North German cities that controlled much European shipping, took over Norway's foreign trade—its main source of income. Norway's mastery of the sea was lost, and the country sank into poverty. Iceland and Greenland, acquired a century before, could no longer be supplied. The population in Iceland survived, but the Greenland colony perished.

In 1397, Queen Margrethe of Denmark set up the Union of Kalmar, uniting Sweden, Denmark, and Norway under her rule. The union lasted until 1523, but Norway's dependence on Denmark continued for nearly another 300 years.

The loss of national independence did not mean loss of personal freedoms. While nearly all the rest of Europe was dominated by the feudal system, most Norwegians remained free. The Norwegian farmer in particular became a symbol of Norway's past and of national independence. The country's forests became a new source of income when the British and Dutch sailed across the oceans in ships built of Norwegian timber. An independent middle class arose in the cities, the economy prospered, and shipping revived.

The drive for independence gained momentum in the 18th century. The turning point came with the Napoleonic Wars in the early 19th century. Denmark sided with France, while most of Norway's trade and other interests lay with England, which was suddenly called the enemy. The Norwegians resented the Danish policy that so neglected the interests of Norway. On May 17, 1814, at Eidsvoll, near Oslo, an elected assembly declared Norway's independence and signed a constitution. Inspired by the American Declaration of Independence and the ideals of the French Revolution, it was the most liberal constitution in Europe at the time. With some amendments, it is still in force today.

Later in 1814, Norway was forced to accept a union with Sweden. Even so, it continued to retain its constitution, and the average Norwegian enjoyed political liberties that were unknown in the rest of Scandinavia. In 1905, the union with Sweden was peacefully dissolved by mutual consent, and a Danish prince, Carl, was elected king (as Haakon VII) of independent Norway.

During the long reign of King Haakon VII (1905–57), modern Norway took shape. Social legislation was passed, with old-age pensions and other benefits for workers. The educational system was expanded to include more vocational and technical schools. Life in Norway grew prosperous and stable.

Then, in April 1940, in spite of Norway's declared neutrality, Germany invaded in a surprise attack. King Haakon refused to surrender, and finally escaped to London to set up a government-in-exile. Vidkun Quisling, a Norwegian whose name has come to mean "traitor," led the government in Nazi-occupied Norway. Throughout the five years of German occupation, nearly all Norwegians participated in the resistance movement. Their protests began with strikes and passive rejection of Nazi rule, but later took the form of large-scale industrial sabotage. At the end of the war, King Haakon was joyfully welcomed back to his newly liberated country.

The postwar reconstruction was efficient and quick. Norway's standard of living continued to rise, and during the 1950s and 1960s, a number of laws greatly increased social benefits. Large oil and natural gas deposits in the North Sea also added to Norway's prosperity.

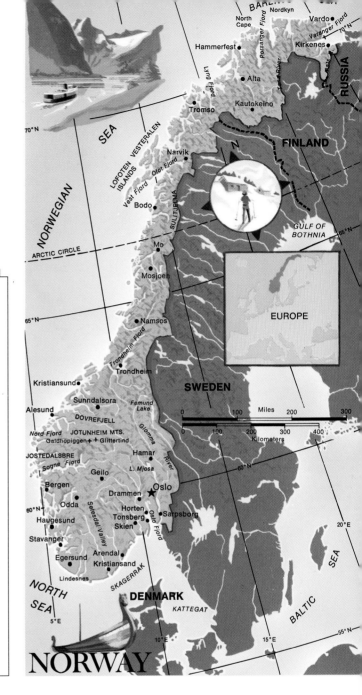

FACTS AND FIGURES

OFFICIAL NAME: Kingdom of Norway.

NATIONALITY: Norwegian(s).

CAPITAL: Oslo.

LOCATION: Western part of the Scandinavian peninsula. **Boundaries**—Barents Sea, Russia, Finland, Sweden, North Sea, Norwegian Sea.

AREA: 125,181 sq. mi. (324,219 sq. km.), mainland; 149,426 sq. mi. (387,014 sq. km.), including possessions.

PHYSICAL FEATURES: Highest point—Galdhøpiggen (8,097 ft.; 2,468 m.). **Lowest point**—sea level. **Chief rivers**—Glåma, Lågen. **Major lakes**—Mjøsa, Femundsjø.

POPULATION: 4,500,000 (2002; annual growth 0.3%).

MAJOR LANGUAGE: Norwegian.

MAJOR RELIGION: Evangelical Lutheranism.

GOVERNMENT: Constitutional monarchy. **Head of state**—king. **Head of government**—prime minister. **Legislature**—Storting.

CHIEF CITIES: Oslo, Bergen, Trondheim, Stavanger.

ECONOMY: Chief minerals—petroleum, natural gas, iron ore, pyrites, copper, zinc, lead. **Chief agricultural products**—oats, other grains, beef, milk, livestock. **Industries and products**—oil and gas extraction, food processing, shipbuilding, wood pulp, paper products, refined metals, chemicals. **Chief exports**—petroleum and petroleum products, machinery and equipment, metals, chemicals, ships, fish, raw materials. **Chief imports**—machinery and equipment, chemicals, metals, foodstuffs, manufactured consumer goods.

MONETARY UNIT: 1 Norwegian krone = 100 øre.

NATIONAL HOLIDAY: May 17 (Constitution Day).

GOVERNMENT

Norway is a constitutional monarchy whose government is based on the Constitution of 1814, with subsequent amendments (the most recent amendment was approved in 1884). The executive power held by the king is actually exercised by a cabinet headed by a prime minister. Cabinet members, although appointed by the king, govern with the approval of the Parliament, or Storting—Norway's 165-member legislative body, which is elected every four years by a popular vote. For certain purposes, the Storting divides itself into two separate chambers, and elects one-fourth of its membership to an "upper house," or Lagting. The judicial branch of government is the Norwegian Supreme Court, or Høyesterett.

ECONOMY

Beginning in the early 20th century, the thousands of rivers, waterfalls, and streams that rush down from Norway's towering mountain ranges were harnessed to produce electric power for homes and industry. Norway today has more kilowatt-hours of electricity per inhabitant than any other country in the world. Because of this, whole new industrial centers have grown up across the country. Chemicals, refined metals, and high-quality finished goods, such as tape recorders, office machinery, and electronics equipment are exported.

The sea is still important, however; Norway's merchant fleet is among the largest in the world. And, as in Viking days, fishing is still a major economic factor, although the number of fishermen is relatively small. In 1993, Norway renewed whale fishing, despite international protests. Whale steaks are a traditional Norwegian delicacy, and whale oil has been used in the manufacture of products such as soap and perfumes. New uses for whale oil are being explored. Moreover, since the 1970s, the sea has yielded an enormous wealth of oil and natural gas—so great that these commodities now account for about one-third of all Norwegian exports. Since these deposits are expected to be exhausted some time after 2020, Norway has been saving its extra earnings in a special Government Petroleum Fund.

Because so little of Norway's land can be farmed, agriculture has been declining in importance. Norway must import most of its grain from foreign trading partners, but extensive domestic dairy farming has supplied the nation with a surplus of dairy products.

Another traditional Norwegian industry is forestry. At one time timber was the country's principal export. Forests still cover much of the country, and they are maintained by the addition of more than 100 million saplings every year—most of them planted by Norwegian schoolchildren and university students. Timber is processed for export and turned into paper, pulp, and a variety of other products.

THE PEOPLE

Finally, as in Viking days, Norway's most valuable raw material is its people. The country has a population of about 4.5 million and statistics show that some 80 percent are blond and blue-eyed; that most are tall and athletic; and that of all the peoples in the world, only Icelanders have a longer life expectancy.

Norwegian culture today is a blend of the traditional and the modern. The Vikings had a highly developed artistic feeling, and their sense of craftsmanship has been preserved through the centuries in Norway's folk art, which can be seen in many open-air museums.

As far back as the 9th century A.D., a form of oral literature flourished in Norway. This was later developed and written down in Iceland, including the sagas of Norway's kings, which contain most of what is known of Viking history. However, what is known abroad today of Norwegian literature dates mostly from the 19th century, when the plays of Henrik Ibsen and Bjørnstjerne Bjørnson were introduced into world literature. In the 20th century, the writers Sigrid Undset and Knut Hamsun won the Nobel Prize for literature. The 19th-century composer Edvard Grieg, the 20th-century expressionist painter Edvard Munch, and the sculptor Gustav Vigeland have also won international renown.

Gabled construction was typical of Norway's medieval stave churches.

Education

Norway was one of the first countries to eradicate illiteracy, and since then Norwegians have been well aware that education holds the key to the future. The educational system is highly developed, but great efforts are being made to meet the fast rising demand for education. The young Norwegian enters school at the age of 7 and remains in school for a minimum of 9 years. Most students continue after that, going into technical, vocational, industrial, or commercial schools, or to colleges and universities. Education in Norway is free at all levels.

Tax money is used to finance the educational institutions—and taxes are higher in Norway than in most other countries. But the Norwegian feels that he is getting something back. Tax money is also used so that every citizen can live in comfort and security, without fear of misfortune. This is not a political issue in Norway. It is more a reflection of a general belief that everybody has a duty towards his neighbor if he is in trouble. This has not been left to chance and improvisation, but is part of a system that all Norwegians consider rational and fair, giving everybody an equal opportunity to live decently.

The Oslo Town Hall (right) opened in 1950 to commemorate the 900th anniversary of the city's founding.

One example is Norway's health program. Norway has a system of compulsory health insurance that covers the entire population and even foreigners who live there. It provides unlimited free medical care, unlimited free hospitalization in modern and comfortable hospitals, liberal cash allowances, and many other benefits. Doctors have their private practices and welcome the health insurance plan, which means that everybody can afford to see a doctor, whether it is the family physician or a specialist. The cost is split four ways—among the employee, the employer, the state, and the local community.

Similar plans exist in many other areas, providing insurance, for instance, against unemployment and disability. And today the retired Norwegian is entitled to a minimum pension that corresponds to about two thirds of his average annual income during his 20 best earning years.

This is the background against which the Norwegians live. Though they do not believe they have solved all their problems, they do believe that if the Norwegian can live under the best material conditions, he will also be able to give his best contribution to Norway's growth.

CITIES

Oslo. Norway's capital and its industrial, commercial, and cultural center is Oslo. It has all the characteristics of a bustling modern city as well as some of the aspects of a peaceful country town. This is largely because of its location at the end of the Oslo fiord and because of the nearby woodlands and hills.

Most public buildings are clustered around Oslo's main street, Karl Johans Gate, which leads from the main railway station up to the Royal Palace. In this town center are found the Lutheran Cathedral, the Storting (parliament), the National Theater, the National Gallery of Arts, the Museum of History, and the old university buildings. The main government buildings and the Supreme Court are only a few steps away, as is the harbor, which is guarded by Oslo's medieval Akershus Castle and the modern City Hall.

The park along the main street is called the Studenter-Lunden, the "student's grove," though most students have moved away to a new university campus built on the outskirts of the town. But the Student's Grove, dotted with open-air cafés during summer, remains the center both of cultural life and Oslo's amusement life. The Opera House is a short walk away, and the city's three repertory theaters and many movie houses are found nearby. Across the street from the grove, the Oslo Philharmonic performs in the old University Hall. Karl Johans Gate itself is lined with bookstores and fine shops. Since most Norwegians speak English, bookstores and newsstands carry a large selection of literature in English. The stores offer selections of contemporary furniture, crystal, silver, ceramics, furs, handmade fabrics, and sweaters—all the products that have contributed to Norway's reputation as a home of good design and craftsmanship. Some of Norway's best restaurants are found there, and though most offer an international menu, it is still easy to sample Norwegian food, like seafood specialties, reindeer steak, or the traditional cold table with its scores of tempting dishes.

Bergen, Norway's chief port on the North Sea, was the country's cultural center for centuries.

Vessels like the 1,000-year-old Oseberg ship were used by Norway's Viking ancestors to raid northern lands.

Among Oslo's attractions are the Vigeland sculptures in Frogner Park, a collection of more than 150 groups of bronze and granite sculptures depicting the cycle of human life. This monumental work was commissioned by the city of Oslo from Norway's best-known sculptor, Gustav Vigeland. Across the city's harbor is the Bygdøy peninsula, with a number of museums. Perhaps the most famous is the Viking Ship Museum, where three 1,000-year-old Viking ships are preserved, together with many Viking artifacts. The ships look as if they could sail today. A large open-air folk museum is also found on Bygdøy, with groups of authentic old farm buildings, as well as a stave church from the 12th century. In the Polar Exploration Museum is the *Fram,* the ship used on expeditions by Norway's explorer-statesman Fridtjof Nansen, and by Roald Amundsen in 1911, when he became the first man to reach the South Pole. Next door is the Kon-Tiki Museum, which shows the famous balsa raft on which Thor Heyerdahl crossed the Pacific in 1947.

These skiers are practicing a sport Norway is said to have invented.

Other Norwegian Cities. During Norway's early history, Bergen and Trondheim vied with each other for the designation as the nation's capital. Today they rank as Norway's second and third largest cities. The picturesque **Bergen** is located on the southwest coast, about 190 miles (300 km.) from Olso, on a small fiord surrounded by seven mountains. It has been a trade center for almost 1,000 years and is proud of its history, which can be felt everywhere—from Haakonshallen, the medieval banquet hall of the kings of Norway, to the Bryggen (Quay) from the Hanseatic period. Bergen is the home of Norway's second university and its College of Business Administration and is one of the world's leading centers of oceanographic research. Each spring thousands of visitors flock to its international festival of music, drama, and arts, when some of the concerts are held in Edvard Grieg's home, Troldhaugen ("troll's hill"), near the city. Bergen is also the starting point for tours of the great fiords, where the intense blues and greens of the crystal-clear waters reflect fruit orchards near sea-level and snow-clad mountain peaks high above.

In the Middle Ages **Trondheim**, farther to the north, was Norway's religious center. The city's skyline is still dominated by the Nidaros Cathedral, which is considered the finest Gothic church in Scandinavia. Trondheim is the home of Norway's Institute of Technology and of the University of Trondheim. The country's fourth university is in Tromso, in the far north, long a starting point for Arctic exploration.

A string of charming cities and towns lie along the Norwegian coast. **Stavanger**, in the southwest, is an important industrial center and has perhaps the most successful blend of old and modern architecture in the whole country. **Alesund**, north of Bergen, is Norway's largest fishing port and calls itself the herring capital of the world. And **Hammerfest** has the distinction of being the northernmost city in the world. All of them have good schools, libraries, and museums, and if they do not have orchestras, art galleries, and theaters of their own, visits are organized by a number of government-sponsored institutions. Even in a small place, life can be varied and full.

Daily Life in Norway

Norwegians start the day with a hearty breakfast, and therefore have little need for a heavy lunch. School is usually over by 1 or 2 P.M., and offices close at 4 P.M. Shops and factories close by 5 P.M. After an early dinner, there is ample leisure time left over for sports and outdoor activities. Many, if not most, city families have cottages on the seaside or in the mountains, which they use for swimming, sailing, fishing, and hunting. Norway's national sport, however, is skiing. Prehistoric rock carvings over 4,000 years old show skis in use in Norway, and a 2,500-year-old ski is on display in a world-famous ski museum in Oslo. In the 19th century, Norwegians introduced skiing as a sport to the rest of the world. They still win many medals in the winter Olympic Games.

Although Norwegians today take modern conveniences as a matter of course, there are some who do not lead the typical life of an industrial society. In the far north, a few nomadic Lapps still enjoy their traditions, following their reindeer herds from pasture to pasture. Years ago, the reindeer provided meat and furs for tents and clothing. Today, the sale of reindeer meat is the Lapp's main source of income. But modern life has reached the Lapps, too. The Norwegian government has built a special school and cultural center at Kautokeino, and radios and modern communications have brought the Lapps closer to the 21st century. (An article on LAPLAND appears in this volume.)

LOOKING TOWARD THE FUTURE

In the early 2000s, thanks to its oil and natural gas deposits, Norway is one of the wealthiest countries in the world, and a leading petroleum exporter. Since it is expected that the nation's oil resources will be exhausted within several decades, Norway is already preparing for this situation by placing their surpluses into a special fund. All their historic experience has taught them to manage their resources very carefully and to always be prepared for lean years.

Following the Nazi occupation during World War II, Norwegians abandoned their traditional neutrality and, in 1949, joined the North Atlantic Treaty Organization (NATO). The country, however, is currently not a member of the European Union (EU). As early as 1972, Norwegian voters rejected joining the EU's precursor, the European Community (EC). In another referendum, in 1994, they voted against membership in the EU mainly to preserve their small-scale farming and fishing industries. Despite this, Norway is not isolated from the rest of the continent, and maintains busy contacts with most European nations. It also belongs to the European Economic Area (EEA), established in 1991, which represents the world's largest common market.

Norway is not only a wealthy nation, but it is also considered to be one of the most environmentally "healthy" countries in the world, with clean air, rivers, and great expanses of unspoiled woodlands. Because the population is so small and homogeneous, there are few serious political or social disputes.

LARS LANGAKER, Cultural Attaché, Royal Norwegian Embassy Information Service

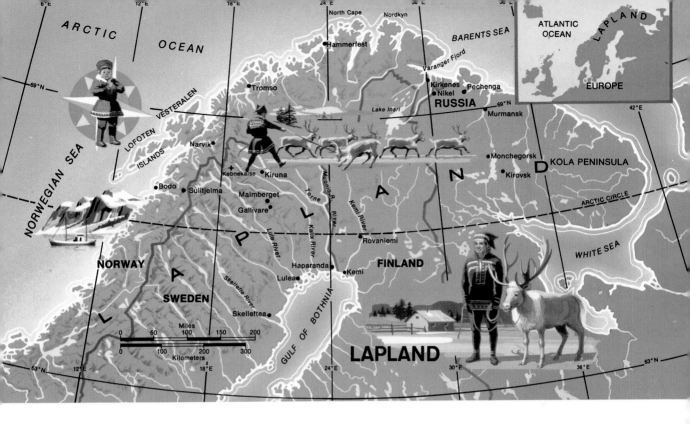

LAPLAND

Lapland is a region of some 150,000 sq. mi. (390,000 sq. km.) that cuts across northern Norway, Sweden, Finland, and the Kola Peninsula of Russia. There, at the very top of Europe, live 60,000 to 70,000 Lapps—30,000 to 40,000 in Norway, 20,000 in Sweden, 6,000 in Finland, and 2,000 in Russia. These people, who call themselves Sami, have made this harsh environment their home for thousands of years, and over the centuries have adapted to it. Today, there are also Swedes, Norwegians, Finns, and Russians living in Lapland.

The Lapps probably arrived in northern Europe at the end of the last Ice Age. They were gradually pushed into the Arctic Circle by the Finns, Norwegians, and Swedes. The Lapps were isolated by the severe conditions in which they lived. But slowly they developed resources for making life easier in their unique northern homeland. They learned to tame and breed wild dogs and reindeer. They invented skis.

THE LAND

In the vast area above the tree line, there are seemingly endless snowfields and alpine mountains. Along the Arctic coastland there are gaunt, rocky cliffs. Inland are deep rivers with dangerous rapids and spectacular waterfalls, and sparkling finger-shaped lakes with thousands of islands. There are boundless marshlands and dense forests.

The Sun does not set over Lapland for 2 to 5 months of the year. The regions closest to the North Pole have sunshine for the longest periods. The Sun dips close to the horizon, filling the sky with glorious color. In midwinter, when conditions are reversed, there are a few hours

A **Lapp** boy in traditional costume beside the family tent.

A **Lapp** family admires one of its prize reindeer.

of twilight at midday, but the sun does not rise at all for 6 weeks or more.

Economy. The development of mineral resources in Lapland has brought thousands of new people to the area. One of the largest deposits of high-grade iron ore in the world is located at Kiruna in Swedish Lapland. Norway has iron mines near Kirkenes, and other metals are mined in Swedish, Russian, and Finnish Lapland. In northern Norway fish is a very valuable export. The rushing rivers are the site of many hydroelectric plants that supply power to Sweden and Finland.

THE PEOPLE

Lapps are known by the area in which they settled. The coastal or sea Lapps of Norway and the river Lapps of Sweden and Finland live in permanent homes and are mostly fishermen. The forest Lapps may have small reindeer herds, but today they combine reindeer breeding with fishing, simple farming, or working in the mining or timber industries. They do not wander far from their settlements.

Some Lapps live in cities and make their living from a thriving tourist industry. Because of the moderating effect of the Norwegian Current, Lapland has a much milder climate than parallel regions in northernmost Canada, Alaska, and Siberia. This encourages thousands of visitors to flock to Lapland to see the midnight sun, to ski, camp, and hike in the magnificent wilderness, and to observe the Lapp way of life.

Once all reindeer-breeding Lapps were nomads, with no permanent homes. Families moved south to the forests in winter. In summer they went north to escape the ferocious swarming mosquitoes and to reach the tundra, the plains on which moss and lichen—the reindeer's food—grow over permanently frozen subsoil. Today, family migrations are shorter or have almost ceased.

Not long ago skis and boat sleds pulled by reindeer provided the nomads with their only transportation over the frozen wastelands in winter. In summer the Lapps walked, but the reindeer carried their packs. The reindeer gave them milk. Some were also slaughtered for food and for their hides. The pelts, sewn with thread made from reindeer sinews, became clothing, shoes, and blankets and were used for the tepeelike tents. Reindeer bones and horns were shaped into implements and utensils. In Lapp a large reindeer herd is *aello*, "what one lives on." Today reindeer are bred for their pelts, and for their meat.

Tourists and workmen have brought the trappings of the modern world to Lapland, but the Lapps still follow many of their old ways of life. Families are close-knit, and devotion is lavished on the children. The Lapp language (which is related to Finnish) has a wealth of special ways to express affection between children and parents, between husband and wife, and between friends. The language also reflects the Lapps' deep feeling about nature. Special words describe states of weather and types of valleys, rivers, and lakes. There are countless words for the beloved reindeer, including a different name for the male reindeer for each of the first 6 years of life. Though there is little written Lapp literature, there is a rich store of legends and fairy tales that tell of the beauty and the hardship of life at the edge of the habitable world.

Reviewed by MIKKO IMMONEN
Former Consul, Consulate General of Finland, New York

Stockholm, Sweden's capital, is a city built on islands.

SWEDEN

Sweden shares the Scandinavian peninsula with its neighbor, Norway. There, at the top of Europe, the Swedish people have created for themselves a prosperous, peaceful, democratic kingdom where they enjoy one of the highest standards of living in Europe.

Unlike many other European nations, Sweden has never known a large-scale foreign occupation, and has not been at war since 1814. In the hope of ensuring their prosperity and independence, the Swedes cling to their policy of neutrality and depend on their self-reliance and strength.

THE LAND

Sweden, one of the largest nations in Europe, is a long, narrow country. Geographers often divide it into three main parts: Gotaland in the south, Svealand in the center, and Norrland in the north. Gotaland, traditional home of the Goths, includes the most southern of Sweden's provinces, Skane. There, on 2.5 percent of the land, live 12 percent of the Swedish people. Skane, which enjoys Sweden's most pleasant climate, is a natural garden. There, amid gently rolling fields and peaceful villages, is Sweden's best agricultural land. Skane also has miles of white, sandy beaches along its coast. Many resorts and the important port of Malmo are located on the coast.

North of Skane rise the Swedish highlands—a rugged, wooded land-scape. This area is damper and cooler, and the forests begin here. The land is stony and the soil thin. This is where most Swedish glass, furniture, and handicraft industries are located.

Svealand is considered the middle section of the country although it is still in the bottom half of Sweden. Here are the great forests that are supposed to have separated the two ancient rival tribes, the Svear and their southern neighbors, the Goths. There are also iron deposits here, and this is where most of Sweden's metal plants and steel foundries are.

Most of the more than 100,000 lakes of Sweden are in this central region. Some, such as Lake Malar, Lake Vatter, and Lake Vaner, are extremely large.

Sweden's two largest cities, Stockholm, the capital, and Göteborg, the port city, are in Svealand. They are connected by the picturesque Gota Canal, a remarkable inland waterway, only about one-third of which is actually composed of canals. The remainder is a chain of rivers and lakes that form one of the loveliest areas in Scandinavia. Svealand also includes Dalarna, a historic province of Sweden, with lovely mountains and the beautiful Lake Silja.

Norrland, the third area of Sweden, covers about two-thirds of the country. This sparsely populated northern land contains Sweden's highest mountains, including Kebnekaise, its highest peak. Norrland is considered the last open frontier in Europe. It is Sweden's big reservoir of natural resources. The great forests feed the string of sawmills, pulp mills, and cellulose factories on the coast. The enormous waterfalls provide the electric power for most of Sweden. The giant iron mountains give Sweden one of the world's most important sources of iron ore.

The nothern highlands extend from central Sweden up beyond the Arctic Circle. This is the heart of Lapland, although Lapland is a vast area that also includes part of Norway, Finland, and Russia. Some 10,000 Lapps live in Swedish Lapland, and many still follow their herds of reindeer on annual migrations to the mountains in the spring and to the lowlands in the fall. (An article on LAPLAND appears in this volume.)

Off the east coast in the Baltic are two large limestone islands, Gotland and Oland. Oland is rich in archeological remains, Viking ship burial sites, and prehistoric forts. Both islands have a great variety of lovely and unusual flowers. Gotland is a trip back six centuries in history to the times of knights and monks. On the island is Visby, the only walled city in northern Europe and one of the best preserved anywhere.

Climate. Although it lies far north, Sweden has a more moderate climate than one would expect. It is warmed by the prevailing southwesterly winds and by the extension of the Gulf Stream current that brings the warm water from the West Indies to the North Atlantic.

But in such a long, stretched-out country, there is naturally a fairly wide variety of climate. "Last year summer happened on a Thursday" is the standard joke in Sweden. In the far north summer lasts only about six weeks, but during that time the midnight sun never sets. In midwinter, for the same period of time, there is almost total darkness. In Lapland snow lies on the ground from August to June. In the south, summer weather is mild and pleasant and lasts from about May to September. By September it is chilly, and in the winter it snows frequently.

Resources. Ore, forests, and water are Sweden's great natural riches. More than one-half of the country is wooded. The favorable climate makes it possible for trees to grow everywhere except on the high mountains in the north. The major rivers of Sweden flow generally southeast from the mountains to the Gulf of Bothnia. Rivers flow through the forests, making it comparatively easy to float the logs down to factories and mills on the coast. A great deal of money, however, has been spent on building good roads, and today logs are often transported by truck.

It seems that where there are no trees in Sweden, there is water. Lakes cover nearly nine percent of the country's area, and the rapids on the rivers supply Sweden with large amounts of hydroelectricity.

Some mines are found in central Sweden, but in the northland there are whole mountains of iron ore. Northern Sweden also has deposits of copper, lead, and zinc.

Sweden does lack some important resources. It needs to import oil, coal, and coke, but the ingenious Swedes have used what they have the most of—iron ore, water, and forests—to build a great industrial nation. Since most available waterpower has been harnessed, however, Sweden has begun to utilize atomic energy. Several nuclear plants are in operation, but further development of this energy source is uncertain because questions about the safety of nuclear generators to produce electricity have led to political controversy.

THE PEOPLE

The population of Sweden is very homogeneous, but there are two distinct minorities: the Finns and the Sami (or Lapps), who live in the north. In recent years, Sweden has also opened its doors to many immigrants, including people from the former Yugoslavia, Turkey, and Greece.

Religion. The people of Sweden also share the same religion. About 87 percent belong to the state church, which is the Evangelical Lutheran Church. There is complete religious freedom, but by law, the king must be a member of the state church.

Language. The Swedish language is related to the languages spoken by the Norwegians and the Danes. All are related to German. The Swedish alphabet is like that of English, but also includes three additional vowels, å, ä, and ö, which come at the end of the alphabet.

Education. In 1842, earlier than in most countries, education was made compulsory. Students must now attend school from the age of 7 to 16. After the basic cycle, students can enter the higher-education system, which was reorganized in the early 1990s. About one-third of all students are enrolled in academic or vocational training programs. Sweden has 37 institutions of higher learning, including the University of Uppsala (established in 1477) and the University of Lund (in 1668). Vital parts of the educational system are the Scandinavian folk high schools, designed specifically for adult education.

Way of Life. The Swedes are extremely hardworking. But they also know how to play. In the summer, they leave their offices early and often take three-day weekends. All workers are entitled to four weeks of paid vacation leave.

Swedish people love sports. Soccer is the national game. Camping, bicycling, motoring, skiing, sailing, tennis, and golf are all very popular. All Swedes are required to take gymnastics in school, and many Swedes continue the exercises afterward since they take great pride in being physically fit.

About 80 percent of the Swedish people live in apartment houses. Because of the high cost of heating during the long winter months, it is more economical to build apartment houses than it is to build individual

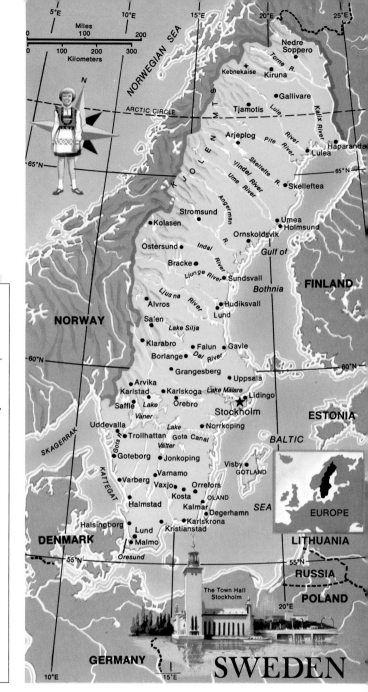

homes. However, many Swedish families have cabins in the woods to which they escape whenever possible.

Sweden is not a classless society, but because of high taxes and wide social benefits, it is a society in which differences hardly seem evident. Ways of living do not vary much from one part of the country to another. The fair-minded Swedes see to it that telephone subscribers in Stockholm pay the same rate for installing a telephone as do the Lapps, for whom it may be necessary to run 50 mi. (80 km.) of wires. Most people have automobiles. Most people live in attractive flats. All see the same television programming. All go to the same state-run schools, take the same examinations, draw similar social-benefit grants, and earn salaries not too different from those of their neighbors.

Sweden has highly productive farms and abundant forestland, despite being as far north as Alaska.

Generally speaking, the Swedish people are determined to find a way for everyone to realize his or her greatest potential. Many sum up the Swedish way of life by saying Sweden is a country of balance and moderation, a country of *lagom,* which means, roughly: not too little, not too much, but just about right.

A large proportion of Swedish married women work full- or part-time outside the home. Since domestic help is almost unknown, the majority of married women with children find it necessary to stay home until their youngsters are old enough to start school. There are free day-care nurseries, but these facilities are used mainly by working mothers who are the sole support of their families.

Whether at home or in a restaurant, Swedish food is delicious and well-prepared. Perhaps the best-known contribution of Sweden to international cuisine is the smorgasbord. This legendary feast—which has been known to satisfy even the heartiest appetites—consists of a seemingly endless array of fish, meats, salads, and cheeses, from which diners select courses until they have eaten their fill. Smorgasbord is usually accompanied by beer. Should any room be left over for dessert, there are tiny, delicate Swedish pancakes, sugared and served with whipped cream and a sauce made of lingonberries, or mountain cranberries. Swedish cooks also take pride in their preparation of the fresh fish that abound in northern waters and in such dishes as *köttbullar,* or Swedish meatballs, which enjoy worldwide popularity.

Writers. Because few foreigners speak Swedish, many of the great past and contemporary writers are unknown to the rest of the world. Only through translation have their works become familiar beyond Swedish shores. Selma Lagerlöf, the first woman to receive the Nobel prize for literature, is probably Sweden's best-known writer. At her death at the age of 82, in 1940, she left a great body of work which ranges from *The Story of Gösta Berling,* a novel based on legends of her native Varmland, to the children's books about Nils, a youngster who traveled on the back of a wild goose and thus learned about the geography, culture, and history of Sweden and of foreign lands. August Strindberg's plays, such as *The Father,* and *Miss Julia,* have had a lasting effect on the development of drama in the Western world. Another great Swedish dramatist, Pär Lagerkvist, wrote stark plays about the plight of man, violence, and wars. He also wrote novels and poems.

Art. In Sweden there are some 2,000 runic inscriptions engraved by Viking artists on boulders, on the face of the bedrock, or on flat, upright stones. In these intricate patterns, done in the country's earliest days, we can see the beginning of Swedish interest in art and design.

The Swedes have always been noted for their wood carvings and sculptures. Sweden's best-known modern sculptor was Carl Milles, who died in 1955. Many of his exuberant works can be seen in a beautiful setting overlooking the waters of the Baltic in Millesgarden, in Lidingo, a suburb of Stockholm.

Sweden's architects have long designed buildings that demonstrated their feeling for the natural beauty of wood, stone, and other materials. The early medieval log buildings, the simple churches of the Middle Ages, the austere castles of the 16th century, and the mansions of later days all had the strong, clean lines and elegant simplicity that are evident in modern Swedish concrete, glass, and wood structures.

Swedish crystal is world renowned for its delicate designs and unusually vivid colors.

Films. Swedish culture today is probably best-known to the rest of the world through the films produced in Sweden. Since the 1940's the work of Swedish directors has been acclaimed by critics everywhere. Arne Sucksdorff's *The Great Adventure* and *A Jungle Tale* and Ingmar Bergman's *The Seventh Seal, Wild Strawberries,* and *Through a Glass Darkly* are considered classics of the screen.

SWEDISH CITIES

More than 80 percent of the Swedish people live in cities and towns, and the process of urbanization is still continuing. There are three metropolitan areas: greater Stockholm, Göteborg and surrounding areas in the west, and Malmo and its neighboring cities in the south.

Stockholm. Stockholm today is truly the center of Sweden and Swedish life. It is the seat of the government and the center of business and culture. It is an important manufacturing city as well. Seen from a plane the lovely city seems to be made of many separate pieces all floating on blue water and interlaced by an intricate network of bridges. Actually, the Queen of the Waters, as Stockholm is known, is built on a whole group of islands where the fresh water of Lake Malar meets the Baltic Sea. Founded in the 13th century, Stockholm became the capital of Sweden in 1634. The Old Town (Gamla Stan) is on an island in the center of the city, and it is from this island that the modern city grew. The Old Town, which still retains its medieval street plan, includes the Royal Palace, a masterpiece of classical design.

The rest of Stockholm is modern, busy, and crowded. All of it seems to be clean, sparkling, and carefully planned. It is hard to mention all

Pedestrian shopping mall in Stockholm combines efficiency and the best of modern design.

These are just a few of the sculptures in the Millesgarden, outside Stockholm.

the treasures of Stockholm and its environs. The museums are a delight to visit, since their collections are displayed with great technical skill.

The Royal Academy of Music, founded in 1771, is one of the oldest on the continent outside of Italy, and the Royal Opera dates from 1773. It plays one of the longest seasons in the world. Close to the city is the famous Drottningholm Court Theater. Built in 1766, Drottningholm is the world's only complete 18th-century theater that has survived and is used just as it was in earlier times for operas and ballets.

Skansen, a beautiful 60-acre (24 hectares) park a few minutes from the center of town, is really a great open-air museum. More than 100 old buildings brought from all over Sweden have been reconstructed there.

Göteborg.   A seaport on the Kattegat at the mouth of the Gota River, Göteborg is Sweden's second largest city and greatest port. It is also a historic city. Dutch town planners were brought in to build it in the 17th century, and their influence is apparent in the old circular canals. The charming Gotaplatsen (Gota Square) is dominated by Carl Milles' fountain sculpture of Poseidon, the Greek sea god. Göteborg is a busy center of auto manufacturing and ball-bearing production. It has an ultramodern shipyard that produces supertankers.

Malmo.   Sweden's third city is on the Oresund opposite Copenhagen. From the end of the Middle Ages until 1658, when it became Swedish, Malmo was one of the leading cities of Denmark. The central city retains its medieval street plan, but the city has spread out and also has some of Sweden's most interesting modern housing projects. An important port, Malmo is also a shipbuilding and manufacturing city. It has many notable buildings, including the finest Gothic church in Sweden, the 14th-century Church of Saint Peter.

ECONOMY

Early in the 20th century, Sweden was one of the most backward countries in Europe. Conditions were so bad that more than one-fifth of the population emigrated to America. In a truly remarkable leap forward, the Swedish people, in a relatively short period of time, created a prosperous industrial nation with almost full employment, where a large share of the national production is exported.

The early industries were based on Swedish forests and minerals. Swedish inventors aided in developing industries by devising products and perfecting techniques to aid in their manufacture. In the 19th century, J. E. Lundström invented the safety match. And in 1866, Alfred B. Nobel invented dynamite and began to accumulate the fortune that enabled him to establish the prestigious Nobel prizes. Other Swedish inventions include ball bearings, new types of steam turbines, methods of electrical transmission, and other products.

Shipbuilding, a traditional industry, is still important, but more important today is the manufacture of cars, buses, and trucks. The Volvo and Saab automobiles have gained worldwide reputations for their reliability. Some of the finest steel in the world is made in Sweden, and many products made from high-grade steel are exported.

The Swedish economy has expanded into other fields as well. The IKEA stores, selling modern, practical furnishings for homes, can now be found in many countries. The Ericsson company, an electronics producer, is one of the largest in its field.

Göteborg is Sweden's leading port and home to its largest shipyards. Only Japan leads in shipbuilding.

Iron ore from the north is used to make high-quality steel—an important Swedish export.

By the early 21st century, Sweden has also become the most wired—and wireless—nation in Europe. More than half of its citizens have access to the Internet, and young entrepreneurs are making Sweden a European leader in the digital revolution. Communication has always been important in this country of great distances (back in 1900, Stockholm had more telephones than London or Berlin), and because virtually all Swedes know English, they have quickly mastered Information Age technology. After experiencing a low point in the early 1990s, Sweden's overall economy is now growing at a rate that is outpacing those of most other European Union (EU) countries.

Agricultural Products. Only 7 percent of the land in Sweden is arable, and only about 2 percent of the people are now employed in agriculture. Most of the farming is done in the southern part of the country. By the use of soil studies, improved seed, artificial fertilizers, and mechanization, Sweden has managed to produce record harvests. Most of the farms are very small, but almost all are participants in cooperatives that market products and provide farmers with equipment. It is remarkable that with so little farmland, Sweden feeds itself so well.

GOVERNMENT
Although Sweden has a king, he exerts no political power and is no longer even crowned. He is the titular head of the state, while real responsibility rests with the prime minister, who is the leader of the majority party in the Parliament. The present king is Carl XVI Gustaf, who succeeded his grandfather, Gustav VI Adolf, in 1973.

The Riksdag, or parliament, became a permanent institution in 1435. One of the oldest legislative bodies in the world, it has one chamber elected by all citizens 18 years or older. The Social Democratic Labor Party (Socialdemokratiska Arbetarepartiet, or SDAP) has been the ruling party almost continuously since 1932, the exceptions being 1976 to 1982, and again from 1991 to 1994. A man symbolizing the rule of SDAP and the creation of the famous Swedish welfare state was Olaf Palme, who became head of the party and prime minister in 1969, at the age of 42 (at that time the youngest prime minister in Europe). In 1986, Palme was assassinated in Stockholm, while he was returning with his wife from a movie. The mystery of his death remains officially unsolved. Since 1996, the SDAP leader and prime minister has been Göran Persson.

Welfare State. Since the early 20th century, the Swedish people have been developing a wide range of social-welfare benefits for all citizens. Government-provided services include free health care, free college tuition, child-care benefits, unemployment provisions, and pensions for everyone over the age of 67. Such benefits are expensive, and taxes are consequently quite high. In 1993, with the economy reeling from the skyrocketing costs of cradle-to-grave benefits, Sweden began to reevaluate its all-encompassing social programs. The tax code was reformed and corporate taxes were lowered, but the benefits are still quite generous.

After joining the European Union, Sweden had to bring its social system in line with the European Union's criteria. Nevertheless, the country refused to adopt the common European currency, the euro, in 1999.

HISTORY

The land that is now Sweden emerged late from the retreating ice cap. Tribes of hunters moved north, and for many years two tribes, the Goths in the south and the Svear in the eastern part of central Sweden, waged war. Ultimately, in the 9th century A.D., the two tribes were united. The Swedish name for Sweden, *Sverige,* can be translated as "kingdom of the Svear."

During the time of the Vikings (A.D. 800–1050), these fierce sea warriors went on long expeditions to trade and to wage war. The Swedish Vikings sailed eastward across the Baltic Sea. Some of them even traveled down the Russian rivers as far as the Black and Caspian Seas. By the 10th century the Swedish Vikings had established trading posts there. The name "Russia" may come from the word "Ros," the name of the Swedish Vikings who lived along the Baltic, north of Stockholm.

Christian missionaries visited Sweden during this time, but it was not until the 12th century that Christianity was firmly established. During the 11th and 12th centuries, Sweden gradually became a united kingdom. Working to convert the Finns, the Swedes developed Finland as a part of Sweden. In 1397, the Kalmar Union united all the Nordic lands—Denmark, Norway, and Sweden—under a Danish queen, Queen Margrethe. The Swedes feared Danish domination, and warfare broke out in the 15th century. In 1523, Sweden became independent. Until 1814, a long series of terrible wars between Denmark-Norway on one side and Sweden-Finland on the other marked Scandinavian history.

Gustavus Vasa, a young nobleman who had led the Swedes in their struggle against the Kalmar Union, was elected king in 1523. He took the title Gustavus I, and until his death in 1560 he did much to lay the

Gripsholm Castle, in southern Sweden, was a favorite residence of King Gustavus I.

foundation of modern Sweden. It was during his reign that Sweden broke with the Catholic Church and Lutheranism became the state religion. His grandson, known as Gustavus Adolphus, who ruled from 1611 until 1632, led an enormous political and military expansion. Under his leadership, Swedish armies played an important role in the Thirty Years' War. By the end of his reign Sweden could regard the Baltic Sea as a Swedish lake.

Swedish power was constantly challenged by Russia, Saxony-Poland, and Denmark-Norway. In 1700 they joined to attack the Swedish kingdom. The young Swedish king Charles XII won spectacular victories, but his plan to attack Moscow led to a catastrophic defeat at Poltava in 1709. This marked the beginning of the end of Sweden as a great power.

Gradually Sweden was forced to give up its Baltic territories. In 1809 the Swedes lost Finland, a country they had held since the 12th century. At this time Sweden was in a desperate economic condition and feared invasion by the Danes from the south and west and by the Russians from the east. A revolution deposed the monarch, and the Swedes drafted a constitution and elected Jean Baptiste Bernadotte (1763–1844), a general in the French Revolution and later one of Napoleon's marshals, to be their crown prince. He succeeded in 1818 as King Charles XIV.

Under Crown Prince Bernadotte the Swedish armies fought against Napoleon. By the Treaty of Kiel in 1814, Sweden received Norway from Denmark. The union of Sweden and Norway lasted until 1905, when the Norwegians demanded and received their independence.

In the early 1900s Sweden embarked on a great drive for liberalized government and economic development of the country. At the same time, the Swedes became determined to make neutrality the keystone of their foreign policy. During World War I, Denmark, Norway, and Sweden declared their neutrality. When World War II broke out, they did so again. Denmark and Norway were invaded. Sweden escaped. All during the struggle, Sweden did much to aid its Scandinavian neighbors and served as a haven for refugees.

During the 1980s, the presence of Soviet submarines in Swedish waters led to tense relations between the two countries. Relations worsened following the 1986 nuclear-reactor explosion in Chernobyl, which spread radiation throughout Western Europe and particularly Sweden. During the late 1980s, Sweden was beset by a number of environmental problems. In 1988, an increase in algae levels severely damaged the west coast's marine ecosystem. Then a virus decimated the seal populations of the North and Baltic Seas.

Neutrality. For more than 150 years, Swedes have been living in peace, and they wish to go on doing so. Sweden's neutral state is supported by substantial military power. The Swedes have used their natural resources to aid their defense planning. Vast underground shelters, said to be safe even during a nuclear attack, have been carved out of Sweden's rocky terrain. They are used in many practical ways—for parking lots, warehouses, and even gymnasiums. Defense expenditures are large for such a small nation, and there is universal military service.

Yet Sweden has always been in the forefront of all peace efforts. A strong supporter of the League of Nations in the past, Sweden is today a strong supporter of the United Nations (UN). Swedish troops have served with peacekeeping missions in Somalia, Macedonia, Lebanon, Israel, and elsewhere. Count Folke Bernadotte lost his life in 1948 in Israel, where he had gone as a UN mediator. Dag Hammarskjöld, the second secretary-general of the UN, died in an accident in 1961 on his way to the Congo.

Sweden, Norway, Denmark, Finland, and Iceland are known as the Nordic countries. Since the 1950s, the Nordic Council has met to discuss and recommend parallel legislation and administrative actions. Relations among these five countries are so close that any Nordic citizen may freely cross the border into any other Nordic country to take up work or residence and is entitled to social-security benefits while there.

The Swedes have often been criticized for remaining aloof in their neutrality, and for being smug about their accomplishments. But along the path that took Sweden from being a great power to a welfare state, there were many hardships. The Swedish people have attained what they have through a willingness to work hard and to pay the price in high taxes for their improvements and benefits.

Joining the World. In recent years Swedes have come to realize the potential benefits of joining the European integration process. After the European Community (EC) changed its name to the European Union (EU) and established a common market of goods, labor, and capital in 1993, Sweden decided to become a member, and did so in 1995. Together with Great Britain and Denmark, however, Sweden has not yet adopted the euro, which, in January 2002, replaced the currencies in 12 EU countries.

Sweden has become more cosmopolitan in other ways as well. As of the early 2000s, it remains the third-largest exporter of pop music, after the United States and Britain. The now-defunct (but still enormously popular) ABBA, artists Sturmark and Meja, and such bands as the Cardigans are known around the world.

ULRICH HERZ
Secretary-General, International Peace Bureau, Geneva

In winter in Finland, reindeer are often used to pull sleds.

FINLAND

Sisu is a Finnish word that means "spirit," "courage," "patriotism," "tenacity," and "determination," and it is the word that best describes the people of Finland.

THE LAND

Since about one third of Finland lies north of the Arctic Circle, the Finns live in one of the most northerly nations in Europe (and the world). Yet Finland today enjoys a high standard of living from every point of view—economical, social, and cultural.

Although Finland lies farther north than the distant wastes of northern Labrador, it has developed modern industry, agriculture, and cities. The Fennoscandian Peninsula, which Finland shares with Norway and Sweden, juts out of continental Europe into the Atlantic Ocean. Southwesterly winds from the Gulf Stream bring warmth and moisture to the land. The waters of the Baltic Sea and the Gulf of Bothnia also contribute to the maritime quality of Finland's climate. As a result, no part of Finland is covered by permanent snow, ice, or ground frost. Temperatures are generally mild, and even during February, the coldest month of the year, temperatures in the north average about 5 degrees Fahrenheit (−15 degrees Celsius).

Finland has an area slightly less than that of the state of Montana. Many rivers thread the land. Its coasts are heavily indented and fringed by some 30,000 islands. Along the western coast especially, another unique aspect of Finnish geography can be observed—land emergence. Since the last Ice Age, about 8,000 years ago, the land has

One of Finland's 60,000 lakes.

been gradually rising from the sea at a rate of about 3 to 4 ft. (1 m.) every century, adding miles of land to Finland's area every 100 years.

Lakes and Forests

Finland has more than 60,000 lakes, which comprise about nine percent of the country's area. Many of them are in central and southeast Finland, where the land was shaped and folded into ridges and depressions by the glaciers of the past Ice Age. The largest of Finland's lakes, and the center of its lake system, is Saimaa, near the Russian border. The Saimaa Canal, extensively rebuilt after World War II, links the industrial city of Lappeenranta on the south shore of the lake with Vyborg, a Russian port on the Baltic.

North of Lake Saimaa, near the town of Savonlinna, stands Olavinlinna ("Saint Olaf's castle"). Built in 1475 as a watchtower facing east, Olavinlinna is the best-preserved medieval fortress in northern Europe. Now, however, the castle walls echo not with the sounds of battle but with the music of the opera festival that is held there every July. Not far from Olavinlinna is Punkaharju, where a road winds for about 5 mi. (8 km.) along a narrow rise of land topped by some of the tallest pine trees in the world. Punkaharju—the word means "primrose ridge" in Finnish—has inspired many poets, artists, and musicians. Overlooking a dazzling view of lakes and islands, it has been described as the soul of Finland and is one of the country's main tourist attractions.

ECONOMY

Since Finland has no coal or oil, waterpower—or "white coal"—is the source of much of the country's electricity. The lake system's major task, however, is carrying wood—Finland's most valuable natural resource. After the timber is cut, huge rafts of logs are floated to the mills,

Olavinlinna, a castle in southeastern Finland, dates from the 15th century.

where they are turned into pulp and paper; to the factories, where they are made into fine furniture; or down to Baltic ports for export to countries around the world. Forests cover about three-quarters of Finland's total land area.

About 8 percent of the land is suitable for farming, and even this small amount had to be won over the years from forests and swamps by backbreaking labor. Today, although the majority of Finnish farms are small—only a few hundred are larger than 250 acres (100 ha.)—every bit of usable land has responded so well to careful tillage that the country is almost self-sufficient in food production. Most of the farms are owned and run by individual families.

The soil resources are modest, but Finland has the advantage of long days during the growing season. In the south in late June, the Sun shines for some 18 to 19 hours daily. In the extreme north, well above the Arctic Circle, the Sun remains above the horizon for more than 70 consecutive days during the year.

Hardy types of grain that ripen during the short growing season are raised extensively, and Finland is able to supply almost 90 percent of its own grain needs. Since the early 1900s, however, dairy farming has become more important than grain farming. Finnish farmers also raise such vegetables as beets, carrots, cabbage, turnips, spinach, and lettuce. Apples, especially cold-resistant varieties, are grown over a wide area, but pears, cherries, and plums succeed only in the south, where the climate is mildest. Potatoes are the only crop that grows in the far north.

During the 20th century. Finland was transformed into a modern industrialized nation from a country that had long been dependent on farming and forestry. Until the fall of the Soviet Union in 1991, a large percentage of Finnish foreign trade was with that superpower. The disruption of these economic ties caused a short-lived recession. A Finnish

Forests are Finland's most valuable natural resource. Cut timber, bundled into rafts, is floated downstream to paper mills, furniture factories, or to Baltic ports for export.

company called Nokia correctly predicted that the future was in communications, and began producing cellular phones. Soon, the company became the mainstay of the country's economy and, by 2000, a billion people around the globe used their cell phones.

Finland's integration into the international economy has also been bolstered by its joining the European Union (EU) in 1999, and later adopting the eruo as its national currency.

THE PEOPLE AND THEIR HISTORY

The origin of the Finns is unknown, although linguistic studies have shown that the Finnish language is related to Estonian and, more distantly, to Hungarian. Finland's recorded history actually began during the Middle Ages, at a time when most Finns lived by hunting and farming, and the country consisted of a group of settlements located mainly along the rivers, within 200 mi. (320 km.) of the south coast.

At the turn of the millennium, Finns were keeping abreast with the rapidly changing world. More than two-thirds of them have cellular phones and almost half are connected to the Internet. The educational system has been modernized, and a greater percentage of young people attend college, compared to most other European countries.

Finland and Sweden

In 1155, King Eric IX of Sweden decided to convert the land of the Finns to Christianity. He sent the Bishop of Uppsala, at the head of an army, across the Gulf of Bothnia. This was the first of three Swedish crusades to Finland. Within about 100 years, most of the Finns had accepted Christianity. Since they had had no national government, there was little resistance and Finland was easily absorbed by Sweden. In this period, cathedrals and fortresses were built and towns grew up around them, including Turku, on the Aura River in southwest Finland. Finland's first university was founded there in 1640. The city was also the center of Roman Catholicism in Finland and, after the Protestant Reformation in the 16th century, of the Lutheran Church. Turku was the capital of Finland until 1812, when Helsinki became the capital.

The inclusion of Finland in its kingdom was an important factor in Sweden's rise to power in the Baltic, a power it was able to maintain against all challenges through the 17th century. In 1703, however, seeking increased trade with European nations and what he called a "window looking on Europe," Czar Peter the Great of Russia founded the city of St. Petersburg (later Leningrad, but since 1991 St. Petersburg again). He built his city on land he had taken by force from Sweden. Throughout the 18th century, Finland remained a focal point in the struggle between Sweden and Russia, and it was repeatedly invaded by Russian armies, especially between the years 1713 and 1721.

In the 18th and 19th centuries, the first awakenings of nationalism took place in Finland. The two leaders responsible were Henrik Gabriel Porthan and Elias Lönnrot. Porthan was a historian who tried through his writings to create an awareness of Finland's own special heritage as a nation. Lönnrot spent many years traveling all over Finland, collecting the legends and tales that had been handed down by generations of Finnish folk poets. In 1835 he published the first edition of the *Kalevala,* the long poem that became Finland's national epic.

Finland and Russia

By the time of the Napoleonic Wars, Swedish power in the Baltic had disappeared almost entirely. In 1808 the King of Sweden refused to join Napoleon I's blockage of England. In retaliation, Napoleon persuaded Czar Alexander I to invade Finland. In 1809, after more than 600 years, Sweden had to give up Finland to Russia.

Again the Finns were not actually conquered. Finland became part of Russia as an autonomous state. Finland was allowed to keep the constitution that had applied to all of Sweden before 1808. The legal rights of Finland's citizens remained unchanged. The Lutheran Church remained the state church. A Finnish government council was set up in Helsinki, the new capital, and a delegation of Finns was sent to the Russian capital to advise the Czar on Finnish matters. The Czar of Russia, under the title Grand Duke of Finland, ruled Finland as a constitutional monarch. So at first Finland seemed to have gained by its inclusion in the Russian Empire. At the same time, other changes were taking place. Farming was being modernized; a nationwide school system was introduced (1866); and railroads and industry came to Finland as they did to the rest of Western Europe.

Yet in the second half of the 19th century, other trends appeared. The spirit of nationalism began to spread. During the Crimean War (1854–56), some young Finns, dreaming of independence, joined the British Navy to fight the Russian fleet in the Baltic. After the war, though Czar Alexander II had granted Finland liberal reforms, Finland's self-

Highly productive family farms have made Finland nearly self-sufficient in agriculture.

FACTS AND FIGURES

OFFICIAL NAME: Republic of Finland.

NATIONALITY: Finn(s).

CAPITAL: Helsinki.

LOCATION: Fennoscandian Peninsula. **Boundaries—** Norway, Russia, Gulf of Finland, Baltic Sea, Gulf of Bothnia, Sweden.

AREA: 130,127 sq. mi. (337,030 sq. km.).

PHYSICAL FEATURES: Highest point—Mt. Haltia (4,357 ft.; 1,328 m.). **Lowest point—**sea level. **Chief rivers—**Kemi, Oulu, Tornio, Muonio, Pats, Ounas, Kokemäki, Kymi, Vuoksi. **Major lakes—**Saimaa, Oulu.

POPULATION: 5,200,000 (2002; annual growth 0.2%).

MAJOR LANGUAGES: Finnish, Swedish (both official), Lapp, Russian.

MAJOR RELIGIONS: Evangelical Lutheranism, Greek Orthodoxy.

GOVERNMENT: Republic. **Head of state—**president. **Head of government—**prime minister. **Legislature—**unicameral Eduskunta.

CHIEF CITIES: Helsinki, Tampere, Turku.

ECONOMY: Chief minerals—copper, zinc, iron, silver. **Chief agricultural products—**cereals, sugar beets, potatoes, dairy cattle. **Industries and products—**metal manufacturing, shipbuilding, wood processing, copper refining, foodstuffs, chemicals, textiles, clothing. **Chief exports—**paper and pulp, machinery, chemicals, metals, timber. **Chief imports—**foodstuffs, petroleum and petroleum products, chemicals, transportation equipment, iron and steel, machinery, textile yarn and fabric, fodder grains.

MONETARY UNIT: 1 euro = 100 cents.

NATIONAL HOLIDAY: December 6 (Independence Day).

government and the freedom of its citizens were in danger. After 1890, a policy of Russification went into effect. Russian was made the official language; Finland's army was absorbed into the Russian army; the power of Finland's Diet (parliament) was restricted until it was no more than a rubber stamp of Russian policies; and strict censorship was imposed on the press. By the beginning of World War I, in 1914, the Finns had lost much of their freedom. When the Russian Revolution brought the end of czarist rule in Russia, in 1917, Finland declared itself independent.

Independent Finland

The period between the two world wars was a time of progress for Finland. Land reforms were passed, and most of Finland's independent family farms date from this time. Industrial production more than tripled in volume and quadrupled in value. Finland's trade also expanded greatly. Some of Finland's other natural resources, such as copper and nickel, were first developed at this time. Finnair, the national airline, was founded. The shipbuilding industry grew, and Finland soon led the world in the construction of icebreakers and similar ships.

Although there had been an attempted revolution by Finnish Communists in 1918, in general, Finland enjoyed marked political stability after independence. Numerous welfare measures were put into effect.

The national school system that had been in place since the 19th century was expanded at this time. In 1921, compulsory education was introduced; school attendance is now obligatory between the ages of 7 and 16. Finland's universities and professional schools also expanded, and the number of vocational schools and adult-education centers increased. During this period, too, the first attempts were made to bring education to the Finnish Lapps and to make them part of Finnish life. (An article on LAPLAND appears in this volume.)

The Winter War and World War II. In 1939, the Soviet Union demanded that Finland cede parts of its territory for the defense of Leningrad (now St. Petersburg). Finland refused and was invaded. Although they were faced with overwhelming odds, the Finns defended their liberty so resolutely that British Prime Minister Winston Churchill said of them, "Finland alone—in danger of death, superb, sublime Finland—shows what free men can do." The heroic resistance was led by Field Marshal Carl Gustav Emil von Mannerheim. United by love of their country, the Finns were able to withstand the unusually severe winter better than the poorly trained Soviet soldiers. Using specially trained ski troops camouflaged in white, the Finns held back the Russians for about four months. Finally, they were forced to accept the harsh treaty imposed by the Soviet Union, and to give up vital areas of southeast Finland.

In June 1941, Germany attacked the Soviet Union. Finland entered World War II fighting alongside Germany, but only to regain its lost territories. (Finland refused to take part in operations that served German, rather than Finnish, aims.) Although they were successful at first, eventually the Finns had to accept another treaty dictated by the Soviets. Under the terms of the treaty, Finland paid the Soviet Union some $300 million—in ships, industrial machinery, locomotives, and, most important, fully equipped paper and woodworking factories.

Recent History. During the Cold War years, Finland was careful not to provoke its powerful Soviet neighbor. Much of the country's economy was tied to the Communist nations, and so when the Communist regimes collapsed, it required a major realignment. In a 1994 referendum, Finnish voters approved the government's proposal to join the EU. This helped Finland to reorient and expand its markets. Furthermore, government and community support for education and research, and development of new information technologies, have moved Finland from the 38th place in international economic competitiveness, in 1995, to fifth in 2000. Since January 1999, Finland has also been part of the European Monetary Union (EMU), and on January 1, 2002, fully adopted the new currency—the euro—for all cash and retail transactions.

Impressive economic growth in recent years has challenged the traditional values of this largely egalitarian society; the accumulation of wealth was never a priority for Finns in the past, and many still prefer a pleasant, easygoing lifestyle over material possessions.

Government. Finland's head of government is the president, who is elected every six years by 301 electors, chosen by universal suffrage. In 2000, they elected Tarja Halonen, the first woman president of the country. Finland's single-chamber legislature is called the Eduskunta.

Helsinki, Finland's capital and largest city, is the site of the imposing Lutheran cathedral (background).

CITIES

Helsinki. Much of Finland's history can be read in the buildings and streets of Helsinki, often called the "white city of the north." It became the capital in 1812, when Czar Alexander I decided that Turku was too far from Russia and chose instead a small city on the Baltic. He supervised much of the planning and architecture of the new capital. A German architect, C. L. Engel, was chosen to design many of the buildings, including those surrounding Great Square—the Government Palace, the University, and the Great Church, whose tower is visible from ships approaching the harbor. In 1894 a statue honoring Czar Alexander II— "Friend of Finland"—was erected in the square.

But even today Helsinki remembers its beginnings as a small port and fishing center. Every morning the traditional harbor market is still held, and among the crowded stalls sea gulls can be seen picking up scraps while ducks paddle and dive below the docks nearby.

Elsewhere in the capital there are the clean, sweeping lines that have made Finnish architecture famous around the world. The Helsinki Olympic Stadium, designed by Alvar Aalto, is used for the track-and-field events in which the Finns have excelled since the days of Paavo Nurmi, the great runner who was called the "flying Finn." The National Museum, on Mannerheimintie ("Mannerheim street"), and the Helsinki Railroad Station were both designed by Eliel Saarinen, who later emigrated to the United States. Both Eliel and his son Eero made important contributions to 20th-century architecture in the United States.

Helsinki's new, white-tile National Theater is the center of the performing arts in Finland. The works of Finnish playwrights of the 19th century, such as Aleksis Kivi, are popular, but the majority of plays put

On Aland Island in the Gulf of Bothnia, a craftsman makes pottery for the tourist trade.

A statue of Paavo Nurmi, a Finnish runner who won seven gold medals, stands by Helsinki's Olympic Stadium.

Boldly colorful Marimekko cottons are only one example of fine Finnish design.

Helsinki's Sibelius Memorial captures the spirit of his music and of Finland.

Helsinki's harbor, choked with midwinter ice.

on are by non-Finnish authors. The Finnish book industry is based in Helsinki, publishing almost 7,000 books per year, including the novels of the 1939 Nobel prize winner, Frans Eemil Sillanpää, and the contemporary Mika Waltari.

In Helsinki's restaurants, some of the country's characteristic foods can be sampled—Karelian pie, made of ground meat, rice, and melted butter; small, succulent crayfish taken from Finland's sparkling waters; desserts made from the yellow cloudberry, which grows only in Scandinavian countries; and the special golden liqueur called Mesimarja, made from the fruit of the Arctic bramblebush. The city's shops sell the pottery and glassware of Arabia and Iittala, the brightly printed fabrics and fashions of Marimekko, Artek, Vuokko, and Finn-Flare, and all the other products that have earned Finland its reputation as a home of good design.

Visitors to Helsinki can enjoy trips out to the fortress of Suomenlinna (Sveaborg), which has been guarding the harbor since the 18th century. They can take walks along the esplanade near the harbor, and relax at one of its outdoor restaurants. On May 1, they can watch the traditional May Day fun, when university students drape the statue of Havis Amanda (a symbol of Helsinki) with flower garlands and place a white graduation cap on her head. The students also take part in Finland's Independence Day celebrations every December 6. There is a torchlight procession during which one Finnish flag is carried for every year since 1917.

Visitors can also try a sauna, one of the oldest and best-known Finnish traditions. No one knows quite how the sauna got its start, but it seems to have been a part of Finnish life for centuries. It is estimated that there are close to 1,000,000 saunas in Finland today, and they are often used more as a social occasion or a form of relaxation than as a bath. Families often invite friends to enjoy their saunas together.

The word "sauna" means "dry heat bath," and in its most traditional form the sauna is a specially constructed wooden cabin, where stones are heated almost red-hot and water is thrown on them to control the humidity. There are several benches, or shelves, in the sauna, and the higher the bench, the hotter the air. The sauna is usually followed by a cooling dip in a lake or pool—or in winter, by a frosty roll in the snow.

In summer, Helsinki offers fine beaches near the city for swimming

Tapiola, near Helsinki, typifies the best of Finnish architecture.

and sunbathing, and visitors and residents alike flock to sports stadiums to watch *pesäpallo* ("nest ball"). This game, which has been called Finland's national sport, is a form of baseball.

Tapiola.   Some 4 mi. (6 km.) from Helsinki is Tapiola, a garden city dating only from 1960. Named for one of the legends of the *Kalevala*, Tapiola was designed by a team of architects and planners to provide the best that modern city life could offer—efficiency, comfort, and beauty in its homes and offices, streets and parks. It is another example of how the Finns not only try to make the best of what they have, but add something special to it.

Espoo.   Espoo, Finland's second-largest city, is located just west of Helsinki, in an area that has been inhabited since 3500 B.C. Notable buildings include a beautiful church dating from 1458 and a structure originally built in 1911-13 as the studio of the artist Akseli Gallen-Kallela; this castle-like edifice is presently the home of the Tarvaspää Museum. The Helsinki University of Technology, which was founded in 1908, also is located in Espoo.

Tampere.   Between lakes Näsi and Pyhä, northeast of Turku, is Tampere, Finland's third-largest city and the home of many of its industries. Because all its factories are run by hydroelectricity, however, Tampere is not a typical industrial town. It, too, has wide, clean streets, many lovely parks and gardens, and modern apartment houses. Even the factories seem close to nature, built among trees, gently rolling hills, or on the lake shores. Tampere is also the starting point of many lake-steamer routes to the north and south.

Turku.   Turku, the fourth-largest city in Finland, stands near the mouth of the Aura River on the Gulf of Bothnia. Because of its location, it was natural that Turku developed into a seaport. As early as the 13th century, Turku carried on trade with the cities of the Hanseatic League and other Baltic ports. Turku is still a busy port today, with a harbor that is kept ice-free year-round.

Turku is Finland's oldest city and was the country's first capital. Its cathedral dates from the 13th century and contains the tombs of many great Finns. In the Luostarinmäki section of the city, spared from an 1827 fire that almost leveled the city, the old houses have been turned into a crafts museum and workshop.

The city is the site of two universities, one teaching in Finnish and the other in Swedish. Turku's position as a cultural center is maintained by its Concert Hall, one of the most modern in Finland.

Hämeenlinna.   Hämeenlinna, about 50 mi. (80 km.) from Tampere, is one of the lake ports on the southern route. It is also the birthplace of Finland's great composer Jean Sibelius (1865–1957), whose music carried Finland to the world and who came to be a living symbol of his country. His tone poems *En Saga, Finlandia,* and *Tapiola* and his symphonies and other compositions all seem to contain more than Sibelius' deep love for Finland. They contain the wind howling through the pine trees and the sun glancing off the waters of 60,000 lakes; they contain the ancient legends of the *Kalevala;* they contain all of Finland's history of hardships and all the promise of its future. They contain *sisu,* which has made Finland what it is today.

JOHN H. WUORINEN, Author, *A History of Finland*
Reviewed by HALLBERG HALLMUNDSSON, Translator and Editor

Vineyards cling to the hillsides of Portugal's upper Douro Valley, the home of port wine.

PORTUGAL

Flying over the coast of Portugal, the westernmost country in Europe, one can see, at the end of the long shoreline that projects into the Atlantic, a point of land called Cape Saint Vincent. The cape, the southwesternmost point in Europe, was for centuries the extreme limit to which Europeans dared to venture. Beyond this point, the legends said, the sea was filled with monsters and dangers beyond description, and one was in danger of sailing off the edge of the flat earth into a vast nothingness.

It remained for the Portuguese to show that great lands and unbelievable wealth lay across the mysterious sea. In the late 15th and 16th centuries, the Portuguese mariners—the astronauts of their day—explored two-thirds of the then-unknown world. Their discoveries made Portugal a leading imperial power. For a time, this small country was the heart of one of the world's largest and wealthiest empires.

Portugal held on to its overseas empire longer than any other European colonial power. It was not until 1974, when political change swept the country and a new government came to power, that Portugal decided to give up its vast territories. The last remnant of the once great

Oxen help launch a traditional fishing boat. Portugal is one of the world's leading fishing nations.

empire, the tiny overseas province of Macao, was returned to China in 1999. Apart from its mainland territory, Portugal now comprises the Azores and Madeira islands in the Atlantic Ocean. The African territories that Portugal governed for centuries are today independent nations, and the country's current leaders are emphasizing a future linked to Western Europe rather than faraway lands.

THE LAND

In a few hours in Portugal, one may drive from the high, cold, almost barren mountainous areas to the southern coast of the country, where summer never ends. Portugal occupies about one-sixth of the Iberian Peninsula, which it shares with Spain, its only neighbor. The boundaries between Spain and Portugal are formed partly by rivers, including the Minho in the north and the Guadiana in the southeast. Two other important rivers, the Tagus and the Douro, rise in Spain and flow through Portugal to the Atlantic Ocean.

The Tagus River (Tejo in Portuguese), divides the country into two distinct parts. The northern half of the nation is mostly mountainous and includes the highest range in Portugal—the Serra da Estrêla—whose loftiest peak, Pico da Serrá, stretches 6,532 ft. (1,991 m.) above sea level. The Serra da Estrêla region is noted for its resorts and for its mineral resources. Moving west from the mountainous interior, one comes to the foothills dotted with small farms, olive groves, and vineyards.

The warm, dry, sunny upper valley of the Douro River in northern Portugal is the home of the country's most famous wine—port. There, on steep, terraced vineyards that resemble giant staircases, the grapes are

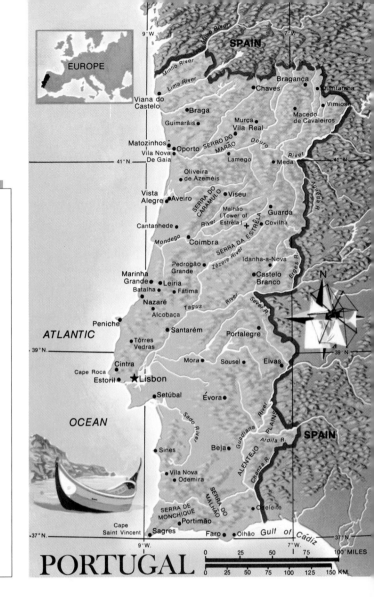

PORTUGAL

grown and harvested. After the grape juice has been allowed to ferment for a time, brandy is added, and the port is put into oak casks. The casks of new wine are brought by oxcarts to the Douro River and then floated on flat-bottomed boats downstream to Oporto, Portugal's second largest city. The wine is graded and stored in caves until it achieves the proper color and flavor for export.

South of the Tagus River, Portugal becomes a land of rolling plains and plateaus. This is the area of the latifundia, huge estates where the owners employ as many as 100 workers, who live on the estate or in nearby villages. Although the soil is poor, this is the grain-growing center of the nation. Here, too, sheep, goats, and cattle graze, and horses and bulls are bred for bullfighting. There are also olive groves, rice plantations, and forests of cork oak. Portugal is the world's largest producer of cork. There are also forests of chestnut, eucalyptus, and pine. Portugal exports much resin, turpentine, and other wood products. In the mild, subtropical climate of the Algarve in the far south, almonds, dates, figs, carobs, oranges, and pomegranates are grown.

Madeira and the Azores: the Island Provinces

The Madeira islands and the Azores are included in mainland Portugal for administrative purposes; however, both groups of islands received limited autonomy in the wake of the 1974 revolution. The Madeira islands, which lie about 600 mi. (960 km.) southwest of Portugal in the North Atlantic Ocean, are famous for their scenery and as a year-round resort. The capital and chief city, Funchal, is on the largest island, also called Madeira. Madeira wines and delicately embroidered linens are the islands' best-known products.

The Azores, about 1,000 mi. (1,600 km.) west of Lisbon, have also been important as a stopover place for travelers between Europe, Africa, and the Western Hemisphere. Today, their location and magnificent scenery make them a popular tourist attraction. Grains and fruit are raised on the islands, and fish are taken from the sea. A controversy erupted in 1986 when Portugal's armed forces objected to a provision in the new autonomy statute that permitted the Azores the right to have their own anthem and flag. The president vetoed the new law the day before it was to take effect. This action sparked the reemergence of a right-wing, separatist Front for the Liberation of the Azores.

The Former Overseas Territories

At one time, Portugal governed overseas territories that were 23 times the size of Portugal itself. Officially these territories were considered to be overseas provinces or states. Portugal ruled a vast area in Africa: Portuguese Guinea (now Guinea-Bissau) on the west coast of Africa; the Cape Verde Islands off the west coast; São Tomé and Príncipe, a group of islands lying in the Gulf of Guinea off west-central Africa; Angola in southwest Africa; and Mozambique in southeast Africa.

Angola and Mozambique were by far the largest and most valuable of Portugal's overseas provinces, with fertile farmland, good fishing grounds, and considerable mineral resources, including oil, copper, and diamonds. Guinea-Bissau was the first of the African territories to win independence, in 1974. The other Portuguese possessions gained their independence in 1975. (Separate articles on ANGOLA, CAPE VERDE, GUINEA-BISSAU, MOZAMBIQUE, and SÃO TOMÉ AND PRÍNCIPE appear in Volume 1.)

Portuguese Timor, the eastern part of the island of Timor in the Malay Archipelago, was one of the Asian territories of Portugal. East Timor, as it was sometimes called, became part of Indonesia in 1976, but in 2002, it gained full independence (see EAST TIMOR article in Volume 2). Portugal lost its territories in India, including Goa, in 1961, but kept the last remaining territory, Macau—at the mouth of the Canton River off China's southeast coast—until December 1999. Macau was then turned over to the People's Republic of China, and became a special administrative zone with considerable autonomy.

THE PEOPLE

The Portuguese people are a mixture of several different groups. The earliest people known to have inhabited the peninsula were the Iberians. They were later joined by the Celts. In time the Phoenicians, Greeks, and Carthaginians arrived and set up coastal settlements. The most aggressive of these invaders were the Carthaginians, and it was to

Women flock to dockside markets to buy freshly caught fish, a staple of the Portuguese diet.

fight them that the Celtiberian people called on the Romans for help. The Romans came, but they, in turn, tried to conquer the region. They were strongly opposed by a warlike tribe called the Lusitanians, who managed to resist the Roman conquest for nearly two centuries but were finally overcome about the 1st century B.C. The Romans were defeated by the Germanic tribes, and they, in turn, were pushed out by the Moors from North Africa in the 8th century A.D. Out of these conquests and reconquests ultimately came the nation of Portugal and a people united by their language and by their religion—Roman Catholicism.

In describing the people of Portugal writers often dwell on the profound Portuguese melancholy, which is said to stem from ages of struggles and sorrows and is eloquently expressed in Portugal's famous songs, the fados. Sung with guitar accompaniment, the fados tell of too-early death, of cruel lovers, of past heroes, of a great bullfighter killed in the arena. They are summed up in the untranslatable Portuguese word *saudade*, which describes a state of mind in which one is yearning, longing, or recalling the past with resignation.

Despite this aura of melancholy the Portuguese find joy in many things. Their heritage of riches can be seen in the tapestries, gold works, and decorative tiles—*azulejos*—in the churches and palaces. Beauty and decoration play a role in their daily life, too. The wife of a poor farmer may embroider her tablecloths exquisitely. The driver carves the yoke of his oxen and paints it in brilliant colors.

It is a treat to be invited into a country home in Portugal for a lunch that comes out of a gleaming copper kettle and is accompanied by a local wine. The items in the diet are limited, but their variations may be great. Corn is a staple, and fish is more important than meat. Codfish is the most common dish, and a good cook will claim she can prepare *o fiel amigo* (the faithful friend), as the codfish is called, in at least 365 ways—one for each day of the year.

Tourists are drawn to the many sandy beaches that line Portugal's long Atlantic coastline.

Sports

Portugal is internationally famous for the excellence of its soccer teams, some of which have achieved top rankings in European and world contests. Each team has fiercely loyal and noisy fans numbering in the thousands. The soccer games and the *totobola* (football pools) based on them are among the most popular amusements of the Portuguese today.

But the major attraction for the person in the street is still the Portuguese bullfight. The traditional *corrida* (bullfight) is a contest between a charging bull and a horseback rider—swerving, turning, and always returning to a frontal attack to prove mastery over the bull. The bull is not killed in the Portuguese bullfight. *Pega*—tackling of the bull by hand—is unique to Portugal. In the bullring, a team of agile and courageous young men led by a captain tackles the bull face-to-face. On foot, they defy the bull, seizing its horns in their bare hands, subduing it, and bringing it to its knees. These men are amateurs who play this dangerous game for the sport, not for money.

Education

There have been compulsory education laws in Portugal since 1911, but they were not strictly enforced until the early 1930s. Today, there is little or no illiteracy in the population under 50 years of age and approximately 10 percent in those over 50. This is because an intensive effort has been made in the field of adult education, and a certificate of primary education is required for even the lowest category of jobs.

There are six universities in mainland Portugal. The oldest, the University of Coimbra, was founded in Lisbon in 1290 and moved to Coimbra in the 16th century. Two other universities, at Lisbon and Oporto, were founded in 1911. The remaining universities are at Aviero (founded 1973), Minho (founded 1974), and another at Lisbon (founded 1974). The Technical University of Lisbon was founded in 1930, and the Catholic University was opened in Lisbon in 1967.

Cities

Ever since 1147, **Lisbon** (Lisbõa) has been the political center of Portugal. One of Europe's oldest cities, Lisbon is built on seven hills overlooking the wide mouth of the Tagus River, a great natural harbor. About one tenth of the population of Portugal lives in Lisbon, which is the commercial and industrial hub of the country.

Much of the beauty of the city is a credit to the master plan drawn up by the Marquês de Pombal, who was prime minister in 1755 when an earthquake, fires, and huge waves destroyed two thirds of Lisbon. One of Pombal's plans resulted in one of the most beautiful squares in Europe, Praça do Comercio ("commerce square"). A series of arcaded buildings, built in the late 18th century, face the square on three sides. The fourth side is open to the river.

Lisbon, like many old European cities, is a city of contrasts. There are broad avenues, handsome modern buildings, and lovely pastel stucco apartment houses. There are also old sections of narrow, twisting streets, ancient areas (some of which escaped the earthquake) with old churches, and little old shops that sell antiques. Some of Lisbon's streets are so steep that elevators take you from one level to another; others have cable cars or cogwheel-driven streetcars. The major distraction to Lisbon's charm is the widespread presence of political slogans and graffiti that began appearing on walls and buildings following the April 1974 revolution that ended a half-century of authoritarian rule.

There are many famous sights for the visitor in Lisbon. Some of the pavements of the important avenues are tiled in black and white mosaics, arranged in attractive designs. The most famous historic monuments are in the area called Belém, where King Manuel I had the great monastery church Os Jeronimos built in the 16th century. It rises on the site of a small chapel to which the early navigators came to pray before sailing into the unknown. It is a national shrine. Vasco da Gama, who is supposed to have prayed at this spot on the eve of his historic voyage to India in 1497, is buried there, as is Luis Vaz de Camões, the Portuguese poet of the 16th century who wrote the epic *Os Lusíadas*. The heart of this poem concerns the voyage of discovery around the Cape of Good Hope to India and the deeds of Da Gama and his band of mariners.

The church of Os Jeronimos is a masterpiece of Manueline architecture, a style developed in Portugal during the late 15th and early 16th centuries and named after King Manuel I. It is an exuberant elaboration of Gothic style that was made possible by the wealth coming from the trade with the Orient. Manueline buildings can be recognized by the masses of intricate stone carvings of ropes, seashells, anchors, compasses, globes, and other symbols of Portugal's mastery of the seas.

The suburb of Belém also has the Tower, an exotic Manueline monument built on the exact spot from which the ships sailed forth on their voyages of discovery. In 1960, to commemorate the 500th anniversary of the death of Prince Henry the Navigator, the Monument of Discoveries was unveiled. Portugal's leading maritime explorers, with the Prince at their head, are depicted on the monument.

A short distance inland from Lisbon is **Cintra,** a town of lovely old stucco houses set in magnificent gardens. At Cintra there are old palaces, for this was once a favorite place for the kings and nobility to pass the summer. Also close to Lisbon, but on the coast, is **Estoril,** the center of Portugal's fashionable resorts on the Costa do Sol (coast of the sun). There the rich, and some exiled royalty from other European lands, have built lovely homes of red, blue, pink, orange, and yellow stucco and tiles that shimmer in the brilliant sun.

Portugal has many old cities, all worth a visit. **Oporto,** the second largest city and the center of the wine industry, has several notable Romanesque churches, and it is also the home of the Museum Soares dos Reis, which displays almost all the works of the great 19th-century sculptor and painter Soares dos Reis, as well as paintings, goldsmiths' work, and porcelains.

North of Oporto is **Braga,** which is famous for its churches. The city of **Évora** traces its history to the Romans and the Moors. There are the remains of a Temple of Diana from the 1st or 2nd century B.C., the great cathedral in Gothic style from the 12th century, and many other monuments.

In central Portugal is the village of **Fátima,** with its national shrine in honor of Our Lady of the Rosary of Fátima. Roman Catholics have made pilgrimages to Fátima since 1917, when three shepherd children reported seeing the Virgin Mary there six times. Portugal's devotion to Roman Catholicism is also reflected in the fact that it is one of only a handful of nations in the world that bars divorce.

ECONOMY

The days of the great voyages of discovery and colonization have passed into history, but many Portuguese still earn their living from the sea. They are the fishermen who provide the Portuguese with the chief source of protein in their diet and the raw material for their important canning industry. The sea abounds in fish, but the open ocean is often brutal and fishing can be a dangerous occupation.

At Nazaré the fishermen take their frail boats directly through the ocean surf in search of sardines and other fish. On the southern coast, in the Algarve province, and around the Azores, they go out mainly for tuna. For centuries, Portuguese fishing fleets have set out each spring for the distant seas off Newfoundland known as the Grand Banks. They return late in summer, heavily laden with codfish. The cod is salted and stored in the ships' holds. Upon arrival in Portugal the salted fish is stripped, cured, and dried, to become the national dish, *bacalhau.*

Portugal is expanding its fishing industry by granting loans for modernizing equipment, but occasionally one can still see the women at the fishing ports mending nets, which they hold taut with their bare toes; and the *varinas* (fishwives) still take their wares from door to door, carrying the fish in baskets on their heads.

The Rossio, a square in central Lisbon, honors the heroes who helped secure Portugal's independence.

Portugal has long been among the poorest West European countries, but in recent decades, its economy has been fully modernized and diversified. Only about 10 percent of the working population is now employed in agriculture, forestry, and fishing, and about 60 percent work in the services industries.

Portugal is moderately rich in minerals, but some are difficult to mine. The most important are wolframite (the source of tungsten), iron, copper, and such nonmetallic minerals as marble, limestone, and slate. There is also some low-grade coal. A natural-gas pipeline from Algeria was opened in 1997.

Successive development plans have provided northern Portugal with a network of dams that generate much-needed power and provide irrigation. The best-known of these dams are Castelo do Bode, Belver, and Idanha on the Tagus and its tributaries. In the basin of the Douro River, a joint Portuguese-Spanish effort has built a vast hydroelectric complex serving both Spain and Portugal. Two oil refineries have been built, one at Matozinhos, near Oporto, in an area that also produces steel and petrochemicals, and another near Lisbon. A modern steel mill is located across the Tagus River from Lisbon. In 1979, a petrochemical complex began operations at Sines, south of Lisbon. These improvements, and the April 25th Bridge (formerly the Salazar Bridge) spanning the Tagus and linking Lisbon with the southern half of the country, symbolize a Portugal that has entered the modern industrial era.

In addition to the fish-canning, cork, and wine industries, Portugal now produces cotton and woolen textiles, metal products, cement, chemicals, paper, soap, glass and glassware, and drugs. However, much

Oporto, Portugal's second-largest city, lies on the terraced banks of the Douro River.

of Portugal's industry is still in small factories and workshops, such as those where textiles are made, linens woven and embroidered, and rugs custom-made. Tourism provides Portugal's economy with its largest single source of foreign exchange. In addition, substantial amounts of money are received from Portuguese who work in other parts of Western Europe, Brazil, and North America and send back earnings to their families at home.

HISTORY

Modern Portuguese history began with the wars fought against the Moors, who occupied the country in the 8th century A.D. In spite of the occupation of the country by the Muslim Arabs, the Christian faith remained firmly established. The Christian nobles had retreated to the mountainous regions of the northwest, and it was not until the 11th century that they began to push the Moors back toward the south. Many young knights, motivated by faith, warrior zeal, and ambition, came from other lands to join in the wars. So it was that Henry, a young Burgundian, came from France in the 11th century, distinguished himself in battle, and gained a bride, the Princess of the Kingdom of León, who had the territory between the Douro and the Minho Rivers. This territory was called the country of Portugal, because one of the centers of this region was located near the mouth of the Douro River at a place called Portucale. The name is probably derived from the Latin for port—*portus*—and Calle, the name of a castle that overlooked it. Portucale gave its name to the nation of Portugal.

In 1139 the able son of Henry of Burgundy, Afonso, declared himself Afonso I, the first monarch of Portugal. Afonso I rallied a group of northern European Crusaders to his cause. They had been on their way to the Holy Land when a storm swept them to the mouth of the Douro. With their help, Afonso recaptured seven Moorish citadels, including the city of Lisbon. In a daring raid, like a modern commando attack, he swept across the Moors' territory and recaptured Cape Saint Vincent.

Afonso's successors completed the work of pushing the Moors out of the peninsula, and by the middle of the 13th century the boundaries of Portugal were firmly established.

One of the most remarkable of the early Portuguese kings was King Diniz (reigned 1261–1325), who was called O Rei Lavrador—"the farmer king"—because of his interest in agriculture. Among his many achievements was the planting of pine forests to prevent erosion. These forests later provided masts and timber for the explorers' ships. Diniz also wrote poetry in Portuguese and published royal edicts and documents in Portuguese at a time when only Latin was used for such writing. He also founded Portugal's first university.

The Explorers

The actual beginning of the great Portuguese voyages of discovery is hard to pinpoint. There is no mystery, however, about the leader who inspired the great voyages. He was Prince Henry the Navigator, who founded a naval arsenal at Sagres, near Europe's southwesternmost corner, to serve as a base of exploration. He then added an observatory and a school for geography and navigation. From 1418 until his death in 1460, he surrounded himself with cartographers, astronomers, instrument makers, mathematicians, and pilots. He sent crews to chart seas, study winds and currents, draw up harbor maps, and build caravels—ships designed for long voyages. With the maps, instruments, ships, knowledge, and inspiration bequeathed to them by Prince Henry, the Portuguese gradually sailed farther and farther down the coast of Africa. In 1488, Bartholomeu Dias reached the Cape of Good Hope, at the tip of Africa, and found that the coast turned northeast there. In 1498, almost 40 years after Henry's death, Vasco da Gama found the route to the riches of India that Columbus and so many others had searched for in vain.

The Portuguese had found the way to bring to Europe the silks, spices, gold, and other treasures of Asia without risking the dangerous overland caravan route or raids by those who controlled the Mediterranean waters. The Portuguese mariners took over the spice trade of the Orient from the Arabs and amassed great wealth. They started settlements on the Indian coast. The Portuguese introduced their language, their customs, and their faith to people in distant lands. Their missionaries preached Christianity in India and as far east as Japan. They also introduced firearms to those lands. From China they brought home the use of tea and fireworks, and left behind Portuguese words that became part of Chinese and other Oriental languages.

Competition between Spanish and Portuguese explorers became intense, and in 1494 the two countries signed the Treaty of Tordesillas. They divided the non-Christian world by drawing an imaginary line from pole to pole. What lay east of the line was given to Portugal; the land west of the line was Spain's. Fortunately for Portugal, when Pedro Alvares

The Monument of Discoveries in Lisbon commemorates Portugal's leading role during the Age of Exploration.

Cabral, accompanied by Bartholomeu Dias, reached Brazil in 1500, that area fell within the Portuguese claim. Missionaries and pioneers followed Cabral, pushing deep into the Amazon jungle of Brazil to found settlements, raise sugarcane, and mine the gold, silver, and diamonds that provided Portugal's fantastic wealth for decades.

In the 16th century the Portuguese empire stretched from the coast of China to Brazil, from North Africa to the Pacific Ocean. Portugal monopolized the spice trade and sent sailors, settlers, merchants, administrators, and priests to its far-flung holdings. But Portugal was a country of only 2,000,000 people, and many of its most gifted men died in these far-off lands. Furthermore, much of the profit from the imported wealth went to guard the distant settlements and to keep open Portugal's widespread sea-lanes.

Portugal's Decline

Portugal's good fortune ended suddenly. In 1578, King Sebastian led the Portuguese armies in an expedition to Morocco. Dreaming of a new crusade, he led his men to battle the Moors in the Moroccan desert. He was killed, and only a few of his men survived the slaughter. In 1580 the weakened country, torn by internal struggles, was annexed by the Spanish, who ruled until 1640. In that year John of Braganza, taking advantage of Spain's involvement in other wars, succeeded in ousting the Spanish and became King John IV of Portugal.

During the 1700's there was again a brief time of great prosperity in Portugal, with the resources of Brazil supplying the wealth. But in 1755,

Lisbon was almost destroyed by an earthquake, and it took the country a long time to recover. During the Napoleonic Wars it was invaded by the French Army. The King and royal family fled to Brazil, and for a short time the capital of Portugal was in Rio de Janeiro. After Napoleon was defeated the royal family returned to Portugal. During this period the vast empire had begun to fall apart. In 1822, Brazil declared its independence, and thus Portugal's single greatest source of wealth was lost.

The entire 19th century and the early part of the 20th century was a time of economic and political disaster in Portugal. The sudden stoppage of wealth from Brazil caused financial difficulties that led to heavy borrowing from England. The liberal ideas of the French Revolution, brought to Portugal by the invading armies of Napoleon, inspired the people to fight against absolute rule. Violent partisan struggles, civil wars, and continuous agitation led to chaotic conditions and a growing movement towards republicanism. The King and his heir were assassinated in 1908, and two years later Portugal became a republic.

During World War I Portugal was one of the Western allies against Germany. But Portugal had such severe economic problems that freely elected governments faced great difficulties. In the 16 years after the republic was proclaimed in 1910, Portugal witnessed repeated coups d'etat, and 46 governments followed one another in quick succession. Political turmoil continued to disrupt the nation's life until 1926, when Marshal António Oscar de Fragoso Carmona took over the government.

In 1928, Carmona appointed António de Oliveira Salazar, a professor at Coimbra University, as minister of finance to help stabilize Portugal's economy. In 1932, Salazar became premier and, with his powers extended by the new Constitution of 1933, headed the government for 35 years. Forced to retire due to illness, he was succeeded by Marcello Caetano in 1968. Salazar died in 1970.

Years of Change

During Salazar's years as premier, Portugal had a generally stable but authoritarian government. Under the constitution then in effect, Portugal was described as a unitary and corporative republic. There was a president as head of state; a legislature, the National Assembly; and an advisory body called the Corporative Chamber. It was Salazar, however, who ruled Portugal during this long period. Only one political party was officially permitted.

Soon after Marcello Caetano became premier he extended the vote for women. Previously only women who were heads of families or independent professional workers were permitted to vote. In 1969 the election law was amended to place women on an equal footing with men. Caetano also curbed the political police, permitted greater freedom of discussion, and relaxed the laws of censorship.

But many Portuguese desired more widespread political and social reforms. The question of the overseas provinces in Africa also aroused great controversy. For many years the Army had been fighting a bitter and costly war against African nationalist groups in Portuguese Guinea (Guinea-Bissau), Angola, and Mozambique who were seeking independence. The war was unpopular with many people who believed that the provinces should be allowed their independence. They felt that the enormous sums of money spent in keeping them under Portuguese rule would be better spent in such areas as education, housing, and industrial development at home.

In 1974, a group of army officers opposed to the continuation of the war in Africa overthrew the government of Premier Caetano. A provisional government, made up of members of the armed forces, was established. One of its first acts was to recognize the right of the African provinces to independence. The new leaders of the country also promised to restore democracy to Portugal. However, conflict soon arose as to what kind of government Portugal was to have. A struggle for power developed between the Communists, allied with extremist radical groups, and the Socialists. A wave of unrest swept the country, and the already weakened Portuguese economy was further disrupted by political instability.

The Democratic Era

Even though many governments have held power since 1974, Portugal gradually moved into the sunshine of democracy from the shadows of turmoil that engulfed the country after Caetano's removal from office. Several factors caused this transition. Of crucial importance was the continual support for democratic forces provided by members of the European Community (EC) and by the United States. In addition, Socialist leader Mário Soares, who twice served as premier before winning the presidency in 1986, championed democratization and opposed extremists within both the armed forces and the Communist Party. Reforms introduced by Soares in the early 1980s opened up an economy afflicted by years of high tariffs, red tape, subsidies, outdated management practices, and state intervention in economic affairs.

Entry into the European Community in 1986 vastly broadened export opportunities for Portugal. By the mid-1990s, the European Union (EU)—the organization that succeeded the EC—had furnished Portugal with billions of dollars in aid for modernization. Throughout the decade, Portugal had one of the fastest-growing economies in Europe. The combination of political stability, economic growth, and flexible policies sparked a sharp increase in foreign investment from other EU states.

Contributing to the country's stability was the 1987 election of Social Democrat Aníbal Cavaço Silva as prime minister. A university professor and economist, he worked to end an era of "state paternalism" by encouraging free enterprise. In 1989, the parliament removed Marxist language from the 1976 constitution. Cavaço Silva and the Social Democratic Party were returned to power in 1991.

General elections held in October 1995 marked the end of the 10-year rule of the Social Democratic Party, as the Socialist Party assumed power. Their leader, Antonio Guterres, became prime minister and vowed to pursue a number of economic and social reforms. In 1999, he was elected for a second four-year term, but his party lost the legislative majority to the Social Democrats during elections in March 2002. In 1996, presidential elections were won by Socialist Jorge Sampaio, the former mayor of Lisbon, who was reelected to the presidency in January 2001. Economic growth continues to be robust, and Portugal replaced its national currency with the euro in January 2002. The country is also proud of its first Nobel laureate, José Saramago, who received the Literature Prize in 1998.

GEORGE W. GRAYSON, College of William and Mary

The Alhambra, a Moorish palace in the city of Granada, was built in the 14th century.

SPAIN

Spain is a peninsula. This geographic fact alone suggests two basic truths about the country: its isolation and its deep historic involvement in the affairs of the world. Spain's greatness and its tragedies have been shaped by this contradiction between its geography and its history.

Spain's geographical isolation comes from the seas and the mountains. Spain is attached to the continent of Europe only by a narrow neck held in the high collar of the Pyrenees. The rest of Spain is surrounded by seas, except for the rectangle of Portugal, with which it shares the Iberian Peninsula. In the south the Strait of Gibraltar barely separates Spain from Africa. In the east its shores are bathed by the Mediterranean.

Spain's physical isolation from the world is mirrored in the isolation of one region from another within Spain—a separateness caused by the mountain chains. From the northern ranges of the Pyrenees to the southernmost peaks of the Sierra Nevada, the country is crisscrossed by mountains and creased by valleys. From the air it looks like a huge sheet of paper crumpled by the hand of God.

Spain's involvement in all the great currents of world history comes, on the other hand, from its central position at the crossroads of conquest and trade routes. From prehistoric to modern times, the Iberian Peninsula has been the prize of invading armies from Africa, in the south, and Europe, in the north. Spain has been not only the target of invasions but a pathway for invasions directed at other lands. It was occupied by the Romans, the Carthaginians, the Visigoths, the Arabs, and the French. Phoenicians and Greeks established trading posts on Spain's coasts and helped to settle some of its great towns and cities.

An historic link between Europe and North Africa, Spain is both European and North African in culture, temperament, and appearance. France's Emperor Napoleon and some geographers have said that Africa begins at the Pyrenees.

But Spain has been more than a continental stepping-stone or a victim of centuries of conquest. In its long history, Spain conquered and held together a majestic empire. Spain created new civilizations across the world. And Spain has enriched the world with its culture.

Spain has seen its own civilization and personality nearly erased by many wars during its long history and by a bloody and devastating civil war in the 1930s. But despite these trials, Spain has kept a powerful identity of its own. There are few countries in the world that offer the variety and beauty that exist in Spain.

THE LAND

Spain, the fourth-largest nation in Europe, with which it is becoming increasingly integrated, occupies five-sixths of the Iberian Peninsula. Almost square in shape, Spain measures about 500 mi. (800 km.) from north to south and about 600 mi. (960 km.) from east to west. At its narrow southern tip, Spain is separated from Africa by the 8-mi. (13-km.)-wide Strait of Gibraltar. Tiny Gibraltar, at the eastern end of the strait, is a British possession. In the northeast is the tiny republic of Andorra, which is jointly ruled by the Spanish bishop of Urgel and the president of France. (Both ANDORRA and GIBRALTAR are described in separate articles in this volume.)

Metropolitan Spain includes the provinces on the peninsula, the Balearic Islands in the Mediterranean, and the Canary Islands in the Atlantic off the northwest coast of Africa.

The two most important geographical facts about Spain are its mountainous terrain and the limited rainfall that affects all except the northern provinces. The heart of Spain is the huge central plateau called the Meseta (tableland), which is divided between Old and New Castile. The Meseta is surrounded and dissected by mountain ranges. The highest mountains in Spain are the Pyrenees in the northeast and the Sierra

SPAIN
ATLANTIC OCEAN
BAY OF BISCAY
FRANCE
PORTUGAL
MOROCCO
ALGERIA
ANDORRA
MEDITERRANEAN SEA
BALEARIC SEA
BALEARIC ISLANDS
Gulf of Lion
Gulf of Cádiz
Gulf of Valencia
Strait of Gibraltar
Cape Trafalgar
Cape Gata
GIBRALTAR (U.K.)
PYRENEES
CANTABRIAN MOUNTAINS
GALICIAN MTS.
MESETA
SIERRA DE GUADARRAMA
SIERRA DE GATA
SIERRA DE GREDOS
MONTES DE TOLEDO
SIERRA MORENA
SIERRA NEVADA
Miño River
Duero River
Ebro River
Tajo River
Tagus
Guadiana River
Guadalquivir River
Pico de Aneto
Mulhacén
La Coruña
Santiago de Compostela
Vigo
Gijón
Oviedo
Covadonga
Altamira Cave
Santander
San Sebastián
Bilbao
León
Burgos
Pamplona
Huesca
Olot
Valladolid
Zamora
Zaragoza
Tarrasa
Barcelona
Tarragona
Tortosa
Salamanca
Segovia
Ávila
San Lorenzo del Escorial
Madrid
Escalona
Torrijos
Talavera de la Reina
Lagartera
Toledo
Aranjuez
Cuenca
Vinaroz
Valencia
Mérida
Ciudad Real
Alicante
Ríotinto
Córdoba
Murcia
Cartagena
Huelva
Seville
Guadix
Granada
Jerez
Cádiz
Marbella
Málaga
Torremolinos
Almería
Adra
Algeciras
Tarifa
Palma
MAJORCA
MINORCA
IVIZA
FORMENTERA
Belmonte Castle, Cuenca
Seville
EUROPE
AFRICA
CEUTA
MELILLA
CANARY ISLANDS
Miles
0 100 200
0 100 200 300
Kilometers
N
12°W
9°W
6°W
3°W
0°
3°E
42°N
39°N
36°N

FACTS AND FIGURES

OFFICIAL NAME: Kingdom of Spain.

NATIONALITY: Spanish.

CAPITAL: Madrid.

LOCATION: Southwestern Europe. **Boundaries**—Bay of Biscay, France, Balearic Sea, Mediterranean Sea, Gibraltar, Gulf of Cádiz, Portugal, Atlantic Ocean.

AREA: 194,884 sq. mi. (504,750 sq. km.).

PHYSICAL FEATURES: **Highest point**—Mulhacén (11,411 ft.; 3,478 m.). **Lowest point**—sea level. **Chief rivers**—Ebro, Duero, Tajo (Tagus), Guadiana, Guadalquivir.

POPULATION: 41,300,000 (2002; annual growth 0.1%).

MAJOR LANGUAGE: Spanish.

MAJOR RELIGION: Roman Catholicism.

GOVERNMENT: Parliamentary monarchy. **Head of state**—king. **Head of government**—president of the government. **Legislature**—Cortés Generales (Congress of Deputies and Senate).

CHIEF CITIES: Madrid, Barcelona, Valencia, Seville.

ECONOMY: **Chief minerals**—coal, lignite, iron ore, uranium, mercury, pyrites, fluorspar, gypsum, zinc, lead. **Chief agricultural products**—grains, vegetables, olives, wine grapes, sugar beets, citrus fruits, beef, pork. **Industries and products**—textiles and clothing, food and beverages, metals, chemicals, shipbuilding, automobiles. **Chief exports**—cars and trucks, foodstuffs, other machinery and manufactured goods, other consumer goods. **Chief imports**—machinery, transport equipment, fuels, semifinished goods, foodstuffs, consumer goods, chemicals.

MONETARY UNIT: 1 euro = 100 cents.

NATIONAL HOLIDAY: October 12 (National Day).

SANTANDER
VIZCAYA
ÁLAVA
GUIPÚZCOA
LA CORUÑA
OVIEDO
LUGO
LEÓN
PALENCIA
BURGOS
NAVARRE
LOGROÑO
HUESCA
LÉRIDA
GERONA
ORENSE
PONTEVEDRA
ZAMORA
VALLA-DOLID
SORIA
ZARAGOZA
BARCELONA
TARRAGONA
SEGOVIA
GUADALAJARA
SALAMANCA
ÁVILA
MADRID
TERUEL
CASTELLÓN
CÁCERES
TOLEDO
CUENCA
VALENCIA
CIUDAD REAL
ALBACETE
BADAJOZ
ALICANTE
CÓRDOBA
JAÉN
MURCIA
HUELVA
SEVILLA
GRANADA
ALMERÍA
CÁDIZ
MÁLAGA
CANARY ISLANDS
SANTA CRUZ DE TENERIFE
LAS PALMAS DE GRAN CANARIA
BALEARIC ISLANDS

Small villages lie nestled in the Pyrenees, the mountains that separate Spain from the rest of Europe.

Nevada (snowy range) in the southeast. Mulhacén, the highest peak in Spain, is in the Sierra Nevada. The Cantabrian Mountains rise on the northern and northwestern edge of the Meseta. The Sierra Morena (dark range) is at its southern edge. The Meseta itself is divided by the Sierra de Gredos, the Sierra de Guadarrama, and the Montes de Toledo.

There are only a few lowland areas in Spain besides the narrow coastal plain. The largest lowland area is the valley of the Guadalquivir River in the south. Other rivers such as the Douro, Tagus, and Guadiana have carved their way through rocks and canyons as they flow across Spain and Portugal to empty into the Atlantic Ocean. The Ebro, in the northeast, empties into the Mediterranean Sea. The Ebro is sometimes called the Nile of Spain because, like the Egyptian river, it brings life-giving water to its parched valley. The northern coastal lowland is the site of a number of ports and industrial cities. The larger lowlands on the Mediterranean coast are the site of such important cities as Barcelona, Valencia, and Cartagena.

Climate. Northern and northwestern Spain are the only parts of the country with adequate precipitation. In this region moisture-bearing winds from the Atlantic bring rain to the land. The year-round temperatures are mild without extremes of hot or cold.

Parts of the Sierra Nevada mountains in southern Spain are snow-covered throughout the year.

As one moves south from the moist, fertile northern regions, Spain's climate becomes typically Mediterranean. Winters are usually mild and somewhat rainy. Summers are very hot and dry. The average annual rainfall for Spain is 20 inches (50 centimeters)—the lowest in Western Europe. With the exception of northern Spain, the lack of fertile soil and water continues to make life a struggle for survival.

Mineral Resources. The shortage of rain and good soil are partially made up for by Spain's impressive variety of mineral resources. They include iron, coal, and zinc in the Cantabrian Mountains in the north; copper from Ríotinto in the southwest; mercury, which is found near the Sierra Morena; as well as lead, manganese, gold, silver, and tin. Spain lacks sufficient oil, but a vast potential power source to take its place has been found in the mountain streams that are being harnessed for hydro-electricity.

The Islands of Spain

The Balearic Islands lie 50 to 190 miles (80–300 kilometers) off the east coast of Spain. The Balearics are made up of three large, densely populated islands—Majorca, Minorca, and Iviza—and several smaller islands. The capital, Palma, is on the island of Majorca. The magnificent scenery and mild climate of the islands have made them into popular year-round resorts.

The Balearics, like so many other Mediterranean islands, have a history of conquest and reconquest. Prehistoric ruins linger side by side with traces of later settlers—Iberians, Phoenicians, Greeks, Carthaginians, Romans, Byzantines, Moors, and Spaniards. Today, the income from tourism is supplemented by that from farm products such as olives, grapes, cereals, almonds, and citrus fruits. Pigs and sheep are grazed. Among the province's other products are lignite, marble, lead, salt, gravel, and timber from the extensive pine forests. Shoes, ceramics, and metal products are manufactured on the islands.

The Canary Islands lie 680 miles (1,100 kilometers) southwest of Spain and about 70 miles (110 kilometers) west of Morocco. The islands are divided into two provinces, Santa Cruz de Tenerife (which is made up of the islands of Tenerife, Gomera, La Palma, and Hierro) and Las

The Spanish island of Majorca in the western Mediterranean receives over 3 million tourists annually.

The sandy Mediterranean beaches of the Costa del Sol near Gibraltar have become a major resort area.

Palmas (which includes Grand Canary, Fuerteventura, and Lanzarote islands and six islets). For the most part the climate is warm and pleasant and a variety of crops, including bananas, sugarcane, citrus fruits, and vegetables, are raised. Shipping and tourism are increasingly important to the islands' economy. (For more information about the CANARY ISLANDS see Volume 1.)

Overseas Territories

The Spanish empire disappeared long ago, and the age of European colonialism is over. Of its once-great empire, Spain today retains only two tiny enclaves in North Africa. The geographic nearness of these small territories makes it relatively easy for Spain to govern them. There is also a touch of sentimentality about Africa, with which the destiny of Spain was interwoven for so many centuries.

At the end of World War II, Spain renounced its sovereignty over what had been Spanish Morocco, now part of the Kingdom of Morocco. Along with other European powers and the United States, Spain also withdrew from the multinational administration of Tangier on Africa's northernmost tip.

After fighting a brief war with Morocco in 1957 to retain the enclave of Ifni on Morocco's Atlantic coast, Spain ceded it voluntarily in 1969. In the previous year it granted independence to Spanish Equatorial Guinea and the island of Fernando Po (now Bioko). Together, they became the Republic of Equatorial Guinea, a tiny country in which Spain continues to have powerful interests. (There are articles about MOROCCO and EQUATORIAL GUINEA in Volume 1.)

Spain's last large territory in Africa was Spanish Sahara. It is a huge tract of desert land rich in phosphates (which are used in making artificial fertilizers) and possibly oil. The native population consists largely of nomadic Berbers, who live around a number of oases. The Berbers are a people of northern Africa who inhabited that region before the arrival of the Arabs. Spain officially withdrew from Spanish Sahara in 1976. The region, which is now called Western Sahara, was divided between the neighboring countries of Morocco and Mauritania. Mauritania later relinquished its claim to the territory. (A separate article on WESTERN SAHARA appears in Volume 1.)

Ceuta and Melilla. Spain has no intention of giving up the remaining small territories it still governs on the North African mainland. These are the ports of Ceuta and Melilla on Morocco's Mediterranean coast. It was from Ceuta that the Nationalist troops of Generalissimo Francisco Franco crossed the Strait of Gibraltar to Spain to launch the Civil War in July 1936. Since 1939, both of these thoroughly Spanish towns have been an integral part of Spain. They have a population of about 70,000 people each, with approximately 85 percent of the people of Spanish origin. Many of the townspeople are employed in the fish processing and tourism industries, which are the main sources of income. In 1995, the territories became autonomous and now have the same status as the 17 autonomous communities in mainland Spain. In 2002, Morocco briefly occupied the Spanish-claimed islet of Perejil, but the crisis was quickly resolved.

Gibraltar. Gibraltar, the British crown colony that controls the passage between the Atlantic and the Mediterranean, has been the subject of continuing controversy. Britain has held Gibraltar—the fortress, the port, and what has grown into a pleasant and prosperous town of about 25,000 inhabitants—since 1704, when Spain lost the War of the Spanish Succession. The Spanish government has called Gibraltar "The Last Colony in Europe" and demanded its immediate return to Spanish sovereignty. The British held a referendum in 1967 that showed that the overwhelming majority of its inhabitants insisted, in Spanish-accented English, "British We Are and British We Shall Remain." The Spanish government, however, declared the referendum illegal. It gradually imposed tight restrictions on the colony, cutting off all trade with the mainland. The flow of Spanish workers to Gibraltar also was cut off. The border was completely opened again in 1985 and talks on the future of the colony resumed. In July 2002, Great Britain and Spain agreed to share sovereignty over Gibraltar, but the final decision will ultimately belong to the residents of the colony. (See also a separate article on GIBRALTAR in this volume.)

THE PEOPLE

There is, of course, no such thing as a "typical" Spaniard. In fact, there is perhaps no other country in Europe where the differences among people are as deep as among the Spaniards. The division of Spain imposed by its geography, which until recently blocked the movement of populations, has preserved the regional types. It has kept alive the different languages and dialects. And it has preserved old political and cultural differences within the nation.

In a general and oversimplified way, the Spaniards can be divided into three principal categories. The northerners are descended from the Celts who came to the peninsula 12 or 13 centuries before the Christian

Narrow streets lined with sun-baked houses are typical of villages in Spain's Andalusian region.

Era and, perhaps, from the Vikings who came to the peninsula about 1,000 years ago. The southerners are strongly influenced by the effects of the Moorish rule that lasted more than seven centuries. The easterners trace their origins back to the ancient Iberian tribes and then to the Visigoths.

Despite all the physical and cultural barriers, modern labor migrations are beginning to blur the differences, particularly in the industrial areas. The southerners have spilled over into the center and the north, and the northerners into the center and the south. Dark Andalusians and short, rosy-cheeked Galicians now often work side by side with fair Basques and Catalonians. If there is such a thing as a Castilian type it defies precise description. The Madrileño, as the inhabitant of Madrid is called, is the product of what might be described as the first Spanish melting pot, since the capital has traditionally attracted people from all over Spain.

Every spring, Seville is the scene of a colorful Holy Week procession. Most Spaniards are Roman Catholics.

Language. Most nations are united by their language, and at first glance this appears to be true of Spain, whose official language is Spanish. However, three languages are widely used. Catalán, which is related to the Provençal language of France, is spoken in Catalonia in northeastern Spain, along the east coast around Valencia, and in the Balearic Islands. Basque, a language that has no known relatives, is spoken in the Basque Provinces of Álava, Guipúzcoa, and Vizcaya. Castilian, which most people know as the language of Spain, is the dialect of the Meseta, as well as the official language of Spain. Spanish is one of the world's most widely spoken languages because it is also used by almost all South Americans except Brazilians.

Religion. Religion appears to be more of a unifying factor in Spanish life than does language, but this has not always been true. The overwhelming majority of Spaniards are Roman Catholics, and Roman

Catholicism was the state religion of Spain until the adoption of a new constitution in 1978. There are several hundred thousand Muslims (concentrated in the South), a Protestant minority of about 25,000, and a small Jewish community of about 7,500. In 1965, Spanish Jews were allowed to conduct public services for the first time since 1492, the year the Jews were ordered to become Catholics or leave the country. A special law adopted in 1966 officially lifted the government ban on public worship for non-Catholics. Moreover, the Cortes (parliament) has liberalized divorce laws, and abortions are permitted under exceptional circumstances.

The Problems of Regionalism

Despite the growing mobility of the population, regionalism and nationalism have grown, rather than diminished, in recent decades. This is the case in Basque country and Catalonia, and, to a lesser extent, in Galicia and Navarre. There are, of course, deep contradictions in this regional nationalism. A Basque considers himself both a Basque and a Spaniard, and a Catalonian considers himself both a Catalonian and a Spaniard. Since 1977, many of Spain's regions have been granted autonomy, with the broadest powers conferred on Catalonia and the Basque area. This satisfies those who only desire to preserve regional traits and characteristics. But extremists still demand outright separation.

Catalonia. Catalonia's inhabitants speak both Spanish and Catalán. But in the remote villages of Catalonia, one rarely hears Spanish, even though Catalonia has been under the rule of Spain for nearly 500 years. In addition to its own language, Catalonia has developed over the centuries a distinctive culture and a rich literature dating back to the 13th century. The sense of Catalonian cultural identity was later submerged under Spanish influences and surfaced again in a powerful renaissance in the latter part of the 19th century. It has been gaining vitality ever since. This separate identity in culture extends to other aspects of Catalonian life. The Catalonians, and especially the prosperous people of Barcelona, regard themselves as more European than the Castilians of Madrid. This feeling stems from Catalonia's nearness to France and the age-old contacts of the Catalonian traders with the entire Mediterranean world. The selection of Barcelona as the site for the 1992 summer Olympic Games brought Catalonia worldwide recognition.

The industrious Catalonians, along with the Basques, believe that their contribution to the Spanish economy helps support the rest of the country. This is largely true, but not necessarily because of the merit of the Catalonians or the failing of their fellow Spaniards. Such factors as Catalonia's geographical location, which favors trade and industry, and the climate, which has blessed Catalonia with a rich agriculture, are largely responsible for its wealth.

Another factor in this relationship is that Catalonia fought on the losing side in the Civil War. Before the Civil War, under the Spanish Republic, Catalonia was virtually an independent state. Under Franco, who was bent on restoring the unity of the shattered nation at the end of the war, Catalonia lost its separate status. Therefore, Catalonian regionalism was equated with being against the government.

Catalonians have their own divisions among themselves. The Catalonians who inhabit the southern coast, where the Kingdom of Valencia once thrived, are convinced that the Valenciano language is purer than the language spoken up north around Barcelona. The people of the Balearic Islands, however, believe that only they and their cousins in the Ampurdán area on the mainland north of Barcelona have properly preserved the Catalonian language and culture. The Catalán spoken in Majorca is, in fact, rather different from the Catalán of Barcelona.

The Basques. The other major nationality problem in Spain is in the Basque country, located in northern Spain in and around the Pyrenees. The movement for Basque separatism, which originated in the 19th century, has been particularly active in recent decades. The Spanish government has treated the issue of Basque nationalism very seriously. Basques supporting separatism have developed a militant political opposition, which is led by an underground nationalist movement known as the ETA. Since the ETA's formation in 1959, more than 800 people have died in terrorist attacks. Many Basques, however, do not support the separatist cause, and the majority oppose the ETA's use of violence.

The Basques were granted home rule in 1980, when three Spanish provinces were officially joined as the Basque Autonomous Community. Such moves have not stemmed the tide of ETA activities. In late 1998, ETA proclaimed a cease-fire, but after 14 months, renewed hostilities. By mid-2002, about 40 people had died in terrorist attacks. Meanwhile, the moderates in the Basque region seem to have gained more support. In 2002, the Spanish government adopted legislation that would allow the authorities more leeway in dealing with extremist groups.

A parador, or national hotel, overlooks the ocean in Galicia, the most northwesterly region of Spain.

Spain is a constitutional monarchy, and its royal family is enormously popular. In 1995, amid much pageantry, King Juan Carlos I escorted his daughter, Princess Elena, down the aisle on her wedding day.

Navarre. The people of neighboring Navarre practice their own brand of nationalism. During the Civil War much of Franco's support came from Navarre, which remained a significant stronghold of conservative support in his favor. They favor the Carlist branch of Spanish royalty—a branch of the Borbón dynasty—that goes back to the War of the Spanish Succession in the early 18th century. The unrest in Navarre grew so great that in 1968 most of the Carlist princes were exiled from Spain. But the fiercely independent mountain folk of Navarre have not surrendered politically, and their young people are allying themselves with other Spanish rebels.

Galicia. A quieter sort of nationalism survives in Galicia, but it is mainly based on past cultural triumphs. Small groups try to keep alive their impoverished region's special identity. The government has initiated economic projects to end the age-old isolation of the region.

Contrasts and Similarities

The Spanish regionalisms, nationalisms, and separatisms in their varying degrees of intensity are a mirror of the extraordinary diversity of the Spaniards. Perhaps the most striking of all Spanish contradictions is that, despite their profound differences, there is a set of characteristics that unites the Spaniards. They come from different origins and backgrounds, many speak individual languages and dialects, and they look different from each other. Spaniards fight for separate rights and identities, and, not all that many years ago, somewhere between 500,000 and 1,000,000 Spaniards were killed in a civil war. Yet, almost incredibly, together they add up to a nation of people who share eternal virtues and eternal sins.

Pride is one characteristic trait that is shared by all Spaniards. One becomes aware of it as soon as one meets the Spaniards. This does not mean that every Spaniard has delusions of grandeur. It means, instead, that each person has a quiet sense of personal dignity. Since the loss of the empire in the early 19th century, or even before that, Spain developed something of a national inferiority complex in relation to the rest of Western Europe and, later, the United States. But few Spaniards have a personal inferiority complex.

Pride and personal dignity have always been vital for Spaniards, whose lives were always fitted into highly organized and authoritarian societies. The Spaniard accepts a king, a duke, a great landlord, and even a dictator, but never grovels before him. It is a peculiar kind of social democracy that has its roots in Spain's earliest origins. It has survived triumphs and defeats, and may find its death only at the hands of a super-technological society.

The king was simply addressed as Señor (mister). The highest title of nobility in Spain was grandee. The title was always desirable, not for the riches or land that might come with it, but because two special privileges went with the title. A grandee could remain with his head covered in the royal presence, and he was free to call on the king, unannounced, in the middle of the night. A rural landlord still shakes hands with his farm-hands when he surveys his domain. It is said that the Spaniard would be less resentful of a man who tried to kill him than of the man who would be rude to him, that is, failed to show respect for his human dignity.

This Spanish pride has its side effects. One of them is anger. The Spaniard is probably the world's most courteous person—his courtesy may be light and casual to his peers but grave to a stranger. But there is an even ratio between a sense of pride and a capacity for anger. Defied, challenged, or insulted, the Spaniard is quick to react. "Honor" is one of the most commonly used words in the Spanish language, and reaction is quick if a Spaniard's honor is questioned or blemished. All of this tends to explain the stubbornness of the Spaniard at war with a foreign invader or in disagreement with a fellow Spaniard.

Courage, too, is related to pride in the Spanish character. It was a blend of these two traits that kept alive the seamen of Christopher Columbus in their voyages of discovery to the West Indies and permitted the conquistadores to overrun the Inca and Aztec empires with just a small band of men. It made it possible for Vasco Núñez de Balboa to cross the isthmus of Central America and for other discoverers to sail the wild Orinoco River in South America. This courage and pride was present when Spanish soldiers fought across Europe; when King Philip II launched his ill-fated Armada against England; and when Spaniards killed each other in the Civil War.

Pride and courage inevitably breed a sense of romance and adventure as well as the belief that the Spaniard can succeed in any enterprise. The conquest of America seems an impossible venture today. One looks back in amazement at how it was accomplished. But the Spaniards succeeded. It was no accident that in creating Don Quixote as his idealistic but impractical hero that the 16th-century novelist Miguel de Cervantes Saavedra revealed himself as one of Spain's deepest and most perceptive philosophers. He had a profound understanding of the heights and depths of the Spanish soul.

On a different level, all these Spanish traits of character go far to explain why bullfighting is the nation's most beloved public spectacle. Standing alone in the middle of the arena facing the wounded and enraged bull, the matador, glorious in his *traje de luces* (suit of lights), personifies the pride, the courage, and the romanticism of the Spaniard. And the "moment of truth," the instant when death may befall either matador or beast, is the essence of the Spaniard's attitude toward life. It is no wonder that Spain's great heroes, even in this technological age, are matadors—Manolete, who was gored to death in the bullring, and Antonio Ordoñez and Manuel Benítez, "El Cordobes," who continued their colorful careers into middle age.

Way of Life

The Spaniards may be mystical and fatalistic, but they are also the world's most sociable people. A day in any Spanish town, village, or city makes this clear. Every street in every town has its share of bars and cafés and *tascas* (places where one stands at the counter drinking a brandy, a glass of wine, or a beer while eating shrimp, cheese, ham, or sausage and throwing the debris on the floor). No self-respecting village, no matter how poor, would lack a café, and Spaniards will always find a minute during the day to drop in for a drink, a bite, and a chat. It is still common for a worker or a clerk to spend the evening in their favorite café playing cards or chess and discussing the bullfights and soccer. The purpose is simply to be sociable.

Spaniards and tourists alike flock to see the vivid spectacle of the bullfight.

Spaniards like to eat and to eat well. Late and leisurely lunches and dinners are not at all the monopoly of the rich. They are part of the Spanish culture. Each region has its own cuisine. Madrid is famous for tripe and its *cocido,* a rich plate of boiled beef. Valencia and Murcia are the land of the paella, the dish of saffron rice, shellfish, and chicken. The south and Estremadura offer gazpacho, the cold soup of bread, tomatoes, and cucumbers. Catalonia is known for its casseroles, and the Basque country, the delight of the epicure, specializes in fish and seafood. The Basques also patronize eating societies.

One of the outlets for the Spaniard's energy is travel. Since the automobile, the rapid train, and the jet airliner have long since replaced the mule and the donkey as the means of national transportation, the entire country seems to be moving constantly from place to place and from country to country. There seems to be no end to family visits, to calls on faraway friends, and to vacation travel.

The new ideas introduced by the growth of travel, communications, and the immense numbers of foreign tourists have deeply affected Spanish society. The economic growth and the change in the economic patterns have also made themselves felt in ways that were foreshadowed in other industrial nations. For example, thousands upon thousands of young women from the countryside and the lower urban classes have left traditional servant occupations to take better-paying and more respected factory jobs. The rising cost of living, the desire for a car and appliances, the need for money for vacations, recreational activities, and so on are leading young wives to seek office jobs. Unmarried women from the so-called good families have also entered the labor market, something that was almost unthinkable less than a generation ago.

Running the bulls through the streets of Pamplona is the highlight of the city's Fiesta de San Fermin.

Flamenco is an expressive, mostly improvised Spanish dance accompanied by guitar and sometimes by drums.

The growing economic independence of young Spanish women has, in turn, led to a change in age-old customs and social habits. Most women drive cars. The institution of long engagements is giving way to quicker marriages, more on the Western European model. Proof of how times are changing is in the attitude of José Aznar's right-wing party, in power since 1996. One of the professed goals of this government has been to bring more women into the labor force and public life. In 2000, both the Senate and the Congress of Deputies had female presidents.

Spaniards have traditionally been tolerant toward foreigners and minorities, but in recent years, they have become overwhelmed by illegal immigration, most notably from Africa. In 1999, for instance, the Spanish immigration office refused to grant asylum to almost 1 million people from Morocco alone.

CITIES
The contradictions that make the Spanish character and the Spanish landscape so attractive are faithfully reflected in the nation's cities, which elegantly and harmoniously blend ancient and modern, Moorish and Spanish elements.

Puerta del Sol is the historic center of Madrid, Spain's capital city.

Madrid

Since the mid-1950's, Madrid has grown from a quiet and traditional European capital into a thriving, modern metropolis with almost ten percent of the national population. Three quarters of a million automobiles create serious traffic jams where once pedestrians walked serenely. Office and government buildings soar along the Paseo de la Castellana, Madrid's most elegant avenue, which was once lined by the handsome mansions of the nobility. La Castellana has been made longer, and the city itself has expanded outward into rings of suburbs.

A settlement of little importance in Roman times, Madrid was called Madjirith by the Moors who came to Spain in the eighth century. The name and a handful of inhabitants were all the city had until the 16th century, when the site of the future capital was still a forest where wild boar and bears were hunted. The transformation of the forest on the Meseta began in 1561, when King Philip II declared that Madrid was to be the capital of the Spanish kingdom. Although many of his successors considered moving the capital elsewhere, Madrid, with its approximately central location, remained the seat of government, and the city began to grow.

The oldest surviving parts of the city are on and near the Plaza Mayor. Here is the Casa de Panadería—Baking House—built in 1672 as a royal box from which the king and his nobles could comfortably watch fiestas, bullfights, tournaments, and even public executions. The law required the inhabitants of the other houses on the plaza to allow members of the court to sit by their front windows to watch these spectacles if they wanted to. The Plaza Mayor was filled on the great day in the 17th century when five saints—Saint Theresa of Ávila, Saint Ignatius of Loyola, Saint Francis Xavier, Saint Isidore (San Isidro), and Saint Philip Neri—were canonized simultaneously.

A short distance from the Plaza Mayor is Madrid's cathedral, the Church of San Isidro, Madrid's patron saint. Madrileños have a special affection for their saint because, according to legend, one day as he lay sleeping on the farm where he worked, a group of angels came from heaven to finish his chores—a bit of relief city-dwellers hope for also.

The center of Madrid is the Puerta del Sol (gate of the sun). Once a city gate, it is now in the heart of Madrid and is a central point from which all Spanish distances are measured, and from which ten of Madrid's avenues radiate. Following one of them, the Calle de Alcalá, one comes to Madrid's most famous fountain, the Cibele, the Mother Goddess. Farther along, on the Paseo del Prado, is one of the world's greatest museums. Its proper name is the Museo de Pinturas (museum of paintings), but it is almost always called the Prado. It contains an incredible wealth of art, including the work of such great Spanish painters as Velázquez, El Greco, and Goya, as well as a vast collection of Italian, Flemish, French, and German masterpieces.

The abundance of the Prado is complemented by the beauty of the nearby Botanical Gardens with its 30,000 different species of trees, and the Parque del Retiro—a green island in the city that is filled with fountains and has shaded walks, a rose garden, and even a small zoo. The

The Prado, Spain's national museum, houses one of the most important art collections in the world.

Retiro, which was begun by Philip II, is only one of hundreds of sites in the city that were embellished by the Spanish kings. The newest is the Ciudad Universitaria (City University), the vast University of Madrid complex, which was begun by the Spanish king Alfonso XIII in 1928. The university buildings were heavily damaged during the Civil War in the 1930's but have since been rebuilt and are still being expanded, like Madrid itself.

Cities and Monuments Near Madrid

About an hour northwest of Madrid is the Valle de los Caídos—"valley of the fallen"—a stark memorial to the victims on both sides in the Civil War. Not very far from this impressive monument is the Royal Monastery of San Lorenzo del Escorial, which Philip II built as a memorial to his father and to honor a Spanish victory. It is in this vast building—a mixture of royal splendors and monastic simplicity—that Philip spent his last days.

Ávila, west of the Escorial, is one of the great religious centers of Spain and because of its remarkable old walls is one of the most photographed places in the nation. Ávila, which was the birthplace of the great 16th-century mystics Saint Theresa and Saint John of the Cross, won the name of "the fortress that threw back the Reformation" largely because of the tireless efforts of its two saints. Ávila's 11th-century walls, with their 88 towers and 9 gateways, still give the city a fortresslike appearance.

Toledo, southwest of Madrid, is the most splendid of the cities near the capital and is so packed with historic treasures that it has been designated a national monument. As Toletum, the city was important in Roman times and later became a capital of the Visigoth invaders from the north. In A.D. 712 the city passed to the Moors and then in 1085 to Alfonso VI of Castile, who made it the capital of his kingdom. Until Philip moved the court to Madrid, Toledo was the Ciudad Imperial y Coronado —"imperial and crowned city"—a title it is still permitted to use.

The most famous painting of the city, El Greco's *View of Toledo,* is in the Metropolitan Museum in New York City, but the painter's greatest work, *The Burial of Count Orgaz,* and his home, which is now a museum, are in Toledo.

Other evidences of Toledo's colorful past are visible everywhere. Outside the city walls, for example, are the remains of the Roman colony, a medieval castle, and the Fábrica de Armas (arms factory), where the steel weapons for which Toledo has been known since the Middle Ages are still made. Within the walls there is a vivid lesson in Spanish architectural history—the great cathedral, which is called Gothic because it was begun in the 13th century, but which incorporates other Spanish architectural styles as well. Among them are Mudejar, plateresque, Churrigueresque, and neoclassic. Mudejar is the name given to the style influenced by the Moors; plateresque is an early 16th-century form that resembles the delicate work of silversmiths. Churrigueresque is named for José Churriguera, whose extravagant designs marked the high point of Spanish architecture in the late 17th and early 18th centuries. Other notable religious buildings in Toledo are the former mosque, dating from the 11th century and now called Santo Cristo de la Cruz, and the synagogue of El Tránsito.

Spain has had a strong artistic tradition for centuries. One of its most noted painters was Francisco Goya, who painted "Majas on a Balcony" in about 1810.

Daydreamers who have been accused of "building castles in Spain" will discover why when they see the magnificent castles in **Segovia,** which are fully fantastic and beautiful enough to inspire even the most down-to-earth. The most famous is the fortress-castle, the Alcázar, which was

The historic city of Toledo is dominated by its cathedral (center) and the restored Alcázar (right).

El Greco ("the Greek") was one of the world's greatest expressionist painters. His famous "View of Toledo," painted in about 1610, is still renowned for its dramatic imagery.

The Alcázar in Segovia is an outstanding example of Spanish castle architecture.

once the home of Queen Isabella I, and is still a fitting home for royalty. Segovia is also known for its remarkably preserved Roman aqueduct, which has brought water to the city since the 1st century A.D.

Barcelona

There is less of a fairy-tale atmosphere but equally as much history in Spain's second-largest city and leading seaport, Barcelona. Its location on the Mediterranean and its people's *seny*—common sense—are cited as reasons for the city's long and successful history as a center of commerce. In 1992 Barcelona captured world attention as it hosted the Summer Olympic Games.

Barcelona has the reputation of being Spain's most European city, but actually its history has been typically Spanish and reflects the usual procession of conquerors, who seem more often to have been won over by their supposed victims. Barcelona is different in that it became so powerful at one point in its history that even the fish in the Mediterranean were said to be wearing the red and yellow colors of the Catalán capital. Barcelona, like the rest of Spain, started declining in importance in the 16th century, but with the dawn of the Industrial Revolution it began to grow—a process that is still going on.

Financial success has not dulled the charm of the city, with its splendid location on a slope leading down to the sea. In the oldest part of the city, the Gothic Quarter, there are abundant relics of the Roman occupation, including parts of the old city wall. Nearby is the beautiful 14th-century cathedral with its cloisters and gardens, where geese consecrated to the city's patron saint, Eulalia, wander happily. The center of the Gothic Quarter is the Plaza del Rey (king's square) with the Palacio Real Mayor (great royal palace), in whose halls Columbus was presented to Ferdinand and Isabella on his return from his first voyage to America.

Today, as in the 15th century, the seaport is the most important part of the city. Along the Calle de Moncada near the harbor are fine mansions that were formerly the homes of aristocrats. The Pablo Picasso Museum, the future home of the private collection of Spain's most famous modern painter, will be housed in two of these mansions. In the harbor itself there is a replica of Christopher Columbus' flagship, the *Santa Maria,* along with modern ships, large and small, including the coastal craft called *golondrinas* (swallows) and *gaviotas* (sea gulls).

Real birds, as well as flowers, books, magazines, and merchandise of every kind, are for sale along Las Ramblas, an avenue extending from the center of the city to the harbor. Scattered throughout Barcelona are the 15 extraordinary buildings designed by the architect Antonio Gaudí y Cornet (1852–1926), whose works have been hailed as the products of a genius or of a madman because of their remarkable appearance. His most famous work is the Templo Expiatorio de la Sagrada Familia—Temple of the Holy Family—a church, which will, when it is completed in about a century, have 12 towers—one for each of the Apostles—plus a

Las Ramblas, one of the most famous avenues in Europe, is the center of Barcelona's shopping district.

Barcelona's unfinished Church of the Holy Family was designed by architect Antonio Gaudí y Cornet.

higher tower for the Holy Family. Even now the church seems an appropriate symbol of the vital city in which it stands.

Seville

Seville, in southern Spain, is the city that probably best captures the foreigner's imaginary idea of what Spain is like. Here a perfect fusion has taken place between the setting, the climate, and the events of the past, resulting in a city that is as beautiful as it is rich in life, color, and history.

Seville is known to readers as the birthplace of Cervantes' knight, Don Quixote, and to opera-goers as the setting of Mozart's *Don Giovanni*, Bizet's *Carmen*, and Rossini's *Barber of Seville*. But the city is, and has been always, far more than a backdrop for imaginary events. Seville is Spain's leading seaport on the Atlantic, to which it is connected by the Guadalquivir River and by a canal for oceangoing ships. Seville is also an important manufacturing center that produces a variety of goods ranging from armaments to tobacco.

Seville was a thriving commercial center even in Moorish times. In fact, a Muslim historian reported: "If one asked for the milk of birds in Seville it would be found." After the city's reconquest by Ferdinand III of Castile in 1248, it continued to grow, although the mosque and minaret of the Muslims became the cathedral and bell tower of the Christians. The discovery of the New World in 1492 ushered in Seville's greatest period of prosperity because the city held a monopoly on trade with the colonies until the 18th century, when the monopoly passed to Cádiz.

The older part of the city with its narrow, winding streets and handsome plazas retains the face of the proud past. The Cathedral—the third largest Christian church in the world after St. Peter's in Rome and St. Paul's in London—is known for its art treasures. It is also claimed as the burial place of Columbus. The nearby bell tower, which is called the Giralda, is as familiar a symbol of the city as the Eiffel Tower is of Paris or the Empire State Building of New York City. Other buildings such as Torre del Oro (tower of gold) guarding the river, the Columbus Library with its collection of manuscripts, and the 14th-century Alcazár have given Seville its well-earned reputation for beauty.

The architecture in Seville uniquely blends Spanish and Moorish influences.

Seville's annual Ibero-American fairs celebrate Spain's enduring links with the New World.

Each evening during the Holy Week before Easter, the great cathedral becomes the focus of the processions of hundreds of *pasos*—floats —carrying magnificently carved religious figures. The *pasos* are followed by bands of trumpeters and drummers playing music that has been specially composed for the solemn and magnificent ceremonies. Other festivals throughout the year are highlighted by music, dancing, and bullfighting, which for many people are the essence of all that is most beautiful and dramatic in Spanish life.

Spain's automotive industry is one of the fastest growing manufacturing sectors in the country.

THE ECONOMY

Since the victory of the center-right Popular Party in 1996, the economy of Spain has significantly improved. For years, one of the major problems had been unemployment—which ran up to 23 percent in the early 1990s. It has since been reduced to less than 15 percent (which may still seem high, but many Spanish citizens who collect unemployment benefits actually work). Spain adopted the new European currency, the euro, on January 1, 2002, and is striving to make its economy more flexible, competitive, and open. The liberalization of telecommunications and privatization of the public sector are planned for the next few years.

Economists and sociologists divide Spain into three basic regions—the seven industrial provinces, the central provinces, and the south.

The Industrial Provinces

The principal industrial provinces are Madrid, Barcelona, the Basque Provinces—Álava, Guipúzcoa, and Vizcaya—Cantabria, and Asturias. Madrid, Barcelona, and Vizcaya together produce more than the other Spanish provinces combined.

Madrid, the province in which the country's capital has been situated for four centuries, derives its power and wealth from its political status. As the seat of the government and a trading and financial center, Madrid requires a high level of services. Therefore it provides considerable employment, including work in the construction industry. Since the middle 1950's, Madrid has grown from a quiet and traditional European capital into a thriving modern metropolis. Madrid has an increasingly important industrial complex, emphasizing electronics, food processing, and the manufacturing of consumer products. The rest of the province, however, remains backward. The mountainous topography of the Castilian plateau, the dryness of the rocky soil, and the inadequacy of the water supply in the dry climate is responsible for the generally poor agricultural production.

Barcelona has always been prosperous. This is due to the mild Mediterranean climate and the fact that there is enough rain for rich farm production. In addition, there is the trading skill of its people, plus the industrial growth that began in the 19th century. Today Barcelona is, among other things, Spain's automotive production center. The city has spilled out into a chain of industrial suburbs and satellite towns. South of Barcelona and down the Valencian coast, the wealth is in the great orange groves, and the export of the fruit provides much of Spain's foreign exchange earnings. North of Barcelona is the Costa Brava—"wild coast"—a popular vacation region and an important source of tourist revenues.

Vizcaya, Guipúzcoa, and Álava—the Basque Provinces—benefit from a fairly benign climate and considerable rainfall brought by the winds and the mists of the Atlantic, though the winters tend to be severe. The Basque country is the greenest in Spain. For the Basques the mountains that separate them from the rest of Spain have also served to isolate them in their prosperity. But new highways and air travel are doing away with the isolation. The Basque coast of the Bay of Biscay, which joins the

Valencia oranges originated in Spain. Seedlings are cultivated indoors and later transplanted in orchards.

Cork harvesting in Andalusia. Spain is one of the world's leading suppliers of cork.

Atlantic, and the ports of Bilbao and San Sebastián have oriented this region toward France, Britain, and northern Europe.

The three Basque Provinces hold more industry than the rest of Spain put together. Taken as a whole, the Basque area, with its banks, steel industry, and shipyards, enjoys the highest revenues and personal incomes in Spain. The Basque Provinces, along with Madrid and Barcelona, absorb the bulk of the migrations from the poorer regions. Santander, the capital of the Cantabria province, adjoins the Basque country and is a rapidly developing industrial region. Oviedo, the capital of Asturias (another northern province) has coal mines and industry.

The Central Provinces

The central provinces around Madrid include the agricultural areas of La Mancha, the Estremadura region adjoining Portugal, and Galicia. The small shipbuilding industry and fishing in Galicia do not make up for the poor soil. The mountain-dwellers of Navarre also belong economically to this region.

Aside from the south, these two areas have the highest rates of unemployment, and many people migrate from there to industrial centers in Spain and abroad in search of work. The difference in incomes and living standards between the seven industrial provinces and the central provinces is sharp. But even the central provinces seem to enjoy a degree of relative prosperity compared to the depressed south.

The South

At first sight, the south is the most striking, beautiful, and romantic part of Spain. It has the extraordinary cities of Seville, Granada, Córdoba, Cádiz, and Málaga, where some of Spain's greatest art and architecture are on display. History still seems to live in the shade of the monumental cathedrals, churches, and mosques and in the narrow, winding streets where the shuttered old houses open up on patios full of flowers. The south is the home of the flamenco and the beautiful women who sing and dance it. The region is part of Moorish Africa in Europe. It also is one of the playgrounds of Europe, with the famous resorts of the Costa del Sol—"coast of the sun"—Torremolinos, and Marbella, and has a surface appearance of affluence.

But it is in the south—from Cádiz to Almería and Alicante—that topography and nature and climate have been the most cruel to the Spaniards. The mountain ranges and the lack of roads isolate the poor

Sherry, a white wine fortified with brandy, originated in the Spanish city of Jerez de la Frontera.

villages. The stone-strewn fields produce little, if anything. Riverbeds are often dry the year round; some of them have not seen water in years. Rain—the plague of tourists and the joy of peasants—just does not come. What there is of good land in Andalusia is held by the owners of the vast latifundia—estates—where bulls are raised for the bullfights, horses are bred for the select few, olives are raised, and grapes are grown for the sherry industry. The Andalusian peasants are farmhands or tenant farmers. In provinces like Almería—where, near the village of Palomares, the United States Air Force lost four hydrogen bombs in 1966—there is no good land to speak of. Individual irrigation schemes help to make life possible, as does the land reclamation project along the Guadalquivir Delta, where villages have been built for resettled farmers and their families.

Inevitably, then, the southerners leave the south. During the Spanish age of conquest, they went to the New World as seamen and settlers. Today, they migrate to Madrid, Barcelona, the Basque country, or abroad. But neither the Spanish of the south nor their neighbors in Galicia, Estremadura, or Castile have been broken by hardship. On the contrary, they have emerged as tough, imaginative, and often talented individualists.

HISTORY

An ancient legend says that the first settlers in Spain were Tubal and Tarsis, nephews of Noah. Little, in fact, is known about the beginnings of Spanish history. Evidence of the Paleolithic settlers in the north is contained in the caves of Altamira, near Santander. Here about 15,000 years ago artists decorated the cave walls with remarkable drawings that still retain their beauty. Slightly younger relics of these ancient times are burial mounds of the New Stone Age that were probably made by the people who gave their name to the peninsula—the Iberians.

Beginning in about 900 B.C., Celts crossed the Pyrenees into the peninsula, where they mixed with the Iberians to form the Celtiberian people, whom one Latin historian called *robur Hispaniae*—"the oak of Spain." The strategic location of the peninsula and its resources, such as tin, attracted other peoples as well. The bold, seafaring Phoenicians are known to have established trading posts in the Guadalquivir Valley and along the southern coast. The most important of these was Gades, now called Cádiz. Still another seafaring people, the Greeks, established their own outposts on the peninsula. The Greeks are credited with introducing to the Celtiberians olive and wine-grape culture, coinage, and improved ways of making ceramics.

The Carthaginians, a North African people, also set up trading posts along the Spanish coast, including Cartagena (New Carthage) and Barcelona, which is said to have been named for Hamilcar Barca, the 3rd century B.C. Carthaginian general. As a leading Mediterranean power, Carthage presented a serious threat to its chief rival, Rome. The result was the long and bitter conflict known as the Punic Wars (about 264–146 B.C.). Much of the war was fought on the Iberian Peninsula. Other important actions such as Hannibal's advance over the Alps against Rome were launched from the peninsula. Ultimately, however, the Romans drove the Carthaginians out of the peninsula and made it a Roman province called Hispania, from which the name Spain comes.

The ancient aqueduct at Segovia bears witness to Spain's past as a province of the Roman Empire.

Roman Spain

The mountainous terrain and the independent spirit of the Celtiberians made the complete conquest of the new province a difficult task that took the Romans nearly 200 years. With the rather enlightened rule of the Romans the people of Hispania were given civil and political rights under Roman law. Schools were established, and Latin became the language of the people. The products of the peninsula's mines and farms played an important role in Rome's economy. Cities such as Hispalis (Seville), Caesarea Augusta (Zaragoza), Emerita Augusta (Mérida), Brigantium (La Coruña), and Tarragona were established. About 18,000 miles (29,000 kilometers) of roads, as well as immense aqueducts (such as the one at Segovia) and amphitheaters were built, and many are still in use, a testament to the Roman genius for building. Four Roman emperors—Trajan, Hadrian, Marcus Aurelius, and Theodosius—were born in Hispania. During the so-called Silver Age of Latin literature, from about A.D. 14 to 130, such Spanish-born writers as Seneca, Martial, and Quintilian gained fame throughout the Roman world.

The period of Roman rule from about 200 B.C. to A.D. 400 was the longest era of peace and prosperity Spain has known to this day. A high degree of unity was achieved under Roman leadership that may be thought of as forming the basis of the Spanish nation. As Roman power declined, it was replaced by another unifying force—Christianity. The

Spanish Catholic Church claims to have been founded through the mission of the Apostle Saint James the Greater, whose shrine at Santiago de Compostela still attracts pilgrims from all over the world. Many scholars believe, however, that it was probably Saint Paul who founded the church in Spain on a mission there between A.D. 63 and 67. Whatever the truth may be, from that day to this the Church has been a powerful force in Spanish life.

The Visigoths

In the early 5th century A.D., the Visigoths—West Goths—a Germanic tribe, crossed the Pyrenees and made an easy conquest of the people, whose fighting skills had been submerged during their long, peaceful years as Roman subjects. But even as the Visigoths were extending their conquest of the peninsula, they were being absorbed into the Ibero-Roman culture. Latin remained the language of the people, and Christianity finally became the faith of the invaders as well. After the Visigoth king Reccaredo was converted to Christianity in A.D. 589, members of the higher clergy and the nobility were given a voice in the councils of state. Education, instead of being state-run as in Roman times, was carried on by the Church. On the peninsula, as elsewhere in Europe during the early Middle Ages, the Church helped to preserve classical learning.

The Moors

One more important strain was added to the Spanish melting pot when the Moors invaded Spain in A.D. 711. These Muslims from Morocco had been asked to help settle a conflict concerning which of the

Alhambra Palace in Granada reflects the city's heritage as the last Moorish stronghold in Spain.

Visigoth rivals should reign as king. Within 7 years the Moors and their Arab allies had conquered the peninsula except for isolated pockets of resistance, mainly in the northern mountains. It was there in the north that the Christians began to mobilize for the reconquest—a goal that was not achieved for 8 centuries.

The Muslims gained their greatest power in southern Spain. There, the greatest of the Muslim rulers, Abd-er-Rahman III (891–961), who called himself Caliph of Córdoba and Commander of the Faithful, helped to make the city of Córdoba one of the great European centers of culture and commerce. In addition, agriculture and industry advanced under the Muslims. The cultivation of such products as figs, oranges, lemons, sugarcane, melons, and rice was introduced and remains important today. The old Roman irrigation systems were expanded and improved. Mines were worked. Armor and swords from Toledo and Córdoba, Spanish silks and woolens, leather, and ceramics were traded all over Europe.

The Muslims left only a handful of architectural monuments—the great mosque at Córdoba, the Alhambra at Granada, and the Giralda Tower at Seville. Their most enduring legacy was intellectual. The Muslims brought to Spain and to Europe the culture of ancient Greece, whose last intellectual center, Alexandria, had been conquered by the Arabs in 642. As historians, philosophers, grammarians, and astronomers the Muslims made important contributions to the development of European thinking. Pharmacology and botany became formal sciences as a result of the Muslims' work in these fields, and two forms of trigonometry—plane and spherical—were developed by them in Spain.

The Reconquest

Great as their achievements were, the Muslims were often divided among themselves. As they fought among themselves, they were increasingly susceptible to attack by the Christian forces seeking to reunite the peninsula under the Cross. As the Christians fought their way south, various kingdoms were established—Galicia, Asturias, León, Castile, Aragón, Navarre, and Catalonia. Through marriages and wars, the kingdoms were gradually united.

The steps leading up to the unification of Spain are immensely complicated and are perhaps best summarized in dates—from the first skirmish at Covadonga in 718 through the recapture of the important cities of Toledo (1085), Córdoba (1236), Seville (1248), and finally Granada in 1492. The turbulence and even the romance of the period is perhaps best portrayed in the epic *Poema del Cid*, which describes the heroic deeds of the 11th-century knight-adventurer Roderigo Díaz de Vivar, known as the Cid, who fought both Christians and Muslims but never his overlord, King Alfonso VI of Castile.

Even as the Cid's deeds were becoming legendary, disunity among the Christian kingdoms seemed to make the formation of one nation impossible. The strongest of the Spanish kingdoms were expanding their power in other parts of Europe. Catalonia conquered the Balearic Islands in the early 13th century, and at the end of the same century the King of Aragón took over Sicily, thus beginning Spain's long and complicated adventures in Italy. In the course of the 14th century, Catalán seapower came to the rescue of Constantinople against the Turks and helped make Catalonia a major power in the Mediterranean. In 1443, Aragón added

Exquisite mosaic designs embellish castles and palaces in areas once under Moorish rule.

the Kingdom of Naples to its territories. The stage was set for a powerful, united Spain to become a major power in Europe and in the world for several centuries to come.

Imperial Spain

The marriage of Isabella I, Queen of Castile, to Ferdinand II of Aragón in 1469 symbolized the union of Spain, although that union was not an accomplished fact until 1492 when Granada was recaptured from the Moors. In the same year, Christopher Columbus discovered the New World for Spain. The nation was at the beginning of its greatest era of prosperity and grandeur.

In 1496, Pope Alexander VI rewarded Isabella and Ferdinand with the title of Los Reyes Católicos—The Catholic Monarchs—for their past services to the Church and as an incentive to side with him in Italy. As early as 1478, Isabella had established the Holy Office, or Inquisition, whose chief duty was to make Spain a Christian nation. Non-Christians were told to become Catholics or to leave Spain. Most of the Jews left Spain, but those that remained, and many of the Muslims as well, pretended to be converted while secretly following their old beliefs. The expulsion of the Jews from Spain had serious repercussions on the nation's life. Spain's religious unity was saved, but since the Jews had given the country some of its most distinguished writers, physicians, and almost all of its merchants, both scholarship and the economy suffered when they were driven out of the country.

At the same time, Spain was becoming a world power. Regarding France as their chief rival, Ferdinand and Isabella managed to encircle France through alliances and marriage. Isabella and Ferdinand's children were united in marriage with the royal houses of Portugal, England, and

Austria. The marriage of Ferdinand and Isabella's daughter Juana to Philip of Burgundy, a son of the Habsburg Emperor Maximilian of Austria, resulted in the union of the two crowns; their son began his reign as Charles I of Spain in 1516 and became the Holy Roman Emperor Charles V in 1519.

The Spanish Habsburgs. The results of this royal and imperial splendor in the person of the Spanish king marked at once Spain's most glorious era and the beginning of its decline. Charles V's deep involvement in European affairs cost Spain dearly in manpower and in wealth. Recruitment and taxes increased as Charles battled Francis I of France in a succession of wars, fought to protect Vienna from the Turks, and tried vainly to turn the tide of the Protestant Reformation. Simultaneously, Spanish explorers, seamen, soldiers, and priests were extending the overseas empire. Mexico was conquered by 1522, Peru became a Spanish territory in 1535. By the middle of the 16th century, Spain's flag flew over colonies in California, Florida, Central and South America, and the Philippines, as well as on the coast of Africa.

In 1556, Charles V gave up the throne of Spain in favor of his son Philip II, who also became King of the Indies, the Kingdom of Naples, and the Low Countries. Philip's 42-year reign is noteworthy for great achievements, which seem matched by equally dismal failures. Philip made Madrid the nation's capital. He made the entire peninsula Spanish when he took over the throne of Portugal in 1580, and helped defeat the Turks in the sea battle of Lepanto in 1571. In his other endeavors, Philip was less fortunate. He was engaged in a long and finally unsuccessful struggle to keep the Low Countries Catholic and Spanish. This led him into conflict with England. It was Philip who dispatched the Invincible Armada against Queen Elizabeth I's fleet in 1588—an adventure that ended disastrously for the Spanish Armada and seriously diminished Spain's position as an international power.

The decline of Spanish power continued slowly throughout the reigns of Philip III and Philip IV. Like other monarchs of the time they entrusted much of their power to their advisers who governed for them. In fact when the kings acted on their own the results were often disastrous, as was the case when Philip III expelled almost 500,000 Moriscos —converted Muslims—from his kingdom in 1609. The loss of these able, hardworking citizens had serious economic consequences for Spain. At the beginning of Philip IV's reign, however, Spain was still a great power in Europe. By the time of his death, in 1655, France had become the leading power on the continent and Spain had lost its European territories.

Curiously, it was against this background that the arts in Spain flourished so magnificently that the period from about 1550 to 1680 has come to be known as the Golden Age. Writers, artists, architects, and sculptors, supported and encouraged by the nobles, provided the world with works of authentic genius. The theater gained enormous popularity through the work of such playwrights as Lope de Vega and Pedro Calderón de la Barca. It was in this period, too, that Cervantes published *Don Quixote,* which is considered one of the masterpieces of world literature. In painting there was an equally impressive array of creative talents, including José Ribera, Bartolomé Esteban Murillo, and Francisco de Zurbarán. The giants of art were, however, Kyriakos Theotokopoulos, who is known as El Greco (the Greek) because he was born in Crete, and Diego de Silva y Velázquez.

The Spanish Borbóns. The last Spanish Habsburg king was Charles II, a sad, imbecilic man who could scarcely think, let alone manage a kingdom. When he was near death, he was persuaded to bequeath his realm to Philip, Duke of Anjou, a member of the French house of Bourbon. The immediate result was the War of the Spanish Succession, but the Duke ultimately came to the throne as Philip V. His unsuccessful military activities did little to help Spain back to its former glory. His successors were slightly more successful in their efforts to administer the empire and Spain. Attempts were made to strengthen the economy, improve education, commerce, and industry. But the dominance of France in Europe and the recurrent wars into which Spain was drawn drained away the modest progress provided by these steps. The last of the Spanish Borbóns to reign in the 18th century was Charles IV, an incompetent king, whose wife, together with his chief minister, Manuel de Godoy, ran the kingdom.

The Long Crisis

Goya's graphic portrayals of the brutality of war reflect events in Spain during the period of Napoleon's domination of Europe. Inevitably Spain was drawn into the conflict, first as an ally of France. The results of the alliance included the destruction of the French and Spanish fleets at Trafalgar in 1805 by England's Lord Nelson and then in 1808 the invasion of Spain by French forces. Napoleon's brother Joseph was made King Joseph I of Spain, but this honor was short-lived, as the Spanish people began to wage a heroic guerrilla war against the French. With the help of British forces under the Duke of Wellington, the Spanish were able to drive the French troops out of Spain by 1814.

At the end of the war the Borbóns returned to the Spanish throne, but there was no end to the nation's problems. Strong forces gathered to overthrow the monarchy—a threat met by King Ferdinand VII with reactionary and repressive measures. The struggle between these same forces in Spanish America led to the loss of all the colonies in South America by 1825. Only Cuba, Puerto Rico, and the Philippines remained, and they were lost as a result of the settlement following the Spanish-American War in 1898.

In Spain itself the 19th century continued to be a time of strife and upheaval. A republic was briefly established in 1873, but the next year King Alfonso XII was asked to return to the throne. His son, Alfonso XIII, had the dubious distinctions of having a long reign—1886–1931—and of being the first Spanish king to abdicate without bloodshed. As the century closed, the workingmen of Spain turned hopefully to socialist and other labor parties as a way of solving their problems. Strikes and uprisings were ruthlessly put down by the government.

Revolutionary ideas were widespread and grew in intensity in the early 1920's. A strike in Catalonia prompted the King to permit General Primo de Rivera to become the military dictator of Spain. The Cortes (parliament) was dissolved, although the King remained on the throne. Rivera, who was never popular with the liberals in Spain, was finally overthrown in 1929. In 1931, as the result of a general election, the King was deposed and a republic was established.

The leaders of the republic began the enormous job of providing Spain with political and economic reforms, but it was an almost impossible task in the face of conservative traditions, attacks from the landowners, the Church, and the Army, and the steady radicalization of the left. In 1936, an election was held in which the Popular Front—an alliance of republicans, Socialists, labor, and Communists—won an impressive victory. The victory of the Popular Front was followed by general disorder and triggered a revolt by the Army against the government.

The Civil War of 1936–39 pitted Spaniard against Spaniard, as the Republican followers of the Popular Front battled the troops under the leadership of Francisco Franco. The Nationalists, led by Franco, were supported by the German and Italian dictatorships, while the Soviet Union provided aid to the Republicans. City after city fell to the Nationalists until in 1939, at the cost of between 500,000 and 1,000,000 lives and terrible devastation, Franco became the head of the Spanish state.

Transition From Franco. Franco, who took the title of Caudillo (leader), became the chief of state, the chief of the armed forces, and the leader of the only legal political party, the Falange. In 1947, Franco announced that the monarchy would be restored after his death. Prince Juan Carlos of Borbón y Borbón—the grandson of Alfonso XIII—assumed the throne as King Juan Carlos I after Franco's death, in 1975.

Modern Spain

Political change has come to Spain, but the scars of the Civil War are barely healed. In 1981, firm action by the King put down an attempted rightist coup. Victories in the 1982 and 1986 parliamentary elections ensured the dominance of the Socialist Party, which under Franco had spent more than 40 years of underground existence and opposition.

Madrid's National Palace was built in the 18th century on the site of an ancient Moorish fortress.

Felipe González, the Socialist leader who became premier in 1982, epitomized the new generation of successful Spanish politicians. He was youthful, charismatic, cosmopolitan, and pragmatic. González, fully backed by King Juan Carlos, who formed an important bridge between the old order and contemporary Spain, proved himself to be an activist. He launched initiatives to reduce the size and influence of the armed forces, to preserve his nation's membership in the North Atlantic Treaty Organization (NATO), and to obtain Spain's entry into the European Community (EC) along with Portugal on January 1, 1986.

González viewed membership in the EC as essential both to diminishing his nation's political isolation and to continuing the economic boom that characterized the Spanish economy in the 1960s and 1970s. Large foreign investments coupled with the Spaniards' hard work have helped to industrialize what had been an agricultural country. There has also been the growth of a better-educated managerial class and, as a result, hundreds of thousands of new jobs. An important contribution to the development of service-oriented economy has been tourism: since the last decades of the 20th century, Spain has welcomed between 50 million and 60 million foreign visitors each year.

A seven-year transitional period was established to ease Spain into full participation in the European Community (renamed the European Union, or EU, in 1991). During this period, Madrid continued—although at decreasing levels—to protect its industry, agriculture, and fishing sectors. Meanwhile the EU provided special economic assistance to nine poorer autonomous regions. In 1991, in anticipation of the unified European market, the government began to restructure Spain's unprofitable industrial sectors, and reduced subsidies to these sectors.

Although González was reelected to office in 1990 and 1993, his Socialist Party lost a significant amount of power in general elections. The Socialists' apparent decline culminated in defeat in the elections of March 1996, when a coalition led by the center-right Popular Party gained control of the government. In May 1996, José María Aznar was named prime minister. His government pushed for liberalization, privatization, and deregulation of the economy. On January 1, 1999, Spain was among 11 EU countries that formed the European Monetary Union (EMU), and introduced the new currency called the euro.

Four years later, after economic successes at home and a growing integration of Spain into European politics, Aznar won another election in 2000. Like his political friend Tony Blair (center-left), Aznar (center-right) belongs to the new brand of young European politicians who are not driven by ideological dictates of traditional right and left, but rather by a desire to make their countries open and competitive.

Government

In 1977, Spain held its first free elections in 41 years. A new constitution ratified in 1978 made Spain a parliamentary monarchy. The king is head of state and appoints a premier as head of government. The Cortes (parliament) consists of a 255-member Senate (*Senado*) and 350-member Congress of Deputies (*Congreso de los Diputados*). The country is divided into 19 autonomous communities (*comunidades autónomas*), two of which are the Spanish enclaves of Ceuta and Melilla in Morocco.

GEORGE W. GRAYSON, College of William and Mary

Sparkling streams rush through Andorra's valleys.

ANDORRA

At Christmastime in the Spanish town of Seo de Urgel, the bishop sits down to a princely feast of crisply roasted capon, delicious smoked ham, and fresh mountain cheese. It is an excellent meal, and if the bishop wants to enjoy it again in the new year, he can, for there are still 11 hams and 23 cheeses in his larder. The food comes to the bishop's table from a place high in the Pyrenees to the northeast—the tiny, mountain-bound country called Andorra.

HISTORY AND GOVERNMENT

Andorra has always charmed those who happened to hear of it or visit it. As long ago as 1806, when Napoleon I passed through Andorra on his way to conquer Spain, someone suggested that he incorporate the little country into France. He refused, declaring that Andorra was a "political curiosity" that "must be preserved."

Andorra's capital, Andorra la Vella, seems dwarfed by the mountains around it.

Small Andorran farm villages cling to the land's rocky slopes.

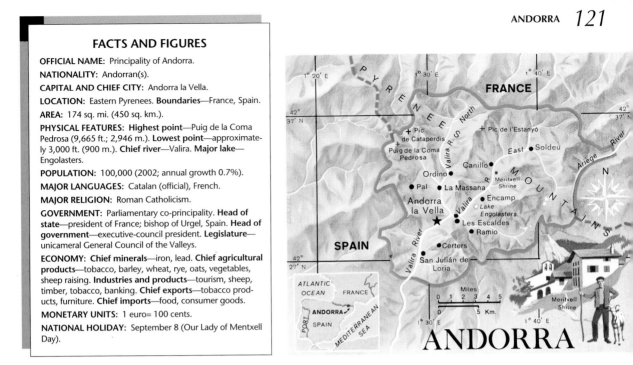

FACTS AND FIGURES

OFFICIAL NAME: Principality of Andorra.

NATIONALITY: Andorran(s).

CAPITAL AND CHIEF CITY: Andorra la Vella.

LOCATION: Eastern Pyrenees. **Boundaries**—France, Spain.

AREA: 174 sq. mi. (450 sq. km.).

PHYSICAL FEATURES: Highest point—Puig de la Coma Pedrosa (9,665 ft.; 2,946 m.). **Lowest point**—approximately 3,000 ft. (900 m.). **Chief river**—Valira. **Major lake**—Engolasters.

POPULATION: 100,000 (2002; annual growth 0.7%).

MAJOR LANGUAGES: Catalan (official), French.

MAJOR RELIGION: Roman Catholicism.

GOVERNMENT: Parliamentary co-principality. **Head of state**—president of France; bishop of Urgel, Spain. **Head of government**—executive-council president. **Legislature**—unicameral General Council of the Valleys.

ECONOMY: Chief minerals—iron, lead. **Chief agricultural products**—tobacco, barley, wheat, rye, oats, vegetables, sheep raising. **Industries and products**—tourism, sheep, timber, tobacco, banking. **Chief exports**—tobacco products, furniture. **Chief imports**—food, consumer goods.

MONETARY UNITS: 1 euro= 100 cents.

NATIONAL HOLIDAY: September 8 (Our Lady of Mentxell Day).

Until 1993, Andorra was a country with three types of government. It was a republic, because it had its own elected parliament. It was a principality, because it had two princes. And it was a suzerainty, for its two princes were also feudal overlords, or suzerains. Then in 1993, the citizens overwhelmingly voted for Andorra's first constitution. Andorra is now a parliamentary co-principality, and the government has separate executive, legislative, and judicial branches.

One of the two princes is the bishop of Urgel; the other is the president of France. Both princes have defined, but strictly limited, powers. As feudal overlords, they still receive an annual tribute from their domain. Because the president of France lives so far from Andorra, he receives a small sum of cash. The bishop receives even less cash, but he gets in addition an annual tribute of food each Christmas, consisting of two capons, two hams, and four cheeses from each of the six districts of Andorra. This payment, called *la quistia* in Catalán, dates back to 1278.

In that year, a treaty was signed at Les Escaldes, Andorra, ending a long struggle over the territory by the bishop of Urgel and the count of Foix. By the terms of this treaty the bishop and the count became co-princes of Andorra. In succeeding centuries, the property of the counts of Foix was transferred to the kings of France and, finally, to the French presidents. The treaty is one of the oldest pacts presently in force. In 1990, Andorra reached an agreement with the European Union (EU) on the free movement of people to and from the country, but it has not yet officially joined the organization.

Andorra's history before the 13th century is not so much fact as it is long-accepted tradition. Andorrans believe that Charlemagne granted them their independence in the 8th century, in return for their help in fighting the Moors in Spain. They also believe that Charlemagne or his son King Louis I named the country—possibly for the Biblical land of Endor. However, the name Andorra may come from the Moorish word *al-dorra*, which means "a thickly wooded place."

LAND AND PEOPLE

The Andorrans are a proud, independent people. Though Spaniards call them *cerrada* ("closed"), and the French have an expression which says that someone who has the tendency to be tight-lipped "acts the Andorran," it may be that Andorrans have developed a certain quiet strength through centuries of living in a difficult land.

Farming is Andorra's traditional way of life, but so much of the land is mountainous that only about 4 percent of it can be farmed. This tiny percentage explains the country's official name—Valleys of Andorra—for the valleys are where the good land is and where Andorrans grow tobacco, grain, fruits, and vegetables. Whole families work side by side on their farms, and schools often do not open in the fall until harvesttime is over. Children also help to tend the many sheep and cows that grow fat grazing the high Andorran pastures in summer.

ECONOMY

Since the 1950s, hydroelectric plants have been harnessing the tumbling mountain streams for power, and Andorra has several small factories that manufacture cigars, cigarettes, matches, sandals, and anisette liqueur. All these are used in Andorra and exported to France and Spain. Andorra's two most famous "exports," however, are not products at all, and both are easier to send over long distances. One is Radio Andorra, which broadcasts in French and Spanish. This station, whose programs consist largely of recorded music, is very popular in both France and Spain. Andorra's other well-known export is its stamps. These are issued by both France and Spain, and are prized by many stamp collectors all over the world.

For years, stamps and radio have been carrying Andorra to the world beyond the mountains, but recently, much of that world has been coming to Andorra. Approximately 12 million tourists visit Andorra annually to delight in its landscape of twisted pines, ancient oaks, glistening lakes, and lush meadows. The roads from France and Spain are plowed constantly and kept open throughout winter, so more skiers can reach Andorra's slopes. Visitors also enjoy annual fiestas like the Bal de Morratxa (held in San Julián de Loria), which features a dance representing the signing of the treaty so long ago. Tourism now accounts for about four-fifths of the nation's income.

ANDORRA'S CAPITAL, MINIATURE OF A MINIATURE

The country's tiny capital, Andorra la Vella, has some 8,000 residents. It is the site of the 16th-century Casa de la Vall ("house of the valley"), where Andorra's 24-member parliament meets. A 4-lb. (2-kg.) key unlocks the door of the old building, which also serves as Andorra's courthouse and prison. The town's shop windows are crowded with attractive merchandise, much of it imported from all over the world. And Andorra la Vella's streets swarm with cars—enough to require a traffic policeman at the busiest intersection.

Like its capital, Andorra is a place where reminders of the past still wait around every corner. It is a country that has enjoyed peace among its mountains for more than 700 years—a country that has been described as "the most peaceful ... in the world."

Reviewed by PRESS AND INFORMATION SERVICE OF THE FRENCH EMBASSY, New Yorks

GIBRALTAR

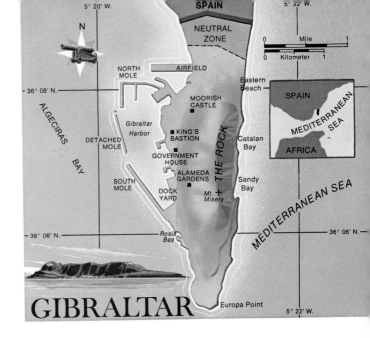

Gibraltar, which covers only 2.3 sq. mi. (6 sq. km.) of land, juts out from southern Spain at the entrance to the Strait of Gibraltar, the narrow waterway that separates Europe from Africa. It is one of the Pillars of Hercules, the ancient name given to the great cliffs flanking the strait. In A.D. 711, Tarik, an Arab Muslim warrior, captured the rock and built a fortress there. The Moors named it Djebel al-Tarik ("rock of Tarik"), which evolved into "Gibraltar." After seven centuries of Moorish rule, the Spanish seized the rock in 1462. In 1704, during the War of the Spanish Succession, the British overran Gibraltar, and in 1713, Spain ceded the fortress to Great Britain "to be held and enjoyed absolutely with all manner of right forever."

Gibraltar is a British crown colony. The commander of the fortress serves as governor-general. There is an elected legislative council and an elected city council to deal with municipal affairs. The language of the more than 27,000 Gibraltarians is English, but most of them also speak Spanish. The inhabitants are descendants of British soldiers who married Spanish women, Maltese who came there to work, Spanish and Portuguese Jews who were driven out of their homelands at the end of the 15th century, and Italians who came to escape conscription into Napoleon's armies. In a 1967 referendum held to allow Gibraltarians to choose between Spain and Great Britain, they voted 12,138 to 44 to remain British.

Since the 1960s, Spain has claimed that the British occupation of Gibraltar is illegal. For centuries, Spanish laborers from nearby towns came daily to work in Gibraltar, but the border was closed by Spain in 1969. It was partially reopened in 1982, and in 1985, the remaining border restrictions were lifted. In July 2002, the British and Spanish governments agreed to share sovereignty over Gibraltar, but the enclave's inhabitants will ultimately make the final decision in a future referendum.

Gibraltar has no agriculture and very little industry. Its income derives mainly from servicing the ships that use the port, light manufacturing, and tourism, which has been greatly developed in recent years. The enclave has also become a renowned international conference center. The town on the lower slope of the rock has a museum, an historic Roman Catholic cathedral, and the ruins of a Moorish castle.

Reviewed by SIR JOSHUA HASSAN, C.B.E., M.V.O., Q.C., Chief Minister of Gibraltar

The scenic Amalfi coast south of Naples is one of Italy's most popular summer resort areas.

ITALY

Italy, an ancient land in south central Europe, is one of the great wellsprings of Western culture. Here the Romans built the capital of their vast empire and where later the Roman Catholic Church chose to make its spiritual headquarters. The Renaissance, or rebirth of classical art, architecture, and philosophy, began in Italy in the 14th century.

All these and other landmark achievements in European history were made against a background of warfare and bloodshed that pitted Italians from one part of the peninsula against those from another and against a seemingly endless succession of invaders. Somehow, in spite of these repeated upheavals, the Italian people survived, united by language and culture. In the mid-19th century, the unity became political as well, and the nation we know as Italy was born.

For the visitor from abroad, Italy provides one surprise after another. The tourist prepared to visit a nation that could well have become a vast museum of Western history finds instead a modern industrial nation. The surprises multiply as one finds Italy more warmhearted, more fascinating, indeed, more of everything than one had expected. At the same time it is one of those unique countries where nearly everybody feels at home immediately. The fine blend of ancient and modern in a setting of beautiful landscapes and exciting cities is an invitation in itself. It is perfectly matched by the Italian people themselves, a nation of born hosts.

THE LAND

The name "Italy" is extremely old. It seems to have been used first in documents of the 5th century B.C. to describe a small territory at the tip of the boot-shaped peninsula that extends into the Mediterranean Sea. Historians used to think that the name came from that of a legendary king, Italo. Many other ingenious and improbable theories have been suggested to explain the origin of the name. No matter what its origins, the name of that small territory at the tip of the boot spread, little by little, to indicate the whole peninsula. By about A.D. 1000 the name designated a region, a dialect, and a culture. But it was not until the mid-19th century that the many separate nations on the peninsula were united into one nation to which the ancient name "Italy" was given.

In the north, where the Italian peninsula joins the European continent, the Alps form an almost continuous natural boundary. The Alps divide Italy from France in the northwest and from Switzerland and Austria in the north. Italy's northeastern neighbor is Yugoslavia.

The Italian peninsula stretches southeast into the Mediterranean Sea from Europe to Africa, with its heel to the east and its toe pointing west. The boot seems poised to kick its largest island, Sicily, from which it is separated by the narrow Strait of Messina. In addition to Sicily, Italy includes the islands of Sardinia and Elba in the Tyrrhenian Sea off its west coast. The island of Corsica in the Tyrrhenian is a department of metropolitan France. There are about 70 smaller islands scattered along the coast in both the Adriatic and Tyrrhenian seas.

Italy's long seacoast is better-known for its beaches and resorts than for its ports, of which only Genoa and Naples are important to international shipping. However, Italy's location with easy access to North Africa, the Balkans, and the Middle East and to the Atlantic, has been vitally important in shaping the country's history and culture.

Two small independent states are within Italy's borders. One is the Republic of San Marino in the northeast, which claims to be the oldest and smallest republic in the world. The other state within Italy is Vatican City, which covers 108.7 acres (44 hectares) in the capital city of Rome. This, the smallest independent nation in the world, is the spiritual center of the Roman Catholic world. (Both SAN MARINO and VATICAN CITY are described in separate articles in this volume.)

Hills, Mountains, and Volcanoes

The most important geographical fact about Italy is that two-thirds is covered with mountains and hills. Considering that the peninsula extends for about 600 miles (970 kilometers) and has an average width of about 90 miles (140 kilometers) from coast to coast, it is easy to visualize how rugged the landscape is. In fact, the mountains and hills have served until recently to keep one region of Italy quite isolated from another. Without traveling too many miles one can still find differences of outlook, custom, dialect, and cuisine. The development of modern transportation and communication facilities is slowly erasing these differences, but it is still quite easy to tell the regional origin of an Italian.

The Alps contain the highest peak entirely within Italy, the 13,323-foot (4,060-meter) Gran Paradiso. But the Wall of Alps has never acted as an effective barrier to aggressive or peaceful invaders. Since earliest times the passes through the Alps into Italy have been used by warriors

FACTS AND FIGURES

OFFICIAL NAME: Italian Republic.

NATIONALITY: Italian(s).

CAPITAL: Rome.

LOCATION: Southern Europe. **Boundaries**—Austria, Slovenia, Adriatic Sea, Ionian Sea, Mediterranean Sea, Tyrrhenian Sea, Ligurian Sea, France, Switzerland.

AREA: 116,305 sq. mi. (301,230 sq. km.).

PHYSICAL FEATURES: Highest point—Mont Blanc (15,772 ft.; 4,807 m.). **Lowest point**—sea level. **Chief rivers**—Po, Adige, Tiber, Arno.

POPULATION: 58,100,000 (2002; annual growth 0.0%).

MAJOR LANGUAGES: Italian (official), German.

MAJOR RELIGION: Roman Catholicism.

GOVERNMENT: Republic. **Head of state**—president. **Head of government**—prime minister. **Legislature**—bicameral Parliament.

CHIEF CITIES: Rome, Milan, Naples, Turin.

ECONOMY: Chief minerals—mercury, potash, marble, sulfur. **Chief agricultural products**—fruits, vegetables, potatoes, olives, grapes. **Industries and products**—tourism, machinery, iron and steel, chemicals, food processing. **Chief exports**—engineering products, textiles and clothing, production machinery. **Chief imports**—engineering products, chemicals, transport equipment.

MONETARY UNIT: 1 euro = 100 cents.

NATIONAL HOLIDAY: June 2 (Anniversary of Republic).

and visitors alike. In the 3rd century B.C. the Carthaginian general Hannibal was able to lead a fully equipped army with elephants across the Alps into northern Italy. This famous invasion was followed by others, each of which has left its mark on the land and people of Italy.

Today, only the most rugged tourists would consider crossing the Alps on foot because excellent highways, tunnels, and railroads link the Italian peninsula with its transalpine neighbors. Among the best-known passes are the Brenner from Austria; the Saint Gotthard, Bernina, Great Saint Bernard, and Maloja from Switzerland; and the Mont Cenis, Mont Blanc, and Little Saint Bernard from France.

Italy's "spine" is formed by the Apennine Range, which stretches from the Ligurian Alps in the northwest down to the Strait of Messina in the south. The mountains of Sicily are considered an extension of the Apennines. Corno Grande, a peak that is in the Gran Sasso d'Italia group east of Rome in the Abruzzi region, rises to 9,560 ft. (2,910 m.) and is the highest point in the Apennines. However, the average height of the range is considerably lower. Although the Apennines were once thickly forested, centuries of indiscriminate tree cutting for building and for fire

Dramatic mountain formations dominate the Dolomite region of the Alps. Many local residents speak German.

Since Roman times, the sheltered shores of Lake Como have provided popular resort sites.

wood have left the mountains nearly bare and very badly eroded. To combat this erosion and to provide Italy with a much needed timber source, the government has launched a long-range reforestation program.

The Apennines are known for their volcanic characteristics—lava fields, earthquakes, and active volcanoes, such as Vesuvius near Naples and Mount Etna near Messina, Sicily. The earliest recorded eruption of Vesuvius occurred in A.D. 79 and destroyed Pompeii. Earthquakes often rock the Italian peninsula and Sicily, wiping out towns and lives in minutes. The most recent, in 1980, left 5,000 dead and 250,000 homeless.

Lakes and Rivers

In addition to the volcanic crater lakes in the Apennines—Bolsena, Bracciano, Albano, and Vico—Italy is noted for its magnificent lake district south of the Alps. The beautiful lakes Garda, Maggiore, Como, Iseo, and part of Lugano are world-famous tourist attractions. Garda is the largest lake in Italy; Maggiore and Como rank as the second and third largest, respectively. Maggiore is known also for its Borromean Islands, one of which, Isola Bella, was transformed by a nobleman from a barren islet into a terraced wonderland rising to surround a palace filled with fine painting and sculpture. Still another lake, Trasimeno, in central Italy, is known for its beauty and because it was there that Hannibal won an important victory against the Romans in 217 B.C.

Italy has many rivers, but only two—the Po and the Adige—are navigable. The 405-mile (650-kilometer)-long Po is Italy's longest river and has the largest drainage basin. The Po rises in the Alps, flows in an easterly direction across the plain between the Alps and the Apennines, and empties into the Adriatic south of Venice. The Po, its tributaries, and an intricate system of irrigation help to make the large north Italian plain the most fertile farmland in the nation.

The Adige rises in the Alps and empties into the Adriatic. Although it is navigable for only about 70 miles (110 kilometers), it has been harnessed to provide hydroelectricity. Other Italian rivers such as the Arno, Tiber, Piave, and Isonzo are well-known because of the cities along their banks and the events that have taken place nearby. The Arno, which is the river of Florence, the leading city of Tuscany, rises in the Apennines and empties into the Tyrrhenian Sea, as does the Tiber, the river that flows through Italy's capital city, Rome. The Piave in the north and the Isonzo in the northeast, both of which empty into the Adriatic, were the sites of fierce battles during World War I.

Islands

Sicily. The largest of Italy's islands, Sicily ranks as the largest and most populous of all the Mediterranean islands. Since 1947 Sicily and such nearby islands as the Lipari and Egadi groups have been governed as an autonomous region of Italy. Mountainous Sicily is known for its magnificent scenery, fine climate, and mineral wealth. Scenically, the most outstanding landmark is Mount Etna, the highest active volcano in Europe. The trip to the edge of the volcano's main crater can be made by cable car, then jeep, and, finally, for the last few yards, on foot. Once atop Etna there is a stunning view of the island, the surrounding sea, and, of course, the awesome crater itself. Etna's first recorded eruption took place in 475 B.C., when the island was colonized by Greeks.

The island has been occupied successively by the Romans, Byzantines, Arabs, Normans, and Spaniards. In the 18th century Sicily, with Naples, became part of the kingdom of Two Sicilies, and it was made part of the newly formed Italian kingdom in 1861. One of Sicily's attractions is the wealth of relics and monuments left behind by some of the earliest settlers. One of the best-preserved Greek temples is at Agrigento; other notable Greek legacies are at Syracuse and Segesta.

Today, however, Sicily is fast recovering from the centuries of foreign occupation, bad government, and the neglect of absentee landlords who once owned much of the land. The fertile island now leads Italy in the production of citrus fruits. Corn, barley, olives, almonds, grapes,

Crowded housing adjacent to sandy beaches is characteristic scenery along the Sicilian coastline.

The small, picturesque island of Ischia guards the approaches to the Bay of Naples.

and cotton are also grown. Tuna and sardine fishing are important to the island's economy. Since World War II, the government and private companies have greatly helped the industrial development of the island. Sicily now produces about two thirds of Italy's sulfur, as well as important quantities of asphalt, rock salt, sea salt, and pumice. Sicily's economic future has been made even brighter by the discovery of one of Europe's largest oil fields.

Sicily's Islands. The Lipari (Aeolian) Islands, Egadi Islands, Ustica, and Pantelleria are part of the autonomous region of Sicily. The Lipari Islands, a volcanic group, take Aeolian, their other name, from Aeolus, the Greek god of the winds, who was believed to store the winds in a cave on one of the islands. Another Lipari island is called Vulcano in honor of the Roman fire god, Vulcan, whose workshop was believed to be there. Stromboli, also in the group, has an active volcano. In the past the islands were used as detention centers for political prisoners, but they are better-known today for their scenery and as a unique place to go skin diving because of the unusually clear water and underwater caves.

Capri and Ischia. These two islands in the Bay of Naples are among Italy's most famous resorts. Capri's scenery, vegetation, and climate have attracted generations of tourists. Even in Roman times, the emperors Augustus and Tiberius found Capri lovely enough to build vacation villas there. Modern visitors seek out the Blue Grotto, which is famous for the strange luminescence of the seawater and can be visited by boat.

Ischia is a volcanic island whose warm mineral springs and superb landscapes have made it a popular health resort. A castle built on 5th-century Greek foundations and the always inviting sea also attract visitors.

Sardinia. About 115 miles (185 kilometers) off the west coast of Italy is Sardinia, the second largest Italian island. Mountainous Sardinia is one of the most dramatically beautiful and least populated parts of Italy. Its dry climate, dense growth of shrubs, cork oak, and heather, and the clear surrounding sea are making it a popular resort. The capital city, Cagliari, is older than Rome. Prehistoric stone fortress-houses called nuraghi are scattered all over the island, but archeologists have been unable to determine exactly who inhabited them.

Sardinia, like Sicily, is an autonomous region. And also like Sicily it is one of Italy's richest mineral resource areas. Zinc, lead, lignite, copper, iron, and salt are mined. Corn, barley, grapes, olives, and tobacco are grown, and cork is exported.

Elba. This small island only 6 miles (10 kilometers) off the coast of Tuscany, is not known either for its iron mines, which have been worked since Roman times, or for its pleasant scenery. Its fame comes from the fact that for one year in its long history of occupation by foreign powers it was a sovereign principality. The brief moment of sovereignty came in 1814–15 when the European leaders banished the French emperor Napoleon there and gave him the tiny island as his own. When he escaped from Elba and failed to reconquer his kingdom, Napoleon was sent to St. Helena, a much more remote island in the South Atlantic, and Elba eventually became a part of Italy.

Natural Resources

Italy lacks most of the resources needed for a modern industrial economy. The fact that Italy's economy is modern and industrial is the result of importing many basic resources, as well as continuous exploration to find existing resources. The ingenious use of outside resources helps to explain how Italy has transformed itself from a predominantly agricultural nation into an industrial one in recent years.

The energy from natural steam jets is harnessed at a giant complex near Pisa and used to create electricity.

One of Italy's important power resources is hydroelectricity produced by harnessing swift-flowing alpine streams. Much electricity is also generated by nuclear reactors. Oil and natural gas are found on the Adriatic coast near Ravenna, on the southern edge of the Po plain, and in Sicily.

Another source of power comes from a unique complex in the Larderello area near Pisa in Tuscany. There the natural high-temperature steam produced by the *soffioni*—steam jets erupting through the earth's crust—has been tapped through deep wells. The steam is then piped to power installations through thermally insulated pipelines and used to operate steam turbines that produce electricity.

Visitors speeding by train from Milan and Genoa to Rome, or vice versa, rarely know that their electric locomotive is powered by steam gushing in geyserlike jets from deep in the earth. And even fewer realize that Larderello—because of its huge, noisy steam jets and boiling mud wells—was for a long time considered a corner of hell on earth. Today, Larderello is a model modern industrial center employing about 2,000 people in a variety of industries—such as power stations (which have been nationalized), chemical plants, and salt refineries. This intelligent exploitation of natural resources is studied by specialists and scientists from all over the world. New Zealand, Iceland, Japan, and Mexico, in fact, have similar installations based on geothermal power.

Only three minerals—mercury, sulfur, and marble—are mined in large enough quantities for export. Italy is, in fact, the world's leading producer of marble. The most famous Italian marble comes from the quarries of the Apuane Alps, a branch of the Apennines that runs along

The Apuane quarries in Tuscany have been a rich source of choice marble since Roman times.

Goats graze near a Sicilian sulfur plant. Sicily was formerly the world's leading supplier of sulfur.

part of the Tuscan coast. The Apuane are a startling sight, rising to about 6,000 feet (1,800 meters) and seeming, even in summer, to be covered with snow. The "snow," of course, is made up of millions and millions of marble chips. Today, the Apuane quarries produce over one third of the world's marble and employ over 100,000 people. The best marble in this region comes from around Carrara. Its beautiful white statuary marble was used by the 16th-century artist Michelangelo.

Climate

Artists, songwriters, and picture-postcard photographers have all contributed to the worldwide fame of the blue Italian sky and the mild climate. Actually it is a little dangerous to make generalizations about the Italian climate because of the length of the peninsula from north to south and the presence or absence of such important geographical features as mountains and lakes. In the north, for example, the Alps act as a shield that keeps the most intensely cold winds out of Italy. At the foot of the Alps, around Lake Como and Lake Garda, the climate is so mild that there are gardens with lemon and orange blossoms.

South of the lakes, in the Po River plain, the climate is more continental. Winters are cold, and summers are hot. In fact, the average winter temperature of Milan, on the northern edge of the Po plain, is colder than that of Paris. Except for the Apennines, central Italy has a typical Mediterranean climate with the heaviest rains falling in spring and autumn. Winters are mild, and summers are hot and dry. It is this part of Italy where the blue skies, indeed the quality of the light, make the land attractive to visitors. In the mountains winter snowstorms are often heavy, but summers tend to be dry, sunny, and pleasant.

As one goes farther down the peninsula to southern Italy and Sicily the climate becomes more and more African, with intense heat in summer and mild, often rainy winters. Occasionally the hot, dust-laden wind called the *sciròcco* blows up from the deserts of North Africa across Sicily and southern Italy.

THE PEOPLE

The Italians of today are descended primarily from the ancient Etruscans and Romans. Throughout the centuries various other peoples have been added to the Italian population, so that mixed with the familiar dark-haired, olive-skinned Mediterranean faces one sees blonde, blue-eyed Italians whose forebears probably came from the north during the barbarian invasions, or later during the various periods of occupation by foreign armies.

Modern Italy is a crowded country. The population is quite homogeneous. A substantial group of German-speaking people, however, live in the province of Bolzano in the north, and a smaller number of Slovenes make their home near Trieste at the northern tip of the Adriatic Sea. These groups and the French ethnic minority in the Val d'Aosta are protected by special statutes. There are also small old communities of people of Greek and Albanian origin. The overwhelming majority of Italians are, however, united by their language, religion, and education.

Language

The Italian language comes from the Latin of the ancient Romans. In fact, a knowledge of Latin helps one to learn Italian because the modern language bears a close resemblance to classical Latin.

Even in Roman times, however, two kinds of Latin were spoken—the language of the educated class and the language of the people who had no schooling. This division grew after the Roman Empire fell in the 5th century A.D., and the Italian peninsula was divided up into many separate states, each of which developed its own dialect. It was not until Dante Alighieri's epic masterpiece, *The Divine Comedy*, appeared in the early 14th century that the Italians began to have a national language. Dante, a native of Florence in the region of Tuscany, wrote his poem in the language spoken by the common people of his city so that more people would be able to understand it than if it were written in Latin. Because of *The Comedy*'s immense popularity its language became the language of all Italy.

Literature, schools, radio, and television have done much to standardize the Italian language, but a visitor who knows Italian from formal lessons may be a bit surprised by what he hears in Italy. A southern Italian may casually drop the final vowels from words or double the initial consonants, especially "b" and "p." A Tuscan farmer may cheerfully change "c" to "h" so that he goes to his hasa—home—perhaps to have an internationally known beverage he calls "hoha hola." There are also regional vocabularies, so that it is interesting to know, for example, that to get watermelon in Florence you ask for *cocomero,* but in Trieste you must request *anguria.* Yet, whatever the words or dialect, Italian is a very musical language because of its beautiful vowel sounds and clearly pronounced consonants. It is appropriate that Italian was the language of the first operas.

The Leaning Tower of Pisa is actually a bell tower in a complex that also includes a cathedral (foreground) and a baptistery (not shown). The tower deviates about 17 feet from the vertical.

Religion

The majority—99 percent—of the Italian people are Roman Catholics, but the Constitution guarantees religious freedom. There are also about 100,000 Protestants, 50,000 Jews, and a small number of Greek Orthodox in Italy.

Since Vatican City, the spiritual headquarters of the Roman Catholic Church, is a separate state within the city of Rome, the Italian government has worked out its relationship with the Church in a series of treaties. Once a vast influential state stretching across central Italy, the Vatican is now a minute, independent state with no temporal power in Italian affairs. The influence of the Church, although declining in recent years as Italy has rapidly become more secularized in its cultural attitudes, remains important. Religious instruction is an optional part of the program in elementary and intermediate schools.

The life of the Italian people is infused with its centuries-old association with Roman Catholicism. This is most obvious in the magnificently designed and decorated cathedrals and churches that are among the nation's most beautiful and inspiring monuments. From the elaborate spires of Milan's Duomo to the smallest country chapel, Italy's churches offer a constant invitation to worship.

The Church calendar is filled with holidays honoring the saints and the great festivals of the religious year. Although each village and city has its patron saint, none has gained such popularity as Naples' San Gennaro, whose day is celebrated also by Neapolitans who have emigrated to other countries. The Feast of the Assumption of the Virgin on August 15th is both a great religious holiday and a signal for the beginning of the two-week period called Ferragosto when many Italians go on summer holiday, and a large number of shops and businesses close.

Each year more Italians are celebrating Christmas in the northern European way, with ornamented trees and the exchange of gifts on December 25th. Many people, however, still keep the older tradition, saving the exchange of gifts for January 6, the Feast of the Epiphany, recalling the gifts of the Three Magi. The Easter holiday is celebrated with church services and at home by feasts of roast lamb or roast kid followed by chocolate eggs and special cakes.

Education

All Italian children must attend school until they are 14 years old. After the five elementary school years, students go on to a *scuola media* —intermediate or junior high school—for three years. This may be followed by five years of secondary school. At this level students have a choice between schools offering courses that emphasize the classics, science, teacher training, or art, and those that emphasize technical studies such as agriculture.

To be admitted to one of Italy's universities to study for the *laurea*, or doctor's degree, a student must pass a difficult examination given by a group of professors appointed by the Ministry of Education, since the government directs all education in Italy. The successful student may choose among some of the oldest and most distinguished universities in the world. They include Salerno, whose medical school dates back to the 9th century; Pavia, whose law school dates from the same century; Bologna, which is younger by about a century; and Florence, a mecca for students from all over the world because of its distinguished faculty.

Pizza, Pasta, and Other Pleasures

When one mentions Italian cooking to most foreigners they almost automatically think of pizza and spaghetti. This is a sad oversimplification, because Italian cooking is as diversified as it is delicious. The centuries during which Italy was a collection of separate kingdoms, duchies, and republics has given the modern Italians a cuisine with many subtle variations. Pizza, for example, is a regional dish that was once served because it was inexpensive, simple to make, nourishing, and tasty.

The ancient Romans both borrowed recipes they discovered all over their large empire and distributed their ideas about cooking wherever their armies went. The best of the Roman recipes survived and were modified during the centuries that followed. In addition, Italy's position at the crossroads of the Mediterranean made it a natural entry point for the foods of the Near East and Africa. Cane sugar, ice cream, sherbet, and such candy bases as almond paste and marzipan were introduced to Italy by the Arabs. The Crusaders returned from the Holy Land with a variety of additions, including the use of lemon juice as a flavoring. By the late Middle Ages the Italians were making leavened bread and some

The Italian culinary tradition is world-renowned. Every region of Italy has its own special dishes.

types of pasta (dough). In fact, dough for making pasta was probably developed in Italy before the 13th century. This is important only because of the widespread belief that the Venetian traveler Marco Polo brought spaghetti to Italy from China.

By the 16th century cooking had acquired the status of an art in Italy. Refinements such as the table fork were introduced. Meals composed of many courses were popular with those who could afford them. And, perhaps most significant of all, two daughters of Florence's leading family, the Medici, married kings of France. Both these noblewomen took their finest chefs to the French court, which thus was introduced to the highly developed Italian cooking.

The introduction of such foods as corn, tomatoes, red peppers, potatoes, and turkey from the New World rounded out the resources of the Italian cook. A typical Italian meal now represents the best of a long tradition of cooking with deep roots extending into the past.

One can begin a meal with one of the delicious antipasti (hors d'oeuvres) such as the rosy, thin slices of prosciutto (ham), mortadella (a kind of bologna), or salami that are particularly popular in the north, or *caponata*, the eggplant appetizer from Sicily. Soups range from thick vegetable soup called minestrone to the peppery *caciucco* of Livorno (Leghorn), which is like a fish stew. The plainest broth is usually made tastier by the addition of cheese and small pasta.

Pasta opens the next course of the meal and sums up the basic Italian food. In fact, there are estimated to be more than 100 different pasta shapes. They can be divided into four categories, depending on whether they are destined for soup, for boiling, for stuffing, or for baking. An ABC of pasta goes from *agnolotti*, *bucatini*, and *cannelloni* to *ziti*. Most pasta names are colorful descriptions of shapes: *agnolotti* ("little fat lambs"), *bucatini* ("little holes"), and *cannelloni* ("big pipes"). Others, like *vermicelli* ("little worms") and *farfalle* ("butterflies"), taste far better than they sound. There are many delicious ways pasta can be prepared, which range from the elaborate lasagne stuffed with meat and cheese and baked in a sauce to the simplest *fettucine al cacio e burro* with its butter, cream, and grated cheese sauce. Internationally, no pasta compares in renown with spaghetti, even though it requires intricate maneuvers to get the long threads from the plate to the mouth. In northern Italy corn flour and rice share the spotlight with pasta as starches.

Beef has always been in short supply in Italy, so the famous *bistecca alla Fiorentina* ("Florentine beefsteak") is the exception to the more general rule that Italians eat little beef. However, fish, pork, chicken, and veal are cooked in a wide variety of ways, including delicate lemon-flavored veal dishes and the more pungent *pollo alla cacciatora* ("chicken, hunter's style"). As accompaniments there is an abundance of vegetables and greens that Italy has made famous.

No meal is complete without bread, which varies in shape and flavor from region to region. There are the golden sticks of *grissini* from the Piedmont, the huge round loaves of Apulia, and the small delicate rolls of Ferrara, to name only a few. Cheese also varies from place to place, as do the wines. And each meal is crowned with fruits: apples from the Trentino-Alto Adige, peaches, pears, and cherries from Romagna, figs and golden plums from Calabria, oranges and tangerines from Sicily, apricots from near Naples. For special occasions there are rich desserts like *zuppa inglese* ("English trifle")—a layer cake drenched in rum with custard and whipped cream—or some excellent ice creams.

Fairs, Feasts, and Festivals

It should be perfectly clear by now that Italians like to eat well. But their joy is complete only if they are in good company. For this reason, Italian folklore—even in the poorer regions—often concerns food and feasts. The smallest town and the largest city, have a fair, or *sagra,* whose main feature is eating. For example, at the *Sagra della Braciòla* ("fair of mutton chops") in Castel San Pietro, a village near Bologna, everybody who comes is given a free, delicious mutton chop that has been roasted over an open fire. At the Ham Fair of San Daniele del Friuli in northeastern Italy, thick slices of the almost-sweet local ham are distributed to whoever happens to be there. At Torre Annunziata, near Naples, there is a Festival of Spaghetti where huge portions of steaming spaghetti in tomato sauce are given away.

Hospitality, as well as sheer joyful eating, is at the core of almost all popular festivals in Italy. There is, for example, a Hospitality Fair celebrated each year at Bertinoro near Forlì in Central Italy. It commemorates the medieval tradition according to which a knight who chanced to pass through the town could tie his mount to a ring on the Column of Hospitality (which still stands in the middle of the piazza). On each ring there was a different coat of arms, so that one could choose his host and be assured of free and lavish hospitality in the palace or castle of the owner of the ring. The tradition has been renewed so that summer visitors can place their cards on the rings and be invited to a home for a dish of pasta and a glass of the good local wine.

Italy's wealth of traditions includes games and pageants that have been handed down unchanged from father to son over the centuries. One of the oldest of these is Florence's *Calcio in Costume* ("costumed soccer"), which has been played in the city since it was a Roman colony and is said to be the ancestor of football. The game was originally Greek and was adopted by the Romans, who, in turn, introduced it in Florence. Today, this spectacular football game is played annually with much of its antique glory revived.

One might say that the Italians—a people whose theatrical tradition goes back at least to the times of the Romans—use games as an excuse to put on a show. *Partita a Scacchi*—"chess game"—is played on the pink and white marble squares of the piazza in Marostica in the Veneto, which is a model of a chessboard. The game is played to commemorate a famous *partita* in which the stake was the daughter of the governor, Parisio. Parisio had forbidden his daughter's two suitors to joust in a tournament for her hand, as was customary then. Instead, he suggested the contest be resolved on a chessboard.

Probably the best-known of all these traditional festivals is the *palio* —a rather wild horse race—run on July 2 and August 16 each year on Siena's oval-shaped Piazza del Campo in the historical center of the town. In this show, music and color play an important role. The *palio* opens with a parade of standard-bearers from each *contrada*—"quarter" —of Siena juggling their banners, whirling and throwing them in the air, and catching them before they touch the ground.

Yet the tourist who comes only to see the horse race may miss the most curious and genuine part of this tradition, which is the ancient ritual that takes place before the race. On the morning of the *palio,* the church

Horse races are the highlight of the Corsa del Palio, a medieval festival held twice each summer in Siena.

Italians are avid sports enthusiasts. Organized bicycle races are common throughout the country.

in each *contrada* is decked with flags, banners, and insignia won from rival *contrade* over the years. At 11 o'clock a special Mass is celebrated in the church, which is attended by all the citizens of the *contrada*, and most important, by the horse that represents the *contrada*. During the rite, the silence and concentration are great, but have nothing to do with devotion. Instead, everyone is anxiously watching the behavior of the horse to see whether or not the omens will be favorable and foretell the horse's victory. In fact, the race is as good as won if the horse's droppings fall in the church. No one would dream of calling this act a sacrilege, let alone of suspecting the priest, himself an ardent supporter of the colors of his *contrada*, of slowing down the service in order to help the horse give a favorable omen.

Sports, Music, and Movies

Clearly, even traditions have their backstage secrets, which perhaps helps one to understand the spirit of a people a little bit better. This is, of course, a difficult job, especially for foreigners, who tend to be impressed by the obvious aspects of Italian life and have little time to investigate what lies behind such a striking mixture of religion and semipagan superstition, ancient wisdom and youthful gaiety.

The Italians' gaiety shows itself in many ways. Their joy in living well is clear from the enthusiasm that marks ordinary events like meals and extraordinary ones like festivals. But it is even more obvious in their passion for sports. Soccer is the national sport, and rival teams have their vocal supporters packing the stadiums. The most popular players are virtually national heroes. Italian athletes also regularly win medals in the Olympics and other international competitions in such events as skiing, bobsledding, and tennis. Long-distance bicycle racing is another sport that has a devoted following in Italy. And in almost every town and resort you can see people of all ages playing bocce, a form of lawn bowling.

The words "Italy" and "music" are almost synonymous, and it is true that nearly all Italians enjoy music. Since Italy is the birthplace of opera, it is probably not too surprising that seemingly every Italian is able to sing at least one aria from the works of 19th- and 20th-century composers Gioacchino Rossini, Giuseppe Verdi, or Giacomo Puccini. Classical music now shares the spotlight with jazz and rock music. Popular singers have their legions of followers, and huge music competitions, such as the one at San Remo, are held annually. The foremost Italian opera singer, lyric tenor Luciano Pavarotti, has brought opera music to huge audiences in his open air concerts. Occasionally he has even shared the stage with pop-music stars.

Since the end of World War II, Rome has become a center of movie production. The first postwar films, with their realistic portrayals of people and their problems, were imitated all over the world. Nowadays Italian movie producers make films of every kind, including some of the best and most realistic Westerns. The works of such serious directors as Vittorio de Sica, Luchino Visconti, Federico Fellini, Michelangelo Antonioni, and Bernardo Bertolucci have won an international audience.

CITIES

Italians joke that they have three capital cities—Rome, the political capital; Milan, the financial capital; and Turin, the industrial capital. One could add Naples and Venice as the tourist capitals. And the list really

Milan, the commercial center of northern Italy, also played a leading role in ancient and medieval times.

Milan's top tourist attraction is the Galleria Vittorio Emanuele II, a covered arcade of shops and cafés.

should be extended to include Genoa, the seafaring capital; Florence, the nation's undisputed cultural capital; and Palermo, which really is a capital—of Sicily; as well as many other cities.

These eight cities are Italy's largest—an important distinction in a country that has been called "a nation of cities" because it has a total of more than 150 towns and cities with a population of over 30,000 each. No matter how great their local pride, the citizens of all the Italian cities now look to Rome as their capital and as the true center of national and political life. (There is an article about ROME in this volume.)

Milan

Milan, the second largest city in Italy and the capital of the province of Lombardy, is not too well loved by the majority of Italians. The Milanese are considered by other Italians to suffer from a self-destructive mania for overwork and success. And the Milanese are often compared to New Yorkers because they seem to run instead of walk. Milan is the one Italian city where one really feels the steady pulse of a productive economy at work. With its skyscrapers, subways, wide avenues, fine shops, and elegant restaurants, Milan is a city solidly planted in the 20th century. It is the most important commercial and banking center in Italy and leads the nation in the production of textiles, chemicals, and metal products, and in printing and publishing. But there is more to Milan than banks and industries. Like all Italian cities, Milan has its great cultural and historical landmarks.

The heart of Milan is the huge Piazza del Duomo ("cathedral"), which was laid out in 1861 at the feet of the magnificent Gothic cathedral. On one side of the piazza is the arcaded Galleria Vittorio Emanuele II with its fine shops, cafés, and restaurants. There the immaculately and dashingly uniformed *carabinieri* (a special army corps that has police duties) watch over an ever-changing parade of Milanese. If one crosses through the Galleria, one comes out on the Piazza della Scala and its most famous building—the Teatro alla Scala. La Scala, as it is called, is probably the most famous opera house in the world.

The city's other important landmarks include the Basilica of Sant' Ambrogio—the 11th-century church built in honor of Milan's first bishop, Saint Ambrose. The Church of Santa Maria delle Grazie is known to art lovers because it is here that Leonardo da Vinci painted his most famous fresco, *The Last Supper*. There are several fine art collections in Milan, including one of Italy's largest, in the Pinacoteca di Brera. The Ambrosian Library and three universities are among the city's best-known contributions to Italy's intellectual life.

Naples

According to an ancient legend, Naples was founded by the siren Parthenope. It was, in fact, founded by the Greeks in the 4th century

In Naples, the narrow streets of the Old Quarter are lined with small, family-owned businesses.

The Bay of Naples is dominated by Mount Vesuvius (right), an active volcano that last erupted in 1944.

B.C. Neapolis, the Greek name for it, means "new city." Naples has always been a vital center of art, learning, and commerce. It ranks as Italy's third largest city. Its magnificent setting on the northern part of the Bay of Naples has inspired great poets like Vergil and street-corner philosophers who have said again and again, *Vedi Napoli e poi muori*—"See Naples and die." The implication is that there is nothing more wonderful to be seen on this earth after one has seen Naples.

Many people have agreed with this idea. The French writer Stendhal said more than a century ago that Naples was "a capital as great as Paris. . . . There is more life here; more noise; the talk is often so shrill, it deafens me. Naples is the real capital of Italy." And to this day, Naples, with its magnificent architectural monuments, crowded markets, and sadly overcrowded slums, is a city of immense vitality. There is a constant noise of traffic, of songs, of voices in energetic conversation.

Today, as Italy's third largest city and second largest seaport, Naples is a market center for the surrounding countryside, as well as the home of such industries as metal production and food canneries and crafts such as glove and jewelry making. The National Museum has a remarkable collection of artistic and historic treasures. The Archeological Museum houses the relics of Pompeii and Herculaneum—the cities destroyed by the eruption of Vesuvius in A.D. 79. The more recent past is recalled in the Church of San Domenico Maggiore, next door to which Saint Thomas Aquinas, the medieval Catholic scholar, once taught. The San Carlo Opera House has been host to some of the greatest musical talents of all time since it was first opened in the 18th century. The city's institute of marine zoology and its aquarium are considered among the best in the world.

Turin

It takes less than two hours to go from Milan, Italy's second largest city, to Turin, the fourth largest, but arriving in Turin, one feels that one is in a new land. This is more surprising because of the fact that Turin is truly Italy's industrial capital and has over 20,000 factories. The largest is Fiat Sp.A., the biggest privately owned industrial organization in Italy. Fiat, founded in 1899, is an international holding company and one of the world's major automobile manufacturers.

Neither the auto industry nor the manufacture of clothing, leather goods, chocolate candy, and vermouth has yet succeeded in overshadowing Turin's old-fashioned stylish charm. Even its shops and restaurants have an air of elegance. In Turin it is easy to feel that France and Switzerland are very near—in fact, they are just across the Alps. Turin's mood is thus a little different from that of any other Italian city. It seems somehow more subdued, more sophisticated and elegant.

All this is in keeping with Turin's important place in Italian history, for it was here—at the Palazzo Carignano—that the idea of a united kingdom was born and proclaimed. The city's most important landmarks are associated with unification. The Palazzo Reale was the residence of the kings of Sardinia, of the House of Savoy, and later, of the kings of Italy. The Basilica of Superga was the royal burial chapel. All these historical landmarks have not overshadowed the present, however, and the Torinese is probably equally proud to tell you that the city has one of the largest sports stadiums in Europe.

The 506-foot-tall Antonelliana Tower soars above the skyline of Turin, a northern industrial city.

Genoa, Italy's leading port, also serves as an important Mediterranean outlet for much of northern Europe.

Palermo

Palermo, the fifth-largest Italian city, is the capital of Sicily and the seat of the regional government. This lovely city with its gentle climate and marvelous location on the Conca d'Oro—a fertile plain at the edge of the sea—has had a tormented history. The city's founders, the Phoenicians, were followed by a long procession of invaders. After the Phoenicians came Carthaginians, Romans, Vandals, Visigoths, Ostrogoths, Byzantines, Arabs, Angevin French, Swabian Germans, Norman French, and Spaniards. The Byzantine, Arab, and Norman styles of art and architecture are still evident in buildings, among which the most famous are the Palatine Chapel of the Royal Palace, with its exquisite Byzantine Mosaics, and the Chiaramonte and Sclafani palaces.

The once drowsy provincial capital, dozing amid the ruins of the past, has become a bustling center of trade and industry. In addition to its important seaport, Palermo has a number of industries that range from the production of steel and macaroni to that of furniture, textile, glass, cement, chemical, and perfume. It is the city's beauty and wealth of historic sites, however, that attract an increasingly large number of tourists each year. Officials are still struggling to eradicate the city's poverty-ridden slums. In 1992, the Italian government took dramatic steps to eliminate the organized crime operations.

Genoa

Genoa is Italy's leading seaport and sixth-largest city. Its one rival for the claim of being the chief Mediterranean port is Marseilles, France. Millions of tons of cargo annually pass through the port's modern harbor facilities, which can handle 100 ships at a time. In addition, Genoa is

Italy's leading shipbuilding center and has iron and steel works. It also produces one-quarter of the nation's soap.

Genoa, like Naples, has a magnificent setting on a large harbor, and, also like Naples, its history goes back to ancient times. Genoa reached the height of its power as a maritime republic during the Middle Ages. During the Crusades, Genovese merchants had warehouses in such remote outposts as the Crimea, Constantinople, Syria, and North Africa. Genoa was defeated by its rival, the republic of Venice, in the 14th century, but beautiful palaces, churches, and stately gardens still recall Genoa's past glory. Mementos of Genoa's most famous son, Christopher Columbus, include the house in which the great explorer is supposed to have been born.

Venice

Venice, considered one of the world's most beautiful cities, was founded by refugees fleeing from barbarian invaders in the 5th century A.D. The refugees chose well. Their hiding place grew into a city built on over 100 islands in the Lagoon of Venice at the northern end of the Adriatic Sea. Venetians called their city the Bride of the Adriatic and proudly spoke of being wedded to the sea, for it was the sea that brought them wealth. With its strategic location at the crossroads of east-west trade, Venice grew into a great maritime power. Its fleets reached the distant ports of the Near and Far East and returned laden with silk and

In Venice, gondolas ply the canal beneath the Bridge of Sighs, across which prisoners were led to interrogation.

brocades, gold and spices. The wealthy traders built superb palaces along the famous canals that run through Venice in place of streets. During the 15th and 16th centuries, such renowned artists as the Bellini family, Giorgione, Paolo Veronese, Titian, and Tintoretto lived and worked in this unique and fascinating city.

The discovery of a sea route around Africa in the 15th century marked the beginning of Venice's decline: the city no longer had a monopoly on the spice trade. Yet the city's splendor has endured. Its inhabitants practically live on the water, and are connected to the mainland only by a railroad bridge and an automobile causeway.

Today, the sea, once the source of Venetian wealth and greatness, threatens the city's existence. The magnificent buildings facing the water are all endangered by the current of the canals, which is increased by the motorboat traffic, and by the seawater that slowly erodes the foundations of buildings. The city sank by 10 in. (24 cm.) over the course of the 20th century—a much faster rate than when only gondolas and rowboats cruised the canals. The vibrations caused by the *vaporetti* (water buses) and other motorboats strike at the city's foundations. Industries in the area around Venice are slowly draining the underground water, thus helping the formation of depressions. Gas fumes, added to dampness, and the salt air itself are slowly eating into the marble and stone of the buildings and the bronze of the monuments. To combat this steady deterioration, in late 2001, so-called Project Moses was initiated. This plan was designed to protect the city with mobile floodgates at the entrances to the Venice lagoon, and after careful consideration, it finally got the "green light" from the Italian government.

Florence. Florence, the birthplace of the Renaissance in Italy, also unwillingly had its destiny changed by water—not by sea, however, but by the Arno River, which cuts the city into two unequal portions.

Piazza San Marco, the largest square in Venice, is noted for its Byzantine basilica and lofty clock tower.

Birthplace of the Renaissance, Florence has countless art treasures, including its bell tower and cathedral.

On the night of November 4, 1966, while everybody was asleep, the river broke its banks, completely flooding the part of the city that is richest in history and art, and covering everything with a thick layer of water, mud, and oil. In several places downtown, the level of the water was over 30 feet (9 meters). Monuments, works of art, unique and irreplaceable masterpieces, churches, elegant shops, museums, and libraries full of invaluable manuscripts and texts were flooded and defiled.

After a few days, when the waters finally receded, it was possible to evaluate the damage suffered by the city. Called the Athens or the Citadel of Italian culture, Florence has throughout history been the home of many of the greatest artists, poets, scientists, and architects of all times. The list extends from Dante Alighieri to Michelangelo to Galileo, and many of their works were damaged—some almost beyond repair.

In the days of the flood, Florence received touching proof that its place in the history of art and ideas was recognized all over the world. Students and workers, specialists and laymen, poor people and rich people worked shoulder to shoulder. They succeeded in rescuing from the dirty mud many precious documents, many great works of art. The National Library of Florence is indebted to them for saving many of its 4,000,000 volumes.

Today, Florence has regained its former appearance. Many of the most visible ravages of the flood have been repaired. There remains only a dark line on the walls of many buildings. And in many downtown streets there is a small plaque with a blue wavy line and the simple inscription, ''Here the Arno, November 4, 1966,'' to mark the level reached by the waters on that terrible night.

Florence seems to be growing outward in rings of highways and upward in blocks of apartment houses. The heart of the old city, however, has remained unchanged for centuries. Narrow streets are now thronged with cars, creating a new problem for all who want to save the city's treasures from gas and noise pollution. Yet the city remains unrivaled in art and architecture. Within the span of a very few blocks there are some of the world's greatest masterpieces. The skyline is dominated by the tower of the Palazzo della Signoria (city hall), Brunelleschi's graceful dome for the Cathedral of Santa Maria del Fiore, and Giotto's campanile. Ghiberti's doors for the nearby baptistery are works of art. The Church of Santa Croce is known for its works by Giotto, Andrea del Castagna, Luca della Robbia, and Donatello, as well as works by many other painters and sculptors. The Church of San Lorenzo, the burial place of the Medicis, who ruled the city-state of Florence from the 14th to the 16th century, is famous for its sculptures by Michelangelo. Florentines and the city's many visitors are constantly discovering new treasures in their city and its distinguished museums—the Bargello, the Pitti, the Uffizi, and many others.

Italy's vineyards and groves produce a billion gallons of wine yearly and a quarter of the world's olives.

The sizable Italian automotive industry, concentrated in Turin, produces many world-famous sports cars.

ECONOMY
Agriculture and Industry

Until quite recently, Italy was a predominantly agricultural country. Thanks to *Il Boom*—the post–World War II growth of industry—only about 5 percent of the working population is now employed in agriculture. The south is the only part of Italy that is still mainly devoted to farming. But farming on the worn-out, rocky soil is difficult and not very productive. Legislation in the post–World War II years has largely eliminated the old system of vast, landed estates (*latifundia*) owned by absentee landlords. The government, through its *Cassa per il Mezzogiorno* ("Southern Italy Development Fund"), a long-range plan for the development of the Italian South, has encouraged industries to move there by offering them lower taxes and loans. The South is steadily modernizing its economy, although many of its people still move out to seek employment in the industrial northern cities or in other countries within the European Union (EU), to which Italy belongs.

The most prosperous farms are in the Po Valley and in the valleys of central Italy. In central Italy the old system of sharecropping (*mezzadria*) has almost completely given way to privately owned or leased farms. Grains, sugar beets, vegetables, fruits, olives, and wine grapes are among the most important products. Although Italy exports fruits and vegetables, it must import the hard wheat used for making spaghetti, macaroni, and other pasta products.

Stylish Italian clothing is made from the high-quality wool and cotton woven at mills in the Po Valley.

Italy's largest, oldest, and most important industry is the manufacture of textiles. Silk is cultivated in the regions of Lombardy, Piedmont, and Friuli-Venezia Giulia. Wool and cotton mills are found in the Po Valley. An offshoot of Italy's textile production is its emergence as a leading clothing exporter. Italian-made suits, dresses, bags, hats, and shoes are sold all over the world.

In addition to textiles, Italy manufactures a wide variety of products including chemicals, petrochemicals, foods and beverages, furniture, and transportation equipment. Lambretta motorcycles, Vespa motor scooters, and FIAT and Alfa-Romeo automobiles have worldwide markets. Ships from the yards at Genoa and Monfalcone, railroad equipment from Milan, and arms from Brescia are other important Italian products. Steel, TV sets, washing machines, refrigerators, computer equipment, typewriters, and tires also are produced in great volume and exported.

Since 1933 about one-sixth of the Italian economy has been financed by a system of state holding companies (the IRI: Institute for Industrial Reconstruction). Many economists complain, however, that this "parastate" sector of the economy is the least efficient part.

Italy was among the first six countries that formed the European Economic Community (EEC); the treaty marking the first step toward European integration was signed in Rome in 1957. Its membership in this organization has helped Italy to maintain a favorable balance between its imports and exports. In January 1999, Italy and 10 other countries belonging to the EU, successor to EEC, adopted a common currency known as the "euro." The Italian economy is greatly helped by the annual peaceful "invasion" of more than 50 million tourists.

The labor force in post-World War II Italy has been highly organized along ideological lines. Thus, the Communists have a powerful CGIL (Italian General Confederation of Labor); the Socialists have UIL (Italian Union of Labor); and the Christian Democrats have the CISL (Italian Confederation of Organized Workers). The big industrialists have their own *Confindustria* (Confederation of Industrialists). In the 1980s, organized labor lost much of its strength as the nation shifted from an industrial to a more service-centered kind of economy.

Transportation and Communication

Italy's railroads; its postal, telegraph, and telephone systems; and some of its radio and television stations are state-owned. The railroad system, which began with a 5-mi. (8-km.) track linking Naples and Portici, is now a modern network covering nearly 12,500 mi. (20,100 km.) and is mostly electrified.

Within Italy, a network of *autostrade*—"superhighways"—has been built since World War II. Considered one of the world's best highway systems, this network has helped to break down the ancient regional differences and has literally paved the way for economic growth all over the country. Planned to cover 4,350 mi. (7,000 km.), the Italian highway network eventually will be linked to Sicily by a bridge across the Strait of Messina. Italy's national airline is Alitalia, and the country has one of the largest merchant fleets in Europe.

GOVERNMENT

From the time of its unification until 1946, Italy was officially a monarchy. However, from 1922 until 1943, Benito Mussolini's Fascist dictatorship held all real power, and the king ruled in name only. In June 1946, the Italian people voted to make their government a republic.

According to the constitution that went into effect in January 1948, Italy is "a democratic republic founded on work." Italy's Parliament is made up of two houses, the Chamber of Deputies (630 members) and the Senate (326 members, 315 of them elected). All members of Parliament are elected for five-year terms by universal suffrage on the basis of proportional representation (that is, each party gets seats in proportion to its popular vote). Additional special members of the Senate include former presidents and others who may be appointed by the president for special merit in such fields as science, the arts, and economics.

The president of the Italian Republic is chosen for a seven-year term by a two-thirds majority of Parliament. The president appoints the prime minister, who in turn selects the heads of the various ministries. This government must then win approval from both houses of Parliament. The constitutional court has the power to pass on the constitutionality of all proposed legislation.

A large number of political parties are represented in the parliament, including about 10 national parties and several lesser groups. They range from the neofascist Italian Social Movement (MSI) and the ultraconservative Monarchist Party on the far right, to the small, hard-line Proletarian Democratic Party, which stands to the left of the Italian Communist Party.

Until 1994, a neofascist candidate had never held a ministerial position in a postwar government. In 1994, however, five members of the neofascist National Alliance Party became ministers. That same year, media magnate Silvio Berlusconi founded a center-right movement named Forza Italia (Let's Go, Italy!), which soon gained popularity and, in 1995, transformed itself into a political party.

Italy's Communist Party, traditionally one of the largest in Europe, has lost considerable strength. In 1991, it renamed itself the Democratic Party of the Left; a small minority resisted the change and turned into the more hard-line Communist Refoundation.

Italy's governments since World War II have had to be formed from a coalition of parties. Until 1992, these coalitions were usually led by the Christian Democratic Party. Since then, the Italian political scene has been in turmoil, beginning with a massive anticorruption campaign known as "clean hands," which shook up the traditional political establishment and led to a landslide victory of Forza Italia in 2001. Its leader, Silvio Berlusconi is the country's richest man. His victory has provoked unease both in Italy and abroad. Although Berlusconi himself has been investigated for a number of offenses—including tax evasion and bribery—his main electoral promise was to rid the Italian political system of long-standing corrupt practices.

The constitution provides for the use of the initiative and referendum. Since the 1970s, these lawmaking tools have been used often. For example, they have upheld such controversial measures as the legalization of divorce and abortions under certain circumstances, and they have made it difficult for the government to commission the building of more nuclear-power plants.

The Constitution of 1947 authorized the creation and election of 20 regional governments, thus reversing the highly centralized system of administration that had been borrowed from France in 1861. Initially, however, such governments were actually set up for only five "special status" regions (Sicily, Sardinia, Trentino-Alto Adige, Val d'Aosta, and Friuli-Venezia Giulia). Not until 1970 did legislation implement the remaining 15 regional governments.

There are also 94 provincial governments, each with its own parliament and executive. The most important units of local government are the communes, run by mayors and councils. They depend heavily on appropriations from the central government.

HISTORY

Little is known about the early history and settlement of Italy. It is known definitively, however, that invasions were part of Italy's story from the beginning. Greek colonies probably were established in Sicily and southern Italy in the 8th century B.C.

It is also known that a remarkable people called the Etruscans were living in central Italy by about 800 B.C. These mysterious people, whose language has been only partly deciphered, had a highly developed culture. They may have introduced the wine grape, olive, and chariot to Italy. Their skill at working metals such as iron, bronze, and gold provided the basis of their trade. The Greek name for the Etruscans, *Tyrrhenoi*, lingers in the name of the Tyrrhenian Sea off Italy's west coast and in the name of their chief region, Tuscany.

Ruins at Selinunte from the 7th century B.C. bear testimony to the Greek influence on pre-Roman Italy.

The Gauls from the north and the Romans from the south conquered the Etruscans, whose last important stronghold fell in 396 B.C. It was the threat of further Gaulish invasions from the north that brought the peninsula under Roman rule. From this base Roman power grew until it included most of Europe and parts of the Near East. The approximately 1,000 years of Roman rule made Italy the center of the known world, and long after the Roman Empire fell to the barbarian invaders in A.D. 476, the Roman ideal of a Europe united by one law and one language—Latin —lived on, mainly through the Roman Catholic Church.

The Dark Ages

During the 5th and 6th centuries the Roman Catholic popes tried to provide political and spiritual leadership for the people of the peninsula. It was mainly through their efforts that the Lombards, a Germanic tribe who had taken over most of northern and central Italy, were kept out of Rome. The Lombards' final defeat came with the help of the Franks, led by Pepin and then by his son Charlemagne. As a reward for his services, and to extend the authority of the Church, Pope Leo III crowned Charlemagne as the first emperor of the Romans on Christmas Day, 800.

After Charlemagne's death, the kingdom he had built was divided and subdivided. The only continuous power remained in the hands of the popes. Italy itself was chopped into a thousand fragmented units that were poorly governed, and invaders struck from all sides.

Although the peninsula seemed ungovernable, various nobles took the title of King of Italy. The last to do so for many centuries was Berengar II, the Marquis of Ivrea in the Piedmont. When Berengar failed to unite the people behind him, he ceded "the kingdom" to Otto I of Germany. In 962, Otto, like Charlemagne before him, was crowned emperor. His vast domain, the Holy Roman Empire, was to survive in one form or

Pompeii, buried by a volcano in 79 A.D. but now excavated, provides a portrait of life in Roman times.

another, with one or another German or Habsburg king on the throne, until the early 19th century.

In actuality, the empire was impossible to rule efficiently in those days of poor roads and primitive communications. Few of the emperors had the time to rule their German domains and the land across the Alps as well. The result was that Italy was part of the empire in name only and developed quite independently.

Just how ineffective the empire was in unifying the Italians soon became clear. The fortified northern cities, the popes' domain, and the separate kingdom of the Two Sicilies in the south each represented what amounted to a distinct country. The cities were moving toward independence. The papacy struggled to retain its power. And the south, in the hands of French and Spanish overlords, slowly sank beneath the weight of a strict feudal rule that made the majority into poor peasants and only a few into rich landholders.

The Growth of the City-States

Throughout the 12th and 13th centuries, the north grew increasingly prosperous as a result of the increased trade that had begun with the Crusades. Cities like Venice, Florence, Genoa, Pisa, and Milan grew into powerful independent city-states. Trade with the cities of northern Europe and the Orient in turn stimulated the growth of such industries as textile manufacturing, metal processing, and shipbuilding and eventually the growth of banking. The new rich loaned money at enormous rates of interest and became not only richer, but more powerful, as the Medici banking family of Florence proved by becoming the rulers of the city between the 14th and 18th centuries.

By the 14th century, the wealthy people of the city-states had more money and more leisure. A rebirth of interest in classical Greek and Roman literature, art, and ideas stimulated a period of unparalleled artistic and scientific growth in Italy. This period, which in Italian was called the *rinascimento*—"rebirth" or "renaissance"—made Italy a center of European culture between the 14th and the 16th centuries. In literature the Renaissance began with Dante's *The Divine Comedy* in the early 14th century. The poet Francesco Petrarch, the storyteller Giovanni Boccaccio, and the political commentator Niccolò Machiavelli are probably the best-known of his successors. In art the period opened with the paintings of Giotto and the sculpture of Nicola Pisano and reached its greatest heights in the works of Sandro Botticelli, Paolo Uccello, Fra Angelico, Masaccio, Leonardo da Vinci, and Michelangelo.

Foreign Rulers

The magnificence of the Renaissance cities and the arts they fostered were not matched by political developments. Unity was as remote as ever. The powerful cities engaged in petty wars for supremacy. Within the cities, two political parties vied for power. They were the Guelfs—the supporters of the Pope—and the Ghibellines—the supporters of the emperor's party. This constant fighting finally weakened the cities and made them easy prey for foreign conquest.

Throughout the first half of the 16th century, Italy was a pawn in the political chess game played to determine whether Spain, France, or Austria would rule the peninsula. By the end of the Italian wars in 1559, Spain had won. But when Spanish power declined during the 18th century, Austria took over the rule of most of Italy.

Stone and brick buildings are typical of many Italian hill towns including Assisi, the home of St. Francis.

Italy was in the forefront in the development of operatic music and the ornate baroque architecture of the 16th and 17th centuries. Galileo, the great astronomer and physicist, gained international acclaim in the face of the papal Inquisition, which denounced him for arguing that the sun is the central body around which the earth and other planets revolve.

In the 18th century, intellectuals from several parts of Italy were conspicuous in the Enlightenment, a movement that sought to bring about rational legal and economic reforms by enlightened despots. Cesare Beccaria of Milan, an advocate of more humane punishment for criminals, was perhaps the most influential Italian writer of this period.

The French Revolution of 1789 had a profound effect on the Italians. The establishment of the French republic made them aware of the need for national unity among the Italian people. When Napoleon Bonaparte led his armies into Italy in 1796, he was welcomed as a liberator. Although French rule was often strict and ruthless, reforms were made that had an important effect on Italian history. Republics were founded with constitutions and representative assemblies. For the first time since the fall of Rome, Italians saw that they could live together as one nation.

Napoleon's defeat at Waterloo in 1815 seemed at first to turn back the clock. At the Congress of Vienna in the same year the European powers met to determine the details of the peace settlement. Austria's Prince Metternich scornfully dismissed Italy as "a geographical expression." In the south the Bourbon kings of French origin, who had been settled in Naples since 1735, became the rulers of Naples and Sicily. The Papal States were restored to the popes. Lombardy, Veneto, and some smaller states were returned to Austria. The House of Savoy was given the rule of Piedmont, Sardinia, and Savoy as the kingdom of Sardinia.

But the movement for national unity did not die. The *Risorgimento* ("resurgence"), as the movement for unification was called, was divided into three groups. The radicals, under Giuseppe Mazzini, hoped to establish an Italian republic. Conservative Catholics wanted to unify the country under the popes. The moderates rallied behind the House of Savoy. Although the Austrians tried to suppress these movements, it was too late. Even opera-goers expressed their sentiments by shouting "Viva Verdi," which not only stood for the patriotic composer, but also meant "Long live Vittorio Emanuele, Re d'Italia."

Vittorio Emanuele (Victor Emmanuel) II, King of Sardinia, did become the king of Italy, largely as a result of the efforts of his prime minister Conte Camillo Cavour. Cavour sought to have the constitution made more liberal, raised taxes, and strengthened the army. He won a place for his kingdom as a European power by sending troops to fight on the side of Britain and France in the Crimean War of 1854. In 1858, Cavour made an agreement with Napoleon III of France by which France would supply troops to help the Italians drive the Austrians out of Italy. In return, Sardinia would cede Nice and Savoy to France.

When Austria declared war in 1859, the Italian and French forces won victories at Magenta and Solferino. Austria's power in Italy was broken. By 1860 all of northern Italy, except Veneto, became part of the kingdom of Sardinia. In the same year, Giuseppe Garibaldi landed on Sicily and defeated the army of the kingdom of Naples, crossed to the mainland, and took Naples. With the exception of Rome and Veneto, all of Italy was united. In 1861, Vittorio Emanuele was declared King of Italy.

Bologna combines the typically Roman checkerboard pattern of streets with distinctly medieval architecture.

The Kingdom of Italy: 1861–1922

The last steps of unification were completed when Veneto was annexed in 1866 and the Papal States in 1870. In July, 1871, Rome became the kingdom's official capital. The Pope withdrew to the Vatican, the small part of Rome that includes the St. Peter's Church. It was not until 1929 that the Vatican City was recognized as independent.

The formation of the kingdom did not solve Italy's age-old problems: the lack of basic industrial resources such as iron and coal, a population too large for the country to support, and the sheer weight of years of foreign occupation, leaving little experience of self-government. However, the new government worked quickly to make Italy a 19th-century power. Railroads were built, a merchant fleet was soon sailing, and the economy was sound. Thousands of emigrants left to settle in other lands, thus reducing the problem of overpopulation. But the Italian government wanted more: It wanted the nation to be like the other great powers, which meant having colonies in Africa. Hoping at the same time to solve its remaining overpopulation problems, Italy chose to expand into Eritrea and Somaliland, a move that drained it of money and manpower. The Italian forces suffered a serious defeat at Aduwa in 1896. In Italy itself the closing years of the century were marred by workers' unrest.

The new century began ominously with the assassination of King Umberto (Humbert). He was succeeded by his son Vittorio Emanuele III, and a degree of stability was gained under the political leadership of Giovanni Giolitti, who helped develop democratic parties and processes in Italy. In 1911, however, Italy went to war with Turkey to gain Tripoli in North Africa. This is sometimes considered the first step toward the Balkan Wars that led to the still more terrible World War of 1914–18.

Italy entered World War I on the side of the French and British in 1915, when it was promised certain Austrian territories in the north and northeast. After suffering a heavy setback in 1917, the Italians won a decisive victory at Vittorio Veneto in 1918, which led to the surrender of Austria-Hungary.

The Fascist Regime: 1922 to 1943

The Paris Peace Conference of 1919 granted to Italy the Trentino and the adjacent South Tryol (Alto Adige), Trieste and its province as far as the Julian Alps, Istria, and some of the islands off the Yugoslav coast. But some Italians wanted more. Thus, the poet and war veteran Gabriele D'Annunzio led a group of volunteers in 1919–20 to seize the city of Fiume on the Adriatic. It was not until 1924 that Yugoslavia relinquished it to Italy.

In the parliamentary elections of 1919 the Socialist Party became the largest political force, while the Catholics (newly organized in the Popular Party) emerged as the second largest group. The Liberals, who had dominated politics, were now in sharp decline.

There was also economic turmoil. Militant labor unions called numerous strikes in the industrial cities. In the rural areas of the Po Valley there was also much unrest among the newly-organized farm workers, who had expected land ownership. Both the landlords and factory owners objected to any concessions to the strikers. Thus, revolution seemed almost inevitable.

At this point it was relatively easy to accept the promises of Benito Mussolini, an ex-Socialist who had organized in 1919 a Fascist party of war veterans and had promised to destroy "bolshevism" and restore "law and order." When his black-shirt militias started to march on Rome in October, 1922, the timid king appointed him premier.

Under Mussolini, all other parties and the independent labor unions were dissolved. Many of their leaders were arrested or forced into exile. Parliament was restructured into a Fascist corporate system that regulated both industry and labor. The press was censored, and schools were made instruments of Fascist teaching. In spite of this repression, the theatrical Fascist leader (*Il Duce*) and his dictatorship were supported enthusiastically for many years by most Italians.

Mussolini negotiated agreements with the Pope in 1929 that recognized the independence of Vatican City and made Roman Catholicism the "official" religion of the Italian State. In 1933, during the global economic depression, Mussolini established the Institute for Industrial Reconstruction (IRI), which provided state financial aid for banks and industries in danger of bankruptcy. This led to a system of state capitalism in Italy that embraced about one-sixth of the economy and provided well-paying jobs for members of the ruling party. Mussolini's other accomplishments included the draining of malarial marshes and the construction of highways, port facilities, stadiums, and government buildings.

But Fascism led to war. In international affairs Mussolini conquered Ethiopia (1935–36), withdrew from the League of Nations, allied with

Rome's Vittorio Emanuele II Monument, dedicated in 1911, centers around the Tomb of the Unknown Soldier.

Hitler's Germany, intervened on the side of General Franco in the Spanish Civil War (1936–39), and seized Albania (1939). In June, 1940, Mussolini belatedly joined Hitler's Germany in World War II. In October, 1940, Italy invaded Greece and in 1941 declared war on the Soviet Union and the United States.

By mid-1943, Fascist Italy had lost its African territories, its economy was in a shambles, and its armies were almost destroyed. In July, Allied troops landed in Sicily and soon conquered the island. This led to Mussolini's arrest by King Vittorio Emanuele and Army Marshal Pietro Badoglio on July 25, 1943. The Fascist era was over. In September the new government signed an armistice with the Allies.

For the next 20 months, Italy was split in two and torn by civil war. The Allies liberated southern Italy and persuaded the royal government to declare war on Germany. In the northern half of the peninsula, Hitler seized control, rescuing Mussolini and setting him up as the head of a new Italian Social Republic. This puppet regime was strongly resisted by anti-Fascist "Committees of National Liberation" and by an underground network of Italian partisans who, with arms parachuted in by the Allies, helped to pin down the enemy. In late April, 1945, as Allied forces finally liberated the north, Italian partisans caught and executed Mussolini.

The Postwar Democracy

War-torn Italy made a dramatic economic recovery with help from the United States. By the end of the 1940's the country had straightened out its finances, rebuilt its transportation system and industries, launched land reforms, and was ready to begin the modernizing "economic miracle" of the 1950s.

Although Italy had helped the Allied cause from 1943 to 1945, it was treated as a defeated country when the peace conference met in Paris in 1947. It lost all its overseas colonies, and it had to turn over to what was then Yugoslavia the city of Fiume and some of the Slavic-populated provinces of northeastern Italy. The disputed city of Trieste at the head of the Adriatic Sea finally reverted to Italy after years of difficult negotiations.

The major political question was what to do with the monarchy. The country voted in favor of adopting a republican form of government. The voters also elected a constituent assembly to draft a new constitution, which went into effect on January 1, 1948.

Italy's postwar governments were dominated by the Christian Democrats until 1992, when an anticorruption campaign led to the collapse of the established political system. Since then, the governments have included ex-Communists, members of the Green Party, and even neofascists. In May 2001, a new period may have begun with the resounding electoral victory of Silvio Berlusconi's Forza Italia.

Italy's parties have been deeply committed to the cause of European economic, military, and political integration. Thus, Italy was a charter member of the Organization of European Economic Cooperation that administered Marshall Plan aid (1947–51), an original signatory of the North Atlantic Treaty Organization (NATO) (1949), of the European Coal and Steel Community (1951), and of the European Economic Community (Common Market) in 1957. The latter has gradually enlarged, renamed the European Union (EU), and by 2002, had 15 members. Italy has reaped benefits from these organizations, as its investments, workers, and products now move freely within this immense trading bloc.

Massive population shifts were among the most important aspects of postwar Italian history. The desire of southern Italians to improve their standard of living led in the 1950s to the outmigration of more than 1 million young men and their families. Similar numbers moved out in the 1960s, the 1970s, and the 1980s. Most of the migrants settled on the edges of large industrial cities in northern Italy, but others moved on across the Alps to seek jobs in northwestern Europe. Meanwhile, Italy itself became a place of immigration for thousands of Muslims from North Africa and the Middle East.

The Modern Era

The years 1968–69 marked the onset of a chaotic, violent period in Italian history. The postwar "baby-boom" generation was reaching maturity, only to find that the overcrowded universities were unable to accommodate them adequately. The unrest quickly spread into the labor unions, which in 1969 extracted from employers huge wage increases that were to be linked to the rising cost of living. The Italian government sought to reduce some of the unrest by restructuring and expanding the universities, lowering the voting age to 18, introducing tax reforms, and setting up the 20 regional governments provided for in the Constitution.

The worst crisis occurred in 1978, when the leftist Red Brigade terrorists kidnapped and murdered Aldo Moro, a Christian Democratic leader who had served several times as prime minister. The center-left

Modern hotels and service areas are found along the *autostrade,* Italy's superb highway system.

government redoubled its efforts to suppress terrorist activities. By the late 1980s, many Red Brigade members had been apprehended.

Meanwhile, in 1978, the government responded to the growing women's movement and legalized divorce and abortion under certain circumstances. The Vatican agreed in 1984 to revise the Lateran Concordat of 1929 with the Italian state. As a result, the state would no longer enforce ecclesiastical laws on social issues.

Italy's political climate has recently undergone extreme change. In the early 1990s, the public lost confidence in the center-left parties after accusations of corruption. In March 1994, a rightist coalition called the Freedom Alliance captured the majority in legislative elections, and tycoon Silvio Berlusconi was sworn in as prime minister. In December 1994, he was forced to resign due to a number of damaging scandals. The following month, an interim government was formed. In May 1996, former Communist Romano Prodi gained the premiership and formed the center-left "Olive Tree" coalition government. Berlusconi retained his prominent position within the Freedom Alliance and, in the May 2001 elections, dramatically returned to power. His controversial allies are two extremist parties, one with fascist leanings and the other the nationalistic and anti-immigration League of the North.

In 1999, Italy played a key international role when NATO strikes against Kosovo and Yugoslavia were launched from 11 Italian bases. In "Operation Rainbow" in Albania, Italy helped cope with the massive flow of refugees from Kosovo.

The country continues to rank high in the worlds of fashion, entertainment, automobile manufacturing, high technology, and finance. Italy is also known worldwide for its hospitality to tourists, and the country remains a popular destination for foreign visitors.

CHARLES F. DELZELL, Vanderbilt University

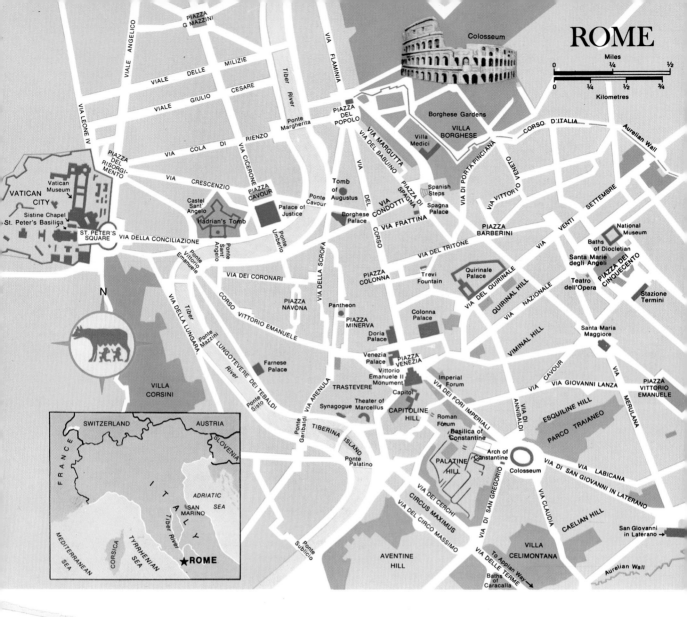

Rome

Rome, Italy's capital and largest city, is a magical mixture of ancient and modern, pagan and Christian, which annually attracts millions of visitors from every country of the world. Inevitably the founding of so great a city has been surrounded by myths and legends. According to the best-known of these, Rome was selected by the gods as the site of a new capital after the fall of Troy. Aeneas, a Trojan prince, was told by the gods to take his followers to the west. After suffering terrible hardships, the Trojans settled near the present city of Rome.

The legend goes on to tell of events in the 8th century B.C. when a priestess, who had been sworn to chastity, gave birth to twin sons whose father was the god of war, Mars. As punishment for her sin, the priestess was ordered to abandon her children on the banks of the Tiber River. A she-wolf found Romulus and Remus, the twins, and nursed them until they were taken in by a shepherd who raised them. The boys vowed that when they grew up they would build a city on the Tiber.

It was Romulus, so the legend goes, who drew the first boundaries of the city with his plow. The twins and their nurse, the she-wolf, have become the symbols of the ancient city's beginnings. A statue of the babies being suckled by the wolf—a copy of the original—stands atop the Capitoline Hill, one of the seven hills on which the city was first built.

From the original seven hills (the Aventine, Quirinal, Capitoline, Palatine, Caelian, Viminal, and Esquiline on the left bank of the Tiber) Rome grew to cover other hills on the right bank. Almost as if it had been inspired by Romulus' words—"My Rome shall be the capital of the world"—the city grew in size and splendor. From a collection of rough shacks at a bend in the river, Rome became the capital first of a republic and then of a great empire. Its motto was *Senatus Populusque Romanus*—"The Senate and People of Rome." The initials SPQR are still used in Rome today and can be seen on everything from taxicabs to manhole covers.

It was during imperial times—the early centuries of the Christian Era—that Rome reached its greatest importance and magnificence. The Romans proudly called their city Urbs—The City—implying that it was the ideal city. When the empire embraced nearly all the known world at the peak of its power, Rome was known simply as *caput mundi*—"the head of the world."

The Emperor Augustus, who ruled from 27 B.C. to A.D. 14, boasted that he had found a city of bricks and left a city of marble. The imperial city was, in fact, a mixture of handsome public buildings, elegant private homes, and slums. As the center of the vast empire the city was the home not only of the ruling classes but of merchants prospering from building and trade, emissaries from all over the empire, nobles, soldiers, slaves, and country people who hoped to find wealth in the capital. The tourist of ancient times would have been shown many of the landmarks the modern visitor seeks.

Atop the Palatine Hill were the palaces of the emperors Augustus and Tiberius. (It is from "Palatine" that the word "palace" comes.) At the base of the hill was the Forum Romanum, the first of the city's public squares. Built on the site where Romulus was said to be buried, the Forum became a city within a city, with public buildings, temples, and shops. In the Forum is the Golden Milestone from which the remarkable network of Roman roads fanned out. And it was in the Forum that the Senate met and that Julius Caesar was assassinated on the Ides of March, 44 B.C.

Later, emperors extended the Forum Romanum into the larger and more stately Imperial Forums. This was the center of the city that ruled the world. Nearby was the enormous Colosseum and across the river the tomb of the 2nd-century A.D. emperor Hadrian, which is now called Castel Sant' Angelo. Marvels of the city were the aqueducts that brought the Romans water and the great sewer called the Cloaca Maxima, part of which is still in use. The approximately 1,000,000 people who lived in the imperial capital were protected by police and fire fighters. The homes of the wealthy were heated and had a system of running water. Truly, for the wealthy, as the Roman writer Cicero observed, "There [was] no place more delightful than home."

St. Peter's Basilica, the largest church in the world, stands near the Tiber River. Although Rome enjoys a generally mild Mediterranean climate, the city is nonetheless subject to an occasional snowfall.

By day a popular diversion was going to the public baths. The largest, the Baths of Caracalla, named for the 3rd-century emperor, is now being used as an open-air opera house. Besides offering Romans cold, warm, and steam baths in the *frigidarium, tepidarium,* and *caldarium,* the building contained stores, libraries, gymnasiums, and offices —everything a Roman gentleman might need.

The wealth that poured into Rome from all over the empire was far from universally distributed. By the 2nd century A.D. one half to one third of the population was on the equivalent of what is now often called welfare. They were given bread to eat and circuses to attend to distract them from thoughts of revolution. As many as 385,000 Romans of all classes would pack into the Circus Maximus to watch chariot races, acrobats, clowns, and bands of musicians. An even more popular spectacle was the combat between gladiators and such wild animals as lions, tigers, and panthers at the vast Colosseum.

THE CENTER OF CHRISTENDOM

The wealth and power that had made Rome the capital of an empire and a rich and cosmopolitan city disappeared under the repeated attacks of barbarian invaders from the north. The imperial court was moved to Constantinople in the 4th century A.D. Christianity, which became the official religion of the empire in A.D. 380, provided the city with its new leaders. From the 6th until the late 19th century, Rome was ruled first by the bishops of Rome and then by the popes. Rome became the focus of the Christian world—a mecca for devout pilgrims who risked every kind of danger to reach the city that was for them a holy goal. No longer citadels of imperial power, the ancient monuments decayed. The great buildings of the emperors were stripped of their marble facings to make lime. Water was taken from the Tiber while the aqueducts fell into ruins. The Forum Romanum became a haven for squatters and pastureland for cattle.

The rebirth of interest in ancient times during the Renaissance in the 15th and 16th centuries led Italians to turn to their ancient capital for inspiration. Under the leadership of enlightened popes, the treasures of the ancient city were systematically uncovered, classified, and restored. The study of the arts and archeology was encouraged. Artists were employed by the popes to design and decorate churches.

The historic and strategic importance of Rome, rather than artistic considerations, made the city and the Papal States, of which it was a part, an early target for Napoleon Bonaparte's troops. The city was involved in a seesaw battle between the Pope and Napoleon for supremacy between 1798 and 1814. In the years between 1815 and 1861, during the political maneuvering and wars that led to the unification of Italy, Rome remained under papal rule except for a brief period in 1848–9. Nearly a decade passed after the Italian kingdom had been formed before the King's troops took possession of the city. Finally, in 1871, Rome was declared the capital of Italy. The Pope considered himself a prisoner of the Italian King in the city that used to be his own. This was the beginning of the so-called Roman Question that was not resolved until the Lateran Treaty was signed in 1929. The treaty created the independent state of Vatican City under the sovereignty of the pope. (See the article in this volume on VATICAN CITY.)

The Pincian Hill affords a dramatic view of the Piazza del Popolo (foreground) and the Roman skyline.

ROME AT WORK

Rome, unlike such other capitals as Paris or London, is neither an industrial nor a commercial center. It is, in fact, the heart of the vast and complicated bureaucratic activities of the Italian Government. Rome was chosen as the capital of the newly united nation a century ago because it was the city that best symbolized Italian unity, not because of its industrial leadership. Even so, many Italians, especially in the highly industrialized north, continue to criticize Rome for being essentially a nonproductive city. "Milan produces and Rome eats," they say, but they overlook the historical and political reasons for the city's condition. As a matter of fact, after Rome was annexed to the kingdom of Italy, the first governments made and maintained a policy of keeping industry out of the city because they thought it was unbecoming to the capital.

Many Romans work for the national government or are involved in the large tourist industry. A substantial number of residents of Rome are members of the Roman Catholic religious orders that have their headquarters in the city. Other important activities are printing and publishing, banking and insurance, clothing and fashion, and moviemaking.

Throughout its history Rome has been the chief tourist goal in Europe. From ancient times to the present the city has been a magnet for artists, writers, pilgrims, and people who wanted simply to see what could provoke even such a restrained and dignified man as Henry James to say on his arrival in Rome: "At last—for the first time—I live!" Satisfied by the city's abundant beauty and vitality, or exasperated by its noise and traffic, visitors continue to swarm over the city, providing employment for thousands of Romans, from hotel-keepers to guides.

The Italian movie industry centers around Cinecittá, southeast of Rome. Moviemaking was begun in 1937, but the coming of World War II and then bomb damage delayed the center's development. It was not until the 1950's that the movie industry began to grow, making the names of such directors as Federico Fellini, Michelangelo Antonioni, and Vittorio De Sica synonyms for fine movies. The addition of a special Italian product, the so-called "spaghetti Westerns"—accurate replicas of the American Westerns down to the last branding iron—helped expand and enrich the Italian movie industry to the point where it is a very important industry in Rome.

The growth of Rome, as well as internal Italian migration, stimulated the building industry, which now employs the largest number of workers. Vast new apartment complexes, office buildings, and shopping centers have been built since the end of World War II. Even so, building has not kept pace with the city's growth. A city of a little more than 690,000 inhabitants in 1921, Rome is now home to more than four times that many Italians and is continuing to grow at a rapid rate each year. Many of the newcomers are from impoverished regions in the south of Italy and are unable to find employment. As a consequence, several thousand people still live in *baracche*—shabby shacks—on the outskirts of the city. Some of the migrants find work in the city's smaller industries—food processing, glass manufacturing, pharmaceutical production, and similar activities—but many remain unemployed or find only part-time work with which to support their families.

As the nation's capital, Rome is naturally the center of the Italian communications industry. Another of Rome's well-known industries, high-fashion clothing, is also one of its youngest, since it only developed in the years after World War II. Rome now vies with Paris and New York as a producer of pace-setting styles. Related industries such as the design and manufacture of accessories and cosmetics have also developed.

Luxury apartment buildings line the streets of Parioli, a fashionable suburb of Rome.

THE ROMAN'S ROME

Administratively, Rome is divided into districts called *rioni* in the city and boroughs, *borgate,* in the suburban areas. The inhabitants of the picturesque Trastevere district, on the right bank of the Tiber, claim to be the *romani di Roma,* the only "true Romans" in the city. As a matter of fact, today the population of Rome is made up predominantly of *burz-zurri* (as government officials and other newcomers are called). The "true Romans" have found some consolation in forming a club, the Association of the Romans. Yet Rome has been an effective melting pot where newcomers are able to blend into a Roman way of life.

The Romans are essentially optimistic, gay, and easygoing. They are among the least nosy and most tolerant people in the world. A major contradiction in their easygoing nature becomes apparent when they drive cars. A Roman behind the wheel or riding a motorscooter seems to have no concern whatsoever with traffic rules or the right-of-way of other drivers. The Roman seems to base his driving exclusively on speed and noise, aiming at bypassing whatever vehicle precedes him and counting essentially on his "good eye" and reflexes, which in most cases, luckily, are excellent. For the visitor, driving in Rome is usually a nightmare, unless he decides to put into practice the old saying, 'When in Rome do as the Romans do.''

The Romans speak *romanesco,* a dialect very close to the Italian language, although rich in words of its own and marked by its own peculiar accent. Even well-educated Romans tend to drawl and to speak with a basso voice that seems to come from somewhere in the belly.

Good company, conversation, open air, food, and wine are the basic ingredients of the joy of life to the Romans. Roman cuisine is delicious, but not particularly refined or elaborate. In fact, it comprises a variety of savory dishes that originated in the countryside around Rome. One eats well everywhere in Rome, in the deluxe restaurants as well as in the most humble trattorias. There seems to be a sudden mushrooming of restaurants in summer, when their tables invade the sidewalks. Musicians walk from restaurant to restaurant, playing and singing popular Roman songs. At night it is not uncommon to see entire families sitting outside an inexpensive trattoria to which they bring their food in paper bags, limiting their orders to wine and occasionally a huge portion of pasta to be shared by everyone.

The Romans like outings very much. In the city one of their favorite goals is the Borghese Gardens with its well-known museum and world-famous zoo. Among their favorite places are the beaches or the pine forests near the sea outside the city limits. Other attractive places near Rome are the towns of the Castelli Romani (Roman castles) on the Alban Hills, which contain the Pope's summer residence at Castel Gandolfo, an astronomical observatory, and a nuclear research center. The hills also are known for the delightful local wine produced there.

The entire city is served by buses and streetcars. There is also the Metropolitana, the subway system that runs from Termini railroad station in the center of Rome through E.U.R. (Esposizione Universale di Roma), a suburb to the south of the city, to the port of Ostia. The subway's growth has been delayed because subway excavations reveal ancient treasures that must be saved or because vibrations from drilling threaten the existence of monuments above ground.

Since the time of the Roman republic, roads have radiated from Rome, each named after the consul that built it. Connecting Rome with many other commercially and militarily important cities of the peninsula, most of them ended on the west or east coast. The consular roads, which were masterpieces of engineering, are still used today. For centuries they formed the major national road network. It is only in recent years that they have been surpassed by modern highways. Rome is linked to all the major roads converging on it from all parts of the country by a loop encircling the city. Rome is also the heart of the national railroad network and is thus connected with the major Italian and European cities. Leonardo da Vinci International Airport at Fiumicino, near the sea, links Rome to all the countries in the world.

THE VISITOR'S ROME

Rome is an enormously colorful and alluring mixture of the old—the Rome of ancient times, the Middle Ages, the Renaissance—and the new.

For example, arriving in Rome by train, one enters the city through the modern Stazione Termini. A few yards from the entrance are the remains of the Servian Walls, named for the legendary 6th-century B.C. king, Servius Tullius. Across the large Piazza dei Cinquecento facing the station are the Baths of Diocletian, part of which is now an archeological museum, and part the 16th-century church of Santa Maria degli Angeli.

Indeed, almost everywhere in Rome there is this rich mixture. In addition, cultural life is intense. Rome is the site of the largest university in Italy, a Catholic university, and some other religious universities, as well as many Italian and foreign cultural and scientific institutions, among which is the American Academy. There are several very important museums, art galleries, and libraries. The old artists' district near Piazza di Spagna, where many famous Italian and European writers,

Many famous artists and writers have lived in the buildings alongside the magnificent Spanish Steps.

The ancient Colosseum was the scene of the famous gladiator fights in the early days of the Roman Empire.

such as the 19th-century English poet John Keats, lived, still houses many studios where painters and sculptors are working.

Theatrical and musical activities are also popular, with a concert season at the Teatro Argentina (Argentina Theater) and an opera season at the Teatro dell'Opera. In summer open-air concerts are held at the imposing 4th-century Basilica of Maxentius and Constantine and operas at the spectacular remains of the 3rd-century Baths of Caracalla, which has one of the world's largest open-air opera stages.

Although Rome today is a vast city, its traditional center is an area of about 1 square mile that extends from Piazza Venezia and touches the Tiber, Piazza del Popolo, and Piazza Barberini. Here are the fashionable boutiques and jewelry and shoe shops of Via Condotti and Via Frattina; the antique dealers of Via dei Coronari; the art galleries and studios of Via del Babuino and Via Margutta. One can find respite a few hundred yards away from the main avenues and streets in some quiet, almost deserted street or a small square where the silence of centuries seems to hover. This can happen in the very heart of the city, or in more remote spots such as the old Appian Way, which is studded with ancient Roman relics.

Even the busiest streets seem to take a rest in the early part of the afternoon. Offices and shops close between 1 and 4 P.M., while the Romans enjoy a meal and perhaps take a little siesta at home unless they join the crowds in the busy restaurants and outdoor cafés. In summer, these are the hottest hours of the day. Rome appears almost

Legend holds that tourists who cast coins into the Trevi Fountain will return to Rome one day.

deserted, except for a few isolated people roaming the streets or the flock of tourists that bravely carry on with their guided or self-guided tours. Most visitors quickly learn the secret of mastering these hot hours. They walk on the shady side of the street, watching out for the first quiver of the tree leaves, a sure indication that the *ponentino,* a cool breeze, is blowing from the sea.

Rome at night is fascinating. Most of the city is silent, although the silence may be broken suddenly by a car horn, the buzzing of motor-scooters, or the howling of members of Rome's enormous colony of cats.

At night such familiar places as the Trevi Fountain and the Piazza Navona, the long oval baroque square with its three central fountains, seem to grow larger and more beautiful. The Via dei Fori Imperiali, flanked by the Forums and facing straight towards the massive Colosseum, seems to regain its stately grandeur under the floodlights. There are, of course, places like the Via Veneto with its outdoor cafés, where life still goes on as if it were daytime, and there is an endless procession of sports cars and people walking to and fro who want to see and to be seen.

Day and night, visitors are drawn to the Trevi Fountain, where according to tradition, they must throw a small coin to insure that they will return to Rome. The basin of the beautiful, baroque fountain is always full of the coins of travelers who are sad to leave and hopeful that they will be able to return soon to the bewitching city on the Tiber.

NELLO SPADA, Author, *Garibaldi and the Red Shirts*

SAN MARINO

San Marino holds the distinction of being the oldest republic in Europe, and it is certainly one of the smallest, as it occupies only 24 sq. mi. (61 sq. km.). In fact, San Marino is the third-smallest independent state in Europe, after Monaco and Vatican City.

LAND

San Marino's territory, roughly rectangular, drapes over the craggy peak and slopes of Mount Titano, an eroded mass of limestone with an elevation of 2,421 ft. (738 m.). It is surrounded on all sides by the countryside of north-central Italy. Two streams, the Ausa (Aussa) and Marano, flow through San Marino's territory, draining into the Adriatic Sea to the northeast. Its climate is temperate, with temperatures ranging from 19° F. (–7° C.) in the winter to 80° F. (27° C.) in the summer.

HISTORY AND PEOPLE

San Marino traces its origins to A.D. 301, when a Christian stone-cutter named Marinus is said to have settled on Mount Titano with his followers to escape religious persecution. Present-day San Marino holds Marinus as its patron saint, and honors him each September 3.

The republic expanded slowly down the mountain slopes, and now includes part of the valley floor. The Sanmarinese came to see the smallness of their home as a virtue. Indeed, in 1797, they declined an offer of

The tiny nation of San Marino sits atop Mount Titano in Italy.

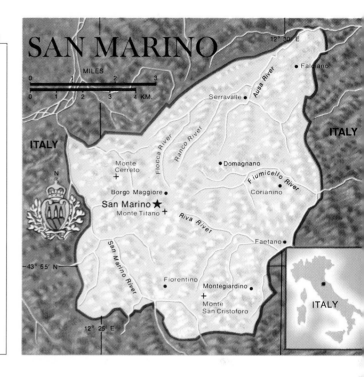

FACTS AND FIGURES

OFFICIAL NAME: Republic of San Marino.

NATIONALITY: Sanmarinese.

CAPITAL: San Marino.

LOCATION: Northern central Italy.

AREA: 23 sq. mi. (60 sq. km.).

PHYSICAL FEATURES: Highest point—Mt. Titano (2,457 ft.; 749 m.).

POPULATION: 30,000 (2002; annual growth 0.3%).

MAJOR LANGUAGE: Italian.

MAJOR RELIGION: Roman Catholicism.

GOVERNMENT: Republic. **Head of state**—two captains regent selected every 6 months from Great and General Council. **Head of government**—secretary of state. **Legislature**—unicameral Great and General Council.

ECONOMY: Chief agricultural products—grains, grapes, maize, olives, cheese, livestock. **Industries and products**—tourism, textiles, electronics, ceramics, cement, wine. **Chief exports**—wine, ceramics, building stone, lime, wood, wheat. **Chief imports**—consumer manufactures, food.

MONETARY UNIT: 1 euro = 100 cents.

NATIONAL HOLIDAY: September 3 (Anniversary of the Foundation of the Republic).

additional territory from Napoleon I explaining that the country's diminutive size and relative poverty made it an improbable target for conquest by its larger and more powerful neighbors.

Just as Mount Titano provided an island of safety for Marinus and his followers, the citizens of the republic have repeatedly given sanctuary to exiles and refugees. During the battles leading up to the unification of Italy in 1861, Giuseppe Garibaldi and some of his followers hid briefly in San Marino. During World War II, San Marino remained neutral.

GOVERNMENT

In 1862, San Marino and Italy signed a treaty of friendship. The two nations have a customs union. San Marino uses the Italian language and currency. However, San Marino has an entirely independent government. The heads of the government are two captains-regent who preside over the 60-member Great and General Council for a term of six months. The same representatives may not be reelected to the office until three years have passed. The captains must accept the office to which they are elected or their citizenship and possessions will be taken from them.

The tiny republic, with its love of medieval laws and ceremonies, surprised the world in 1945 when it voted in a Communist government. The only Communist government in Western Europe stayed in power for 12 years, though without collective farms or state controls. Since 1957, San Marino's government has moved along democratic paths. In 1992, San Marino gained membership in the United Nations.

ECONOMY

Today, as for many years past, San Marino's economy is based on its income from tourism, agriculture, and a variety of products. Tourists pour into San Marino from the nearby parts of Italy by auto, bus, and heli-

The Government Palace, one of many attractive buildings in San Marino.

copter to spend a day or more looking at the mountaintop capital city, with its narrow old streets, turreted medieval buildings, the 14th-century Church of St. Francis, the Government Palace, and the museum in the Valloni Palace. Another attraction for visitors is the opportunity to write and mail postcards bearing the beautiful and highly prized stamps that annually add a considerable amount of money to the republic's income.

Agriculture and cattle raising are the main sources of income. The slopes of San Marino are covered with vineyards and meadows where cattle graze. The factories of San Marino produce a variety of products for export, such as woolen and silk textiles, tiles, varnishes, ceramics, and building stone. Only a handful of San Marinese still practice Saint Marinus' craft of stonecutting, but all of them honor his dream of freedom and independence.

Reviewed by CHARLES RÉ, Consul of San Marino (New York)

St. Peter's Basilica, the largest church in the world, is the focal point of Vatican City, the world's smallest independent nation. Above, thousands gather in St. Peter's Square to greet the pope, the leader of the Roman Catholic Church and the Vatican's head of state.

VATICAN CITY

Vatican City is not a city at all, but a sovereign state. The smallest independent nation in the world, Vatican City covers only 108.7 acres (44 ha.) and is entirely surrounded by Rome, the capital of Italy. Vatican City is ruled absolutely by the pope, who is also the bishop of Rome and the spiritual head of the world's more than 1 billion Roman Catholics. The present pope, John Paul II (Karol Wojtyła, born in Poland), was elected in 1978.

As the heart of the Roman Catholic Church and as one of the great cultural treasure-houses of the West, Vatican City is nearly always filled with lay and religious visitors from every corner of the globe. It is not only the center of one of the world's great religions, but an inexhaustible source of beauty and inspiration.

THE LAND

Vatican City takes its name from an isolated ridge to the west of Rome's fabled seven hills. The city's southeast boundary is formed by St. Peter's Basilica and the great keyhole-shaped St. Peter's Square. The rest of the Vatican's borders is marked by walls that were built between the 9th and the 17th centuries. Within these walls lie not only the spiritual and administrative center of the Roman Catholic Church, but also a library and museums containing extraordinary treasures. In addition, the walls enclose large gardens, a variety of civic buildings, the offices of the Roman Catholic Church, and homes and apartments.

The Vatican also controls "territory" outside the walls, including several basilicas or churches, residences, administration buildings, seminaries, and universities in Rome and the pope's summer villa at Castel Gandolfo, in the Alban Hills outside Rome. These properties enjoy the status of extraterritoriality—that is, independence from the governments of Rome and of Italy.

HISTORY

The tiny nation of Vatican City and its estimated 890 inhabitants are all that is left of the centuries-old Papal States, which once had more than 3 million people and covered some 17,000 sq. mi. (44,000 sq. km.), stretching from the Adriatic to the Tyrrhenian Sea. In 1870, the armies of the king-

dom of Italy entered Rome. The pope, Pius IX, felt that the new Italian government held his territory illegally. In protest, he became a voluntary prisoner in the Vatican. His four successors continued this policy until 1929, when the Lateran Treaty, between the Vatican and the Italian government, recognized Vatican City as a sovereign and independent state.

Since 1929, Vatican City, like other nations, has had a diplomatic corps. Its envoys, appointed by the pope, are known as nuncios or internuncios. In 2002, the Vatican maintained diplomatic relations with more than 150 countries, and was a member or observer in two dozen international organizations.

PEOPLE AND ECONOMY

Most of the people who reside in Vatican City itself are priests and mem-

An elaborately decorated bronze canopy stands high above the main altar inside the basilica. The altar is situated over the tomb of Saint Peter, the first Pope. Skylights and stained glass (background) help illuminate the vast interior.

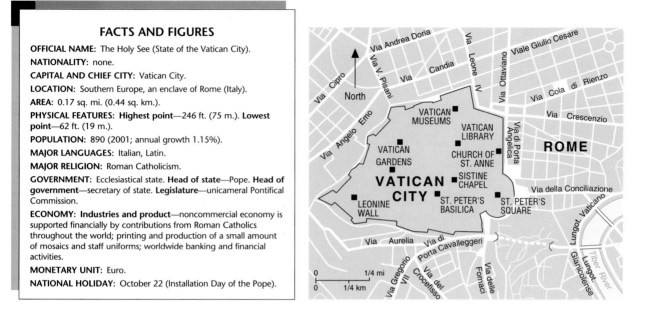

FACTS AND FIGURES

OFFICIAL NAME: The Holy See (State of the Vatican City).

NATIONALITY: none.

CAPITAL AND CHIEF CITY: Vatican City.

LOCATION: Southern Europe, an enclave of Rome (Italy).

AREA: 0.17 sq. mi. (0.44 sq. km.).

PHYSICAL FEATURES: Highest point—246 ft. (75 m.). **Lowest point**—62 ft. (19 m.).

POPULATION: 890 (2001; annual growth 1.15%).

MAJOR LANGUAGES: Italian, Latin.

MAJOR RELIGION: Roman Catholicism.

GOVERNMENT: Ecclesiastical state. **Head of state**—Pope. **Head of government**—secretary of state. **Legislature**—unicameral Pontifical Commission.

ECONOMY: Industries and product—noncommercial economy is supported financially by contributions from Roman Catholics throughout the world; printing and production of a small amount of mosaics and staff uniforms; worldwide banking and financial activities.

MONETARY UNIT: Euro.

NATIONAL HOLIDAY: October 22 (Installation Day of the Pope).

bers of religious orders. Several hundred laypeople—church and civic officials, secretaries and clerks, tradespeople, domestic staff members, and their families—also make their home in Vatican City.

The governor of Vatican City, who is appointed by the pope, heads the executive and legal offices as well as the postal, telegraph, telephone, tech-

The museums, libraries, seminaries, and palaces within the Vatican's boundaries are connected via the manicured walkways that crisscross the magnificent Vatican Gardens. Most of Vatican City is enclosed by walls.

Pope John Paul II (above, center) exchanges gifts with Queen Elizabeth II, the British monarch. As an independent nation, Vatican City maintains a diplomatic corps.

nical, and economic services. He is assisted by the counselor-general to the state; judicial tribunals (the legal system is based on canon, or church, law and the laws of the city of Rome); and the Victualing Board. This board, as its name suggests, buys all the food necessary to feed the inhabitants (Vatican City is too small to produce agricultural goods), and provides the state's hygiene services.

Like other, much larger states, the Vatican issues its own stamps (with the same values as Italian postage). Its post office is considered among the most efficient in Europe. The Vatican also has its own automobile-registration plates, as well as a bank, electric-power station, and a railway station served by the Italian railroad system.

Vatican City even has its own army: the Swiss Guards, organized in the 16th century. They number about 100, perform various protective duties, and serve as the personal guard of the pope. Then, as now, the guards are Roman Catholic men from Switzerland. Their colorful uniforms of blue, gold, and red are said to have been designed by Michelangelo, the great Italian Renaissance artist.

The Vatican's radio station, which has the call letters HVJ, is one of the most powerful in Europe. It was designed by the inventor of the radio, Guglielmo Marconi, and was supervised by him until his death in 1937. Today, the station, with its staff of about 200, broadcasts to nearly every country in the world in more than 30 languages. Vatican City's daily newspaper, *L'Osservatore Romano,* deals with religious and political news and is widely read because it is considered to reflect the official views of the pope on church issues and on world affairs.

PLACES OF INTEREST

St. Peter's Basilica, the world's largest church, is believed to be built over the tomb of Saint Peter, chief of the 12 Apostles, who were the first followers of Jesus Christ. Tradition has always held that Saint Peter, whom Roman Catholics consid-

The Swiss Guards—the Vatican's "army"— dress in colorful uniforms said to have been designed by Michelangelo.

er the first pope, was martyred on Vatican Hill and buried there in A.D. 67. This tradition was given substance in recent years by the discovery of what some experts believe to be Saint Peter's tomb and bones. In the 4th century A.D., Constantine, the first Christian Roman emperor, built a basilica on the spot where the tomb was believed to be. The present basilica was begun in 1506 and was completed in the early 17th century, according to the designs of a number of master architects, notably Michelangelo, who drew up the plans for the magnificent dome, and Giovanni Lorenzo Bernini. St. Peter's is the burial place of numerous saints, popes, kings, queens, and princes. It also contains priceless works of art, of which the most famous is

Although in the hills outside Rome, Castel Gandolfo (above), the summer papal residence, is considered the territory of Vatican City, and therefore not under Italian jurisdiction.

Michelangelo's *Pietà*. Surprisingly, the parish church of Vatican City is not St. Peter's, but a much smaller church dedicated to Saint Anne.

The huge square, or piazza, in front of the basilica is really an ellipse formed by two great colonnades designed by Bernini. The square, which can accommodate 200,000 people, is always crowded to capacity on Christmas, Easter, and other major holy days in the Christian calendar.

Alongside St. Peter's are the Papal Palace, where the pope lives and receives distinguished visitors from around the world; the Sistine Chapel; the Vatican Museums; and the Vatican Library. The chapel, which takes its name from Pope Sixtus IV (1414–84), for whom it was built, is one of the outstanding artistic attractions in Vatican City. In addition to frescoes by some of the greatest artists of the 15th century, the Sistine Chapel is the setting of Michelangelo's superb ceiling and wall paintings. The ceiling portrays Michelangelo's vision of the Creation, the story of Adam and Eve, and the biblical Flood. Twenty-two years after he completed these paintings, Michelangelo returned to the chapel to depict the *Last Judgment* on the wall behind the altar. It is considered one of his most powerful works. The Sistine Chapel paintings were restored to their original splendor during the 1990s.

The Vatican Museums contain one of the world's greatest collections of ancient sculpture and vast collections of paintings by the old masters. The Vatican Library, which was founded in the 15th century, is the oldest public library in Europe and one of the outstanding libraries of the world. It contains an estimated 1 million printed books, 7,000 incunabula (the earliest printed books), and 90,000 manuscripts.

FATHER JOSEPH I. DIRVIN, C.M., Assistant to the President, St. John's University

Valletta, Malta's capital, has two natural harbors. Its fortifications were built by the Knights of St. John.

MALTA

Malta is a land of history, political intrigue, and legends. The island once served as the base of the crusading Knights of Malta, who wielded the power of the sword to defend this island of Christianity against the Muslim Ottoman Empire in the 16th to 18th centuries.

LAND
The Maltese archipelago lies 57 mi. (92 km.) south of Sicily in the Mediterranean Sea. Its large main island, Malta, is about 17 mi. (27 km.) long and 9 mi. (14 km.) wide; the other islands are Kemmuna (Comino), Gozo, and the uninhabited islets of Kemmunett (Cominotto) and Filfla. The main island is composed of limestone.

THE PEOPLE AND THEIR HISTORY
Malta may have been part of the land bridge that once linked North Africa to Italy. It is filled with the archeological, architectural, and artistic treasures of the people who once lived there. Stone Age temples have been unearthed, and remains of Neolithic and Bronze Age men

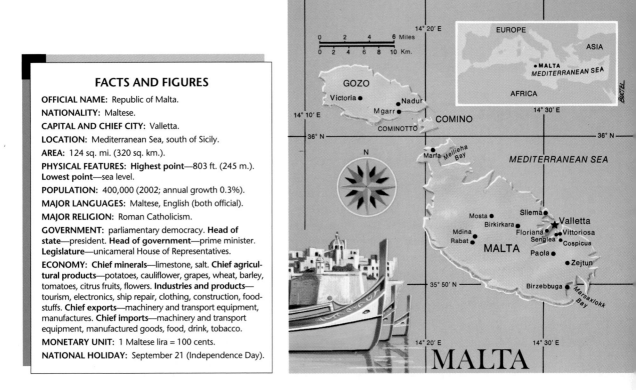

FACTS AND FIGURES

OFFICIAL NAME: Republic of Malta.

NATIONALITY: Maltese.

CAPITAL AND CHIEF CITY: Valletta.

LOCATION: Mediterranean Sea, south of Sicily.

AREA: 124 sq. mi. (320 sq. km.).

PHYSICAL FEATURES: Highest point—803 ft. (245 m.). **Lowest point**—sea level.

POPULATION: 400,000 (2002; annual growth 0.3%).

MAJOR LANGUAGES: Maltese, English (both official).

MAJOR RELIGION: Roman Catholicism.

GOVERNMENT: parliamentary democracy. **Head of state**—president. **Head of government**—prime minister. **Legislature**—unicameral House of Representatives.

ECONOMY: Chief minerals—limestone, salt. **Chief agricultural products**—potatoes, cauliflower, grapes, wheat, barley, tomatoes, citrus fruits, flowers. **Industries and products**—tourism, electronics, ship repair, clothing, construction, foodstuffs. **Chief exports**—machinery and transport equipment, manufactures. **Chief imports**—machinery and transport equipment, manufactured goods, food, drink, tobacco.

MONETARY UNIT: 1 Maltese lira = 100 cents.

NATIONAL HOLIDAY: September 21 (Independence Day).

have also been found. The island was held in succession by Phoenicians, Carthaginians, and Romans. The Maltese still take pride in an event that occurred during Roman domination of the island. In A.D. 60, Saint Paul, on his way to the imperial capital of Rome, was shipwrecked on Malta, at a bay that now bears his name. This is the traditional date of the conversion of the island to Christianity. Today most Maltese are members of the Roman Catholic Church.

In the 9th century the Arabs began their 220-year domination of Malta. Maltese, the language of Malta, is akin to Arabic, with traces of Italian and other languages. In 1090 a Norman count subdued the Arabs in Sicily and took the island of Malta. For 440 years Malta was an appendage of Sicily. Eventually it came under the control of the Holy Roman Emperor Charles V.

In 1530 Charles V gave Malta to the religious and military order of the Knights of St. John of Jerusalem (known also as the Knights of Malta). The Knights, originally a hospital order established to defend and care for wounded Crusaders, came to Malta after they had lost their bases in Jerusalem and Rhodes. For 268 years they policed the Mediterranean, making Malta a military base in their fight to halt the expansion of the Ottoman (Turkish) Empire. In the year 1565, the Turks laid siege to Malta with an army of about 30,000 men in nearly 200 ships. The islanders were outnumbered five to one, but they managed gallantly to hold the island as an outpost of Christian Europe. Shortly thereafter, Jean Parisot de La Valette, Grand Master of the Knights and the leader of the defense, built a great harbor-fortress on the rocky promontory and named it Valette, or, as it is now known, Valletta. It is the capital of Malta and a living memorial to the great wealth and artistic taste of the Knights.

Napoleon I seized Malta in 1798, and in 1800 the British came into control. Until 1959, Malta was a key link in the defense of the British Empire. The island prospered, with most of its inhabitants directly or indirectly involved with the British Royal Navy. During World War II, Malta endured more than 2,000 bombing raids. In memory of the terrible suffering and heroic action of the people, the entire population of Malta was awarded the George Cross in 1942 by King George VI of Great Britain.

Although most visitors know Malta as a peaceful place, its internal politics since World War II have been quite divisive. Two major parties—the socialist Malta Labor Party and the conservative Nationalist Party—have bitterly wrestled for control of the nation's government.

From 1971 to 1987, the ruling Labor Party tried to curtail the traditional influence of the Roman Catholic Church. The Nationalists took over in 1987, and remained in power until 1996. In December 1989, after most of the Communist regimes in Eastern Europe had collapsed, Malta hosted the first summit meeting between U.S. President George Bush and the Soviet President Mikhail Gorbachev. During the Nationalists' tenure, Malta also applied for membership in the European Union (EU) and joined the North Atlantic Treaty Organization's (NATO's) Partnership for Peace.

In another shift of powers, the Labor Party won by a slim majority in 1996, and shortly after taking over, withdrew the nation's request for membership in the EU. Two years later, in 1998, the Nationalists won again and renewed the EU application—even though the people of Malta continue to be divided on the issue of membership.

GOVERNMENT

Malta won internal self-government in 1947 and complete independence in 1964. It became a republic in 1974. The legislature is the House of Representatives. The House elects the president, who is head of state, for five years. The president appoints as prime minister, or head of the government, the leader of the majority party in the House.

ECONOMY

Malta lacks rivers, lakes, minerals, and raw materials, except for the yellowish limestone used for building. There are few trees. Winters are occasionally cold; summers are hot, dry, and cloudless. The rainfall comes mostly in the fall and early winter. The number of sunny hours the islands enjoy is a major asset. The islands' rocky surfaces are covered with 3 or 4 ft. (about 1 m.) of soil. Maltese farmers have to struggle to grow anything, but they do raise potatoes, tomatoes, onions, melons, cereals, grapes, citrus fruits, and other vegetables, as well as clover and hay to feed their cattle, sheep, and goats. They also export flowers, and there is a small fishing industry.

The Maltese have found a good natural resource through the combination of a pleasant climate and great historical richness. Tourism accounts for 27 percent of Malta's gross domestic product and employs one-third of its workforce. Visitors come from around the world to catch a glimpse of the great relics of the past—fossil remains of prehistoric animals, Stone Age temples, medieval palaces and cathedrals, and the tombs of the Crusaders.

Reviewed by HUGH H. SMYTHE, *Former United States Ambassador to Malta*

The Parthenon, one of the greatest achievements of classical Greece, overlooks Athens from the Acropolis.

GREECE

Greece occupies a unique place in the minds of modern people. The ancient Greeks played a dominant role in the development of classical civilization and helped lay the basis for all European and European-inspired civilizations throughout the world. Thus modern Greece is regarded as the fountainhead of Western civilization. The Greek city-states of the classical era are remembered for their contributions to art, architecture, literature, religion, philosophy, and education. And above all, ancient Greece is looked upon as the inspiration for our modern theories of democracy.

It is not just classical Greece, however, that has influenced the modern world. Toward the end of the classical era the Greek city-states fell under the domination of Rome; but in conquering the Greek world the Roman Empire absorbed and adapted much of the Greek culture, thereby expanding and making permanent Greek ideals. Furthermore, out of the Roman Empire of the East there eventually developed a Greek medieval empire that we today call the Byzantine Empire. This empire, one of the most durable political entities ever to exist, lasted from A.D.

A canal now cuts through the Isthmus of Corinth. In ancient times, ships were dragged across the isthmus.

330 to 1453. Initially the empire's rulers used Latin in administration, but by the 7th century the empire had been reduced to essentially Greek-speaking areas of Europe, Asia, and southern Italy. The Byzantine Empire left its imprint not only on modern Greece but also on all European civilization. Its capital at Constantinople (modern Istanbul) was for many centuries the greatest city in Europe and surpassed Rome as the center of Western culture and learning.

During the 11th century the Byzantine Empire started to weaken militarily and economically. It lost many of its major core territories to outsiders (especially the Muslims) who sometimes themselves left their impact on Greek culture. As the years went by, the disintegration of the empire continued. From the late 13th century the Ottoman Turks, a people who had come out of Asia, began encroachments that became ever more successful. By 1453 the Turks had taken Constantinople, and the Byzantine Empire collapsed. Thereafter until the 19th century, Greece was under Turkish domination, but as the years went by opposition to Ottoman rule grew. Finally, independence triumphed; in 1821 the Greeks revolted, and in 1832 a tiny independent Greek kingdom was founded. From this kingdom the modern Greek state developed and expanded.

THE LAND

Geographically, Greece is located in southeastern Europe at the southernmost tip of the Balkan Peninsula and encompasses hundreds of islands scattered through the eastern end of the Mediterranean Sea. To the north, mainland Greece borders Albania, Macedonia, Bulgaria, and Turkey. In other directions, Greece is surrounded by the Mediterranean and its various subdivisions: the Ionian Sea, the Aegean Sea, and the Sea of Crete.

It took more than 100 years to bring together the lands—both continental and island—that constitute the modern Greek state. When Greece first became an independent kingdom in 1832, the state consisted of the Peloponnesus, the Cyclades, and a little territory to its north, including Euboea. The Ionian Islands were ceded by Great Britain in 1864; Thessaly and a tiny part of Epirus were handed over by the Ottoman Empire in 1881; Crete, Epirus, Macedonia, and many of the Aegean islands came from the Turks with the settlements of the Balkan Wars of 1912 and 1913; Western Thrace came from Bulgaria after World War I; and finally (1947) the Dodecanese Islands were ceded to Greece by Italy after World War II.

Throughout Greece, small squares and parks are favorite places to meet friends and pass the time.

FACTS AND FIGURES

OFFICIAL NAME: Hellenic Republic.

NATIONALITY: Greek(s).

CAPITAL: Athens.

LOCATION: Southeastern Europe. **Boundaries**—Albania, Macedonia, Bulgaria, Turkey, Aegean Sea, Mediterranean Sea, Ionian Sea.

AREA: 50,942 sq. mi. (131, 940 sq. km.).

PHYSICAL FEATURES: **Highest point**—Olympus (9,570 ft.; 2,917 m.). **Lowest point**—sea level.

POPULATION: 11,000,000 (2002; annual growth 0.0%).

MAJOR LANGUAGES: Greek (official), English, French.

MAJOR RELIGIONS: Greek Orthodoxy, Islam.

GOVERNMENT: Parliamentary republic. **Head of state**—president. **Head of government**—prime minister. **Legislature**—unicameral Parliament.

CHIEF CITIES: Athens, Salonika, Piraeus, Patras.

ECONOMY: **Chief minerals**—bauxite, lignite, magnesite, oil, marble. **Chief agricultural products**—wheat, olives, tobacco, corn, barley, sugar beets, tomatoes, wine, tobacco, potatoes, meat, dairy products. **Industries and products**—tourism, food and tobacco processing, textiles, chemicals, metal products. **Chief exports**—manufactured goods, foodstuffs, fuels. **Chief imports**—manufactured goods, foodstuffs, fuels.

MONETARY UNIT: 1 euro = 100 cents.

NATIONAL HOLIDAY: March 25 (Independence Day).

The Mainland

Mainland Greece is divided into two uneven parts by the Gulf of Corinth. To the north of this gulf are the historical subdivisions of Attica, Boeotia, Thessaly, Epirus, Macedonia, Western Thrace, and the Chalcidice Peninsula. To the south of the gulf is the Peloponnesus, a peninsula that until modern times was connected by land to the northern areas by the Isthmus of Corinth. In 1893, the Corinth Canal was opened, cutting through that isthmus and connecting the Gulf of Corinth with the Saronic Gulf to its east. Today, the Peloponnesus is completely surrounded by water, and ships travel directly from the west through the Corinth Canal to the Aegean Sea. The Peloponnesus itself includes areas with such ancient names as Arcadia, Laconia, Achaea, Argolis, and Messenia. In medieval times, the Peloponnesus was called the Morea, a name that is still occasionally used.

The topography of mainland Greece varies, but mountainous conditions prevail over much of the territory. The Pindus Mountains dominate in the northwest and the Taygetus Mountains in the southern Peloponnesus. Although mountains, hills, and valleys are to be found throughout the country, there are quite fertile areas suitable for farming in places like Thessaly, Arcadia, and Boeotia. Nonetheless, there has generally been insufficient fertile land to sustain the population. This is one reason why many Greeks either turned to the sea for their livelihood or emigrated to territory around the Mediterranean and later all over the world. Emigration from Greece in the late 19th and 20th centuries has been particularly high, resulting in substantial numbers of Greeks settling in the United States and elsewhere.

Mainland Greece, like Italy and Spain, reflects the climatic conditions of the Mediterranean. Many of its areas are extremely hot during the summer months. In the winter mountainous areas, especially in the north, can be very cold with considerable snowfall. Even the mountains of the southern Peloponnesus suffer severe cold and winter conditions at times. Most of the rain falls in the spring, and the summer and fall tend to be extremely dry.

The Greek Islands

Mainland Greece is bracketed by hundreds of islands that, like the continental part, vary greatly in topography and climate. The two largest islands are Crete to the south and Euboea to the east. Euboea, also

Mykonos and other Greek islands are noted for lovely harbors and dazzling white buildings.

With its mild climate and ancient and medieval ruins, the island of Rhodes is a major tourist mecca.

known as Negropont (the name given it in medieval times), lies to the east of the mainland and is separated from it by a narrow channel.

Some of the Greek islands are included in groupings that have their own distinctive names. To the west are the Ionian Islands, of which the best known are Corfu, Cephalonia, Ithaca, and Zakynthos (or Zante).

The Cyclades. In the Aegean Sea are the Cyclades (which comes from the Greek word for circle, because the ancient Greeks considered them a circular group of islands with Delos as the great commercial and political center). The largest island in the Cyclades is Naxos. It is associated with the ancient story of Theseus, who killed the Minotaur on the island of Crete with the help of Princess Ariadne, whom he abandoned on Naxos.

Another of the Cyclades, Thera, also called Santorin, is noted for its geological formations and its many volcanic eruptions. An ancient city, believed to have been destroyed by the great volcanic eruption of 1400 B.C., is being systematically excavated.

The Sporades. Two other groupings of islands in the Aegean Sea are the Northern Sporades and the Southern Sporades. Euboea is one of the Northern Sporades. Another is the island of Skyros, most famous perhaps because the English poet Rupert Brooke (1887–1915) is buried there. Also in the Northern Sporades is Mykonos, which is notable for its windmills and numerous whitewashed churches, chapels, and houses. Mykonos is one of the most popular of the Greek islands with summer tourists.

The most important islands of the Southern Sporades are the Dodecanese, which in Greek means "twelve." In fact, there are 12 main islands and a number of smaller ones in the group. They lie off the southern

Turkish coast, and the most important of them is Rhodes. There in ancient times was built the great bronze statue of the sun god Helios, which has come to be known as the Colossus of Rhodes, one of the Seven Wonders of the Ancient World. No trace of it survives. Rhodes has seen many conquerors over the centuries. In 1309 it was taken by an order of Crusaders, who fortified the island and established their headquarters there. In 1522 the island was surrendered to the Ottoman Turks. On Rhodes some of the medieval fortifications and other buildings have been restored.

The island of Patmos is important in Christian history. Church tradition holds that around A.D. 95, St. John the Evangelist was exiled to Patmos. There he saw his vision of the Apocalypse and dictated his account of it to his disciple St. Prochorus. The Apocalypse, also called the Book of Revelation, is part of the New Testament.

To the north are three islands famous in Greek history: Samos, Chios, and Lesbos. Samos was a great cultural center in the 6th century B.C. and claims Pythagoras as a native son. Chios, which claims to be the birthplace of Homer, was noted in ancient times for its fine sculptors and poets. In the late Byzantine period, Chios fell (1261) into the hands of the Genoese. The Ottoman Turks captured it in 1566; and in 1822, during the Greek Revolution, it was the scene of a great massacre when the Turks murdered the entire Christian population. The massacre was widely publicized and did much to bring Europeans and Americans to the side of the Greeks in their quest for independence from the Turks.

Lesbos (also known as Mytilene) is included by some geographers in the Southern Sporades. Its name is forever associated with the great woman poet Sappho and other poets of the 7th century B.C.

On the island of Astypalaia, whitewashed houses climb a hillside to the ruins of a centuries-old citadel.

Crete. In the southern Aegean is the largest Greek island, Crete. Crete has a splendid heritage from ancient times to the present. It was the site of an early Mediterranean civilization called the Minoan, after the legendary King Minos, whose palace was in the city of Knossos. The Minoan civilization influenced other parts of the Greek world. The palace at Knossos was excavated and restored in the early 20th century and is today one of the top tourist attractions of Greece.

Crete remained part of the Greek world in the classical era, and later it fell under the Roman and Byzantine empires. From 823 to 960 it was held by the Arabs. The Byzantines retook it but later lost control to Venice early in the 13th century. In 1669, it was surrendered to the Ottoman Turks after a long war. During the period of Venetian occupation, Crete produced one of the greatest artists of all time. His name was Kyriakos Theotokopoulos, but he is best known to the world by his Spanish nickname, El Greco.

Crete, the largest Greek island, is largely agricultural. Modern farming methods are not widespread.

In modern Greece, traditional costumes and folk dances are generally limited to holidays and celebrations.

THE PEOPLE

The Greeks refer to themselves as Hellenes, and Greece can be referred to as Hellas, the Greek word for the country. The inhabitants of Greece live in widely divergent locales, from the tiniest villages to great, sprawling cities like Athens. With the advent of advanced technology in transportation and communications, distinctions between city and country people have almost disappeared. Information is accessible to almost everyone throughout the country. The usual dress in urban settings is much like that known everywhere in the rest of the world. In agricultural and remote rural areas forms of dress are sometimes based on the old styles, but in general the traditional Greek costumes are worn only at festivals, parades, and other social events. The famous Evzones that guard the presidential palace and the Tomb of the Unknown Soldier in Athens wear a distinctive *fustanella* uniform; it is distinguished by a kiltlike skirt and distinctive shoes called *tsarouhia*. At one time, a century or more ago, the *fustanella* was the customary men's wear.

Modern Greek culture and civilization are an amalgam of the many influences that have been combined through the centuries. The classical tradition is visible in the remnants that abound in the country and in the reverence the Greeks show toward their heritage. The Byzantine influence is seen in the living presence of the Greek Orthodox Church as an integral part of society as well as in the architectural and artistic works that continue to be inspired by Byzantine forms. Folk traditions, music, literature, and crafts exhibit influences that stem from the classical, Byzantine, and modern periods.

It is the Greek language that binds all of this together, so that in the 20th century, Greek civilization has emerged as a multifaceted yet vibrant whole. One only needs to cite the works of three Greek writers: the poet

George Seferis, who won the Nobel Prize for Literature in 1963; Odysseus Elytis, another distinguished poet, who won the Nobel Prize in 1979; and Nikos Kazantzakis, author of *Zorba the Greek* and numerous other works and Greece's most famous modern novelist. The influence of such writers extends beyond the borders of their native Greece.

Religion

It is estimated that about 98 percent of the Greek population belongs to the Greek Orthodox Church, a Christian denomination that is an integral part of the Eastern Orthodox Church, which was separated from the Roman Catholic Church in 1054. At that time each branch excommunicated the other.

Over the centuries the two churches for the most part merely tolerated each other. Gradually, relations between them improved. Though still separate, in 1965 both "committed to oblivion" the excommunications of 1054; and thus there is at present greater cooperation between them. In the same spirit of cooperation the Greek Orthodox Church has developed friendly relations with Protestants and non-Christian sects outside the country. Yet when Pope John Paul II visited Greece in 2001, his reception was decidedly lukewarm.

Special breads and other delicacies are prepared for Easter, the major feast of the Greek Orthodox Church.

For Greeks generally, membership in the Orthodox Church is seen not only as a matter of religious devotion but also as a part of being ethnically Greek. There is special pride and reverence in the fact that the New Testament was written originally in Greek, and it is this untranslated form of the Bible that is still used in Greek Orthodox services in Greece today.

The Greek Language

The modern Greek language is the result of developments over many centuries. At the time of Greek independence in the 19th century two forms of modern Greek were espoused by different factions. The purist form, called the *katharevousa,* was used for literary endeavors and not for everyday conversations; it tried to emulate classical Greek as much as possible. The other form was the language of ordinary speech, called the demotic, or *dimotiki,* which varies greatly from classical Greek but is still recognizably its offshoot. At times the whole question of which form—*katharevousa* or *dimotiki*—should be given precedence in literature and education became intertwined with Greek political issues. Recently, however, the demotic has gained wide acceptance in written as well as in spoken discourse.

Education

Today, universal education in Greece is strongly stressed, and the curriculum of primary and secondary schools is closely monitored by the national government. As a result of those efforts the country today has a literacy rate of 95 percent. At the top of the education system is the University of Athens, founded in 1837, only a few years after Greece gained independence. It became a catalyst for a nationwide system of higher education that today includes a number of other universities and numerous technical, trade, and specialized colleges. Under Greek law, no private universities can exist.

Cities

Athens.   As the capital city and the economic and cultural center of Greece, Athens plays a dominant role in all aspects of Greek life. Named for the goddess Athena and once the jewel of classical Greek civilization, Athens was much less important in Byzantine times and was reduced to little more than a village during the Ottoman period. It was not even the first capital of the Greek republic; Nauplia, on the Peloponnesus, was. But the seat of government was soon removed to Athens, and from that point the growth of the modern city began. Although it grew throughout the modern era, it had its greatest explosion of growth in the period after World War II. In village after village all over Greece, the young people deserted the family home in search of jobs and economic advancement in Athens. Often, they were followed by the rest of the family. As a result, today Athens is a sprawling, overcrowded city with inadequate public services and serious pollution problems. Yet the city still remains a magnet for Greeks from the rural areas and possesses a vibrancy found only in the world's great cities. It is the center of Greece's economic life, and much of the nation's shipping passes through its port of **Piraeus.**

Athens is the site of many world-famous relics from Greek history. The best known of these is the Parthenon. It is located, along with other

Despite its ancient roots, modern Athens has a contemporary look much like other European capitals.

glories of classical Greece, on the Acropolis, the ancient citadel of the city. It was originally a shrine dedicated to the goddess Athena, and it was converted to a Christian church during the Byzantine era. Incredibly, the building survived in almost perfect condition until the 17th century. Unfortunately, however, during an Ottoman-Venetian war in 1687 the Turks used the Parthenon as a storage site for munitions, and Venetian gunboats bombarded it, reducing it to the ruins we know today. Its frieze, known today as the Elgin Marbles, was removed in the early 19th century by the English Lord Elgin and is today in the British Museum. Athens boasts many other famous remnants from its classical, Roman, and Byzantine eras. Among the relics of the classical era are the Agora, the Erechtheum, and the Theater of Dionysos. From the Roman period, Hadrian's Arch dominates its location. From the Byzantine era is the 12th-century Small Cathedral, or Old Metropolitan Church. The Kapnikarea Church is another outstanding example of Byzantine architecture. The National Museum in Athens displays glorious art from all over Greece.

Among the modern structures in Athens is the Parliament Building, located on Syntagma (Constitution) Square, the city's most important public space. Originally built as a royal palace for King Otto I (reigned

1832–62), the first king of modern Greece, it was converted to a building to house the Greek parliament in the 20th century. It was in front of this building in 1844 that revolutionaries forced King Otto to grant the nation a constitution. Athens is also the site of the Olympic Stadium, which was built for the first modern Olympic Games in 1896.

The Plaka, at the base of the hill on which the Acropolis sits, is the old section of Athens. Its winding, narrow streets give an idea of what the city must have been like toward the end of the Byzantine era, the period of the Crusades, and during the Turkish occupation. The Greek government has recently paid much attention to the restoration and preservation of the Plaka, and it is one of the favorite tourist attractions of Athens, with many shops, restaurants, and night clubs.

Salonika. The second largest city in Greece is the great Macedonian city of Salonika, also known as Thessalonica. Throughout its long history it has been the cultural, religious, and commercial capital of the north. It was especially important during the Byzantine era, and its museums are filled with masterpieces of Byzantine art that rival those found in Istanbul. Modern Salonika remains an important commercial center, and its port is second only to Piraeus.

Patras. The greatest seaport in the Peloponnesus, Patras is also a major industrial center. It produces textiles, paper, tires, wines, and chemicals. Led by its bishop, Patras was the first city in the Peloponnesus to rise against the Turks in the Greek revolution of 1821.

Pandrosou Street in the Plaka, an older section of Athens, is lined with shops selling handmade goods.

The monastery atop Mount Athos has twice as many monks as all the other Greek monasteries put together.

Mount Athos. A fascinating locale in northern Greece is the Christian community of Mount Athos, located on the tip of the Chalcidice peninsula. This all-male religious community consists of 20 monasteries and is governed under a theocratic system that functions as a separate administrative entity within Greece. The first monastery on Mount Athos was founded in 963, and its religious communities have survived since that time.

Historic Cities. **Delphi**, on the mainland northwest of Athens and situated between Mount Parnassus and the Gulf of Corinth, was one of the most significant religious centers of ancient Greece. It was here that the Delphic Oracle was consulted on great matters of state. Many elaborate temples were built at Delphi and filled with treasures by various Greek city-states.

The Peloponnesus is the site of several of the most important cities of ancient Greece. **Olympia,** like Delphi, was a religious center, and it was here that the original Olympic Games were held. **Tiryns** is the location of the ruins of an important 13th century B.C. military fortress. **Mycenae** is one of the most ancient cities in Greece. It flourished from about 1600 B.C. to 1100 B.C., during the Bronze Age, and was the legendary capital city of King Agamemnon. **Corinth** was probably founded in the 9th century B.C. and became a bustling commercial center. It was destroyed in 146 B.C., and in 44 B.C. Julius Caesar built a new city on the same site. Corinth continued as an important city during the Byzantine, Venetian, and Turkish eras. Much of the city was destroyed by earthquake in the 19th century and modern Corinth was built in 1858 inland from the ancient site. Although modern **Sparta** is quite a small city, it is the site of the most important city-state on the Peloponnesus during classical times.

THE ECONOMY

The multifaceted Greek economy includes agriculture, industry, shipping, mining, and tourism. Even more than most economies, that of Greece has always been vulnerable to outside pressures. In the 20th century it has felt the effects of the Balkan War of 1912 and 1913, World War I, the Greek-Turkish War of the 1920's, the worldwide depression of the 1930's, World War II, and the Greek Civil War of the 1940's.

Agriculture remains a significant part of the Greek economy despite insufficient arable land and the fact that many young people do not seem to want to go into farming, opting instead for life in the city. Major crops include grapes for wine and raisins, olives, figs, wheat, and citrus fruits. Other fruits, rice, and vegetables are also grown. Cotton and tobacco are important crops for export. Sheep are the primary livestock.

Greece is not blessed with rich mineral resources. Bauxite is an important mineral. Marble, lignite, magnesium, and nickel are also mined. Recent discoveries of oil near the Aegean island of Thassos have led to serious disputes with Turkey over oil rights in the area.

The much-indented coastlines of Greece and its islands have made fishing an important way of life.

Shipping remains an important factor in the Greek economy, and most of the great fortunes made in Greece come from the flotillas of tankers sailed by Greek shipowners. Industrial production lags behind that of the nations of Western Europe. Greece does produce cement, steel, textiles, refined sugar, and ships.

Greece joined the European Community (EC) in 1981, but the expected boost to the economy did not occur immediately. In the late 1990s, however, after the EC grew to 15 members and changed its name to the European Union (EU), the Greek economy improved dramatically. In January 2002, Greece adopted the new currency, the euro.

Tourism. At least since the 18th century, adventurous European travelers have sought out the glories of classical and Byzantine Greece. Today, tourism is a major factor in the Greek economy. Foreigners still come to Greece to seek out its magnificent ruins and historical sites; but many more come to enjoy swimming, fishing, boating, and cruising among the Greek islands. Fostered by governmental support, the Greek tourist industry has grown enormously since World War II. The Athens international airport is one of the busiest in the world. Luxurious cruise ships carry foreign tourists from one Greek island to the next.

THE GOVERNMENT

Since 1974, when the monarchy was overthrown, Greece has been a republic; its official name is the Hellenic Republic. Under its constitution, ratified in 1975, the head of state is the president. Legislative authority is vested in a unicameral parliament (*Vouli*), or national assembly. Parliament, made up of 300 deputies elected by universal suffrage, chooses

The volcanic island of Thera is thought by some to be the site of the legendary continent of Atlantis.

The spectacular Palace of Minos at Knossos, Crete, discovered in this century, was built before 1400 B.C.

the president for a five-year term. Actual executive power, however, rests with the prime minister and the cabinet of ministers, who form the government. They are chosen from among members of the parliament.

Administratively, Greece is subdivided into 51 prefectures, or departments (*nomoi*). They in turn are divided into smaller units. There is also an autonomous region, Mt. Athos. The minister of the interior appoints a governor, or prefect (*nomarchis*), for each department; thus there is a great deal of central control of local governments. Mayors and other officials are elected locally.

Greece has a highly structured, complicated judicial system. Included are the Special Supreme Tribunal, which specifically deals with constitutional issues; the Council of State, which serves as an appellate court for administrative acts; and the Supreme Court, which despite its name does not function like the U.S. Supreme Court. There are also various specialized judicial bodies, such as tax courts.

HISTORY

Greek-speaking peoples first migrated down the mainland of what is now Greece around 1900 B.C. Coming in contact with the already thriving Minoan civilization of Crete, they developed their own civilization, now known as the Mycenaean. This flourished from around 1600 B.C. to around 1150 B.C. This era of periodic instability was the setting for the two great masterpieces of ancient Greek literature, the *Iliad* and the *Odyssey*. Both poems were written down between 800 B.C. and 750 B.C., based on oral traditions. The blind poet Homer has always been credited with writing them. They form the first great literary works of the ancient Greeks and two of the most influential works in Western civilization. In the *Iliad*, Homer describes the siege of Troy to secure the

Ancient Greeks flocked to Delphi to ask advice of the oracle, through whom the gods spoke.

release of the exquisitely beautiful Spartan queen, Helen, who had been captured and carried away by Paris, son of Priam, king of Troy. Thus the stage was set for the Trojan War, an event that most historians accept as having taken place about 1250 B.C. The *Odyssey* traces the wandering of Odysseus, ruler of Ithaca, in his efforts to return to his home after the end of the Trojan War.

Greece's Golden Age

The ancient Greeks did not establish one unified country. Instead they established city-states, each called a *polis*, which were self-governing and independent. Often they warred with one another, the two most persistent enemies being Athens and Sparta. All the city-states, however, would from time to time go to war with another *polis*.

Although the Greeks are credited with inventing the democratic form of government, not all of the city-states were democratic in form. Sparta, for example, was during most of its predominance an aristocratic and a military regime. Even Athens, the most famous of all the democratic city-states, relied on slavery for its economic well-being. Only male Athenian citizens participated in the democracy.

All the Greek city-states had high levels of culture, and Greek civilization spread to colonies throughout the Mediterranean world: from the Black Sea to Spain and from Italy and southern France to North Africa.

Athens served as a kind of catalyst among the city-states, and what emerged was one of the greatest civilizations the world has ever seen. Architecture reached splendid levels. The Parthenon, built between 447 and 432 B.C., was the most spectacular of many beautiful temples that were erected throughout Greece. Seldom has any period in time seen such a profusion of talented people as in classical Greece. Among them were the Athenian leader Pericles; the philosophers Socrates, Plato, and Aristotle; the sculptor Phidias; the dramatists Sophocles, Aeschylus, Euripides, and Aristophanes; the poet Pindar; and Herodotus, the "Father of History."

The rivalry between Athens and Sparta erupted into the Great Peloponnesian War in 431 B.C. It finally ended in 404 B.C. with a great victory for Sparta, which emerged as the ruler of all of Greece. It was to be a short-lived rule. Wars with Persia to the east and with the Greek city Thebes left Sparta—and all of Greece—open to conquest from the north.

The Hellenistic Period

In 338 B.C., King Philip II of Macedonia was able to bring the once-proud Greek city-states under his control. The Macedonians were a kindred people to the Greeks. They spoke a form of Greek, and their rulers considered themselves to be true Greeks. Philip's son, Alexander the Great (reigned 336–323 B.C.), conquered vast areas of Europe, Egypt,

Tourists walk through the ruins of the agora in Corinth, one of ancient Greece's leading city-states.

Steps leading to a church at Mistras are typical of the architecture required by the stony Greek terrain.

and Asia, reaching as far as India. Alexander's conquests spread Greek civilization and language throughout the Middle East. The Greek-based civilization that then developed is called Hellenistic to distinguish it from the classical Greek period that ended with the Macedonian conquests.

After Alexander's death his empire was divided among his generals. The Greek city-states formed several leagues and by the 220's had become mostly independent again. Clashes with the Macedonians and the expansion of Rome hindered these attempts to maintain independence.

The Roman Period

With the decline of Macedonian power and the rise of Rome the Romans intervened repeatedly in Greek affairs particularly from the 220's B.C. By 146 B.C. the Greeks were effectively under Roman domination and would remain so for centuries. The Romans, however, were captivated by the beauties of Greek civilization, and Greek forms and ideals had such an important influence on Roman culture that even today people speak of the fusion as Greco-Roman. Christianity was fostered among the Greeks by the missionary journeys and works of St. Paul. He preached at such places as Athens, Corinth, Philippi, and Thessalonica (Salonika). It was in the first centuries of Christianity that the Roman period melded into the Byzantine era of Greek history.

The Byzantine Empire

In 330 A.D. the Roman Emperor Constantine I founded the city of Constantinople, which he erected on the site of the ancient Greek city of Byzantium. Constantinople became the capital of what was to become the Byzantine Empire. Greek had always remained the language of culture in the eastern Roman Empire. Following Constantine's reign the eastern parts of the empire increasingly separated from the western territories. Gradually they split into two parts: the Western, with its capital at Rome, and the Eastern, with its capital at Constantinople. As the Roman Empire weakened, much of its eastern territories were lost to Islamic conquerors. By the 7th century A.D. what had been the Eastern Empire was reduced to an essentially Greek-speaking core centered around Constantinople.

For many centuries this still-powerful Byzantine Empire had an enormous impact on Europe and the world around the Mediterranean basin. As Rome declined, Constantinople became the center of art, architecture, literature, education, commerce, and religion. At Constantinople resided the most important bishop of the Eastern Church, the Ecumenical Patriarch; even today members of the Greek Orthodox Church and other Orthodox churches consider the Ecumenical Patriarch the spiritual leader of the Church. Missionaries sent out from the Greek Church in Constantinople converted many people of Eastern Europe to Christianity, including the Russians, the Serbs, the Rumanians, and the Bulgarians. Thus, through the Church, Greek influence covered virtually all of Eastern Europe.

By the 11th century the Byzantine Empire had begun to weaken internally in the face of increasing outside pressures. Christian Crusaders, who came from Western Europe initially to take over "infidel lands" in Palestine, annexed lands controlled by their fellow Christians, the Byzantine Greeks. Westerners like Normans, Venetians, and Genoese took over great sections of Byzantium. Even the capital city of Constantinople was held by Western Europeans from 1204 to 1261, when the Byzantines retook it.

By that time the empire had lost its momentum, however, and the Byzantines were never able completely to dislodge Western European leaders who had set up their own little states in parts of what is today modern Greece. Athens became the Duchy of Athens and Thebes, ruled by people of Western origins. Most of the residents of the Greek islands became vassals of various ruling princes of Western Europe. And a new power had emerged in the area; from the 14th century the Ottoman Turks began encroaching on both the Byzantine Empire and its Western European conquerors.

The Ottoman Turks

Constantinople fell in 1453, thus ending the political existence of the Byzantine Empire. Subsequently, the Turks brought under their control all the Greek-speaking parts of Europe and Asia Minor except for one major area, the Ionian Islands. These remained under Venetian domination for hundreds of years (until 1797). After the Napoleonic era, they became a British protectorate.

Otherwise, the Greeks came under the domination of the Ottoman Turks. Sultan Mohammed II the Conqueror, the Turkish ruler who took Constantinople in 1453, gave to the Ecumenical Patriarch certain political and religious rights over the Greek Orthodox subjects of the empire. This helped the Greeks retain a recognizable ethnic identity in an empire that was otherwise almost wholly Muslim. Relatively few Greeks were converted to Islam, and the Greek Orthodox Church thus helped keep alive a separate national feeling among the Greeks.

The conditions of the Greeks varied from place to place in the Ottoman Empire. Some were downtrodden and exploited; others grew wealthy in commerce. Still others reached high position in the government even though they remained Christian.

The Quest for Independence

Still, many Greeks chafed under Ottoman domination, and as the ideals of nationalism that were unleashed by the French Revolution in the 18th century spread into Greek-speaking areas, the revolutionary spirit developed among the Greeks. The result was a full-fledged revolution against the Turks in 1821. With the help of Great Britain, Russia, and France, and after numerous bloody battles, Greece became an independent kingdom in 1832.

During the revolution many foreigners who were pro-Greek, including a few Americans, either helped the cause from outside or went to Greece to fight with the rebels. They were called Philhellenes, and the most famous of them was the English poet Lord Byron. His death in Greece in 1824 made him a Greek national hero, inspiring many others to join the Greek cause.

The Greek Kingdom

With independence, a Bavarian prince named Otto was chosen by the Western powers to be the first king of modern Greece. It may seem strange that the Greeks would accept a foreign-born king after they had thrown off the Turkish yoke. There were several reasons for this, among them that no Greek rebel had emerged as the clear leader of the country. Perhaps most important, it was believed that an outsider connected by birth to the great royal houses of Western Europe would give the struggling new nation the prestige it would need among the other royal rulers of Europe. Otto was the son of King Ludwig I of Bavaria, the first European monarch openly to support the Greek cause. Lastly, Otto was young enough so that he could acclimate himself to the country and become, in effect, Greek.

Otto turned out to be a strong Greek patriot. He supported a concept called the Great Idea, which envisaged tiny Greece as the nucleus for a larger Greek state that would recreate the old Byzantine Empire at the expense of now weak Ottoman Turks. Although mild-mannered, Otto was also authoritarian. An uprising in 1843 forced him to accept a national constitution. Nevertheless, his authoritarianism increased, and in 1862 he was forced from the throne.

In medieval times, the Crusaders built castles in Greece to protect their routes to the Holy Land.

Otto was replaced in 1863 by a Danish prince—elected by the Greek National Assembly—who assumed the Greek throne as George I of the Hellenes. The new king, like King Otto, espoused the Great Idea and in fact saw his kingdom enlarged three times during his reign.

During the last years of his rule, King George entrusted the prime ministership to one of the most remarkable leaders of modern Greece. Eleutherios Venizelos, a Cretan by birth, had fought the Turks on his native island, where he won wide acclaim. As prime minister, Venizelos rejuvenated Greece; he paid attention to internal administration and built up the army and the navy. He oversaw the revision of the constitution, and he skillfully built up a network of connections with Greece's northern neighbors against the Ottoman Turks.

The Balkan Wars. It was under these circumstances that the first Balkan War broke out in 1912, and Greece was a major participant in it. With Venizelos as the political leader and King George's son, Crown Prince Constantine, at the head of the army, Greece won unparalleled victories. As soon as Constantine had taken Salonika from the Turks, King George went to reside there to show that even before the peace treaty, Greece considered the city Greek. It was in Salonika that the king was assassinated by a madman in March, 1913 as he walked through the streets.

Constantine I came to the throne as a martyr's son and as the first Greek-born king in centuries. In June 1913 a second Balkan War commenced. Again Constantine and Venizelos worked together to secure enormous victories and new territories for Greece.

World War I. Unfortunately, World War I broke up the close relationship between king and prime minister. Venizelos favored joining the Allies (Great Britain, France, and Russia) against Germany, Austria-

Just off the lush Ionian island of Corfu lie several tiny islets, one of which houses a small monastery.

Hungary, and the Ottoman Empire. Constantine, whose wife, Queen Sophie, was a sister of the German Emperor William II, wanted Greece to remain neutral. Constantine was branded pro-German; Venizelos resigned from office, led a revolution, and forced the king to abdicate in 1917. Constantine's second son then became King Alexander I of the Hellenes. Venizelos returned to office as prime minister and won a brilliant series of military and diplomatic victories. They culminated in Greek troops entering Constantinople along with the other Allied forces when the Ottoman Empire lost the war and faded from history. In addition, Venizelos won from the Allies the right to occupy the Greek-inhabited city of Smyrna, in Asia Minor, thus signaling the fact that Turkish territory in Asia Minor was not immune from the Great Idea.

The 1920's and 1930's. Then everything collapsed. King Alexander died tragically as the result of an infection from a monkey bite. Venizelos lost at the polls, and King Constantine was restored to the throne by popular vote. The Turks, despite their defeat in World War I, attacked the Greeks at Smyrna and drove them out. Constantine was forced to abdicate once again (1922), this time in favor of his oldest son, who became King George II of the Hellenes. The military disaster in Asia

Minor had left Greece a weakened, disrupted country. The Great Idea was destroyed forever, and George II was forced to leave Greece in 1923.

From 1924 to 1935, Greece was a republic. Most of those years were turbulent, except for a period from 1928 to 1932 when Venizelos once again gave the country a stable government. The monarchy was restored in 1935 in the person of George II, but the following year all governmental power fell into the hands of a military dictator named John Metaxas.

World War II. Metaxas was still at the helm in October 1940 when Fascist Italy under Benito Mussolini invaded Greece. The valiant defense by the Greeks, which continued after Metaxas' death in early 1941, led to a German invasion from the north in 1941. King George II and his government were forced into exile.

During the Nazi occupation, resistance groups developed, the most important being EAM with its army ELAS. They were communists who tried unsuccessfully to take over the government in 1944 when Greece was liberated.

The Greek Civil War and Cyprus. At the end of World War II, King George II was once again restored to the throne in a 1946 plebiscite. He died in 1947, and his brother, the youngest son of Constantine I, became king as Paul I. In the meantime the communists had begun a civil war that lasted until 1949 when, with decisive American aid, it was crushed.

During King Paul's reign there emerged a man who ranks with Venizelos as one of the two great modern Greek statesmen. Constantine Karamanlis became prime minister in 1955. He stressed economic development and a settlement of the Cyprus question. Cyprus was a British

Plays in ancient Greece were performed in semicircular theaters, the ruins of which can still be seen.

colony with a population about 80 percent Greek and 17 percent Turkish. The Greek Orthodox Archbishop of Cyprus, Makarious III, became the leader of a movement for *enosis,* or union, with Greece. *Enosis* was bitterly opposed by both the Turkish Cypriots and by Turkey. Karamanlis negotiated with the British, Turkey, and the Cypriots, and as a result Cyprus became an independent republic in 1960. (There is an article on CYPRUS in Volume 2.) Hostility over this issue continues to impair Greek-Turkish relations. After a quarrel with King Paul I and his German-born wife, Queen Frederica, Karamanlis resigned in 1963.

The Rule of the Colonels. The absence of Karamanlis marked the beginning of a long political crisis in Greece. King Paul died in 1964, and his son succeeded as Constantine II. Constantine found it increasingly difficult to cope with an unstable political situation. In April, 1967, a group of military officers known as the Colonels took over the government and established a dictatorship. The king valiantly tried to oust them from power in December 1967, but he failed and was forced into exile.

Meanwhile, the Cypriot problem continued. The two factions, Greek and Turkish, could not live together harmoniously. In response to the Colonels' efforts to force union on Cyprus, Turkey invaded the island in 1974 and took over approximately 40 percent of the island. In Greece, this led to the Colonels' downfall. Karamanlis returned from his long exile, became prime minister again, and reestablished democracy.

From this palace in Corfu, the British administered the Ionian islands during the 19th century.

In 1932, the Old Palace in Athens, formerly the monarch's residence, became the Parliament Building.

The Greek Republic

In 1974, the monarchy was rejected by plebiscite, and Greece was declared a republic. Karamanlis remained as prime minister until 1980. His foreign policy was focused on a close relationship with Western Europe and the United States, and Greece joined the European community (EC).

In 1981, a Socialist government came to power. Andreas Papandreu, leader of the Socialist party (PASOK) served as prime minister until 1989. Then, until 1993, a conservative New Democracy Party was in power and Karamanlis became president in 1990. Meanwhile, Papandreu and several of his associates were arrested on corruption charges, although Papandreu was acquitted in January 1992. In October 1993, PASOK won in the parliamentary elections and Papandreu became prime minister again. Shortly after that, Greece held the rotating presidency of the European Union and often was at odds with other member nations, particularly because of Greece's trade blockade against neighboring Macedonia over nationalistic issues. In January 1996, Papandreu resigned due to ill health and was replaced by Costas Simitis. In April 2000, PASOK won the parliamentary elections for the fifth time.

Prime Minister Simitis has managed to improve relations with Greece's traditional enemy, Turkey, and has also pursued an increasingly pro-European approach. About 1,000 Greek troops served in the peacekeeping force in Kosovo. In 2000, the country began to prepare for the 2004 Olympic Games, to take place in Athens for the third time in modern history.

GEORGE J. MARCOPOULOS, Tufts University

Vast, gently rolling plains cover nearly the entire Polish countryside.

POLAND

Since the beginning of its history more than 1,000 years ago, Poland has often suffered because of its geography. Poland, which takes its name from *pole*, a West Slavic word meaning "field," is in fact one vast area with no natural frontiers or defenses on the east or the west. Only the Sudetes and Carpathian mountains in the south and the Baltic Sea in the north provide natural boundaries. For centuries the somber landscape of Poland has been the setting for warring armies. From the 17th century on, the nation has been conquered, partitioned, and destroyed time and time again. But throughout Poland's history, its people have acted out the words of their national anthem (composed and written in 1795–96), which begins, "Poland will not be forsaken while we live. . . ."

THE LAND

On the north of Poland is the 326-mi. (525-km.)-long Baltic Sea coastline. The rest of the country is part of the great plain that extends from the North Sea across Europe to the Ural Mountains in Russia. The gently rolling plains rise gradually to the south, where, at the border with the Czech Republic, they meet the low Sudetes and, at the Slovakian border, the lofty Carpathian mountains. This is one of the most picturesque regions of Central Europe. The High Tatra Range of the Carpathians is a national park where one may see chamois, red deer, bears, lynx, wolves, eagles, and black storks. The nearby Ojców National Park, with its great woods and high cliffs, contains about 50 caves in which primitive people may once have lived and where remains of prehistoric giant deer, hyenas, lions, and mammoths have been found. Just northeast of the Tatra Range is the Pieniny Range. Within this range is another national park where plants grow that are found nowhere else in the world and where more than 1,800 species of butterflies exist.

Deep woods still cover more than one-fourth of Poland. The country is also dotted with thousands of lakes. The Masuria region, in the northeast, with dense, high trees and countless sparkling lakes, is a fine hunting, fishing, boating, and camping area. In the Białowieski Forest, in eastern Poland, are 485 sq. mi. (1,256 sq. km.) of the last remaining lowland primeval forest in Central Europe. It includes a famous national park, once the private property of Poland's kings, where the only surviving European bison roam in complete freedom, fantastic lime trees grow, and huge eagles swoop and soar overhead.

The winters are cold, damp, and snowy, and the summers cool in this land of fields, woods, and rivers. The mighty Vistula (Wisła), the main river of Poland, rises in the Carpathians, carves a roundabout route that forms a huge letter *S*, and empties into the Baltic Sea after traveling 680 mi. (1,094 km.). The Vistula, with its tributaries the Bug and the Pilica, drains about two-thirds of the land. Light boats can sail up the river as far as Cracow (Kraków), except during the winter months, when the Vistula is frozen. Warsaw, the nation's capital, is situated on the west bank of the Vistula. Coal and lumber are transported on the river. West of the Vistula are the Oder and Neisse rivers, which rise in the Sudetes, flow separately, and then combine to empty into the Baltic. The canals that link the main river systems serve as industrial delivery routes.

A religious procession in Podhale. The Catholic Church plays a vital role in the lives of many Polish citizens.

THE PEOPLE

Poles are noted for their Old World gallantry. Men habitually bow and kiss women's hands and present roses on every possible occasion. Poles are great patriots, proud of their long history and many accomplishments. Prior to World War II, about 3 million Jews and large numbers of Ukrainians resided within Poland. Today, only a few groups of minorities remain, mostly Germans, Ukrainians, and Belorussians.

Religion. Most of the people are devout Catholics. Church attendance in Poland is among the highest in the world. About 90 percent of the children born in Poland are baptized in the Catholic Church. In addition, there are a great number of priests, and many new churches have been built in recent years. The elevation of Karol Wojtyła, a Polish cardinal from Cracow, to the papacy in 1978 lifted the morale of Poles and gave them the confidence to challenge Communist rule.

In post-Communist Poland, the Catholic Church has lost some of its influence; it no longer represents a rallying point against the atheistic ideology propounded by Marxism-Leninism. Furthermore, many Poles strongly oppose the church's teachings on contraception.

Way of Life. Traditionally, Poland has been characterized by significant differences between city and country life, and these continue to be quite apparent. While most larger cities bustle energetically and offer a rich selection of cultural pursuits, many villages appear ancient and undeveloped, as if they were from the distant past.

In some ways, Poland has changed almost beyond recognition since the fall of Communism; areas that once appeared shabby or neglected now teem with giant shopping malls and busy superhighways. Even so, many distinctive traditions remain, making Poland unique among its European neighbors.

Education. There is virtually no illiteracy in Poland. Education is compulsory for eight years, after which a student can enroll in a general secondary school or a vocational school. Poland has about 140 institutions of higher learning, including 11 universities.

Literature and Music. Poland boasts a distinguished literary tradition. Adam Mickiewicz (1798–1855) is best known for the epic *Pan Tadeusz (Sir Thaddeus)*. Poland claims four Nobel laureates in literature—Henryk Sienkiewicz, who won the 1905 prize for his novels, including *Quo Vadis?;* Władysław S. Reymont, author of *The Peasants,* who won the prize in 1924; the poet Czesław Miłosz, who has lived in the United States from 1960 and who received the prize in 1980; and the poet Wislawa Szymborska, the laureate in 1996. Several authors born in Poland but writing in other languages have also won international acclaim: Joseph Conrad at the turn of the century; Isaac Bashevis Singer, who left Poland in 1935 and received a Nobel Prize in 1978 for his stories about Polish Jews; and Jerzy Kosinski, who lived in the United States from 1957 until his death in 1991. The best-known contemporary Polish authors are the science-fiction writer Stanisław Lem and the former dissident novelist Tadeusz Konvicki.

There are many large repertory theaters and countless small theaters and cabarets noted for their political satire. The Polish movie industry has won international fame, particularly with films by Andrzej Wajda, which include *Man of Marble* and *Man of Iron* (the latter about Solidarity).

Some say that to hear the truest voice of Poland's tragedies and triumphs, one must listen to the music of Frédéric Chopin (1810–49), whose waltzes, études, ballades, sonatas, and nocturnes were often based on old folk themes. Polish folk songs are lighthearted and sad at the same time. Many folk dances—such as the polonaise, mazurka, krakowiak, and others—are still danced today, while at the same time, almost every Polish village also has a contemporary-music club. Western rock and movie stars are well known and popular.

CITIES

Warsaw (Warszawa). For centuries, the Poles prided themselves on their intellectual ties to the West, especially to France and Italy. Many consider Warsaw an eastern, smaller version of Paris. Located in the heart of Poland, Warsaw is the largest city in the country, the center of trade and industry, and one of the liveliest capitals in Central Europe. It is famous for its institutions of higher learning, especially the University of Warsaw; its theater and concert halls; and its great museums and libraries. Warsaw's music festivals, particularly the Chopin competition, attract some of the most gifted young artists from around the world.

Occupation by the Nazis took its toll on Warsaw. Much of the city was left in ruins by the German army at the end of World War II. The rebuilding of the Old Town was modeled on more than 300 pictures of Warsaw that had originally been painted by the Italian artist Bernardo Bellotto (1720–80). Warsaw's reconstructed palaces and handsome 18th-century mansions today house government agencies and academies of arts and sciences. Among the city's best-known landmarks are the Cathedral of Saint John, which dates from 1360, and Casimir Palace, the home of the University of Warsaw, founded in 1818. One of the finest modern buildings is the radium institute and hospital built in honor of Marie (Marja) Skłodowska, a Polish girl who went to France, married Pierre Curie, and with him discovered radium. They shared the Nobel Prize in Physics in 1903. Eight years later Marie Curie won the Nobel Prize in Chemistry, becoming the only person to win prizes in both categories.

Cracow.   The capital of Poland until 1609, Cracow remains one of the intellectual centers of the country and one of Europe's most beautiful historic cities. In Cracow the charm of a medieval town blends with the bustle of the 20th century. The royal castle of Wawel, located on a hill overlooking the Vistula, was built nearly 1,000 years ago. Its majestic chambers are filled with a rich collection of tapestries and other medieval art objects. The Gothic cathedral next to the castle contains the tombs of most of the country's kings and other famous personages. Many poets are buried there, since, according to old Polish tradition, great poets are equal to kings.

Cracow is also the home of the Jagiellonian University, which was founded in 1364 and has become a leading center of culture and learning in Central Europe. It has produced some of the world's greatest scholars, including Nicolaus Copernicus (1473–1543), the astronomer who was the first scientist to postulate that Earth revolves around the Sun. His labo-

Cracow, the former capital of Poland, retains much of its medieval atmosphere.

Scores of modern buildings have been built in Warsaw since World War II, when the city was nearly leveled.

ratory has been preserved in the medieval part of the campus and is still used by the university.

Located close to the industrial area around Katowice, Cracow has unfortunately become a victim of reckless development. Pollution is destroying many monuments, and outdoor statues are disintegrating. Poland will need massive international aid to stop this deterioration.

ECONOMY

Before World War II, Poland was largely an agricultural country. Today, because of the growth of industries and the movement of young people to the cities, only 30 percent of the population remains in the countryside. When the Communists came to power, they tried to establish a system of collective agriculture. Polish farmers resisted, forcing the Communists to dismantle most of these cooperatives in 1956 and to allow private ownership of farms.

Today, agriculture produces about 7 percent of the gross national product, but it employs a quarter of the working population. Thanks to government support after 1989, many farmers have been able to build new houses for their families, but overall productivity remains low. Many peasants still sow by hand, reap the grain with scythes, and milk their cows manually. The main agricultural products are wheat, barley, and sugar beets; some grain and fodder must be imported.

Potatoes, cabbages, beets, mushrooms, dairy products, and some meat—mostly pork—form the bulk of the Polish diet. Favorite dishes include *bigos,* a mixture of sauerkraut and sausage; *kielbasa,* smoked sausage; *barszca,* beet soup served with many meat and vegetable accompaniments; and *kolduny,* a pastry with meat filling. Polish ham and bacon are widely exported, as is Polish vodka, made from potatoes and grain.

Poland has extensive coal deposits, but it must import petroleum and iron ore. Other natural resources include lead, zinc, natural gas, lignite, salt, copper, manganese, uranium, phosphates, and sulfur.

By the mid-1950s, the Communists had nationalized all industry, trade, and banking. Steel production centered around the city of Nowa Huta, a textile industry developed in Łódź, and huge shipyards on the Baltic began to produce ships for sale all over the world.

After workers' riots in the early 1970s, the government announced plans to modernize the Polish economy. Unfortunately, the reforms were badly mismanaged, and led to overall impoverishment throughout the country. In the 1970s and 1980s, the standard of living declined.

In 1990, the first post-Communist government introduced a radical "shock therapy" to transform the economic system. Price controls were abandoned, and subsidies to industries, agriculture, and households were slashed. The initial results were stores filled with goods that few people could afford, three-digit inflation, and rising unemployment.

In 1994, however, Poland's economy began to recover, and by the end of the decade it was growing at the fastest rate in the region. The private sector has replaced state enterprises, and the financial situation of one-half of the population has improved. Most families now have kitchen appliances and television, and the number of main telephone lines increased from about 6 million in 1995 to over 10 million by the early 2000s. Yet Poland is still a relatively poor country, compared not only to Western Europe, but also to the Czech Republic and Hungary.

Trade with Russia, for years the major partner, dwindled to almost a trickle after the Russian financial crisis of 1998. About two-thirds of all Polish foreign trade in 2000 was with European Union (EU) countries.

A dry dock at Gdańsk, Solidarity's birthplace. In 1998, the shipyard was sold to a shipbuilding consortium.

Advanced and efficient assembly techniques have helped Poland to streamline its automobile industry.

Since the early 1990s, Poland—eagerly preparing to join the EU—has been introducing the necessary changes in legislation. It expects to become a member of the organization in 2004.

HISTORY

Slavic tribes probably inhabited some regions of present-day Poland as early as 2000 to 1000 B.C. In the 10th century, Prince Mieszko married a Christian princess from Bohemia (today part of the Czech Republic) and accepted her faith for himself and his people. Conversion to Christianity marked Poland's entrance into Western civilization.

In the next few centuries, under the rule of the Piast dynasty, Poland fought numerous wars with its neighbors and suffered from internal conflicts. In 1386, however, the Poles united with the Lithuanians and emerged, under the powerful Jagiellonian dynasty, as one of the strongest states of Central Europe.

The 16th century was Poland's golden age. The commonwealth stretched from the Baltic to the Black Sea and reached almost to the gates of Moscow. Universities were built. Brilliant literature was written. The church had great influence in state affairs. Many Jews driven out by neighboring countries were welcomed in Poland, where the gentry, uninterested in handicrafts and trading, encouraged the Jews to become shopkeepers and traders. During this period the nobility, who made up about 10 percent of the population, acquired immense independent political power. After 1572 they elected the king. Theoretically, each member of the nobility was eligible to be chosen as king. In addition, any member could stop the proceedings of the parliament (Sejm) or block any law by saying "veto," the Latin for "I forbid." The unrestrained use of this veto power gradually paralyzed the entire government. The weakness of the government and internal disorders (such as the peasant uprising against Polish domination in Ukraine in 1648–49) invited foreign intervention from neighboring Russia, Prussia, and Sweden. These wars drained the country's scattered strength and poorly used resources. Even so, there were occasional victories. The Poles believe they were saved from Swedish conquest in 1655 by the Miracle of Częstochowa. A 40-day siege of the fortified monastery at Jasna Góra is said to have ended because the abbot held up a portrait of the Madonna that the people believed had been painted by Saint Luke. To this day the monastery, the holiest Polish shrine, is visited each year by about 200,000 pilgrims. Poland's last important ruler, King John III Sobieski, was a brilliant military leader. He helped save Europe from Turkish invaders by defeating them at Vienna in 1683.

Decline and Downfall

But Sobieski could not save his own country from internal decay. From the time of his death in 1696 until early in the 20th century, the Poles had no real self-government.

In 1772 part of Poland was divided among the Russians, Prussians, and Austrians. A second partition by Russia and Prussia in 1793 carved up most of the rest of the country. There were various attempts at revolt. In 1794 Thaddeus Kosciusko (Tadeusz Kościuszko), a Polish general who had fought in the American Revolution, tried to unite his countrymen to drive the Russians and Prussians out of Poland and to free the peasants from serfdom. The Poles fought fiercely, but were defeated, and in 1795 the country was partitioned for a third time by Russia, Prussia, and Austria. Poland disappeared from the map of Europe. In the part controlled by Russia, Poles repeatedly rebelled against their overlords, but were always defeated. During these difficult times, only the Roman Catholic Church kept alive the spirit of the Polish nation.

Independence and Two World Wars

In the late 19th century, Polish emigrants in Paris, London, and New York formed groups to work for a free Poland. They cooperated with various political associations inside the partitioned country. At the beginning of the 20th century, this drive for independence was led by Józef Piłsudski, founder of the Polish Legions during World War I; Ignace Paderewski, the famous Polish pianist; and Roman Dmowski, leader of the National Democratic Party.

The Treaty of Versailles in 1919 established Poland as a fully independent republic, and Józef Piłsudski became the first president of the new state. In the next two decades, economic and political problems and boundary disputes with the neighboring countries plagued Poland. In 1926 Piłsudski took complete power, and then ruled as a virtual dictator until his death in 1935.

Although Poland concluded a 10-year nonaggression treaty with Germany in 1934, Nazi forces attacked the country on September 1, 1939, without formally declaring war. Two days later Britain and France, which had promised to protect Poland, declared war on Germany. World War

II had begun. While German forces launched their blitzkrieg ("lightning war") on Poland from the west, the Soviet Union struck at Poland from the east. Again the Poles fought stubbornly but in vain. Germany took the western part of Poland, the Soviet Union the eastern part. In 1941, when Germany attacked the Soviet Union, all of Poland came under German occupation.

Hitler had sworn he would obliterate the country, and he almost succeeded. More than one-fifth of the people were killed or died as a result of the war. Of the major cities in Poland, Warsaw was 84 percent destroyed, Wrocław 80 percent, and Gdańsk and Gdynia 50 percent. Every third person lost his farm, home, or apartment. Despite the suffering, many thousands of Poles were involved in a large, well-organized resistance movement, which supplied the Western Allies with information about Nazi troop movements and sabotaged German war efforts.

No group in Poland suffered more than the Polish Jews. In 1940 the Germans herded 500,000 Jews from Warsaw and nearby areas into a part of the city around which high walls were built. In April 1943, the surviving Jews rose in revolt. The battle of the Warsaw Ghetto lasted one month,

A monument in the former Warsaw Ghetto honors Jews killed in the 1943 uprising against the Nazis.

and only 200 Warsaw Jews survived. Near Cracow is Oświęcim (Auschwitz), the site of the most infamous Nazi concentration camp, where Dr. Josef Mengele performed his appalling human medical experiments and where about 1.5 million inmates were systematically murdered in the gas chambers.

Other camps at Birkenau and Treblinka were also huge "death factories." Poland lost most of its political leaders, educators, and intellectuals in concentration camps. The country also lost more than 1 million of its workers, most of whom were deported to slave-labor camps in the Soviet Union.

When the Germans were finally turned back by the Russians, the Soviet army invaded German-controlled Poland. Late in the summer of 1944, as the Soviet armies approached the Polish capital, the people of

Warsaw rose up against the Germans, expecting the advancing Soviet troops to come to their aid. Instead, the Soviets stayed on the east bank of the Vistula River, and Warsaw was reduced to rubble.

Rule by the Communists

As a result of the war, Poland was "moved" to the west: the Soviet Union took over former eastern Polish lands, and Poland was given former German territories east of the Oder and Neisse rivers. The shift involved a huge population transfer, with about 6 million Germans leaving the country and some 7.5 million Poles moving from east to west.

Another result of the war was the gradual Communist takeover, which was complete by late 1948. Mass political arrests followed, and a Soviet-style constitution was adopted in 1952. Yet popular support for the regime was less than halfhearted. (Poland was one of the few Soviet satellites that never built a monument to Stalin.) In 1956, worker riots led to the elevation of Władysław Gomułka, a nationalist Communist leader, to the post of first secretary of the Communist Party and to gradual liberalization of the regime. Collective farms were broken up and returned to their owners, and relations with the church improved. This trend was reversed in the late 1960s and, during another wave of worker riots in December 1970, at least 44 people were killed.

In 1978, Polish national feelings were greatly boosted by the elevation of Karol Wojtyła, the archbishop of Cracow, to the papacy. When Pope John Paul II visited his homeland in 1979, he was welcomed by millions. This upsurge of pride strengthened the resolve of many Poles to challenge the Communist regime. A new wave of strikes in 1980 resulted in the formation of new independent trade unions, named Solidarity, which was led by a Gdańsk electrician, Lech Wałęsa.

During 1981, Solidarity grew to a 10-million-member movement. Pressed by the Soviet Union, the new first secretary of the Communist Party, General Wojciech Jaruzelski, declared martial law in December 1981. He suspended Solidarity and arrested some 10,000 people. All freedoms and rights gained in the previous 15 months were abolished.

The government ended martial law in 1983, the same year that Lech Wałęsa received the Nobel Peace Prize. While the economic conditions kept deteriorating, Solidarity, although banned, continued its activities. Communist leaders gradually realized that the only way to overcome the brewing crisis was through national reconciliation, and began talks with Solidarity. The Communist era formally ended in August 1989 when Solidarity member Tadeusz Mazowiecki became prime minister.

Post-Communist Poland

The exhilarating year of 1989, which brought the collapse of other Eastern European Communist regimes as well, ushered in a new era for Poland and with it, new problems. The Solidarity movement split and many former friends became bitter opponents. A "shock therapy" economic reform was instituted that led to huge inflation and massive unemployment. Lech Wałęsa became president in late 1990, but his initial popularity soon declined in the face of economic hardship.

Former Communists, who renamed their party the Alliance of the Democratic Left, capitalized on popular discontent and won roughly 20 percent of the popular vote in parliamentary elections held in 1993. They

The labor union Solidarity led the struggle for more freedom for the Polish people.

became the nation's strongest party and later completed their comeback when their candidate, Aleksander Kwaśniewski, defeated the incumbent, Lech Wałęsa, in the November 1995 presidential elections. Kwaśniewski's moderate political agenda resembled that of a Western European Social Democratic politician.

In November 1997, Solidarity Action, a conglomerate of about 40 right-of-center parties, won in the parliamentary elections. One of its first measures was a thorough administrative overhaul, giving more power to local authorities. The coalition fell apart in June 2000 because of disagreements over economic policy. In the presidential election of October 2000, Aleksander Kwaśniewski defeated Lech Wałęsa once again, and the latter retired from politics. In September 2001, a post-Communist coalition received overwhelming support from voters, reflecting the general public's disappointment with the scandal-plagued, rightist government.

In March 1999, Poland joined NATO, shortly before the bombing of Yugoslavia. The Polish government fully supported this action.

GOVERNMENT

Poland today is a republic, with a bicameral parliament and a strong presidency. Sejm, the National Assembly, has 460 members, and the Senate has 100 members. In the first few years after the demise of Communism, 29 political parties were represented in the parliament. This number shrank to six after passage of an electoral law that requires 5 percent of the vote to gain representation in the parliament. A new constitution was adopted by Poland in 1997.

Reviewed by EDWARD W. WALKER, Ph.D., Columbia University

Prague is world famous for its beautifully preserved medieval section.

CZECH REPUBLIC

The Czech Republic is the heir to the medieval kingdom of Bohemia and its sister principalities of Moravia and Silesia. For most of the 20th century, the Czech Republic was part of Czechoslovakia, which comprised Bohemia, Moravia, a small slice of Silesia, and Slovakia.

The union of Czechs and Slovaks, two related Slavic peoples, was never quite harmonious, and in the post-Communist era of nationalist disintegrations, it has resulted in a peaceful parting of ways. In reference to the smooth overthrow of Communist rule in late 1989, some journalists dubbed the end of Czechoslovakia a "velvet divorce."

THE LAND

Bohemia is a plateau region of rolling land encircled by the Bohemian Forest, the Erzgebirge (Ore Mountains), and the Sudetes Mountains. This part of the country is drained by the Labe (Elbe) River and its main tributary, the Vltava (Moldau). Prague, the capital of the Czech Republic, lies just in the center of Bohemia. Plzeň, Kladno, Liberec, and Jáchymov are the major industrial cities and towns.

Moravia lies to the east of Bohemia. The Moravian lowland, an important farming and industrial region, is drained by the Morava River, which flows into the Danube, giving the country an all-water route to the Black Sea. Brno, the largest city in Moravia, is a busy industrial center.

Silesia is the name of a historic region that now lies mostly in southwestern Poland and eastern Germany. The narrow, mountainous slice of Silesia in the Czech Republic, north of Moravia, is a vital source of coal and iron. The main industrial city is Ostrava.

During the Communist era, several parts of the country, particularly the northwest and the northeast, were devastated by industrial pollution, but thanks to a series of ecological measures, the countryside has revived markedly in recent years.

THE PEOPLE

The earliest known inhabitants of the present Czech Republic were two Celtic groups, the Boii and the Cotini. The Boii lived in the Bohemian basin, giving it the name it still bears today. In the middle of the 5th century, Slavic tribes from the east settled in the valley of the Elbe, and apparently mingled with the local Celtic population.

Czech is written in the Latin alphabet and is distinguished by a multitude of diacritical marks (accents) that indicate the length of vowels and a soft pronunciation of many consonants.

The word "Bohemian," which is frequently used to indicate a person of artistic, unconventional temperament rather than an inhabitant of Bohemia, was first used in France in the 15th century for Gypsies who were thought to have come to the West from Bohemia. In English, the word appeared in the 19th century.

There are several minorities: Slovaks, often in mixed marriages, who moved to the Czech Republic during the existence of Czechoslovakia; Poles in the north; and a small minority of Germans. The largest minority are the Romanies (Gypsies), who number 200,000 to 300,000.

Religion. The predominant religion of the country is Roman Catholicism, but there are also a number of Protestant churches. Although the freethinking Czechs are religiously lukewarm, churches have become more visible during the 1990s, and some sects, such as the Jehovah's Witnesses, have gained new members. The Jewish community, an important part of Czech life for centuries, is now very small.

Education. Free compulsory education begins at the age of six and lasts nine years. Since the fall of Communism, the educational system has been changing, and private and parochial schools are being established. There are several types of secondary and vocational schools, and more than 20 institutions of higher learning.

Music, Spas, and Sports. The country's spirit, a mixture of cheerfulness, melancholy, and irony, is expressed in the music of its two foremost 19th-century composers, Bedřich Smetana and Antonín Dvořák. The major 20th-century composer is Leoš Janáček, whose symphonies and operas often are performed in the West. People love to sing the moody folk songs in city and country pubs, but the younger generation looks to Western rock stars for musical inspiration.

The great spas of Karlovy Vary, Mariánské Lázně, Františkovy Lázně, and many others have given real or imaginary relief to people from all over the world who came there suffering from a variety of afflictions. Karlovy Vary is a favorite place for affluent Russians, but virtually any Czech can have a spa cure prescribed by a doctor at very little or no cost.

Winter sports have always been popular, especially skiing and ice hockey. When the Czech hockey team won the Olympic gold medal in 1998, the whole country indulged in celebration. The traditional national sport is soccer. During the 1980s, Czechoslovakia produced such top tennis players as Martina Navratilova (who won 18 Grand Slam singles titles) and Ivan Lendl (winner of eight Grand Slam singles titles).

Food. Roast pork with dumplings and sauerkraut is the traditional national dish. Since the 14th century, Czechs have raised carp in numerous ponds, particularly in southern Bohemia. Carp, much tastier than its wild American cousin, is a traditional food for Christmas Eve dinner. Pastry baking (and eating) is a national pastime.

PRAGUE

Prague, the capital, is more than 1,000 years old. Around A.D. 965, a Jewish merchant from Spain described it as a busy town built of stone, where Slavs, Muslims, Jews, and Turks traded their goods. The brightest periods of Prague's history were always those times when the city opened itself to the world. During the reign of Emperor Charles IV in the 14th century, Prague attracted famous architects and sculptors from the rest of Europe. Around 1600, Emperor Rudolf II invited noted astronomers, artists, and musicians to his court. In the 19th century, Prague became a cultural center for the national Czech revival. After 1918 it was again a bustling, vigorous place, full of old charms and contemporary attractions.

Prague always has been a music-minded city. Wolfgang Amadeus Mozart wrote *Don Giovanni* for the German Theater in Prague and conducted the first performance there. Today the music of Mozart and other composers can be heard at countless concerts, particularly during the annual spring music festival.

In the 1920s, Jaroslav Hašek wrote his famous novel about *The Good Soldier Schweik,* who seems stupid but is actually mocking the authori-

The town of Cesky Krumlov is picturesquely set in southern Bohemia, near the Austrian border.

ties. At the same time, the German Jewish Prague writer Franz Kafka envisioned much of the absurdity and anxiety of 20th-century life in such novels as *The Metamorphosis* and *The Trial*.

The post-Communist Prague is a lively city, with a rich cultural and social life and with thousands of foreigners from all parts of the world. Many old buildings in Prague have been beautifully restored, and several sections in the city's center are now pedestrian zones. Prague is less dazzling than such European cities as Paris or London, but it is a magical place that can possess one's soul. Among its many landmarks is one of Europe's oldest synagogues, with 13th-century Gothic architecture. Prague also has great baroque palaces, romantic squares with stone fountains, narrow cobblestone streets, mysterious passageways, and old churches with tombs sunk deep in the ground.

But not everything is old in Prague: the elegant modern subway, glass-walled structures scattered among the historical buildings, and traffic jams remind everyone that this is indeed a modern city.

ECONOMY

The Erzgebirge Mountains, running astride the border between Bohemia and Germany, have for centuries yielded valuable minerals—not only silver, but also tin, lead, bismuth, zinc, and antimony. In 1727, large deposits of pitchblende, a greasy-looking ore containing uranium and radium, were discovered there. It was from Jáchymov pitchblende that the Curies, after years of experimentation, extracted radium.

In the 19th century, Bohemia and Moravia became the most industrialized parts of the Austro-Hungarian Empire. After the formation of Czechoslovakia in 1918, the country began to develop worldwide markets for such products as glassware and textiles. Czech plants also manufactured just about anything that could be made of steel—from railroad rolling stock to machine tools. Four automobile works—Praga, Aero, Skoda, and Tatra—

Much of the new commercial architecture in Prague takes bold steps in the abstract direction.

began to produce and export cars. The Bat'a shoe factories in Zlín, Moravia, became the largest enterprise of this kind in Europe, selling inexpensive mass-produced shoes to many countries. Tomáš Bat'a, the founder of the company, had spent some time in the United States and became an admirer of Henry Ford, whose industrial practices he then adapted in Czechoslovakia. The trademark "Made in Czechoslovakia" became well known throughout the world.

After the War. Soon after the conclusion of World War II, more than 2 million Sudeten-Germans, who had lived for centuries in the Sudetes Mountains near the German border, were expelled from Czechoslovakia. The expulsion was a bitter result of wartime hostilities, but it dealt a heavy blow to the Czechoslovak economy because many of the expelled Germans were highly skilled craftsmen and technicians.

Following the Communist victory in 1948, virtually all economic activities were taken over by the state: railroads, banking, heavy and light industry, and services. Although the country recovered from the war years and new industries were developed, the centralized economy did not perform well, and Czechoslovakia began to lag behind Western Europe; it had been one of the most prosperous countries before 1938. Still, Czechoslovakia had a higher standard of living than most other Communist countries and never experienced really serious shortages.

Toward a Free-Market Economy. The new post-Communist government made progress toward a free-market economy one of its highest priorities, and quickly embarked—under the leadership of Václav Klaus, first finance minister and later premier—on a thorough economic transformation. Large companies were privatized in a complex coupon scheme that seemed to work well until about 1995. It turned out, however, that dozens of unscrupulous entrepreneurs had taken advantage of loopholes and embezzled huge amounts of money from enterprises and banks. In the late 1990s, the country experienced an economic slowdown, but by 2000, the prospects looked better, as an increasing number of international companies established headquarters in this European heartland. The opening of a new Czech nuclear plant at Temelin has been the source of controversy: since the summer of 2000, many Austrians have strenuously opposed the facility.

Under Communism, land was either in collective farms or in state farms. Land is being returned to its previous owners, but some farmers have opted to stay in the collectives. The country has traditionally been self-sufficient in terms of food production.

Since the 1980s, the Czech Republic has made great progress in the field of information technology. Computers are commonplace, and the number of Internet users increases almost daily. Cell phones are also quite ubiquitous: among the nation's 10 million residents, there are 8 million cell-phone users.

An important source of income is tourism. People from more than 100 other countries travel to the Czech Republic each year.

HISTORY

The kingdom of Bohemia took shape in the 10th century, under the patron saint of the country, Saint Wenceslaus. In 1310, a German prince, John of Luxemburg, was elected king, and under the rule of his son Charles, Czechs experienced the most brilliant chapter of their history. Charles became king of Bohemia in 1346, and Holy Roman emperor in 1355. Although brought up in France, he fell in love with Bohemia and made it the center of the empire. Prague's architecture still recalls this era: the most famous of the city's many bridges across the Vltava River, Charles Bridge, was completed in 1357 and is a magnificent structure with its tower gateways and statues of saints. Charles was also the patron of a Prague school of painting. He ordered the development of a Latin-Czech dictionary, and in 1348 he founded Charles University of Prague, today one of the oldest in Europe.

One of the greatest Czechs of all time, John Huss (Jan Hus), was elected rector of Charles University in 1402. A forerunner of the Protestant movement, Huss was a religious reformer, and his teachings brought on a long struggle, partly religious and partly political, called the Hussite wars. Two outstanding leaders of the Hussites were Jan Žižka of Trocnov and George of Poděbrad, who became king in 1458.

After a flourishing period of Czech renaissance in the second half of the 16th century, Czech Protestant armies were defeated in 1620 by Habsburg forces in the Battle of the White Mountain, near Prague. With that defeat, Bohemia and Moravia lost their independence, which was not to be regained for almost 300 years. The battle was one of the first engagements in the Thirty Years' War, between Protestants and Catholics, which wracked Europe from 1618 to 1648.

During the late 18th and early 19th centuries, many of the subject peoples living in the Austrian Empire began to agitate for more freedom and autonomy within the empire. In 1848, there were revolutions in many parts of Europe, including Bohemia. The Czechs did not win all they hoped for, but, by the end of the century, they did obtain a number of political rights. Meanwhile, an intellectual revival and the growth of industry helped create a strong middle class, and the Czechs were reawakening as a nation. At that time, contacts between Czechs and their Slavic neighbors to the east, Slovaks, began to flourish.

The First Republic

After World War I broke out in 1914, various groups of Czech intellectuals and politicians decided to push for independence, and some Slovak leaders came up with the idea of uniting the two nations. In October 1918, Czechoslovakia emerged as one of the successor states of the Austro-Hungarian Empire.

During the time of the so-called First Republic (1918–38), Czechoslovakia was a prosperous democratic state, but the emerging German Nazism eventually undermined it. The country's large Sudeten-German minority—about 3 million people—succumbed to Nazi propaganda and turned into pawns in Hitler's aggressive plans. In September 1938, Britain, France, and Italy signed the infamous Munich agreement, which made the Sudetenland a part of Germany. The amputee Czechoslovakia lingered for six months, and in March 1939 split into an "independent" Slovak state and a German Protectorate of Bohemia and Moravia. In September 1939, World War II began.

The Communist Period. After the war, a brief democratic interlude ended in February 1948 when the Communists took power in a bloodless coup d'etat. Thereafter, all industries and businesses were nationalized and strict censorship was introduced. Purges and show trials in the early 1950s strengthened the party's position. Ultimately, more than 200,000 were imprisoned; tens of thousands had their property confiscated; about 170,000 emigrated; and 248 were executed.

The 1968 "Prague Spring" liberalization movement in the former Czechoslovakia flourished briefly before being crushed by Warsaw Pact troops.

In 1968, under the leadership of Alexander Dubček, the country underwent eight hectic months of liberalization known as the Prague Spring. The efforts to introduce "socialism with a human face," however, were crushed by the Warsaw Pact armies in August 1968, and, for the next two decades, Czechoslovakia had one of the most repressive Communist regimes in Eastern Europe. Among those who suffered most were writers, scholars, and journalists. In 1977, the dissident Charter 77 movement was born; its initiator was the future president, playwright Václav Havel. Meanwhile, readers in the West were reading about Communist Czechoslovakia in books by Milan Kundera, an internationally acclaimed Czech writer living in France.

After 1989's "Velvet Revolution" (above), Czechs enthusiastically moved toward a Western-style economy.

The Post-Communist Beginnings and the End of Czechoslovakia. In late 1989, the Communist regime collapsed during the "Velvet Revolution," and President Havel, an outspoken advocate of open-society principles, became the darling of the population at home and of audiences abroad. Soon, however, euphoria was replaced by Czech-Slovak tensions, which ultimately led to the "velvet divorce": the division of Czechoslovakia into two successor countries, on January 1, 1993.

The Czech Republic. Although most Czechs regretted the end of Czechoslovakia, they turned energetically to the task of building a new society. For several years, the country was in an upswing mood, with rising salaries and people taking vacations in the previously forbidden West. The Civic Democratic Party, led by charismatic Václav Klaus, reassured Czech citizens that the road to prosperity would be short and painless. The government, however, continued to support unprofitable businesses and did not set up clear financial rules, inadvertently providing many loopholes for fraudulent business transactions. In 1997, economic tightening and problems with party financing led to the fall of Klaus' government and widespread dissatisfaction. In early elections the following year, the winner was the Social Democratic Party, which ruled in a quasicoalition with the Civic Democrats. In 2002, the Social Democrats won 30 percent of the vote and the unreformed Communist Party 18 percent. The Czech Republic joined NATO in 1999, and is slated to join the European Union (EU) around 2004.

GOVERNMENT

The Czech Republic is a democratic country, with a largely ceremonial presidency. The chief executive is the prime minister. The Parliament consists of two houses: the 200-member Chamber of Deputies and the 81-member Senate.

IRINA RYBACEK / Reviewed by EDWARD W. WALKER, Ph.D., Columbia University

Castles, cathedrals, and other historic buildings grace Bratislava, Slovakia's capital city.

SLOVAKIA

A small Slavic country in the heart of Europe, Slovakia was for most of the 20th century the less populous and less developed part of Czechoslovakia. The union with the Czechs, although initially proposed by the Slovaks themselves, was from the very beginning a marriage of unequal partners. The post-Communist yearning for national independence resulted in the dissolution of Czechoslovakia on January 1, 1993.

THE LAND

Slovakia borders Poland to the north, Ukraine to the east, Hungary and Austria to the south, and the Czech Republic to the west. It is a beautiful mountainous country, with soaring peaks in the High Tatras of the Carpathian Mountains. In the center of Slovakia stretches another range, the Low Tatras, which are known for their many ski slopes.

The southern part of Slovakia, along the border with Hungary, is a fertile lowland. A generally mild climate makes possible the cultivation of such crops as peppers, melons, and sunflowers.

The largest river of Slovakia is the Danube, which forms the border with Hungary and connects the country with the Black Sea. The Danube's main tributaries are the Váh and the Hron.

THE PEOPLE

Slovaks are descended from Slavic tribes that settled in the area during the 5th and 6th centuries A.D. The Slovak language, which was codified only in the 19th century, is very similar to Czech and belongs to the West Slavic group (together with Polish). A large Hungarian minority (about 600,000 people) lives in southern Slovakia; there are also several hundred thousand Romanies (or Gypsies).

Although Slovakia was part of Hungary until 1918, close contacts between Czechs and Slovaks had already developed during the nationalist renaissance of the 19th century. After the formation of the Czechoslovak republic in 1918, however, the differences between the Czech and the Slovak ways of life and the contrasts between the overall political and economic development of the two parts of the new state caused problems. The Czechs built up Slovak schools, communications, and many institutions, but they also neglected the Slovak economy and often behaved in a patronizing manner. Slovaks resented the Czech patronage, and this animosity eventually led to the formation of an independent Slovak state in 1939.

After the Communist takeover in 1948, the old Slovak resentments were for decades muted by the repressive policies of the Communist regime. Most Czechs were not even aware of these feelings, and tended to see their eastern compatriots as "Czechs who happen to speak Slovak." Despite the initial ecstatic rejoicing over the fall of the old regime in late 1989, a strong revival of Slovak nationalism soon developed. By mid-1992, the two nations had embarked on the road to separation.

Religion.   Traditionally, rural Slovakia has been heavily Roman Catholic. Small Protestant churches have typically attracted Slovaks who felt closer to Czech culture.

Education.   When Slovakia became part of Czechoslovakia, the educational level of the majority of its inhabitants was low. Hungarian authorities had systematically suppressed the Slovak culture for years and, in the late 19th century, even engaged in forceful "magyarization." The major cultural Slovak institution, the Slovak Association, which had been founded in 1863, was suspended in 1875.

After 1918, educational levels throughout Czechoslovakia gradually became comparable, and at present Slovakia has a well-developed educational system, with 14 institutions of higher learning.

Slovaks celebrated when their country and the Czech Republic became separate nations in 1993.

FACTS AND FIGURES

OFFICIAL NAME: Slovak Republic.

NATIONALITY: Slovak(s).

CAPITAL AND CHIEF CITY: Bratislava.

LOCATION: Central Europe. **Boundaries**—Poland, Ukraine, Hungary, Austria, Czech Republic.

AREA: 18,859 sq. mi. (48,845 sq. km.).

PHYSICAL FEATURES: Highest point—Gerlachovka (8,711 ft.; 2,655 m.). **Lowest point**—308 ft. (94 m.), in the southeast. **Chief rivers**—Danube, Váh.

POPULATION: 5,400,000 (2002; annual growth 0.0%).

MAJOR LANGUAGES: Slovak (official), Hungarian.

MAJOR RELIGION: Roman Catholicism.

GOVERNMENT: Parliamentary democracy. **Head of state**—president. **Head of government**—prime minister. **Legislature**—unicameral National Council of the Slovak Republic.

ECONOMY: Chief minerals—coal, iron ore, copper. **Chief agricultural products**—grains, potatoes, sugar beets, hops. **Industries and products**—metal, food and beverages. **Chief exports**—machinery, chemicals. **Chief imports**—machinery and transport equipment, fuels, chemicals.

MONETARY UNIT: 1 koruna = 100 halierov.

NATIONAL HOLIDAY: September 1 (Constitution Day).

Because of greater economic and cultural opportunities, large numbers of Slovaks have always gravitated toward the Czech Republic. There are thousands of mixed marriages, and Czechs and Slovaks remain on very friendly terms, despite the split of Czechoslovakia. Eastern Slovakia, around the city of Košice, is the most pro-Czech region.

Bratislava. Situated on the Danube, the capital of Slovakia is a leading river port. It is an old city, mentioned in written sources as early as the 10th century A.D. It was part of Hungary until 1918, and, from 1526 to 1784, served as the Hungarian capital.

Other Cities. The second-largest city in Slovakia is **Košice,** an industrial center and a seat of three universities. **Trnava** dates from the 13th century, and later was an important trade center.

THE ECONOMY

Historically, Slovakia was a very poor and backward region. Between 1867 and 1914, more than 500,000 Slovaks emigrated, most of them to the United States.

During the Communist era, mammoth industrial enterprises were built, producing mainly steel and various types of armaments. This concentration of heavy industry was a contributing factor to the splitting of Czechoslovakia: a reduction of arms exports in the early 1990s led to high unemployment in several regions. Since 1993, there has been some economic transformation, and in major cities the living standards are higher than during the Communist era. The countryside is much poorer, particularly in places formerly dependent on a single large employer.

HISTORY

The Danube formed the northernmost boundary of the Roman Empire, and Roman legions occasionally entered present-day Slovakia. In the 9th century, Slovakia was a part of Greater Moravia, the first important Slavic state in Central Europe.

Magyars came in the 10th century, and, from the next century onward, Slovakia was part of Hungary, generally known as Upper Hungary. Contacts with Czechs and Moravians to the west were sporadic; during the Hussite wars in the 15th century, for instance, large parts of Slovakia came under the influence of Hussite leaders.

In the 19th century, Slovak intellectuals codified the language, organized national Slovak associations, and began to press for political freedoms. During World War I, a young Slovak general, M. R. Štefánik, together with Czech leaders T. G. Masaryk and Eduard Beneš, set out to create a new state of Czechs and Slovaks. Important support for this goal came from the Slovak community in the United States. The Pittsburgh Agreement of May 1918 confirmed the decision to form a common state of Czechs and Slovaks, to be called Czecho-Slovakia (to indicate that it was a union of two nations). Later, however, the Czechoslovak government adopted the view that there was one Czechoslovak nation.

Despite material and cultural improvements during the interwar period, Slovakia remained in the position of junior partner, and many Slovak nationalists became ardently anti-Czech. These attitudes culminated in the creation of a separate Slovak state in 1939 after the Nazi invasion of Bohemia and Moravia. A Nazi vassal, the state (much smaller than present-day Slovakia, with the southern areas under Hungarian control) was independent in name only.

After the war, Czechoslovakia was reconstituted, and the "Slovak question" was submerged by Communist rule. The constitution of 1960, proclaiming Czechoslovakia a socialist republic, further strengthened the central government of Prague. Slovak dissatisfaction then became one of the factors leading to the short-lived "Prague Spring," a period of liberalization in 1968. One name indelibly linked with these eight months is that of Alexander Dubček, a soft-spoken Slovak Communist who became the head of the Czechoslovak Communist Party in January 1968.

The federalization law, adopted in January 1969, was the only reform of the Prague Spring that survived the Soviet occupation of August 1968. Czechoslovakia thus became a federal republic.

Independent Slovakia. Economic difficulties in the post-Communist transformation of Czechoslovakia led to high unemployment in Slovakia, which in turn fueled anti-Czech sentiment. The populist leader Vladimír Mečiar then negotiated the division of Czechoslovakia.

The "velvet divorce" took place on January 1, 1993, and many Slovaks—particularly the intelligentsia—deeply regretted it. Mečiar's autocratic ways led to his temporary downfall from the premiership in 1994, but he regained his post after early elections later that year. He became embroiled in an ugly political conflict with the country's president. At the same time, several international organizations criticized Slovakia for restrictions of political freedoms. In the 1998 elections, Mečiar was unexpectedly defeated by a democratic coalition, which has significantly improved the country's international standing. Slovakia hopes to join NATO and the European Union (EU) in the foreseeable future.

GOVERNMENT

Slovakia has a 150-member unicameral parliament and a ceremonial presidency. The chief executive is the prime minister.

IRINA RYBACEK / Reviewed by EDWARD W. WALKER, Ph.D., Columbia University

Budapest, Hungary's capital, was originally two cities, Buda and Pest, separated by the Danube River.

HUNGARY

In the heart of Europe is a small nation that for more than 1,000 years has struggled with great powers to remain independent. It is the Republic of Hungary, home of the Magyars, or Hungarians, who speak an Ugro-Finnic language. Hungarian is not related to the three major European language groups—Germanic, Romance, and Slavic.

Hungarians discarded Communist rule in a most undramatic way in 1989 and have been rebuilding their country ever since. They have a tendency to emphasize problems and difficulties, yet by the late 1990s they had completed the fundamental post-Communist transformation. Hungary joined NATO in early 1999.

THE LAND

As a result of World War I, Hungary was reduced to one-fourth of its former size and is now a landlocked country. The Danube River, or Duna in Hungarian, which forms part of the Slovak-Hungarian border, turns south and cuts through the country, flowing in a southerly direction. Most of eastern Hungary consists of an extensive lowland, the Great Plain (Alföld). To the south and west of the Danube River lies Transdanubia (the country across the Danube), a region of undulating hills, wide valleys, and woods of beech and oak trees. To the northwest is the Small Plain, or Little Alföld (Kis Alföld).

In the north of Hungary, in particular in the northeast, hills and ranges of low mountains stand out against the horizon. In the north-central highland belt rise mountains of volcanic origin—the Börzsöny, Cserhát, Mátra, Bükk, and Zempléni— separated by river valleys. These mountains have one of the largest cave systems in Europe, and many visitors come to explore the underground world of stalactites. Mount Kékes, at 3,330 ft. (1,015 m.) the highest peak in the country, rises in the Mátra Mountains.

The Danube, which crosses the Little Alföld, breaks through some low hills and continues south through the Great Plain on its way to the Black Sea. It provides an important trade route between Hungary and its neighbors. The Tisza River, which also crosses the entire country from north to south, joins the Danube in Yugoslavia.

Lake Balaton, in western Hungary, encompasses 230 sq. mi. (596 sq. km.) and is the largest lake in Central Europe. Often called the Hungarian Sea, Lake Balaton attracts about 1 million visitors a year who come to swim, sail, and fish in its lovely fresh turquoise waters. Extinct volcanoes mark the skyline on the northern shore, and in the valleys nearby are old trees, rare plants, and exotic flowers. In the marshland at the southwest corner of the lake, migratory birds come to breed, including snow-white herons, pelicans, cormorants, bustards, and other rare species.

The climate in Hungary is continental, with seasons of almost equal length. More rain falls in western Transdanubia than in the eastern Great Plain, and in the west the winters and summers are more temperate than in the east. It is sunnier in Hungary than in other countries of the same

Towns dating back to the Middle Ages are found throughout the scenic Hungarian countryside.

The imposing House of Parliament, completed in 1903, stands on the Pest side of the Danube.

latitudes, and the long, warm, sunny autumn helps produce fine fruits and sweet wine grapes.

Natural Resources.   Hungary has little mineral wealth apart from extensive deposits of bauxite, the principal source of aluminum. Most of the bauxite is exported, since Hungary lacks the energy resources needed to extract aluminum from the ore. Some hard coal, lignite or brown coal, petroleum, and natural gas are present, but additional amounts of these fossil fuels must be imported. Since the flat terrain provides Hungary with no source of hydroelectric power, coal is used to generate electricity. The coal industry underwent extensive restructuring in the early 1990s. The first Hungarian nuclear-power plant went into operation in 1982; in the late 1990s, almost one-half of the electricity supply was generated by nuclear power.

THE PEOPLE

In the late 9th century A.D., a seemingly endless column of people crossed the northeastern Carpathians into what is now Hungary. These settlers included fierce horsemen wearing long felt coats; pointed, fur-trimmed caps; and leather boots. Their sabers, bows, and quivers hung from their silver-decorated belts. Women and small children, perched atop mounds of carpets and furs, traveled inside some of the large covered wagons, which were pulled by long-horned oxen. Other wagons carried agricultural tools—iron plows, hoes, sickles—as well as the implements of armorers, saddlers, bow makers, potters, and silversmiths. Behind the wagons followed herds of cattle, horses, water buffalo, and sheep. The cattle were driven along by dogs—big white shaggy komon-

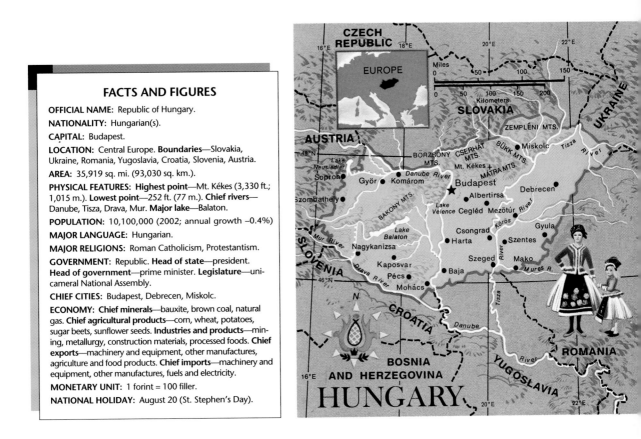

dors and lively little black pulik. The wave of people and cattle descended to the Great Plain.

Historians believe that 500,000 Magyars from the area north of the Black Sea arrived in Hungary during this invasion. It took them about 10 years to absorb or conquer the Slavic and Avar groups who had occupied most of the Carpathian Basin. The conquerors were the ancestors of today's Magyars, who are also known as Hungarians.

Today there are few minorities in Hungary. Germans account for about 0.5 percent; there are also about 600,000 Romanies (Gypsies), some of whom speak their mother language, Romany.

Way of Life. Before World War II, Hungarian society was sharply divided between the ruling classes and the people. Political power was primarily in the hands of large landholders and industrial, military, and religious leaders. Their Hungary was known for its frivolous lifestyle.

When the Communists took over in 1949, they nationalized most of the industry and collectivized the agriculture, thus leveling the differences in wealth. Living standards improved during the 1970s, but the next decade brought increasing social and economic inequalities. At that time, many Hungarians had to hold two or even three jobs to make ends meet. The traditional pessimistic streak in the Hungarian national character, one of the world's highest suicide rates, and the high divorce rate have contributed to a decrease in Hungary's population. There is a great difference between the rapidly modernizing west of the country and the much poorer east. Recently, however, a number of young people, many of them intellectuals, have begun to leave the overcrowded, polluted cities and move to the large open spaces in the Great Plain.

Education. Education is compulsory through 10 grades, and most children start school before the age of 6. Secondary education can be pursued at more than 800 grammar, vocational, and technical schools. Admission to the universities in Hungary is difficult to obtain. Only the best students are accepted. For several years, children of workers and peasants were favored, but today academic qualifications are the main criterion for admission.

Religion. About two-thirds of Hungarians are Roman Catholics; most of the rest are Protestants, mainly Calvinists. Eastern Rite Catholics comprise a tiny minority, no more than 2.5 percent. There are also about 80,000 Jews, most of whom live in Budapest. While the Communists held power, practicing of religion was discouraged. In the late 1970s, however, relations between the state and the Roman Catholic Church improved, and in 1978 Hungary established diplomatic relations with the Vatican, the first Communist country to do so.

Food. One aspect of life that all Hungarians enjoy is preparing and eating good food. Food preparation is both an art and a national pastime, and Hungarian cooks make superb use of spices mixed with meat, fish, and chicken. *Gulyás* (goulash) and chicken paprikás are famous dishes. Red paprika, made of peppers grown in Hungary, is the national spice. Hungary produces and exports wonderful native wines, fine apricot brandy, delicious salami, pâté of goose liver, and delicate pastries.

Sports. Hungarians have always been avid sportsmen. A large percentage of the population is registered in sports clubs, where individuals can participate in track and field events, swimming, water polo, soccer, fencing, weight lifting, gymnastics, shooting, boxing, and wrestling.

Language and Literature. Although a number of individual Hungarian words may sound familiar to Western ears, and though the Roman alphabet is used, the language itself is a unique one. It belongs to the Uralic family of languages, which also includes Finnish and Estonian.

Stress in Hungarian words is placed on the first syllable, and the letters of the alphabet always stand for the same sound, which makes pronunciation relatively easy. Because of the great flexibility of the language (it has 20 grammatical cases), however, translation from Hungarian to other languages is extremely difficult. Many significant Hungarian literary figures are completely unknown except to Hungarians, since the works of only a few have been translated. Sándor Petőfi, who died in 1849 at the age of 26, composed fervent poems in praise of liberty and equality. The 19th-century novelist Mór Jókai wrote to inspire a nation defeated by the Habsburgs of Austria. His thrilling stories are still very popular. Imre Madách, writing at the same time, expressed his ideas in poetic dramas of great power. His most famous philosophical drama, *The Tragedy of Man*, tells the history of humankind as shown to Adam by Lucifer. The poet Endre Ady, who wrote in the early 20th century, revived ancient forms of Hungarian poetry to express in forceful and symbolic language the need for change in Hungary. Hungarians consider Attila József to be their greatest modern poet. His works are scarcely known outside Hungary, however, because of translation difficulties.

The Hungarian writer best known abroad is probably Ferenc Molnár (1878–1952), whose plays have been translated into many languages. The highly successful Broadway musical *Carousel* was based on Molnár's *Liliom*. One of the first leftist intellectuals who denounced Stalinism was

Hungarian-born Arthur Koestler, whose political novel *Darkness at Noon* (1940) is a brilliant analysis of totalitarianism. György Lukacs (1885–1971), a controversial Marxist thinker, was one of the outstanding personalities of European culture. Among contemporary writers, the best-known is György Konrad, whose writings were suppressed in Hungary during the years of Communist rule. Some of his works are available in the West in translations.

Music. Hungarian music developed later than the country's literature, but it soon caught up in importance, enriching the Western world. Franz (Ferenc) Liszt, the 19th-century pianist who created the symphonic poem, also composed concerti, sonatas, ballads, rhapsodies, and études that deeply influenced composers of the following generations. He became the first director of the Hungarian Academy of Music, which has since educated conductors and concert artists who perform in many countries.

Women in costumes reserved for special occasions lead a religious procession.

Two later influential figures in the music world, Béla Bartók (1881–1945) and Zoltán Kodály (1882–1967), studied Magyar folk music. Bartók, using folk music as his source material, went on to create 20th-century masterpieces for individual instruments and for the orchestra. Kodály's great choral works are also rooted in Hungarian folk music.

In Hungary today, traveling Gypsy *(cigány)* orchestras delight people wherever they gather for impromptu entertainment. Concerts and operas are always crowded. Many Hungarian operettas, such as those of Franz (Ferenc) Lehár, who wrote *The Merry Widow,* among others, are very popular.

The Sciences. Hungarians are proud of the large number of eminent scientists their small nation has produced. János Bolyai contributed to modern ideas of relativity and space physics. Ignaz Semmelweis, who discovered the cause of puerperal (childbirth) fever, is known in medical history as the savior of mothers. Two Hungarian physicists, Leo Szilard and Edward Teller, made significant contributions to the development of atomic energy while working in the United States. Three of the five Hungarian-born Nobel prizewinners in science—Georg von Békésy, Albert Szent-Györgyi, and Eugene P. Wigner—lived and worked in the United States.

CITIES

Budapest, the capital city, is home to almost one-fifth of the population of Hungary, and the entire metropolitan area accounts for over one-fourth of the country's people. Located in north-central Hungary, close to the border of Slovakia, Budapest is one of the leading cities in Central Europe. At the hub of Hungary's vast network of roads, railways, and waterways, it is the gateway for travelers whether they come by plane, train, or Danube steamboat or hydrofoil.

The mighty Danube divides both Hungary and its capital. Buda, on the west bank, and Pest, on the east, were once independent cities. They merged in 1873, also incorporating Óbuda, another old town on the hilly west bank of the Danube. Pest, built on flatlands at the beginning of the Great Plain, is more modern than Buda. The city's factories, warehouses, and shipbuilding yards are located on the outskirts of Pest along the Danube. More than 50 percent of Hungary's industry is concentrated in or near the capital.

A uniquely beautiful city, Budapest is graced by eight bridges that cross the Danube. Part of the city is situated on picturesque hills with wooded slopes. Within the city, there are 123 thermal springs, making it the largest spa in the world. Budapest is also a great cultural center, with many theaters, two opera houses, and three major symphony orchestras. And it boasts dozens of good restaurants and elegant, fashionable shops, the best of them on Váci Utca, the equivalent of New York's Fifth Avenue. In the middle of the Danube are islands, including the lovely Margaret Island, with its huge park and famous luxury hotel.

Budapest is a living picture book of Hungarian history. At its northern border are the excavated remains of Celtic settlements from the Copper Age. Close by, within the city limits, are the ruins of Aquincum, the capital of Roman Pannonia, where Valentinian II was proclaimed emperor in A.D. 375. Nearer the center of the city is a recently discovered Roman amphitheater built to hold about 16,000 spectators. Close to it are the ruins of the 4th-century chapel that marked the first appearance of Christianity in the region.

Hungary also contains examples of Romanesque, Gothic, and Baroque architecture. Castle Hill, the ancient seat of Hungarian kings, has been restored to its original style after being bombed in World War II. Next to it is the famous Gothic Coronation Church of Matthias, where the Hungarian kings were crowned. A part of the rebuilt Royal Palace became home to the National Library in the 1970s, while another section houses a great museum. The neo-Gothic Parliament Building, completed in 1903, stands by the river on the Pest side of the city.

Budapest has had public transportation since 1866, when horse-drawn trams were first introduced. Old-fashioned rattling streetcars still can be seen in the streets, but a modern subway built in the 1970s is now the most important means of public transportation.

Other Cities

Pécs, in the south, is both a mining center and a university town. Around the city are Hungary's largest coal mines and uranium mines. Hungary's oldest university was founded there in 1367. Pécs also has a famous 11th-century cathedral. **Miskolc,** a growing industrial town, is the center of northern mining activity. **Debrecen,** in the east, is an old college

The traditional garb of Hungarian shepherds includes long, fleecy, reversible cloaks.

city with historic buildings. **Szeged,** to the west on the Tisza River, has a neo-Romanesque Cathedral Square used for open-air drama and opera performances. Around the square is the Hall of Fame arcade, with busts and reliefs depicting great Hungarians.

ECONOMY

Agriculture. Under Communist rule, almost all farming was done on state farms or in cooperatives where laborers received fixed wages. They raised wheat, rye, corn, potatoes, sugar beets, and tobacco, and were guaranteed a steady income by the state in much the same way as were factory workers. Since 1989, the numbers of private farmers cultivating their own tracts of land have greatly increased.

Hungary now uses more than half of its land for farming, but only about 8 percent of the labor force is employed in agriculture. As in many other countries, young people tend to leave the villages for the cities.

Industry. Largely lacking in the raw materials for heavy industry, Hungary has sought sound industrial development in those industries requiring much skill but little material. Hungary's major industries include the manufacture of machinery, machine tools, and transportation equipment. Electrical appliances, agricultural machinery, trucks, and bicycles are among the chief products. A growing chemical industry exists in Hungary, particularly of pharmaceutical products. Much of the agricultural wealth is processed into canned foods, sausages, and wines.

Economic Reforms. Hungary was the first Communist country to abandon a centrally planned economy. As early as 1968, economic reforms led to some private enterprise and increased contact with the West. Although the changes were somewhat halfhearted, they would prepare the country for the eventual post-Communist overhaul.

Vineyards thrive in Hungary's climate. Some grapes are grown for an unusual wine known as Bull's Blood.

Hungarian Economy Since 1989. Hungary's post-Communist transformation was initially easier than those in other countries. Private enterprise and foreign investment had already begun to grow during the Communist era, and, most importantly, the financial and banking sectors had been brought in line with Western standards. Between 1990 and 1994, about $7 billion flowed into Hungary from the West, more than into all other Central European states together.

Yet even with this help, Hungary underwent another downturn in the mid-1990s. A serious financial crisis forced the government to cut social benefits and introduce various austerity measures. Hungarians had to tighten their belts again, but in a few years the country caught a second breath. Its reform of the social-security system is one of the most progressive in Europe.

Like other developed countries, the percentage of people working in the services industries is increasing and, in 2000, it was about two-thirds of the nation's overall labor force. Hungary has thoroughly modernized its communication system, and Internet use is growing. The number of telephone lines has doubled since the early 1990s.

A promising new source of income is so-called wine tourism, with "tasting" tours of individual wineries in southern Hungary. At one time, Hungarian wines were widely renowned, but during the Communist era, this industry experienced a sharp decline.

In the early 2000s, Hungary has demonstrated strong economic growth, with widespread foreign ownership and investment. By around 2004, the country is expected to join the European Union (EU).

HISTORY

Hungarians date the beginning of their country from A.D. 896, the year of the Magyar conquest, although the Magyars were not the first invaders of the area. It was once a part of the Roman Empire, and was later overrun by Huns, Slavs, and Germanic tribes. After the Magyars established themselves in the region, Stephen I (István in Hungarian) became the first Christian ruler. He asked the pope for recognition as king of Hungary, and on Christmas Day, A.D. 1000, he was enthroned with a crown sent by the pope. Later he was canonized and became the patron saint of Hungary. For more than 900 years, the Crown of Saint Stephen was the crown of the kings of Hungary.

King Stephen organized his state into counties on the model of Charlemagne's empire. When German armies invaded Hungary, he drove them from the country. The Germans made many later attempts to conquer Hungary; each time, they were defeated. In the 12th century, the Hungarians were threatened by the Byzantine (Greek) Empire, but this attempted takeover also failed.

In the 13th century, Mongols (Tatars) swept over Hungary, pillaging and burning the countryside and slaughtering half the population in two years. In 1301 the able Árpád dynasty, descendants of the founder of Hungary, died out, and the French Anjou dynasty began to reign. During the 14th century, under Charles Robert and Louis the Great, Hungary became the leading power in Central Europe.

By the middle of the 15th century, the Ottoman Turks were threatening the Balkan Peninsula, and soon they began to raid Hungary. From 1443 to 1456, the great Hungarian military leader János Hunyadi fought them off. In 1456 he defeated Sultan Mohammed II at Belgrade (now the capital of Yugoslavia), and saved Hungary and Europe from the Turks for another 70 years. His son, King Matthias Corvinus, made Hungary one of the most powerful countries in Europe. His court attracted scholars and artists. He founded a university, the famous Corvina Library, and a fine museum. After his death in 1490, the nobles fought over who was to be his successor, and the country was filled with dissension. The peasants, oppressed by the powerful nobles, rose in revolt in 1514. The uprising was put down with great cruelty. This time the invading Turks found a weakened and divided country. In 1526, on the plains near Mohács, the Hungarian army suffered a total defeat. Even today, Hungarians, when pressed, will say jokingly, "Don't worry; more was lost at Mohács!"

The country was cut apart. Central and southern Hungary, including the capital, Buda, were occupied by the Turks for a century and a half. The west and north came under the Habsburg emperors of the Holy Roman Empire. All that remained of Hungary was Transylvania, now mostly in Romania. The Transylvanian Diet enacted laws providing for extension of the freedom of religion to Calvinists, Lutherans, Unitarians, and Catholics, a revolutionary idea in the 16th century. The ruling Hungarian princes fought the Habsburg king and also secured religious liberty and constitutional rights from the Habsburgs for northern and western Hungary.

In 1686 Buda was recaptured from the Turks by Habsburg forces with the help of armies from other countries of western Europe. The Turks were driven out of Hungary, but the entire country then fell under the domination of the Austrian Habsburgs. Hatred for Austria grew, especially when attempts were made to impose the German language and customs on the Hungarian people. In 1825 a movement was begun by Count István Széchenyi, a Hungarian statesman, to revive the oppressed nation morally, socially, and economically.

In 1848 revolutions erupted all over Europe. Hungary, under the leadership of Lajos Kossuth, rose to demand independence from Austria.

The Austrians, assisted by Russia, crushed the revolt and forced Kossuth into exile. The Hungarians made use of the tactics of passive resistance. They were so successful that the Habsburgs were forced to compromise. The Compromise of 1867 created the Dual Monarchy of Austria-Hungary, with Hungary accepting Austrian Emperor Franz Joseph as king, but Austria agreeing to recognize Hungary's internal autonomy.

The 20th Century

After failing to prevent the war, Hungary, during World War I, fought on the side of Germany and Austria. With the defeat came the loss of nearly 75 percent of Hungarian territory, one-third of all the Magyar people, and half of the country's industry. A democratic revolution broke out, but was unsuccessful. A Communist regime took over briefly. Soon, however, conservatives came back to power under Admiral Miklós Horthy, who reestablished the monarchy without a king. He ruled as regent. The Hungarians, determined to recover their lost territories, turned to Germany and Italy for help. From 1938 to 1941, Hungary, with the aid of Germany, was successful in regaining part of its lost territories. But in 1944, during World War II, the Germans, fearing the Hungarians would try to conclude a separate armistice with the Western Allies, invaded the country. The Soviet armed forces drove the German armies out of Hungary between 1944 and 1945. Hungary once again was forced to give up her old lands, and once again occupation brought wholesale destruction and violence.

A factory worker smooths the undercoat of a bus in the factory's drying room prior to applying the final coat of paint. Buses were an important export item during Hungary's Communist era, with Eastern Europe and North Korea as the chief markets.

In 1945, a democratic government emerged in Hungary, and a republic was officially proclaimed. Land was distributed to the peasants. Within a few years, however, the Communists took over. By 1949, a Stalinist dictatorship had been established under Mátyás Rákosi. Democratic institutions were abolished, and repression was widespread. Years of terror followed.

After Stalin's death in 1953, Rákosi was replaced by Imre Nagy, who released all political prisoners and introduced some freedoms. The Soviet Union became increasingly dissatisfied with developments in Hungary and tried to reverse them, helping Rákosi back to power. The forces of anti-Communism were too strong, however, and on October 23, 1956, an anti-Soviet armed uprising broke out. The Freedom Fighters, as the rebel students and workers became known, were supported by the overwhelming majority of Hungarians. They briefly controlled Budapest, they could not withstand the Soviet army. In two weeks of revolt, about 5,000 to 6,000 Hungarians were killed, 13,000 were wounded, and 20,000 homes were destroyed. In the wake of the uprising, some 200,000 people left for the West, 40,000 were imprisoned, and about 280 were hanged, including Imre Nagy. János Kádár became the head of the new Soviet-sponsored government.

After 1960, a delicate compromise between the nation and the Kádár government took shape. Kádár's economic and political liberalization and his policy of national reconciliation made him the most respected Communist leader. The improving living standards, relatively free travel to the West, and lack of outright political oppression made life in Hungary more pleasant than in much of Eastern Europe. By the late 1980s, however, a sense of political lethargy had become pervasive. Kádár was then shifted to the new ceremonial post of president. His death in July 1989 epitomized the end of an era.

In May 1989, Hungary precipitated the fall of Communism in Eastern Europe by opening its borders with Austria. The Hungarian Communist Party renamed itself and prepared the way for the first multiparty elections in May 1990. The Hungarian Democratic Forum became the leading party, and Árpád Göncz, a writer imprisoned after the 1956 revolution, was elected president. He was immensely popular. In 2000, he was replaced by Ferenc Madl, a university professor.

The first four years of the post-Communist period were marked by a steady economic transformation process but also by increasing economic hardship. Social discontent grew, and the yearning for the good old times of "goulash Communism" led to a sound defeat of the ruling Democratic Forum in the spring 1994 parliamentary elections. The former Communists, now renamed Socialists, won a resounding victory.

Hungary thus followed the path set by Lithuania and Poland, where restructured Communist parties returned to power after the initial transformation period. Ironically, it was up to the Hungarian Socialists to implement a final economic overhaul, which proved difficult for many citizens (real wages went down by more than 10 percent).

In 1998, Hungarian voters opted to change the ruling party yet again, and the Socialists were replaced by a conservative democratic opposition, the Alliance of Young Democrats (FIDESZ). Despite a successful term in office, FIDESZ was voted out of power in 2002—partly because of its highly aggressive campaign and the right-wing, nationalist rhetoric of Prime Minister Viktor Orbán.

Hungary became the first post-Communist country to permit a U.S. military presence on its territory: a supply base was set up in late 1995 in southern Hungary in connection with the Joint Endeavor operation in Bosnia and Herzegovina. In 2000, the country allowed the U.S. Federal Bureau of Investigation (FBI) to set up an office in Budapest in order to help Hungarians fight international crime.

GOVERNMENT

The present National Assembly consists of 386 deputies who are elected to four-year terms. The president, who has mostly a ceremonial role, appoints the prime minister, who heads the government.

ISTVÁN CSICSERY-RÓNAY, University of Maryland
Reviewed by EDWARD W. WALKER, Ph.D., Columbia University

Mountains and rolling hills occupy two-thirds of the picturesque Romanian countryside.

ROMANIA

Romania, on the Balkan Peninsula, is one of the younger nations in Europe. Although the land was settled more than 2,000 years ago, the nation known as Romania (formerly also spelled Rumania) has existed for only a little more than a century. From the late 14th until the mid-19th century, the country consisted of two principalities: Moldavia and Walachia. In 1859 these provinces were united and named Romania. Today Romania includes, in addition to the two original territories, the regions of Banat, Transylvania, Bukovina, and Dobruja.

Between the mid-1940s and December 1989, Romania was a Communist state. In the second half of its Communist period, it was ruled by an autocratic and increasingly megalomaniacal ruler, Nicolae Ceauşescu, who was ultimately deposed and, with his widely detested wife, Elena, was executed in a bloody uprising in December 1989. Romania embarked on a difficult road to democracy and a free-market economy, and by the late 1990s could already claim some results.

THE LAND

On the map, Romania looks like a round pouch with a wide opening in the lower right. The opening is the Black Sea. Romania borders on five countries: Bulgaria in the south, Yugoslavia in the west-southwest, Hungary in the west-northwest, Ukraine in the north, and Moldova in the east. A country of great beauty and diversity, Romania consists of about one-third mountains, one-third hills and plateaus, and one-third plains.

Mountains. The Carpathian Mountains form a majestic semicircle that shelters an elevated plateau. This is the Transylvania tableland, a high area with a cool climate, rich in forest and mineral resources. The area was the home of Prince Dracula, a famous fighter against the Turkish oppressors, who later came to be identified with the legendary Transylvanian vampire.

The Carpathians are divided into the Moldavian Carpathians in the east, the Apuseni Mountains in the west, and the Transylvanian Alps in the south. Numerous fairly low passes break through the high mountains. Romania's highest peak, Negoi, rises 8,361 ft. (2,548 m.) in the Transylvanian Alps.

A girdle of lower hills gradually descends from the ring of mountains. In the spring, these hills are carpeted with flowers—narcissi, anemones, crocuses, daffodils, and forests of lilacs. Sweeping down from the hills are the great, well-watered plains of Romania. In the east lie the Moldavian plains. In the south the Walachian plains contain vast oil deposits. To the southwest is the small Banat plain.

Rivers. The mighty Danube is Romania's chief river. Only the Danube and one of its tributaries, the Prut, are navigable. The Danube not only waters some of Europe's richest soil, but it is also a main artery of national and international commerce. Galați and Braila, two inland ports on the Danube, are used for loading wheat, while the port of Giurgiu is the outlet for the Romanian oil fields. The Danube forms part of the border with Yugoslavia and almost the entire border with Bulgaria. Near the beginning of the boundary with Yugoslavia, the river flows through a deep gorge, the Iron Gate.

Wildlife. Romania has a fascinating variety of wildlife. Surefooted chamois clamber over the highest peaks. Deer, foxes, bears, wolves, lynx, boars, and smaller animals fill the woods. Eagles and falcons can be seen hovering above the crags. The lovely lakes of the Dobruja region, just west of the Black Sea, teem with fish.

Romania's Black Sea coast is lined with luxury hotels and other tourist facilities.

The Danube's broad, marshy delta, where the river empties into the Black Sea, is entirely within Romania. This area of more than 1,000 sq. mi. (2,600 sq. km.) is an immense natural park, providing a paradise for waterfowl. Swans, pelicans, egrets, cormorants, flamingos, wild ducks and geese, night herons, and many other birds abound. More than 60 varieties of fish live in the numerous channels of the delta.

Climate. Romania has a continental climate, with plenty of rainfall, severe winters, hot summers, and long autumns. The southwest enjoys a mild Mediterranean-type climate; in the uplands of Transylvania, the climate is usually moderate. But in many of the inland cities, summers can be intensely hot; and winters, when the north wind, or *crivat*, blows, bitterly cold.

THE PEOPLE

The heart of modern Romania was imperial Rome's Dacia. The Dacians were conquered by the Romans in the early years of the 2nd century. Rome established colonies in Dacia, and they were garrisoned by Roman legions. Most Romanians, about 85 percent, are believed to be descendants of the Dacians and the Roman colonists. The Romanian language is basically a Latin language to which, over the years, the Romanians have added bits and pieces of the Slavic languages spoken by their neighbors.

Hungarians make up the largest minority group in Romania. They live in Transylvania, the western part of the country, and number about 2 million. Under Ceaușescu, the rights of Hungarians were severely limited; even after the revolution, tensions have persisted, affecting Roma-

The exterior walls of the 15th-century Sucevița monastery are beautifully decorated with frescoes.

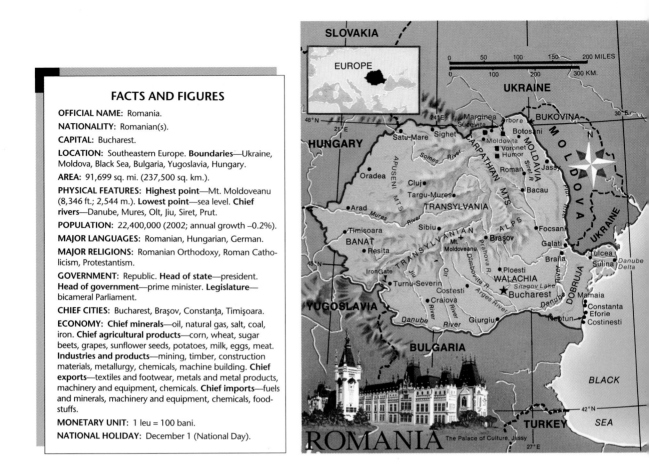

FACTS AND FIGURES

OFFICIAL NAME: Romania.

NATIONALITY: Romanian(s).

CAPITAL: Bucharest.

LOCATION: Southeastern Europe. **Boundaries**—Ukraine, Moldova, Black Sea, Bulgaria, Yugoslavia, Hungary.

AREA: 91,699 sq. mi. (237,500 sq. km.).

PHYSICAL FEATURES: Highest point—Mt. Moldoveanu (8,346 ft.; 2,544 m.). **Lowest point**—sea level. **Chief rivers**—Danube, Mures, Olt, Jiu, Siret, Prut.

POPULATION: 22,400,000 (2002; annual growth –0.2%).

MAJOR LANGUAGES: Romanian, Hungarian, German.

MAJOR RELIGIONS: Romanian Orthodoxy, Roman Catholicism, Protestantism.

GOVERNMENT: Republic. **Head of state**—president. **Head of government**—prime minister. **Legislature**—bicameral Parliament.

CHIEF CITIES: Bucharest, Braşov, Constanţa, Timişoara.

ECONOMY: Chief minerals—oil, natural gas, salt, coal, iron. **Chief agricultural products**—corn, wheat, sugar beets, grapes, sunflower seeds, potatoes, milk, eggs, meat. **Industries and products**—mining, timber, construction materials, metallurgy, chemicals, machine building. **Chief exports**—textiles and footwear, metals and metal products, machinery and equipment, chemicals. **Chief imports**—fuels and minerals, machinery and equipment, chemicals, foodstuffs.

MONETARY UNIT: 1 leu = 100 bani.

NATIONAL HOLIDAY: December 1 (National Day).

nia's relationship with neighboring Hungary. Many Gypsies—who prefer to be called Romanies—also live in Romania, but estimates of their numbers are very approximate (peaking at 2 million). The Jewish and German populations, which used to be quite large, have dwindled because of emigration.

Religion. The Communist government of Romania strongly discouraged religious observance and regulated the church as much as possible, paying church salaries and maintenance. The largest denomination in Romania today consists of members of the Romanian Orthodox Church. Roman Catholics, Calvinists, Jews, and Lutherans are also represented. Emigration to Israel has sharply cut the once-sizable Jewish community to about 18,000 to 20,000 members.

Education. Romanians traditionally regarded their country as an island of French culture in the Balkans. Before the Communist government was established in March 1945, Romania looked to France for cultural, social, and educational inspiration. Schools were patterned on those of France, and French was a required second language.

When the Communists took over the country, the educational system was changed. General education was made free and compulsory for 10 years, for children from 6 to 16. Workers and peasants were brought into the schools, so that almost everyone learned to read and write. The secondary-school system was expanded to include, in addition to the traditional academic schools, technological and teacher-training schools. At the university level, institutions were established to stress training useful to the state—teaching and technology. The study of Russian was compulsory for many years.

Since the 1989 revolution, academic excellence has regained its importance, and Marxism-Leninism is no longer the primary focus of academic education. Technical expertise and economic development are now major educational goals. Romania boasts some 140 institutes of higher learning, including seven universities and a number of institutes that specialize in technical training. The biggest gaps in scholarly literature are being addressed, and modern computer technology is beginning to change the learning process.

Culture. Romania has a rich folklore, whose roots go back centuries. This folk history is expressed in lyric poetry, ballads, folktales, mystery plays, traditional New Year and Nativity plays, and many other forms. Folk music and amateur theatricals have long flourished in even the most remote parts of the country.

Many Romanian writers and composers left Romania to work in France, drawn by its congenial intellectual atmosphere. There they created some of their best works. However, most of them retained, through their work, a close identification with their native land. This is especially true of composer and violinist Georges Enesco, whose best-known orchestral work is the *Romanian Rhapsodies*. Enesco died in 1955. The world-famous playwright Eugène Ionesco, son of a Romanian father and a French mother, lived most of his life in France; he died in 1994. A leading author of the theater of the absurd, Ionesco became widely known to English-speaking audiences with his play *Rhinoceros* (1959).

The most prominent Romanian artist was Constantin Brancusi, the sculptor, who traveled on foot from Romania to Paris, where he worked until his death in 1957. His art, found in the great galleries of the world, sought to capture "the essence of spirit" of the subject. His lovely sculptures of birds eternally poised in flight are elegant, deceptively simple, thin shafts of marble or brass. The museums of Bucharest and Craiova exhibit works created by Brancusi when he was young.

The monasteries in the towns of Voroneţ, Humor, Arbore, Moldovița, and Sucevița are outstanding examples of early Romanian art and architecture. Simple and severe in outline, the entire outer walls of these monasteries are covered with frescoes. These mural paintings, extraordinary displays of creativity and acute observation, depict religious stories, historical events, and local legends. Although they are more than four centuries old, the murals have retained their brilliance and freshness. No one knows the secret of this remarkable preservation.

In the United States, the best-known writer of Romanian origin is Elie Wiesel, whose novels are based on his Holocaust experiences in Auschwitz and Buchenwald. In 1986, Wiesel was awarded the Nobel Peace Prize for his message of "peace, atonement, and human dignity."

Way of Life. About half of the people in Romania still live in or near small villages. Rural life has changed greatly since World War II, and was particularly disrupted in the last years of Ceauşescu's reign when, under the so-called "systematization plan," old villages were torn down and their inhabitants forcibly relocated into high-rise developments. The plan was stopped after the 1989 revolution.

Food. A ubiquitous dish is *mămăligă*, a cornmeal porridge that is eaten twice or even three times a day, often in combination with cheese,

Construction of the grandiose Palace of the People (background) ceased when the Ceauşescu government fell.

salted fish, or bacon. Still a part of Romanian tradition is the distillation of plum brandy *(ţuica)* each fall. Another favorite dish is *imam baiyldi,* an eggplant stuffed with spiced meat or vegetables and covered with tomatoes. The delicious dish takes its name from the legend of the Turkish priest *(imam)* who fainted *(baiyldi)* with pleasure after taking a taste.

CITIES

Bucharest, the capital and largest city of Romania, stands on a plain in southern Romania. A modern city of more than 2 million people, Bucharest is the political, artistic, cultural, and economic hub of the country. It has numerous skyscrapers and blocks and blocks of modern houses; vast sections of the city that consisted of ancient hovels were torn down in the early 1960s to make way for modern apartments.

In the 1980s, a historic part of the city was demolished to make room for a mammoth Palace of the People, a "pet project" of the dictator. This enormous building, with thousands of rooms, remained unfinished at Ceauşescu's death. It is now a cultural and conference center.

Bucharest was the seat of the Walachian princes in the 14th century. In the 16th century, the Curtea Veche Church was built; the Church of the Patriarchy and the Mihai Voda Church were erected in the 17th century, while the Stavropoleos and Cretulescu churches were built in the 18th century.

Before World War II, Bucharest was known throughout Europe as the Paris of the Balkans. Its Parisian-style boulevards were shaded by lime trees and bordered by miles of red, yellow, and white roses. It was a glittering, sophisticated city, filled with cafés, theaters, palaces, and luxury hotels. Today little remains of this prewar elegance.

Cluj is Romania's second-largest city and an important industrial and educational center. It has a rich historic past and is the chief city of

The burning of low-grade coal has made Copşa Mică one of the most polluted cities in Europe.

Transylvania, which, before World War I, was a part of Hungary. Many of its residents are of Hungarian descent.

Constanţa, Romania's chief seaport on the Black Sea, is one of the country's oldest cities. It contains important archaeological sites that relate to its founding more than 2,500 years ago by the Greeks. Later, under the Romans, Constanţa served as an important trading post. The ancient Roman poet Ovid (43 B.C.–A.D. 17) spent the last years of his life in exile in this city. Roman remains, including a ruin noted for its mosaics, are also found in Constanţa.

Many resorts have sprung up on the outskirts of the city to accommodate tourists who are attracted by the sunshine, the miles of fine, sandy beaches, and the warm blue waters. These resorts are located in Mamaia, Eforie, Costineşti, Neptun, Jupiter, and Venus, all on the southern Black Sea coast.

Jassy, the ancient seat of the Moldavian princes, is a major administrative and economic city. The Romanian cultural renaissance of the 19th century flowered there, and the city is still a cultural center. The well-known Cuza University is also located in Jassy.

Timişoara was the site of a massacre by soldiers that provoked the 1989 uprising. It is an ancient town of historical interest; the 14th-century Huniady Castle is nearby. A breathtaking road runs through the Transylvanian Alps and the Carpathians from Timişoara, in western Romania, to **Braşov,** in central Romania. Ruined medieval castles dot the heights, and Gothic churches with massive walls tower over the landscape. In Braşov, a superb 14th-century cathedral and an ancient town hall are still standing.

Ploeşti is the main center of Romania's oil industry. Europe's petroleum industry began there in 1857. During World War II, costly low-level Allied bombing raids were conducted to cut off this vital source of fuel for Germany's war machine. Just north of Ploeşti is the lovely Prahova Valley with its picturesque mountain resorts and lovely lakes.

ECONOMY

Traditionally, Romania has been one of the poorest countries in Europe, despite its rich resources. The land is fertile and the rivers—when not polluted—are filled with fish. Forests supply timber for building, paper production, and export. Among the many varieties of trees are the firs that grow in high altitudes. Fir wood is prized for its resonance and is used in the manufacture of musical instruments.

Mineral wealth includes copper, manganese, uranium, lead, zinc, bauxite, kaolin, sulfur, gold, and salt. The most important mineral product is petroleum. Pipelines from the oil fields run from Ploeşti to Bucharest, Constanţa, and Giurgiu. Other petroleum resources are near Bacău. Transylvania contains the largest natural-gas reserves in Europe. Coal is mined in the Jiu River valley, and iron ore is found in several areas.

Agriculture. When the Communists came to power in 1945, they launched a program to nationalize agriculture. In the following years, some land was divided into small holdings to be worked in farm cooperatives, but most of the better land was held for the huge state farms. Persistent lack of fertilizers and modern machines limited production.

The post-Communist government has begun to return land to private owners; by early 1995, about 80 percent of farmland had been privatized. About one-third of the active population works in agriculture.

Industry. Before World War II, Romania was primarily an agricultural country. Industrial development began after the war, under the direction of the Soviet Union.

On the one hand, Romania made spectacular progress. Industrial output increased at a much faster rate than in the major industrial countries of the world. On the other hand, the costs of rapid industrialization have been incalculable. Other branches of the economy—agriculture, consumer goods, communications, and services—were almost completely disregarded, and huge metallurgical and chemical plants virtually destroyed several regions of the country. Repairing that environmental damage is one of the greatest challenges of post-Communist Romania.

Post-Communist Developments. When the Communist dictator Ceauşescu was deposed and executed in December 1989, the country was in a pitiful state. In order to pay off all foreign debt, Ceauşescu had in the preceding years plunged the country into darkness, both literally and metaphorically: most food was exported and people were undernourished, only 40-watt bulbs were permitted and there was not enough heat. And so while the United States and Western Europe were entering the Information Age, Romania was returning to the Middle Ages.

Since 1990, the country has been trying to transform its economy into a free market system, but it is not easy. In the mid-1990s, production went up, inflation slowed down, and privatization proceeded steadily, yet almost half of the people still lived below the poverty level. By the end of the decade, things had gotten worse again: in 2000, inflation was more than 40 percent, unemployment doubled since 1996 to 12 percent, and there was a widespread banking crisis. Even though Romania has applied for European Union (EU) membership, it will take years before it qualifies—but it can count on EU credits. The International Monetary Fund also approved a sizable loan in 2000. Despite these difficulties, there is a widely shared conviction, both within and outside the country, that the free-market track of the Romanian economy is irreversible.

HISTORY

The history of Romania is a long sequence of conquests and occupations. In the 2nd century A.D., the Romans made Dacia, the region northeast of the Danube, one of their most prosperous colonies. Toward the end of the 3rd century, Goths, Huns, and Slavs invaded the area. Bulgaria was the conqueror during the 7th and 8th centuries, and it was at this time that Eastern Christianity was introduced. Later, warriors from Asia invaded the land.

Moldavia and Walachia, the principalities that, until the 19th century, made up the country that is now Romania, were briefly united with Transylvania by Michael the Bold at the end of the 16th century. He was not able to withstand the might of the Turks, however, and they occupied Walachia and Moldavia. Transylvania was returned to Hungary.

Moldavia and Walachia began to gain a measure of independence after 1856, and in 1859 the two provinces were united as Romania. Violence and unrest, however, continued to plague the country. The peasants were desperately poor, and political corruption was widespread. Complete freedom from Turkish control was won at the end of the Russo-Turkish War (1877–78), but some land was ceded to Russia.

As a result of the Second Balkan War (1913), Romania won a large part of Dobruja from Bulgaria. After World War I, when Romania sided with the Allies, the country doubled in size. It received Transylvania from Hungary, and Bessarabia from Russia.

Between the two world wars, there was constant friction among the various ethnic groups in Romania, and economic conditions were bad. Crown Prince Carol gave up the throne in favor of his son Michael in 1925, only to take it back in 1930. In 1938 Carol set himself up as a dictator, but his rule soon conflicted with the Iron Guard, a terrorist organization with strong sympathies for Nazi Germany.

During World War II, Romania was caught between Nazi Germany and the Soviet Union. After Carol was forced to abdicate by the pro-Nazi government, Michael returned to the throne in 1940, but a dictator, Ion Antonescu, was in control of the government. German troops occupied the country, and in June 1941, Antonescu wiped out the Iron Guard and declared war on the Soviet Union. In 1944, as the Soviet armies advanced, King Michael overthrew Antonescu and entered the war on the side of the Allies. The Soviet Union occupied and seized control of Romania.

The Communist takeover caused a social, economic, and political revolution. The first leaders concentrated on destroying the power of the old ruling classes, chiefly the landowners, and reversing the country's anti-Russian viewpoint. In 1947, King Michael was forced to give up the throne again and go into exile. Prominent anti-Communists were sentenced to prison, and the only opposition, the National Peasant Party, was outlawed.

Romania had never known democratic rule, but was all too familiar with dictators. Thus, the establishment of a small, all-powerful group in control of the government was nothing new. In 1952, Gheorghe Gheorghiu-Dej became premier, and in 1955 he became head of the Romanian Communist Party. He ruled as chief of state and head of the Party until his death in 1965. His successor, Nicolae Ceauşescu, who came to power in 1965 as president of the State Council and secretary-general of the Communist Party, began a program to set Romania free from its total commitment to the wishes of the Soviet Union. His rule, however, was increasingly ruthless, and he placed family members in key positions. His wife, Elena, was hated throughout the country. He ruled through an extensive network of fiercely loyal secret police (known as *Securitate*) and informers.

Post-Communist Romania

The uprising of 1989 in Romania was the only revolt in Eastern Europe that was met by massive force. Hundreds of people died in the fighting, provoked in part by the massacre of protesters by government soldiers in Timişoara. Nicolae Ceauşescu, who only a month before had boasted of the achievements of socialism, was deposed and, together with his wife, executed on December 25, 1989. Lurid images of their bodies were broadcast around the world.

The new rulers of Romania, many of them former Communists, created a political organization called the National Salvation Front (NSF). Its leader was Ion Iliescu, a reformed Communist who became president in 1990. Two years later, a segment of the NSF headed by Iliescu transformed itself into the Party of Social Democracy, which remained in power until 1996. Throughout the first half of the 1990s, there was a great deal of social unrest, due in large part to numerous violent clashes between pro-democracy students and pro-government coal miners.

In late 1996, Romanians voted the Communists out of power. A right-of-center Democratic Convention received a parliamentary majority; geologist and former university president Emil Constantinescu became president. The new government was welcomed with great expectations, but by 2000, its record had been less than successful, characterized by poor economic performance and corruption. In late 2000, Ion Iliescu and his Party of Social Democracy won convincingly during the nation's presidential and parliamentary elections.

There have also been a number of continuing problems concerning the ethnic rights of Romania's large Hungarian minority, which lives mainly in the Transylvania region of the country. For several years, these issues negatively influenced relations between Romania and Hungary. Romania's primary—and to some extent, all-consuming—goal, however, is to join the European Union (EU) and NATO, and therefore it has tried to improve relations with its neighbors.

Former king of Romania Michael I (who had ruled from 1940 to 1948 and then lived in Switzerland) regained his citizenship in 1997. Since then, he has visited Romania regularly and has grown popular among the people, many of whom would like to see him return to the throne. He has named his oldest daughter Margaret to be his successor.

GOVERNMENT

A new constitution was approved by the Romanian Parliament in November 1991, defining Romania as a republic and giving considerable powers to the president. The Parliament has two chambers, and deputies are elected for four years. The constitution also proclaims adherence to the Universal Declaration on Human Rights, abolishes the death penalty, and guarantees the right to private property.

STEPHEN FISCHER-GALATI Editor, *Romania*
Reviewed by EDWARD W. WALKER, Ph.D., Columbia University

The Monument of Liberty dominates the center of Sofia, the capital of Bulgaria.

BULGARIA

Highway E-5, the modern road from Belgrade, Yugoslavia, to Istanbul, Turkey, is built over the old Roman road to the Near East. Running southeast across the country, this road, originally paved with stone slabs four or five steps wide, once separated two Roman provinces. Today, these provinces are united as the Republic of Bulgaria, a country facing new challenges and uncertainties in the post-Communist era.

The Roman road linked the Western and Eastern Roman empires. Later it was an avenue for the peoples invading the eastern parts of the empire, and still later a part of the Crusaders' route to the Holy Land. After the Crusaders, the warriors of Bulgaria and the soldiers of the Byzantine Empire (successor to the Eastern Roman Empire) traveled the road to reach the fields where they met in a succession of bloody battles. During the nearly 500-year-long occupation of Bulgaria by the Ottoman

(Turkish) Empire, the Turks used the ancient thoroughfare to maintain their iron grip on Bulgaria.

Along Highway E-5, as elsewhere in Bulgaria, evidence of settlers and travelers from earlier times can be found. Ancient tombs, Roman stone columns, ruins of Roman spas, Byzantine monasteries, and Turkish mosques dot the countryside. But the travelers and invaders left more than archaeological remnants and historic monuments. They left a people accustomed to violence, disorder, and hardship. They also left a wealth of legend and superstition.

Today, one may still see a collar of blue beads with a rosebud pattern hanging from the hood of a taxi. These collars, used to ward off the "evil eye," once adorned the necks of horses. In remote villages, Bulgarians still celebrate Saint George's Day, the holiday of herders and shepherds. On this day, a lamb is killed, and wine is spilled to bring good health. When the lamb has been eaten, the bones are collected. Half are buried in an anthill, so that the sheep will multiply like ants; the rest are thrown into the river so that the sheep milk will flow like water.

After centuries of facing the East, Bulgarians have become more interested in cultivating relations with the West. Bulgarian trade missions have tried to attract foreign investment to the country, and some democratic values have taken root. In a dramatic turn of events, a center-right movement headed by former Bulgarian king, Simeon II—a successful Western entrepreneur—won the June 2001 elections.

Present-day Bulgaria was once part of the Roman Empire. Many ruins of the Roman period still stand.

THE LAND

Bulgaria is divided into two main agricultural regions by the Balkan Mountains, or "Old Mountains" to the Bulgarians. In the north is the Danubian Plateau, where wheat and other grains, sugar beets, and sunflowers are grown. The Balkan Mountains serve to block the cold winds blowing from the plains of Russia so that in the fertile Maritsa River valley to the south, the winters are mild and rainy and the summers dry and very hot. Tobacco, grapes, cotton, and rice are harvested there. Fruits and vegetables are cultivated in both regions. Winters in the western half of the country, particularly in the mountains, can be very cold.

The country is bordered by Romania on the north, the Black Sea on the east, Turkey and Greece in the south, and Macedonia and Yugoslavia in the west.

THE PEOPLE

Bulgarians are descendants of Turkic Bulgars, who invaded the country in the 7th century A.D. and mingled with resident Slavic tribes, whose language they adopted. Bulgarians are therefore considered Slavs, but they look different from their Slavic relatives: most commonly, they have very dark hair and black eyes. They are fierce patriots and have a keen sense of history.

Muslim Turks, who were forced in the last decade of Communist rule to adopt Christian Bulgarian names, constitute a large minority group in Bulgaria. This assimilation campaign led to a massive exodus of Bulgarian Turks to Turkey.

In the Rhodope Mountains of southern Bulgaria, the dramatic limestone formation known as the Monks (below) attracts many tourists.

FACTS AND FIGURES

OFFICIAL NAME: Republic of Bulgaria.

NATIONALITY: Bulgarian(s).

CAPITAL: Sofia.

LOCATION: Southeastern Europe. **Boundaries**—Romania, Black Sea, Turkey, Greece, Macedonia, Yugoslavia.

AREA: 42,822 sq. mi. (110,910 sq. km.).

PHYSICAL FEATURES: Highest point—Musala Peak (9,596 ft.; 2,925 m.). **Lowest point**—sea level.

POPULATION: 7,800,000 (2002; annual growth –0.5%).

MAJOR LANGUAGE: Bulgarian.

MAJOR RELIGIONS: Bulgarian Orthodoxy, Islam.

GOVERNMENT: Republic. **Head of state**—president. **Head of government**—prime minister. **Legislature**—unicameral National Assembly.

CHIEF CITIES: Sofia, Plovdiv, Varna, Burgas.

ECONOMY: Chief minerals—bauxite, lead, zinc. **Chief agricultural products**—grains, oilseeds, vegetables. **Industries and products**—machine building and metalworking, food processing. **Chief exports**—machinery and equipment, metals, minerals, fuels. **Chief imports**—fuels, minerals, machinery and equipment.

MONETARY UNIT: 1 lev = 100 stotinki.

NATIONAL HOLIDAY: March 3 (Independence Day).

BULGARIA

Of all the peoples of Eastern Europe, only Bulgarians feel a deep and genuine friendship toward the Russians. These bonds were forged by a shared history and culture, as well as by political, military, and economic ties. Above all, they were the result of the Bulgarians' enduring gratitude that in the late 19th century, Russia helped them shake off the centuries of Turkish rule.

Education. At the beginning of the 20th century, more than 90 percent of the people over school age could not read and write. Today there is almost complete literacy in the country. School is compulsory for all children between the ages of 7 and 16. There are 40 institutions of higher learning in Bulgaria.

Under the Communist regime, Bulgarian students were prepared for their role as workers in the Communist society. There was strict control of the entire school day as well as of all extracurricular activities. Back in those days, all students were even required to work part of the time in farming or in industry. In post-Communist Bulgaria, education has undergone many changes. Students are no longer required to study Marxism-Leninism, and many try to arrange scholarships to attend schools in Western Europe and in the United States.

Religion. Under the Communists, churches could not own property, and the appointment of all priests and church officials had to be approved by the government. Although religious practices were discouraged by the government, most Bulgarians remained faithful to their Eastern Orthodox faith. The Turks in Bulgaria, who make up nearly 9 percent of the population, are Muslims. There are also small Jewish, Roman Catholic, and Protestant minorities.

Literature and the Arts. Because of the difficulty of the language, few Bulgarian writers are known to the rest of the world. A novel by Ivan Vazov, *Under the Yoke* (1894), provides such a remarkable picture of life in Bulgaria under the Turks, however, that it has been widely translated and read in many countries.

The icon above portrays Ivan Rilsky, the 10th-century founder of the Rila Monastery in western Bulgaria. The monastery now houses a museum.

Bulgarians are intensely proud of their opera. They have many fine singers, particularly bassos. In a country with about the same population as the city of New York, there are five opera houses, two official music theaters for light opera, and 12 symphony orchestras.

Contemporary art in Bulgaria has not approached the greatness of the country's ancient icon art. Icons, small religious images painted on wood, were introduced into Bulgaria with the adoption of Christianity. The icon artists reflected in their work the great imagination and the love for brilliant colors that were seen also in the beautiful embroidery, weaving, and wood carving done by peasants.

CITIES

Sofia, the capital, is beautifully situated 1,820 ft. (555 m.) above sea level, and looks out onto the towering peaks of the Vitasha Mountains. The city is filled with gardens, parks, and tree-lined boulevards. It is also filled with monuments and museums devoted to the past and the present: the remains of a Roman tower that can be seen in the basement of a Sofia department store; the Church of Saint Sophia, built during the 3rd and 4th centuries; the Archeological Museum; the Museum of Ecclesiastical History; and many others.

In the pleasant cafés of Sofia, a visitor can sip Turkish coffee or sample yogurt, a Bulgarian food that is famous all over the world. Coca-Cola is also available; Bulgaria was the first Soviet-bloc country with its own Coca-Cola bottling plants. Bulgaria also offers a host of aromatic and flavorful native dishes that combine delicious vegetables and meats with oriental spices and herbs. These include bean or cucumber soup, carp stuffed with nuts, a lamb kebab or *giuvetch* (stew), and a dessert of melon or berries. Universally popular is the *shopski* salad, made of tomatoes, peppers, cucumbers, and sharp grated cheese.

Though cafés resound with Western popular music, the famous native dance, the *horo,* is still danced to the music of bagpipes. Supermar-

The Ivan Vazov National Theater in Sofia is named for the founder of Bulgarian classical literature. This stately theater seats 1,200 people.

With the ideal climate for growing roses, Bulgaria has become a leading producer of attar—rose oil used as a base for the world's most expensive perfumes.

kets, cafeterias, motels, and other everyday features of Western life have come to Bulgaria, but it is still far from a truly modern country.

ECONOMY

During the Communist era, Bulgaria was industrialized, but agriculture continues to play a large role in the country's economy. A special bank has been established to provide funds to support small farms and help individual farmers make the transition to a free-market economy. By the late 1990s, almost all land had been returned to private owners.

Roses are one of Bulgaria's most valuable crops. Thousands of varieties are grown in the famous Valley of Roses, in the southern foothills of the Balkan Mountains. More than 200 lbs. (91 kg.) of petals are needed to produce 1 oz. (28 g.) of rose oil, known as attar of roses. This oil, which rises to the surface when rose petals are boiled in water, is extremely expensive and is used in making fine perfumes.

Industry. Timber from the mountains and hydroelectricity from the rivers are only two of Bulgaria's resources. Coal, lignite, iron ore, lead, zinc, copper, uranium, pyrites, chromite, manganese, petroleum, and natural gas are also found. During the Communist era, Bulgaria enjoyed rapid economic expansion. Steel and electric-power production greatly increased, and the oil and petrochemical industry was developed along the Black Sea at Varna and Burgas.

For decades, more than three-fourths of all exports went to the Soviet Union and Eastern European countries. Since these markets collapsed, Bulgaria has suffered great economic hardships. In the mid-1990s, repeated waves of strikes protested the declining standard of living. In 1996, the situation became so dire that, in many towns and villages, bread was rationed.

Economic reforms, particularly the privatization of land and industrial enterprise, began to be implemented in 1992, but government corruption and red tape slowed the process, which again picked up speed in 1997. The hope of Bulgarian economists for increased foreign investment was strengthened by the June 2001 electoral victory of former Bulgarian king, Simeon II.

Tourism. In the last years of the Communist era, Bulgarians tried to bring Western currency into the country by developing their great natural advantages—the magnificent beaches, beautiful mountain ranges, and more than 500 mineral springs. The tourist industry attracted more than 5 million visitors to the country each year, but most of them were other Eastern Europeans. Bulgarian beaches and mountains have great potential for tourism, and some areas are already developing as modern resorts with all the typical Western comforts.

HISTORY

Bulgaria's violent and tragic history began in the 7th century A.D., when the Bulgars, a fierce, warring group of horsemen, rode out of Central Asia. They seized lands near the Danube River, and some spread south to conquer the Slavs. They imposed their political practices on the Slavs, but at the same time adopted the Slavic customs and language. Thus, the Bulgarian nation was born.

The First Bulgarian Empire, founded in A.D. 679, lasted until 1018. During this period, Christianity was introduced into Bulgaria. In the 9th century, disciples of two Christian missionaries, the brothers Cyril and Methodius, known as the Apostles of the Slavs, arrived in Bulgaria. They brought with them an alphabet and a written language and literature. This alphabet, called Cyrillic, is shared by the Russian, Ukrainian, Serbian, Macedonian, and Bulgarian languages, and to this day it provides a strong cultural tie between the people of Bulgaria and their Slavic cousins.

Bulgarian culture flourished during the First Empire, but the people warred with Byzantium constantly. In 1018, Bulgaria was defeated and became part of the Byzantine Empire. In 1186, the brothers John and Peter Asen led an attack on Byzantium and started Bulgaria back on the road to independence and power with the establishment of the Second Bulgarian Empire. During most of the Middle Ages, the Bulgarian czar ruled the major part of the Balkan Peninsula. In 1395, Bulgaria was overrun by the Turks, who then controlled the region for nearly 500 years. The Turks were driven out by Russians in a war that started in 1877. The long years of Turkish domination left traces in the food, names, customs, dress, art, and architecture of Bulgaria.

Modern Bulgaria was created in 1878 with the Treaty of San Stefano and the Congress of Berlin, which ended the Russo-Turkish War. Russia reestablished the medieval frontiers of Bulgaria, but other European powers objected, and only the northern part of the country remained independent. In 1885, the southern part broke away from Turkey, and the country was reunited at last.

After a brief period of peace, Bulgaria first gained and then lost considerable territory in the two bloody Balkan Wars of 1912–13. In World

War I, Bulgaria joined with Germany and Austria-Hungary against the Allies. Again, land was lost. Three wars in six years left the Bulgarians defeated, bitter, and impoverished.

In 1941, Bulgaria joined Italy and Germany and declared war on Great Britain and the United States, but not on the Soviet Union. The king was able to keep his country from active involvement in the war, and Bulgaria was the only Axis power whose Jewish population survived.

On September 5, 1944, a few days after Bulgaria began peace talks with Great Britain and the United States, the Soviet Union declared war on Bulgaria and occupied the country. An armistice was signed in Moscow. A government friendly to the Soviet Union was set up. All opposition was ruthlessly stamped out. Hundreds of high government officials, intellectuals, and other opponents of Communism were put to death or jailed. The young king, Simeon II, was exiled.

From 1946, when Bulgaria was declared a People's Republic, to 1989, it was one of the former Soviet Union's most faithful allies in the Eastern bloc. Todor Zhivkov, leader of the Communist Party from 1954, was the longest-ruling Party boss in the European Communist states. During this era, security forces remained a powerful presence, and newspapers and other media were tightly controlled.

In November 1989, Zhivkov was forced to resign, and several months later, the Communist Party renamed itself the Bulgarian Socialist Party. The first free elections since 1919 took place in June 1990, and the former Communists won. They were defeated by a democratic opposition coalition (the Union of Democratic Forces, or UDF) one year later, but

Each summer, Bulgaria's Black Sea resorts draw thousands of vacationers to the sandy beaches.

Modern hotels and other tourist facilities have helped bring Western currency into the Bulgarian economy.

the new government was soon embroiled in a torrent of internal squabbles, and was soon replaced by a nonpartisan government of technocrats.

During the rest of the decade, the Socialists and the UDF alternated in power, as the country's political scene changed dramatically from the Communist era. Many new Bulgarian politicians are young, some in their thirties, and there was even a woman prime minister in 1994.

The UDF won praise from the European Union (EU) and the World Bank for its economic reforms, although almost one-fifth of Bulgarians were out of work in early 2001. As a result, an organization called the National Movement arose, headed by Simeon II, the former Bulgarian king who was exiled from the country in 1946 at the age of nine. The American-educated former monarch promised to solve the country's major economic problems within 800 days. In the June 2001 parliamentary elections, he won 43 percent of the vote. One year later, however, there was no significant improvement and widespread disappointment among the Bulgarian people was evident.

GOVERNMENT

A new post-Communist constitution came into effect in July 1991. Bulgaria is a democratic republic, headed by a president with substantial executive powers. The first Bulgarian president (the post did not exist under the Communist rule) was Zhelyu Zhelev, a writer and philosopher. After two terms, he was replaced by Petar Stoyanov in 1997, who was then succeeded in late 2001 by former Communist Georgy Parvanov. The government is headed by a prime minister.

Reviewed by EDWARD W. WALKER, Ph.D., Columbia University

The architecture of Tirana, Albania's capital, reflects the city's Turkish influence.

ALBANIA

The 18th-century English historian Edward Gibbon described Albania as "a country within sight of Italy which is less known than the interior of America." Now, more than two centuries later, the interior of America has been thoroughly explored, settled, and voluminously described, but the small, impoverished Balkan country of 3.5 million people has only begun to be known to outsiders.

For decades, Albania was a rigid Communist state. The disintegration of totalitarian control in the early 1990s threw the country into confusion: anarchy and chaos swept over many regions, and old feuds were revived. Thousands fled to Italy and Greece as economic refugees. The failure of an investment pyramid scheme in 1997 led to the fall of the nation's right-of-center government. By 2002, the country had stabilized. A new socialist government has kept Albania out of ethnic conflicts, and is preparing to discuss European Union (EU) membership.

THE LAND

Albania is a narrow strip of land on the west coast of the Balkan Peninsula. It is washed by the Adriatic Sea on the west, and wedged between Macedonia and Serbia and Montenegro on the north and east and Greece on the southeast and south. About 40 mi. (64 km.) away, across the Strait of Otranto, lies the heel of Italy's boot.

The country has three distinct landforms—coastal lowlands, hills, and high mountains. The long lowland coast features stretches of sandy beaches as well as many shallow lagoons and extensive marshes. The stagnant waters in the swampy areas hold the constant threat of malaria. Here and there along the coast can be seen the beginnings of the hills that cover the central part of Albania. The slopes of the lower hills are terraced and carefully cultivated. Some of the major cities and towns are located in this area.

The outstanding geographic feature of Albania, however, is that nearly three-quarters of its surface area is mountainous and mostly inaccessible. The mountains rise to their greatest height in the 9,066-ft. (2,763-m.) Mount Korab, in northeastern Albania. Throughout the centuries, the mountains have served as a natural fortress and refuge for the people. In fact, the Albanians call themselves Shqyptarë ("sons of the eagle"), and many still make their homes in the mountain valleys.

The mountainous nature of the country and its poor soil make it very difficult to grow enough food to feed the population. Wheat and corn are the main crops. Olives, figs, grapes, and citrus fruits are grown in the southern part of the country. Sugar beets, tobacco, and cotton are becoming more important. Raising livestock, particularly sheep, is also important, but grazing land is often quite far from villages or farms.

Climate. Although Albania is small, it has a surprising variety of climatic conditions. The coastal regions enjoy a Mediterranean climate, with mild, rainy winters and very warm, dazzling summers. But these mild temperatures are sharply altered in the hilly inland areas by the harsher climates of the central Balkan Peninsula. Some of the mountain areas are windswept and snow-covered in winter, with precipitation of up to 100 in. (254 cm.) annually in the north. The summer months are cool and bright.

Lakes and Rivers. Albania shares its largest lake—Scutari—with Yugoslavia, and two other large lakes—Ochrida and Prespa—with Macedonia. Many relatively short rivers cross the country, but they usually dry up in summer. Only one of Albania's rivers, the Buene, is navigable. The

Gjirokastër, a town in southern Albania, is the birthplace of the country's longtime Communist leader Enver Hoxha. The region around Gjirokastër produces olives, tobacco, and wheat.

Shkumbî River, which crosses the center of Albania, is thought of as the dividing line between the northern Albanians, who speak a dialect called Gheg, and the southern Albanians, who speak Tosk.

THE PEOPLE

The Albanians are a homogeneous people. They speak Albanian, an Indo-European language that is written with the Roman alphabet. Even though two dialects are spoken, each group can understand the other. About 2 million Albanians live outside the country, in the neighboring Yugoslav province of Kosovo and in the republic of Macedonia.

Traditionally, the Ghegs of the north have been thought of as reserved and taciturn, and they have a reputation as good fighters. Many are tall, handsome, and blond, and all are credited with great courage in defending their mountain homes. Tosks, on the other hand, are a more affable, outgoing people. Since they lived in the path of Albania's many invaders, they met and mingled with other peoples.

A rich oral literature made up of folk songs, poetry, and proverbs plays an important part in the cultural life of the country. The songs are often accompanied by the one-string lute called the *lahuta*.

Religion. Christianity came to Albania in the 1st century A.D. When the Turks arrived in the 14th century, they brought the Muslim religion with them. Waves of conversion followed each Turkish victory until Albania had the largest number of Muslims in Europe.

In 1967 the Communist government closed the country's mosques and churches and claimed that Albania was the first atheist state in the world. Religious buildings were then used as youth-group centers, cultural houses, and even as restaurants. Since 1990, religious life has revived, with Islam, Orthodox Christianity, and Roman Catholicism coexisting peacefully alongside each other.

Education. At the outbreak of World War I, after more than 500 years of Ottoman rule, Albania was one of the most backward countries in all of Europe. After the nation gained independence at the end of the war, some schools were built, but it was only during the Communist period that education became widely available. Albania's first university opened in 1957, offering studies in medicine, law, and other fields.

In the mid-1990s, secondary education was completely reorganized to fit the needs of a democratic society. Although there are eight universities and two other institutes of higher learning, relatively few students continue their studies past the secondary level.

CITIES

Tirana (Tiranë), the capital of Albania, centers on a plaza that bears the name of Skënderbeg—Albania's national hero. In January 1968, the residents of the city commemorated the 500th anniversary of Skënderbeg's death by placing a huge statue of him in the square. For many years, the wide, tree-shaded main street seemed even wider because so few cars were seen on it—a situation that is quite different today. The wooded hills beyond lend a certain charm to Tirana, as do the delicate spires of old mosques. In the old section of the city, along the narrow streets, men can be seen wearing the baggy trousers and sashes of the Turks of bygone days.

A railroad line connects Tirana with its port city of **Durazzo** (Durrës), which is approximately 20 mi. (32 km.) away on the Adriatic Sea. Durazzo is the chief port of the country. Its beach was once the mecca of Eastern European vacationers seeking the sun, but is now becoming increasingly popular with Western Europeans.

Other important Albanian cities are **Scutari** (Shkodër) and **Valona** (Vlorë), which are about the same size as Durazzo.

ECONOMY

Albania has always been an agricultural country. Primitive farming methods were used up to the time of World War II, and families toiled together to share the hard work of the farms.

In the 1950s, the government had to start from scratch in a land devastated by war. With Soviet money, aid, and technicians, new factories were built, including a textile mill, sugar refinery, tobacco factory, and cotton-processing, plywood, and hydroelectric plants. In addition, drilling for oil and mining for copper, coal, and chromium were initiated.

In the early 1960s, after breaking with the Soviet Union over policy differences, Albania turned to China for help. After the Chinese aid terminated in 1978, Albania slowly began to establish economic ties with other countries, particularly its Balkan neighbors.

The collapse of Communist rule during 1991 and 1992 caused an almost total economic disintegration. About one-third of all factories closed, and unemployment rose to about 70 percent.

In 1993, things began to improve. The streets of Albania's capital became crowded with kiosks selling all kinds of items. Cars, once driven only by Communist bosses, were suddenly available, and Coca-Cola—forbidden for years as a symbol of capitalism—became a popular beverage. An investment crisis in 1997 brought Albania to the brink of collapse, and foreign aid became vital to the nation's survival. Economic prospects have brightened, and popular satisfaction with the Socialist government brought the ruling party's second electoral victory in 2001.

HISTORY

The first people in recorded history to inhabit the area that is today Albania were the Illyrians, who set up a kingdom in the 3rd century B.C. The Illyrians were a sturdy people—peasants, warriors, and pirates. The Romans, irritated by the Illyrian pirate ships that harassed their trade, decided to remove the source of trouble, and conquered Illyria in 167 B.C. They never penetrated the inaccessible mountain regions, however. After the Romans, other conquering peoples and races continued to invade the country.

The Long Years of Turkish Rule

The people who had the greatest and most enduring influence in Albania, mainly because their rule was of such long duration, were the Ottoman Turks. The first Turkish invasion of Albanian territory took place in 1385 at the invitation of a petty ruler who had quarreled with one of his neighbors. The newcomers gradually extended their rule over most of the country, after overcoming a good deal of resistance. The most spectacular opposition to Turkish domination was led by the greatest Albanian hero, Gjergj Kastrioti, or Skënderbeg, as he is known.

Skënderbeg, the son of an Albanian nobleman, was sent as a hostage to the sultan's court. There he became a Muslim and joined the Turkish army, in which he had a distinguished career. However, he knew that his people had not fully submitted to Turkish occupation, and he decided to return to Krujë, his family home. He reconverted to Christianity, and the Albanians soon recognized him as their leader. For a quarter of a century, Skënderbeg fought a number of highly successful defensive battles against large Turkish armies. His death in 1468 marked the end of large-scale resistance, although it took the Turks many more years to conquer the entire country. Skënderbeg is a symbol of freedom to the Albanians, and the mainspring of the modern national independence movement.

Independence

Albania declared itself an independent state in 1912, one of the last countries to break away from the dying Turkish Empire. In 1914, Germany's Prince Wilhelm zu Wied was made ruler of Albania. When World War I broke out, Wilhelm left the country. During this war, Albania was occupied at one time or another by the armies of several countries.

A leading figure in the postwar years was Ahmet Zogu, who seized power in 1925 and then proclaimed himself King Zog in 1928. He ruled the country as a dictator, but his years in office were marked by a number of real achievements. The strong centralized government encouraged education and in some ways strengthened the national economy.

Zog formed a close alliance with Italy and encouraged Italian investments. But the Italian Fascist leader, Benito Mussolini, asked Zog for more and more concessions. In 1939, five months before the outbreak of World War II, the Italians occupied Albania and forced Zog into exile. The Germans took over Albania after Italy's defeat in 1943.

A resistance movement, divided into Communist and nationalist branches, grew up during the war years. These two groups struggled for power, and in the civil war that followed, the Communist forces won. Known as the National Liberation Movement, they set up their own government in Tirana with Enver Hoxha as the leader.

The bleak economic conditions in Albania have caused many people to flee the country.

In the next few years, the Communists rebuilt their administration and removed all centers of opposition to their rule. The close ties to Yugoslavia ended when Yugoslav President Josip Tito quarreled with Stalin in 1948. Albania turned to the Soviet Union for protection, but when the latter renewed its friendship with the former Yugoslavia in the mid-1950s, Soviet-Albanian relations soured and were soon completely broken off. Albania then found a friend in the People's Republic of China, but that relationship ended in 1977. The Albanian Communist regime was one of the harshest in Europe. Between 1954 and 1990, some 400,000 people were put in prison, and about 6,000 were executed.

In late 1990, Albania began to wake up from its totalitarian period. Strikes and protests brought down one-party rule, but in the first free elections, in early 1991, the renamed Communists (now calling themselves Socialists) won two-thirds of the vote.

The March 1992 elections brought victory to the Democratic Party, and Sali Berisha, a cardiologist, became Albania's first post-Communist president. He won international respect for his restraint in international affairs, especially for not fomenting the nationalist yearnings of Albanians in Kosovo, but his reputation suffered after voting irregularities and a financial scandal in 1997. That year, the Socialists won the national elections and Berisha resigned. In 1999, Albania became the key operational area for international relief agencies during the NATO bombing of Yugoslavia, when 450,000 refugees from Kosovo flooded the country.

GOVERNMENT

Albania is a democratic republic with a strong presidency and a unicameral People's Assembly of 155 members. Since 1997, the Socialist Party has been in power, winning its second term in 2001. The nation's 32-year-old prime minister, Ilir Meta, is respected throughout the region.

Reviewed by ANTON LOGORECI, British Broadcasting Corporation, European Services

The lovely Gulf of Kotor in Montenegro is an inlet of the Adriatic Sea.

YUGOSLAVIA
(SERBIA AND MONTENEGRO)

Over the course of the past three-quarters of a century, the term "Yugoslavia" has been used to describe a succession of countries in the Balkan peninsula. Since early 2002, the name Yugoslavia has been on the verge of disappearing from maps in favor of "Serbia and Montenegro," thanks to an agreement promoted by the European Union (EU) under which a reorganized, loose confederation of the two regions was formed. All that is left to accomplish this is for the Serbian and Montenegrin parliaments to ratify the agreement.

The "original" Yugoslavia, meaning "Land of South Slavs," was adopted in 1929 for the Kingdom of Serbs, Croats, and Slovenes. Following World War II, from 1945 to 1991, the "second" Yugoslavia was a Communist federation of six republics: Slovenia, Croatia, Serbia, Bosnia and Herzegovina, and Macedonia. It was a favorite vacation spot for European tourists, especially visitors from Germany, many of whom enjoyed the beautiful beaches on the Dalmatian coast and the famous Yugoslav hospitality. In this pleasant country, people of different ethnic backgrounds and religions lived peacefully, side by side. This apparent tranquility, however, was somewhat artificially imposed by the country's pre-eminent ruler, Marshall Josip Broz Tito, a guerrilla hero of World War II, and later a widely popular Communist dictator.

Tito died in 1980, and many correctly predicted that historic ethnic rivalries, suppressed for decades, would soon reemerge. During the 1990s, the region witnessed the worst violence in Europe since World War II. In 1991 and 1992, the "second" Yugoslavia was replaced by five new independent countries: Slovenia, Croatia, Bosnia and Herzegovina, Macedonia, and a "third" Yugoslavia consisting solely of Serbia and Montenegro. Fighting first took place in Slovenia (lasting just a few days), then in Croatia (for several months), and in Bosnia and Herzegovina from 1992 to 1995. The last theater of war was in the Serbian province of Kosovo and Serbia itself: the persecution by the Serbian government (based in Belgrade) of the large Albanian minority in the province of Kosovo prompted NATO to bomb Serbia in 1999. Since then, Kosovo has been occupied by international peacekeeping forces, and is a virtual protectorate of the United Nations (UN)

A new era was ushered in during the fall of 2000, when Slobodan Milošević—the president of the "third" truncated Yugoslavia, and now an accused war criminal who has been largely blamed for inciting the ethnic violence—was defeated in presidential elections. The new president, Vojislav Koštunica, pledged to restore democracy to the country. In June 2001, Milošević was extradited to the international tribunal at The Hague, Netherlands, and his trial began in early 2002.

Meanwhile, the republic of Montenegro, with approximately 650,000 inhabitants, has also been pressing for independence, but the international community remains opposed to further splitting apart the country. A curious solution was settled upon in March 2002: it was decided that this "third" Yugoslavia will devolve into a loose union of Serbia and Montenegro.

THE LAND

The northern third of Serbia and Montenegro, which corresponds roughly to the province of Vojvodina, is a large farming region that consists of a vast expanse of flat and well-watered land where wheat, corn, sunflowers, tobacco, and fruit are grown.

Vojvodina is a part of the fertile Danube lowland that extends into Hungary and Romania. In ancient geological times, the area was the floor of a vast inland sea that was gradually drained by the Danube River.

South of Belgrade, the nation's capital, the country becomes increasingly rugged. Historically, these mountains served as a refuge for the local people during the countless invasions that are part of the region's history. Today, the higher elevations are a source of timber; they are also used to graze cattle. In the south, where the climate is milder, such crops as tobacco, rice, and cotton are grown in the valleys.

Serbia is completely landlocked, while Montenegro borders the Adriatic. There is a beautiful, mostly unspoiled mountainous region in the south, with Europe's largest canyon along the Tara River. The mountain range of Durmitor has been proclaimed a "natural monument."

Rivers and Lakes. The largest river is the Danube, which crosses the country's northeastern corner, flows past Belgrade, and cuts through the Carpathian Mountains at the Iron Gate, a magnificent gorge that has been called one of the greatest natural wonders of Europe. Over the millennia, the Danube has cut a passage through the gorge rock—at the narrowest place, the river is only 500 ft. (152 m.) wide, with cliffs rising on both sides up to 2,000 ft. (610 m.). The Djerlap Hydroelectric Dam, a joint venture of Yugoslavia and Romania, began operation in 1970. The main tributaries of the Danube are the Tisa, Sava, and Morava Rivers. The largest lake, Scutari (Shköder), lies within Montenegro, and is shared with neighboring Albania.

Climate. The country has several climate zones: in the north the weather is generally mild year-round, while the mountainous center and

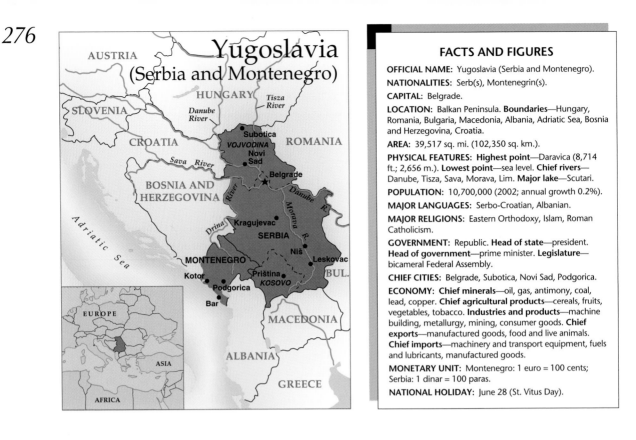

Yugoslavia
(Serbia and Montenegro)

FACTS AND FIGURES

OFFICIAL NAME: Yugoslavia (Serbia and Montenegro).

NATIONALITIES: Serb(s), Montenegrin(s).

CAPITAL: Belgrade.

LOCATION: Balkan Peninsula. **Boundaries**—Hungary, Romania, Bulgaria, Macedonia, Albania, Adriatic Sea, Bosnia and Herzegovina, Croatia.

AREA: 39,517 sq. mi. (102,350 sq. km.).

PHYSICAL FEATURES: Highest point—Daravica (8,714 ft.; 2,656 m.). **Lowest point**—sea level. **Chief rivers**—Danube, Tisza, Sava, Morava, Lim. **Major lake**—Scutari.

POPULATION: 10,700,000 (2002; annual growth 0.2%).

MAJOR LANGUAGES: Serbo-Croatian, Albanian.

MAJOR RELIGIONS: Eastern Orthodoxy, Islam, Roman Catholicism.

GOVERNMENT: Republic. **Head of state**—president. **Head of government**—prime minister. **Legislature**—bicameral Federal Assembly.

CHIEF CITIES: Belgrade, Subotica, Novi Sad, Podgorica.

ECONOMY: Chief minerals—oil, gas, antimony, coal, lead, copper. **Chief agricultural products**—cereals, fruits, vegetables, tobacco. **Industries and products**—machine building, metallurgy, mining, consumer goods. **Chief exports**—manufactured goods, food and live animals. **Chief imports**—machinery and transport equipment, fuels and lubricants, manufactured goods.

MONETARY UNIT: Montenegro: 1 euro = 100 cents; Serbia: 1 dinar = 100 paras.

NATIONAL HOLIDAY: June 28 (St. Vitus Day).

the southern region experience a more continental climate, with cold winters and hot summers. The amount of precipitation is great, particularly in Montenegro. About 10 mi. (16 km.) inland from the Gulf of Kotor is the "wettest place in Europe," a region where the annual rainfall averages 180 in. (457 cm.). However, since limestone, which lines the Gulf coast, is porous, the water runs down through the rocks to form underground channels and rivers.

THE PEOPLE

Two-thirds of the people living in Serbia and Montenegro today are Serbs, but the country's overall ethnic pattern is quite complex. In the northern province of Vojvodina, which adjoins Hungary, there are about 400,000 ethnic Hungarians and also a small Romanian minority. In the southern province of Kosovo, most of the population (nearly 2 million people) consists of ethnic Albanians. The mountaineer inhabitants of Montenegro, numbering about 650,000, are ethnically very close to Serbs, but, during the Communist era, they were classified as one of the nationalities of Yugoslavia. Montenegrins have some traits in common with other European highlanders, such as Scots and Basques.

In other former republics of Communist Yugoslavia, large Serbian minorities lived peacefully alongside their Croat and Muslim neighbors for decades. In the early 1990s, they yielded to nationalist propaganda and, driven by the vision of "Greater Serbia," rose in arms. Even though all warring sides committed atrocities, the Serbs were believed guilty of most of them, particularly against civilians. Altogether, about 250,000 people have been killed or are missing, and more than 2 million have become refugees. Several hundred thousand people left for Hungary, Austria, and Germany, but most refugees remained within the region.

Religion. Two different scripts—Cyrillic and Latin—in the former Yugoslavia reflect the conversion of the South Slavs to two branches of the Christian faith centuries ago. The Croats and Slovenes were converted to Catholicism by missionaries from Rome, while Serbs and Macedonians were converted to Eastern Orthodoxy and later formed the independent Serbian Orthodox Church. A third major religion—Islam—was introduced into large areas of the region by the conquering Turks between the 14th and 16th centuries.

Today, most people are Orthodox, but the large Albanian population in Kosovo is Muslim, and the Hungarian minority in Vojvodina is Roman Catholic. The Serbian Orthodox Church generally supported the Serbs in Croatia and Bosnia and Herzegovina, which gave the ethnic wars an additional strong religious overtone.

CITIES

Belgrade. The capital of the country, **Belgrade** (Beograd in Serbian), lies at the junction of the Sava River and the Danube. It was founded by the Celts in the 3rd century B.C., and later became a Roman fortress called Singidunum. Its location on the east-west route between Europe and the Orient guaranteed that it would be repeatedly destroyed by warring armies. The city is completely modern, but a few reminders of the past have survived through the centuries. By far the most impressive is the mighty Turkish fortress, the Kalemegdan. The National Museum houses a priceless collection of objects, including the Law Code of the 14th-century emperor Stephen Dušan; this code was the first of its kind in the Balkans. The long Turkish occupation of Belgrade is evoked by

Belgrade's contemporary architecture belies the city's long and colorful history.

the mosque known as Bajrakli Džamija. The University of Belgrade was founded in 1838.

Today, Belgrade has a population of about 1.6 million people and is a center of industry and of government administration.

Other Cities. Northwest of Belgrade, in the heart of Vojvodina, lies **Novi Sad,** a modern city remembered as the main center of Serbian nationalism in the 19th century. **Niš,** on the Morava River in Serbia, dates from Roman times, when it was known as Naïssus. The 4th-century emperor Constantine I (the Great), who declared Christianity the state religion of the Roman Empire, was born in Niš. The main city of Montenegro, **Podgorica,** was called Titograd from 1944 until 1992. **Priština,** capital of Kosovo, has been rebuilt as a modern city, but it still carries traces of centuries-long Turkish dominance. The oldest of Priština's mosques, Carsi, was built by the Turkish sultan immediately after the Battle of Kosovo in the 14th century.

KOSOVO

This mountainous region—less than half the size of New Jersey, and with about 2 million inhabitants—is considered by Serbian nationalists to be a "holy land." It was the last theater of the Yugoslav wars of the 1990s; by 2002, although still part of Serbia, Kosovo was in reality a United Nations (UN) protectorate.

During the early Middle Ages, present-day Kosovo was the heartland of Serbia. A "golden age" of sorts ended in 1389 with the legendary battle of Kosovo Polje (Kosovo Field), in which the Serbs were defeated by the Turks. This marked the beginning of Turkish domination of the Balkan peninsula.

In the 17th century, the Serbian population began to leave the area, and was gradually replaced by Muslim Albanians. When the Kingdom of Serbs, Croats, and Slovenes (the precursor of Yugoslavia) was established in 1918, Kosovo became part of it. In the 1920s, a few Serbian colonists arrived, but the population remained mostly comprised of Muslims. In 1974, the province acquired autonomous status, and was formally known as Kosovo and Metohija.

In 1987, even before the collapse of the Communist regimes in Europe, tensions in Kosovo between Muslim Albanians and the Serbian authorities had begun to lead to numerous clashes and violent demonstrations. In 1990, Kosovo's autonomy was abolished, and the Serbs seized direct control.

Throughout the rest of the decade, tensions continued to mount. Then, in the late 1990s, the central government in Belgrade turned its attention toward separatist movements within Kosovo. The campaign escalated to become a systematic effort at "ethnically cleansing" the region of its Muslim Albanian inhabitants. The extreme brutality prompted the United States to intervene and, in 1999, Yugoslavia was subjected to repeated air strikes for 78 days. Afterward, Kosovo was occupied by a UN-backed peacekeeping force, which remains in place indefinitely.

Kosovo was the scene of brutal fighting in the 1990s. Many ethnic Albanians ended up in refugee camps (above).

Today, about 100,000 Serbs still live in Kosovo, separated from the Albanians in ghetto-like communities. A parliament was elected in late 2001, and the winning party was the Democratic Union of Kosovo, headed by moderate Albanian nationalist Ibrahim Rugova. The exact jurisdictions of the parliament and the president have not yet been clearly defined, and the status of the region remains unclear.

ECONOMY

The country's resources include iron, copper, gold, lead, chromium, antimony, coal, zinc, bauxite, natural gas, and oil. The rivers provide hydroelectricity, while the forests are a source of timber. The rich farmland of Vojvodina has made the country self-sufficient in food production.

The Communist Era. At the end of World War II, the country was an agrarian, economically backward country that had been badly damaged by fighting. When the Communists came to power, they first followed the lead of the Soviet Union and tried to collectivize the farmlands, but with little success. In the 1950s, the government—having distanced itself from the Kremlin—abandoned this effort, and farmers were permitted to own up to 25 acres (10 ha.) of land.

In industry, Serbia and Montenegro, like the rest of Yugoslavia, moved from a centrally directed economy to a decentralized system. This "workers' capitalism" seemed successful for some time, but by the late 1980s, it became obvious that even this relatively liberal approach was an inefficient way to run a modern economy.

Recent Developments. Considering the upheavals in the early 1990s, it is remarkable that the economy did not collapse completely. In 1992, as punishment for Belgrade's support of the Bosnian Serbs, the UN imposed an economic blockade on the new Yugoslav state.

In late 1993, inflation skyrocketed to such an extreme that shoppers were using 500-billion-dinar notes to purchase everyday goods. At supermarkets, prices sometimes doubled hourly. In January 1994, the government introduced a new dinar, and the overall economic situation began to improve. Following accords signed in Dayton, Ohio, in late 1995, the blockade was lifted and economic life began to return to normal.

This respite lasted only for a few years: in 1998, in response to increased repression of ethnic Albanians in the province of Kosovo, several Western countries imposed economic sanctions again. And then, in the spring of 1999, NATO planes bombed Yugoslavia for 78 days, destroying bridges, factories, and public-utility plants. Former President Milošević somehow managed to put the country back together in less than a year, through a combination of coercion and "reconstruction taxes." Even so, the patience of the Serbian people finally ran out, as they came to the realization that Milošević's rule had not made them masters of a "Greater Serbia." The country had become a political and economic outcast, isolated from the world, and life was growing more difficult each year. In the fall of 2000, Milošević was voted out of office and the overall reconstruction of the country began, with massive international help. When the former dictator was handed over to the International Tribunal at The Hague in June 2001, the level of financial assistance from abroad increased once again.

The formation of the new loose union of Serbia and Montenegro in March 2002 provides for separate economies in the two regions. For some time, Montenegro had been using the German mark; in January 2002, it switched to the euro. Serbia continues to keep its traditional currency, the dinar.

HISTORY

Slavic tribes moved into the Balkan Peninsula after the 5th century A.D. In the mid-14th century, Serbia became the leading Balkan kingdom, under Stephen Dušan. Turkish rule began with the defeat of the Serbs at the Battle of Kosovo Field in 1389, and soon extended to include most of the region. The longest and darkest chapters in their history describe subjugation to foreign rulers—Austrian, Hungarian, Italian, Turkish, and, briefly in Napoleon's time, French.

In the early 19th century, Serbia, which suffered the most from Turkish rule, achieved a certain degree of independence. Serbian politicians and intellectuals became the most outspoken advocates of the Pan-Slavic movement, which aimed to unite all the southern Slavic peoples. By that time, the Austro-Hungarian monarchy had replaced Turkey as the chief foreign power in the northwestern Balkans.

The Serbian rulers encouraged the formation of underground movements to overthrow Austrian rule in such regions as Bosnia. Gavrilo Princip, the leader of one of these revolutionary movements, assassinated the Austrian archduke in Sarajevo in 1914. This murder led to World War I and the destruction of the 640-year-old Austrian monarchy and its vast empire. One of the new nations to appear on the map of Europe at the end of the war was the Kingdom of Serbs, Croats, and Slovenes.

The newly created kingdom faced enormous problems. Age-old traditions of ethnic rivalries did not die easily, nor were the other parts of the young kingdom ready to turn over their governing power to the Serbian-dominated government. In 1929, King Alexander I tried to solve these problems by dissolving the parliament and transforming the government into a dictatorship called the Kingdom of Yugoslavia. The parliament was reopened in 1931, but various national groups, especially those in Croatia and Macedonia, continued to fight for more independence. Alexander's assassination in 1934 is attributed to Croatian extremists.

Alexander was succeeded by his 17-year-old son Peter; Alexander's cousin Prince Paul acted as regent. The rise of Fascist power in Germany and Italy provided the regency with its greatest threat. In March 1941, after all of its neighbors but Greece had fallen to Hitler and Mussolini, the Yugoslav government signed a treaty with the Italians and Germans. The Serbs refused to accept the treaty and forced the government into exile. Slovenia and parts of Dalmatia were subsequently divided between Germany and Italy, a large part of Macedonia was annexed by Bulgaria, Montenegro came under Italian military rule, and an independent Fascist Croatia was proclaimed, led by the Ustaši Fascist movement.

A guerrilla war then began, and the fighters against the Ustaši, the Germans, and the Italians soon formed two hostile camps: the Chetniks, consisting mainly of Serbian nationalists, and the Communist Partisans, who also included other nationalities. Led by Josip Broź Tito, the Communists ultimately prevailed. By the end of the war, about 1.7 million Serbs, Croats, and Muslims had died—fighting the invaders as well as each other.

Tito's Yugoslavia. In November 1945, the Communists under Tito's leadership formally took over the government. Starting as a faithful Soviet ally, what was then Yugoslavia parted ways with its big Communist brother in 1948. Marshal Tito, by birth a Croat, was a relatively benevolent dictator whose major achievement was to keep the country together. Under his leadership, Yugoslavia was a Communist state (with one party, press censorship, and political prisoners), but it was also more open than other countries under Marxist rulers.

The Milošević Era. When Tito died in 1980, the Yugoslavian nation adopted a collective presidency, and for most of the decade the various ethnic groups lived in peace. In 1987, however, Slobodan Milošević became president of Serbia. Signs of conflict between ethnic Albanians and Serbs soon appeared in the province of Kosovo. Milošević fanned Serbian yearnings for "Greater Serbia" and incited Serbs in Croatia and in Bosnia and Herzegovina to take up arms against the Croats and Muslims. Within the next few years, Yugoslavia disintegrated into five new nations, and full-scale ethnic wars decimated Croatia and Bosnia and Herzegovina.

For its role in the ethnic bloodshed, the new Yugoslavia was expelled from the UN in 1992. Most Serbs, however, continued to believe in their right to an all-Serbian state.

The Dayton Accords of 1995 ended the war in Bosnia and Herzegovina, and the international embargoes and sanctions were lifted. During the winter of 1996–97, anti-Milošević forces within Serbia enjoyed short-lived success after a series of widespread demonstrations against rigged elections forced the government to recognize the opposition victory in the communal elections of 14

Many observers blamed former Serbian leader Slobodan Milošević (at left) for the long war in the Balkans.

large cities. In the summer of 1997, however, Milošević was comfortably reelected to the presidency.

The following year, widespread fighting erupted in Kosovo. The Serbs embarked on "ethnic cleansing," executing numerous Albanians or driving them from their homes. The international community protested, but to no avail. In March 1999, NATO and U.S. warplanes began to bomb the country. After 78 days, UN peacekeeping forces entered the province, and have been governing it ever since.

The Milošević era ended in September 2000, when the dictator who had seemed invincible for so long lost the presidential elections. The slow process of healing began, but huge problems will plague the country for years to come. Ethnic divisions remain, the economy is devastated, and Kosovo and Montenegro yearn for independence.

GOVERNMENT

A new constitution is being prepared, to reflect the new character of the country—tentatively renamed Serbia and Montenegro in March 2002. There will be a small government, a federal president, a common army, and one representative to the UN (with Serbs and Montenegrins regularly alternating in this position), but the economies of the nation's two parts will remain separate. After three years, each of the member states will have the right to leave the union.

IRINA RYBACEK / Reviewed by EDWARD W. WALKER, Ph.D., Columbia University

SLOVENIA

Slovenes rejoiced upon gaining their independence from Yugoslavia in June 1991. Slovenia was spared the strife that beset the other former Yugoslavian republics.

Slovenia, one of the five successor republics of the former Communist Yugoslavia, has largely escaped the violence experienced in other parts of the region, thanks primarily to its ethnic homogeneity and its comparative remoteness from Belgrade. In the early 2000s, the country was ahead of all other post-Communist nations, with its living standards close to those of Austria.

THE LAND

Roughly the size of New Jersey, Slovenia is an Alpine country, dotted with the shimmering, snowcapped peaks of the Slovenian Alps. The Karavanke Mountains rise in the north, and the Julian Alps grace the northeast. The highest peak is Mount Triglav, which means "Three Heads"—one looking to the past, one looking to the present, and the third looking to the future, according to folk legend.

Slovenia contains many small, beautiful lakes and swift streams. Lake Bled, at 1,500 ft. (457 m.) above sea level, has been a favorite spot for years. The castle Bled, on its shores, dates to the times of Charlemagne. In the middle of the lake is a small romantic island, which is said to have been the home of Živa, the Slavic goddess of love and life.

The remarkable 12-mi. (19-km.)-long Postojna Cave outside Ljubljana was carved out of the limestone by an underground river. The cave is known for the fantastic shapes of its stalactites.

Slovenia lays claim to a small piece of the Adriatic coast, between the Italian city of Trieste and the Istrian Peninsula. It stretches for only 29 mi. (47 km.), south of the ancient town of Koper.

THE PEOPLE

The Slovenes belong to the ethnic and linguistic group of the South Slavs, which also includes Serbians, Croats, Macedonians, and Bulgarians. Their language is written in the Latin alphabet.

Even when it was a republic of Yugoslavia, Slovenia was by far the most Westernized part of the federation—in its way of life, its architecture, and the attitudes of its people. Since 1992, the strong, self-confident middle class has adopted many of the same customs as have middle classes in Western nations. Slovenes proudly consider their country the "Switzerland of Central Europe."

The food in Slovenia combines Central European and Mediterranean influences. One favorite local specialty is *ajvar*, a relish of red pepper served with the flat hamburgers called *pleskavica*. From the region around Lake Bled comes *kremna rezina*, a delicious puff pastry dessert reminiscent of the old Austro-Hungarian Empire.

Winter sports are an integral part of Slovenian life. Excellent ski slopes can be found throughout the country, with a plentiful variety of hotels, inns, and mountain cabins.

Slovenia's capital, **Ljubljana,** is an ancient city with its own gentle charm. With a population of about 270,000, it looks very much like other Central European cities. It is well known for its concert and opera performances and as a starting point for visits to the mountains. Ljubljana dates to Roman times; it was founded under Augustus in 34 B.C., and was originally known as Aemona. The city was destroyed in the 5th century A.D. by the Huns, and later rebuilt by Slavs and renamed Luvigana. Ljubljana also boasts numerous baroque buildings and a fortress-like castle on a hill overlooking the city.

ECONOMY

Slovenia was the most industrialized republic of the former Yugoslavia. As soon as the Yugoslav army withdrew from the territory in October 1991, Slovenia established its own central bank and issued its own currency, called the tolar. The transition to a market economy caused some initial difficulties, but by the early 2000s, the country appeared almost indistinguishable from its northern neighbor, Austria. Slovenia expects to join the European Union (EU) around 2004.

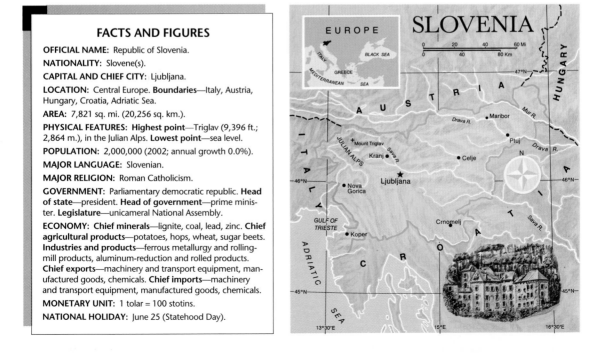

FACTS AND FIGURES

OFFICIAL NAME: Republic of Slovenia.

NATIONALITY: Slovene(s).

CAPITAL AND CHIEF CITY: Ljubljana.

LOCATION: Central Europe. **Boundaries**—Italy, Austria, Hungary, Croatia, Adriatic Sea.

AREA: 7,821 sq. mi. (20,256 sq. km.).

PHYSICAL FEATURES: Highest point—Triglav (9,396 ft.; 2,864 m.), in the Julian Alps. **Lowest point**—sea level.

POPULATION: 2,000,000 (2002; annual growth 0.0%).

MAJOR LANGUAGE: Slovenian.

MAJOR RELIGION: Roman Catholicism.

GOVERNMENT: Parliamentary democratic republic. **Head of state**—president. **Head of government**—prime minister. **Legislature**—unicameral National Assembly.

ECONOMY: Chief minerals—lignite, coal, lead, zinc. **Chief agricultural products**—potatoes, hops, wheat, sugar beets. **Industries and products**—ferrous metallurgy and rolling-mill products, aluminum-reduction and rolled products. **Chief exports**—machinery and transport equipment, manufactured goods, chemicals. **Chief imports**—machinery and transport equipment, manufactured goods, chemicals.

MONETARY UNIT: 1 tolar = 100 stotins.

NATIONAL HOLIDAY: June 25 (Statehood Day).

Compared to other former Communist countries, however, Slovenia has a very strong state sector (about 45 percent of the economy belongs to the state) and very little foreign ownership or investment.

HISTORY

As part of the Roman Empire, the area of today's Slovenia was crossed by the Roman legions on their way north, and later by the Germanic Lombards from the north when they invaded Italy in the 6th century A.D. The territory came under Austrian rule in the 10th century and remained within the Austrian orbit for 1,000 years. The mountain ridges in the east and south once formed the barrier between the Christian world and the Turkish Empire.

The famous Lippizaner horses originated in the town of Lipica (Lippiza), close to the Italian border. In 1580, Austrian Archduke Charles founded the farm that has raised the elegant white horses of the Viennese Spanish Riding School ever since. The horses are taught to perform intricate, almost balletlike steps to the sounds of Viennese waltzes.

Napoleon occupied the area in the early 19th century and created a province called Illyria, after the old Roman province, with its capital at Ljubljana. The territory reverted to Austria in 1813.

In 1918, Slovenia joined the other Balkan nations and became part of the Kingdom of Serbs, Croats, and Slovenes, which adopted the name Yugoslavia (meaning "Land of South Slavs") in 1929. During World War II, Slovenia was carved up by Hitler's Germany and Mussolini's Italy.

The Splitting of Yugoslavia and Independence. Slovenia initiated the disintegration of Yugoslavia in September 1989, when the Parliament proclaimed the republic an "independent state." In April 1990, Slovenian Communists were defeated in the first free elections by a coalition of center-right parties called DEMOS.

In June 1991, Slovenia declared independence, but the Yugoslav government said this was unconstitutional and sent in troops to regain control of international borders. A 10-day war between the Yugoslav army and the Slovenian Territorial Defense resulted in the deaths of 49 people, but a cease-fire stopped the hostilities, and the federal army withdrew. In January 1992, Slovenia was recognized by the European Community, and, in April 1992, by the United States.

Elections in December 1992 resulted in the victory of the leftist Liberal Democratic Party, headed by Janez Drnovšek. Drnovšek had begun his career within the Yugoslav League of Communists and even served as president of Yugoslavia, in 1989. Most of Slovenia's top politicians also have a Communist past, including the president, Milan Kučan. This Communist legacy has not prevented them from leading a smooth transition from a one-party system to a more open society. By the early 2000s, Slovenia had become an orderly, optimistic, and prosperous country. It is the front-runner among the applicants for EU membership, and also hopes to join NATO at some point in the near future.

GOVERNMENT

A new, post-Communist constitution was adopted late in 1991. The lower house of the bicameral parliament has 90 members, the upper house 40 members. The head of state is the president.

IRINA RYBACEK / Reviewed by EDWARD W. WALKER, Ph.D., Columbia University

CROATIA

The walled city of Dubrovnik, once a popular Adriatic resort, sustained much damage (most now repaired) from shelling in the violence that followed the breakup of Yugoslavia.

Croatia went through two dramatic changes within less than a decade. In June 1991, it declared its independence from Yugoslavia, after being part of that multiethnic country for most of the 20th century. Immediately thereafter, a war between the Serbian minority and the newly created Croatian army erupted and lasted until January 1992. Further engagements with the Serbs took place in 1995, and the arch-nationalist Croatian president Franjo Tudjman was hailed as the national hero.

Tudjman tried to suppress all political opposition. He died in December 1999, and less than a month after that, the opposition was overwhelmingly victorious in the parliamentary elections. Under its new president, Stjepan Mesić, Croatia embarked on a road to democracy—but aggressive nationalists continue to exert substantial influence.

THE LAND

Croatia is a country of unusual form, consisting of three distinct, very different parts. The largest area is the inland plateau, which stretches east of the republic's capital, Zagreb; the smallest portion is the westernmost extremity, the peninsula of Istria. The third part of Croatia is the long and narrow southern extremity, which consists of the Dalmatian coast and includes the historic towns of Split and Dubrovnik.

Inland Croatia is mostly low hills and valleys. Its borders are formed by rivers—the border with Hungary in the north by the River Mur (Mura), the border with Serbia in the east by the Danube, and the border with Bosnia and Herzegovina in the south by the Sava.

The hilly and beautiful interior of the Istrian Peninsula is covered with medieval villages that reflect the centuries-long influence of Venice and Austria. The long Dalmatian coast, and the hundreds of islands along it, were a favorite vacation spot for wealthy Europeans long before the massive development of tourism after World War II.

The climate of Croatia varies from mildly continental weather in the inland part to pleasant Mediterranean temperatures in Istria and Dalmatia. Refreshing sea breezes sometimes turn into strong winds called *maestral* that can accompany fierce but short summer storms.

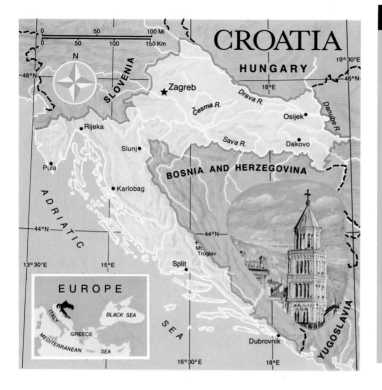

CROATIA

FACTS AND FIGURES

OFFICIAL NAME: Republic of Croatia.

NATIONALITY: Croat(s).

CAPITAL: Zagreb.

LOCATION: Balkan Peninsula. **Boundaries**—Slovenia, Hungary, Yugoslavia, Bosnia and Herzegovina, Adriatic Sea.

AREA: 21,829 sq. mi. (56,538 sq. km.).

PHYSICAL FEATURES: Highest point—Troglav (6,276 ft.; 1,913 m.), north of Split. **Lowest point**—sea level. **Chief rivers**—Drava, Danube, Mur, Sava, Česma, Krka.

POPULATION: 4,300,000 (2002; annual growth –0.2%).

MAJOR LANGUAGE: Serbo-Croatian.

MAJOR RELIGIONS: Roman Catholicism, Eastern Orthodoxy.

GOVERNMENT: Presidential/parliamentary democracy. **Head of state**—president. **Head of government**—prime minister. **Legislature**—bicameral Assembly or Sabor.

CHIEF CITIES: Zagreb, Rijeka, Split, Dubrovnik.

ECONOMY: Chief minerals—coal, oil, bauxite, iron ore. **Chief agricultural products**—corn, wheat, sugar beets, sunflowers. **Industries and products**—chemicals and plastics, machine tools, fabricated metal, electronics, pig iron and rolled-steel products. **Chief exports**—machinery and transport equipment, miscellaneous manufactures, chemicals. **Chief imports**—machinery and transport equipment, chemicals, miscellaneous manufactured articles.

MONETARY UNIT: 1 Croatian kuna = 100 lipas.

NATIONAL HOLIDAY: May 30 (Statehood Day).

THE PEOPLE

Croats belong to the South Slavic ethnic and linguistic group. They speak Croatian, which is almost the same language as Serbian (and therefore was once known as Serbo-Croatian). Croats write their version in Latin script, while the Serbs use Cyrillic.

In Communist Yugoslavia, about 11 percent of the population of Croatia were Serbs; now the percentage is much lower. The legacy of bad blood between these two groups has deep historical roots, with Catholic Croats traditionally leaning toward Western Europe and Orthodox Serbs toward the East. Strengthened during World War II, this hostility was exploited by nationalist leaders throughout the 1990s, when about 1 million people were driven from their homes. Several Croatian generals have since been accused of war crimes by the Hague International Tribunal.

CITIES

Zagreb, the capital of the republic, is also the largest city in Croatia. Originally two separate towns—one on the summit of a hill, and the other on a plain below it—Zagreb became one city in the 19th century. The lower town is now full of shops and cafés, centered around the recently renovated Republic Square. A university, theaters, opera houses, art galleries, publishing houses, and film studios contribute to Zagreb's traditionally active cultural life.

Dubrovnik (formerly Ragusa) led all the cities of Yugoslavia in popularity. Surrounded by 1,000-year-old walls, the old city has red-roofed buildings that add warmth to the glistening whiteness of the village homes. For years, Dubrovnik hosted a festival of operas, concerts, and dances. In September 1991, the city was shelled by the Yugoslav army, but it has since been repaired.

Other Cities. Rijeka, known before World War II as Fiume, was an Italian city until 1945. Located on the Istrian Peninsula, it is a major seaport and tourist center, boasting numerous historical monuments. The Dalmatian city of **Split,** which lies halfway between Rijeka and Dubrovnik, is famous for the remains of the Roman Emperor Diocletian's palace.

ECONOMY

Croatia's inland area, with its deposits of coal, oil, and natural gas, is the industrial and mining region of the republic. The main economic activities in the southern part of Croatia are agriculture and the various services associated with tourism. While it was part of Yugoslavia, Croatia was the second most-prosperous republic, but the upheavals of the 1990s disrupted traditional economic ties and badly damaged factories, bridges, and power lines. It is hoped that Western aid and investment will help bolster the economy.

HISTORY

The Slavic tribes known as the Croats came to the area of present-day Croatia in the 6th and 7th centuries, and, in A.D. 924 or 925, they created their own kingdom under a ruler named Tomislav. In the following century, Croatia extended its dominion over the Dalmatian coast, and, in 1102, it associated itself with the kingdom of Hungary.

When the Turks invaded Hungary in the early 16th century, Croatia joined Austria, but it reverted to Hungarian control in the late 18th century. In 1868, Croatia was granted autonomy by the Hungarians.

As part of the Kingdom of Serbs, Croats, and Slovenes after World War I, Croatia became one of the puppet states of Nazi Germany during World War II. Its Fascist movement, called Ustaši, seized power in 1941, after the invasion of German and Italian troops, and set up an "independent state." Following the establishment of the "Second Yugoslavia" in 1945, Croatia became one of its six constituent republics.

Independent Croatia. On June 25, 1991, the Croatian parliament declared independence, and, a few weeks later, ethnic violence erupted between Serbian irregulars and the newly formed units of Croatian guardsmen and police. Fighting continued until late 1991, causing great human suffering and enormous physical damage. The so-called Republic of Serbian Krajina, about one-fourth of Croatian territory, was proclaimed by rebel Serbs in 1991. The Croatian army regained the area in 1995.

In 1993, Croatia supported Croats in western Bosnia when they fought against the Muslim government. The following year, however, the Croatian government began to participate in international negotiations, which culminated in the Dayton Agreements of 1995 that ended the war in Bosnia and Herzegovina. In the early 2000s, Croatia was looking toward a peaceful future, but repairing the damages caused by years of armed conflict while modernizing the economy remain daunting tasks.

GOVERNMENT

Croatia is a democratic republic with a constitution adopted in 1990. The nationalist Croatian Democratic Union, headed by Franjo Tudjman, was in power throughout the 1990s, but in the parliamentary elections of January 2000, it was soundly defeated by the opposition.

IRINA RYBACEK / Reviewed by EDWARD W. WALKER, Ph.D., Columbia University

The famous arched bridge in Mostar was destroyed in the prolonged civil war.

BOSNIA AND HERZEGOVINA

The people who for centuries have lived in the mountainous and landlocked area of the former Yugoslav republic of Bosnia and Herzegovina are Muslim Slavs, Orthodox Serbs, and Roman Catholic Croats. Under the stern rule of Marshall Tito, the three groups lived in mixed neighborhoods with many intermarriages. Then, in the early 1990s, the country then known as Yugoslavia disintegrated. After Bosnia and Herzegovina declared independence in March 1992, its Serbian population took up arms, and soon the Croats joined the fray. The brutal ethnic and religious war left up to 250,000 dead and 2.5 million refugees. Following the 1995 Dayton (Ohio) agreements, a fragile peace returned, but the country remains divided along ethnic lines. It is a virtual protectorate, with 18,000 NATO troops overseeing postwar reconstruction.

THE LAND

Bosnia and Herzegovina is a country with magnificent mountains that are home to a rich variety of game animals, including deer, bears, and wild boars. The rivers are full of trout, and vineyards are known for their excellent wines. Olive groves and fig trees grow everywhere. Lowlands are few: along the River Sava in the north, the valley of the Neretva in the south, and the Drina Valley in the east. The mountains belong to the limestone Dinaric Alps Range. There is a narrow 12-mi. (20-km.) access to the sea.

The war has brutalized not only the people, but also the countryside. Bosnia and Herzegovina is now full of land mines.

The climate of Bosnia and Herzegovina is mild; along the Neretva River, temperatures are almost subtropical, but in higher elevations, continental influences prevail. The country receives plenty of precipitation.

THE PEOPLE

Before the war, about 44 percent of the inhabitants were Muslim Slavs, descendants of the original Slavic tribes that came to the area in the Middle Ages, and were converted to Islam after the Turks overran the region in 1463. The Serbs, living mostly in the east and northwest, accounted for 31 percent of the population, and the Croats, 17 percent. In 2000, the population was broken down into three ethnic groups: Muslims (38 percent), Serbs (40 percent), and Croats (22 percent).

The future coexistence of the three groups is uncertain. The Balkan peoples have long historical memories, and the atrocities of recent years have sown seeds of hatred for decades to come.

CITIES

Until the brutal siege of 1992–94, **Sarajevo,** the capital of the republic, exemplified the complex mixture of nationalities and religions of Yugoslavia. Set in a narrow mountain valley, Sarajevo's clock tower and the spires of its minarets recall centuries of Turkish occupation. In contrast, the outskirts of the town were built after World War II.

The area has been inhabited since prehistoric times, but the town gained importance in the 15th century under Turkish rule. The 16th century was Sarajevo's Golden Age—more than 70 mosques of great grace and stature were built during this period. Sarajevo gained worldwide attention in June 1914, when a young Bosnian, Gavrilo Princip, assassinated the visiting Austrian Archduke Franz Ferdinand. It was a spark that ignited World War I.

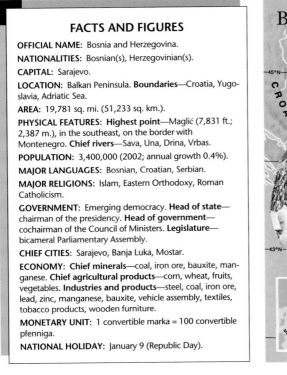

FACTS AND FIGURES

OFFICIAL NAME: Bosnia and Herzegovina.

NATIONALITIES: Bosnian(s), Herzegovinian(s).

CAPITAL: Sarajevo.

LOCATION: Balkan Peninsula. **Boundaries**—Croatia, Yugoslavia, Adriatic Sea.

AREA: 19,781 sq. mi. (51,233 sq. km.).

PHYSICAL FEATURES: Highest point—Maglić (7,831 ft.; 2,387 m.), in the southeast, on the border with Montenegro. **Chief rivers**—Sava, Una, Drina, Vrbas.

POPULATION: 3,400,000 (2002; annual growth 0.4%).

MAJOR LANGUAGES: Bosnian, Croatian, Serbian.

MAJOR RELIGIONS: Islam, Eastern Orthodoxy, Roman Catholicism.

GOVERNMENT: Emerging democracy. **Head of state**—chairman of the presidency. **Head of government**—cochairman of the Council of Ministers. **Legislature**—bicameral Parliamentary Assembly.

CHIEF CITIES: Sarajevo, Banja Luka, Mostar.

ECONOMY: Chief minerals—coal, iron ore, bauxite, manganese. **Chief agricultural products**—corn, wheat, fruits, vegetables. **Industries and products**—steel, coal, iron ore, lead, zinc, manganese, bauxite, vehicle assembly, textiles, tobacco products, wooden furniture.

MONETARY UNIT: 1 convertible marka = 100 convertible pfenniga.

NATIONAL HOLIDAY: January 9 (Republic Day).

In April 1992, the Serbian nationalist forces began to blockade and bombard Sarajevo, and the capital's 560,000 citizens found themselves living in a nightmare, with the death toll increasing each day. The siege lasted until April 1994 and cost Sarajevo 10,000 lives.

Other Cities. Banja Luka, the second largest city in the country, was rebuilt after a severe earthquake in 1969. **Mostar,** the provincial capital of Herzegovina, is named after the beautifully arched Stari Most—Old Bridge—that spans the Neretva River. The bridge was completely destroyed during the war, but has since been repaired. The names of two towns—**Srebrenica** and **Goražde**—became known worldwide because of their prolonged sufferings.

ECONOMY

Bosnia and Herzegovina has mineral deposits of lignite, iron ores, manganese, bauxite, and rock salt, and mining was an important part of the republic's economy. Agriculture has been traditionally based on the cultivation of corn, wheat, potatoes, sugar beets, olives, flax, tobacco, vine products, and fruits.

The war left the economy in ruins. Thanks to massive international help, an economic reconstruction has repaired the most serious damages, but it will be several decades before the country fully recuperates.

HISTORY AND GOVERNMENT

The area was originally inhabited by Illyrians, but during the 6th century A.D., Slavic tribes moved in. By the end of the 1st millennium, the region of present-day Bosnia and Herzegovina was the borderland between Western Latin Christendom and Eastern Byzantine Orthodoxy. By the 12th century, the principalities of Bosnia allied themselves with the Hungarian-Croat monarchy, and the area later became a duchy of Herzegovina (the name derives from the German *Herzog*, "duke").

The Turks came in 1463 and stayed for 400 years, converting most of the population to Islam. Modern Bosnian nationalism emerged in the late 19th century, first directed against the Turks, and then against the Austro-Hungarian Empire, initiating World War I. After the war, Bosnia and Herzegovina became part of the newly formed Kingdom of Serbs, Croats, and Slovenes, which was renamed Yugoslavia in 1929.

Independent Bosnia and Herzegovina. In March 1992, the government declared the republic a "multinational and multireligious community," based on parliamentary democracy and "freedom for all." The Serbian-initiated policy of "ethnic cleansing" and the atrocities by all warring sides have since invalidated this proclamation.

The Dayton Agreements of late 1995 ended the war and provided for a presence of 60,000 NATO troops to oversee the implementation of peace. By 2002, the number of troops had dwindled to 18,000. There is no fighting, but distrust remains between the Serbian Republic and the Bosnian-Croatian Federation. In local elections, voters generally prefer the nationalist parties. Even so, there have been recent encouraging signs that indicate the wounds are beginning to heal. Muslim families are returning to their native villages in Serb-held Bosnia. With Slobodan Milošević in prison in The Hague, the extreme nationalism once common in all three communities has also lessened.

IRINA RYBACEK / Reviewed by EDWARD W. WALKER, Ph.D., Columbia University

Skopje, Macedonia's ancient capital city, has a distinct contemporary flavor—thanks in large part to the massive rebuilding that followed a catastrophic 1963 earthquake.

MACEDONIA

One of the successor republics of the former Yugoslavia, Macedonia shares its name with a historic region that includes a large part of northern Greece. The powerful kingdom of ancient Macedon was the birthplace of Alexander the Great. This distant past complicated the new republic's establishment, because of a claim by Greece that Macedonia was usurping its national symbols. By 1995, the two countries had resolved their dispute. In 2001, Macedonia was shaken by an armed conflict with Albanian insurgents in the north. Under intense international pressure, an agreement was struck between the Macedonian government and the Albanian minority, granting Albanian citizens more rights.

THE LAND

Macedonia is a mountainous country divided in the southeast by the River Vardar, which flows past the country's capital, Skopje, on its way to the Aegean Sea at the Gulf of Salonika. The highest mountains are in the northwest. In the south lie two large lakes, Prespa and Ohrid.

Macedonia enjoys a pleasant, almost Mediterranean climate. In the winter the temperature in Skopje hovers around the freezing point, while in the summer it is about 76° F. (24° C.).

THE PEOPLE

About two-thirds of the inhabitants are Macedonians, a southern Slavic people who speak a language similar to Bulgarian. Most Macedonians belong to the Orthodox Church. Between 25 and 30 percent of the population are Muslim Albanians, who received greater autonomy in 2001. Many Macedonians still celebrate their traditional feasts. The country is known for its carpet weaving, wood carving, and embroidery.

CITIES

Skopje. Housing more than 500,000 people, Macedonia's capital looks very modern, even though it is an ancient town. Known in Roman times as Scupi, it was destroyed in an earthquake in A.D. 518. On a frightening day in July 1963, another strong earthquake damaged or completely destroyed about 80 percent of the buildings and killed more than 1,000 people. A new Skopje was built around the shattered railroad ter-

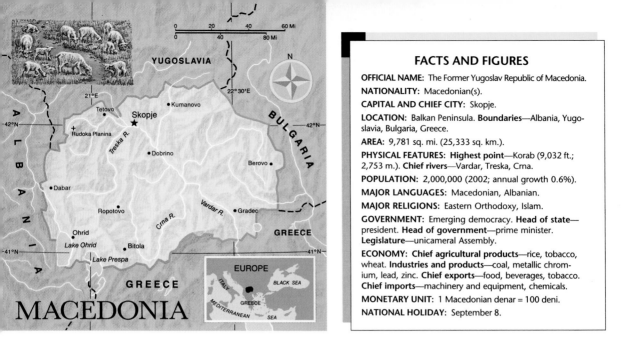

minal, with its broken clock marking the time of the earthquake—5:17 in the morning. Many historic memorials have been completely restored, including the 15th-century Stone Bridge across the Vardar and the Mustapha Pasha mosque.

Ohrid, a small historic town on the shore of Lake Ohrid in southern Macedonia, is the most popular tourist spot in the country. From the 9th to the 14th centuries A.D., it was an important Serbian religious center.

ECONOMY

Although Macedonia's subsoil contains a number of minerals, the country is mostly agricultural. It was industrialized during the Communist era, with most of its industry centered around the capital.

HISTORY AND GOVERNMENT

After the defeat of the Macedonian kingdom, the region became the Roman province of Macedonia. In the late 10th century, Slav tribes established an independent state under Czar Samuilo, centered around Ohrid. This state included much of present-day Bulgaria, but it came to a bitter end in 1014. In a battle with the Byzantines that year, the Byzantine emperor Basil II took 14,000 prisoners, blinded them, and sent them back to Samuilo, who then died of a stroke.

From the end of the 14th century until 1912, Macedonia was part of the Turkish Ottoman Empire. During the Communist period, the first Macedonian schools were opened and new roads were built, but overall the republic remained backward. After becoming independent in 1991, Macedonia was an oasis of peace until 1999, when about 335,000 Albanian refugees flooded the country from neighboring Kosovo during the NATO bombing. In 2001, fighting between Macedonian police and Albanian insurgents claimed dozens of victims on both sides.

Government. Macedonia is a republic with a strong presidency. The unicameral parliament, the Sobranie, has 120 members. In November 2001, a new constitution gave more rights to the Albanian minority.

IRINA RYBACEK / Reviewed by EDWARD W. WALKER, Ph.D., Columbia University

ESTONIA

Tallinn, the capital of Estonia, retains much of its medieval charm.

Between July 1, 1940, and September 6, 1991, Estonia was one of the 15 constituent republics of the Soviet Union, the smallest in population and the third smallest in size. After regaining independence, the country put all its energy into the building of a democratic, free-market system, and by the late 1990s it had become the first success story to emerge from the old Communist empire. Estonia belongs to the first group of post-Communist states that are expected to join the European Union.

THE LAND

Estonia is the most northerly of the Baltic republics. Its squarish shape gives it four borders: the Gulf of Finland to the north, Russia to the east, Latvia to the south, and the Baltic Sea to the west. Estonian territory also includes more than 1,500 islands and islets, the largest of which are Saaremaa (Sarema) and Hiiumaa. The landscape is mostly flat, with low moraine hills, numerous short rivers, and about 1,500 lakes. Only one-tenth of the country rises higher than 160 ft. (50 m.). The largest lake, Peipus (1,390 sq. mi.; 3,600 sq. km.), is shared with Russia.

The climate of Estonia is pleasant, with cool summers and moderate winters. Precipitation levels are usually high, sometimes resulting in flooding. Because of the northern latitude, summer days and winter nights in Estonia are long.

THE PEOPLE

About 60 percent of the inhabitants of Estonia are Estonians, while 30 percent are Russians. The remaining 10 percent consists of Ukrainians and other peoples. Estonians are ethnic cousins to all the Finno-Ugric peoples who migrated to Europe from the Ural hinterlands. These include Finns, Lapps, and Hungarians. Strongly influenced throughout the centuries by the Germans as well as their Finnish and Baltic neighbors, Estonians began to assume their modern identity in the 19th century.

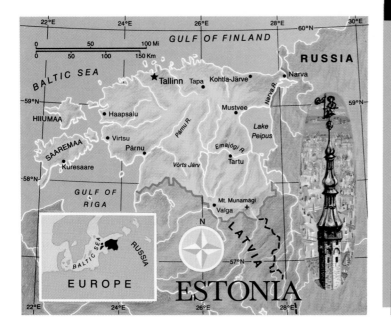

FACTS AND FIGURES

OFFICIAL NAME: Republic of Estonia.

NATIONALITY: Estonian(s).

CAPITAL AND CHIEF CITY: Tallinn.

LOCATION: Eastern Europe. **Boundaries**—Gulf of Finland, Russia, Latvia, Baltic Sea.

AREA: 17,462 sq. mi. (45,226 sq. km.).

PHYSICAL FEATURES: Highest point—Mt. Munamägi (1,042 ft.; 318 m.), in the southeast. **Lowest point**—sea level. **Chief rivers**—Pärnu, Emajõgi. **Major lake**—Peipus.

POPULATION: 1,400,000 (2002; annual growth –0.4%).

MAJOR LANGUAGES: Estonian (official), Russian, Ukrainian.

MAJOR RELIGION: Protestantism.

GOVERNMENT: Parliamentary democracy. **Head of state**—president. **Head of government**—prime minister. **Legislature**—unicameral Parliament.

ECONOMY: Chief minerals—shale oil, peat, phosphorite, amber. **Chief agricultural products**—potatoes, fruits, vegetables. **Industries and products**—shale oil, shipbuilding, phosphates, electric motors. **Chief exports**—machinery, textiles. **Chief imports**—machinery, transport equipment.

MONETARY UNIT: 1 Estonian kroon = 100 cents.

NATIONAL HOLIDAY: February 24 (Independence Day).

During the Soviet era, the republic attracted many immigrants from Russia and Ukraine, who came to work in the newly established industries and to serve as representatives of the central power. This "Sovietization" was deeply resented by Estonians, who had always been the most Western-oriented of all Soviet citizens, even before they gained easy access to Finnish television beamed across the Gulf of Finland.

In November 1991, the Parliament restored a 1938 law that grants citizenship only to applicants who have lived in Estonia for two years and who know the Estonian language. The resident Russians—so long the dominant group in Estonia—are displeased with these policies, but so far there have been no signs of ethnic strife.

Education and Cultural Life. Estonians are cultured, well-educated people who have developed modern literary forms since the 19th century. As early as the 1870s and 1880s, virtually all Estonians were literate, and many were bilingual, fluent in German and later Russian, under Czar Alexander III in the 1880s and 1890s. Tallinn, the Estonian capital, boasts numerous theaters, orchestras, and regular music and song festivals.

During the Soviet era, education was standardized to conform to the ideological dictates of the Communist regime. Now that Estonia is an independent republic, young Estonians are learning for the first time the complete 20th-century history of their country.

CITIES

Tallinn. With a population of roughly 500,000, Tallinn is both a medieval Hanseatic town, full of picturesque winding streets and old buildings, and a modern, smart city with lively cafés, numerous galleries, and western Scandinavian spirit. Every summer the city hosts a number of music and dramatic festivals. Tallinn is also an industrial center and an important grain-handling port.

Dating back to at least the 12th century A.D., the city reached its medieval pinnacle in the mid-14th century. From 1561 to 1721, it belonged to Sweden; then it became part of Russia. Large shipyards were built at Tallinn before World War I. During World War II, 6,000 buildings were damaged.

Foreign entrepreneurs, mostly from Scandinavian countries, are now flocking to Tallinn to set up representative offices for their companies. New private restaurants and cafés serve pastries, cakes, and open-face sandwiches; fancy boutiques offer fashionable clothing and accessories; and streets are often jammed with expensive foreign cars. Tallinn also had the first real supermarket in the former Soviet Union.

Tartu. The country's second-largest city, Tartu (known in German as Dorpat), is a major manufacturing and intellectual center. Tartu is the seat of a well-known university founded in 1632, closed in 1700, and then revived again in 1802. The 19th-century Estonian nationalist revival was centered in this city.

Parnu, a town on the Gulf of Riga, is a favorite resort that prides itself on new and refurbished hotels full of visiting Finns and Swedes.

ECONOMY

Estonia is an industrial country, specializing in the manufacture of precision instruments, textiles, and food processing. Timber products have traditionally been important, but many forests have been badly depleted and can no longer be harvested. The land contains mineral deposits of oil shale, phosphate rock, and peat, along with small deposits of uranium. Industrial development has caused serious environmental pollution in Estonia, as it has in many other parts of the former Soviet Union.

Estonians love music. Many towns and villages sponsor a variety of choral groups and hold annual music festivals.

Agriculture, which was collectivized during the Soviet era, is now returning to private peasant hands. The most important agricultural activities are dairy farming and meat production.

A Success Story. Like other republics of the former Soviet Union, Estonia was economically linked to the vast Soviet market, and the initial period of independence was difficult for the little country, with serious food shortages and an inflation rate that reached over 200 percent. In June 1992, however, Estonia introduced its own currency, the *kroon*, which has since become very stable.

In contrast to its Baltic neighbors, Estonia has greatly profited from its links to Finland and other Scandinavian countries. Finland has become the country's largest foreign partner, and Sweden has supplied most of the foreign investment. Many Estonians who had emigrated and had successful business experiences in the West have returned and are contributing to the rebirth of capitalism in their native country.

The government privatized former state companies and made it easy for foreign investors to open businesses in Estonia. As of 1994, about 60,000 new enterprises had begun operating. The economic recovery has led to the creation of new jobs, and, by the mid-1990s, Estonia had the lowest unemployment rate of any of the Baltic republics. The country's economy is now one of the most open in the world, with almost nonexistent import duties. In 2000, Estonia's economy grew faster than any other economy in central and eastern Europe.

Even though such social groups as pensioners, farmers, and state employees went through several difficult years when they could barely make ends meet, their living standards have begun to rise. In the areas inhabited mainly by Russians, particularly around the city of Narva, economic transformation has been somewhat slower.

HISTORY

The ancestors of present-day Estonians lived in the area since pre-Christian times. Vikings passed through the region on their explorations and trade missions to the Slavic lands to the east, and in the 11th and 12th centuries A.D., Danes, Swedes, and Russians tried unsuccessfully to Christianize and conquer the area. The Germans entered Estonian lands next, and their missionary military orders finally prevailed. By 1227, southern Estonia and most of its islands were controlled by the Teutonic Order; northern Estonia became a part of Denmark.

By the end of the Middle Ages, the land that forms present-day Estonia belonged to Sweden, but in 1721 the Russians—led by Peter I (the Great)—wrested all the Baltic provinces from the Swedish Crown and placed them under Russian rule.

The Estonian national awakening took place in the 19th century, culminating in two decades of independence—from February 1918 to June 1940. When Germany attacked the Soviet Union in June 1941, Estonia was occupied by Germany, but in September 1944, the Soviet Red Army took Tallinn, and Soviet rule was again imposed on the country. To break any resistance, large numbers of Estonians (about 60,000 people) were deported in the late 1940s. During the following decades, Estonia was firmly controlled by the Soviet Union and its ideology.

Independent Estonia. Estonia proclaimed its sovereignty in November 1989. In a referendum in March 1991, almost 80 percent of the voters favored gradual independence. On August 20, 1991—the second day of the attempted Soviet coup against Mikhail Gorbachev—Estonia declared itself independent. In early September the State Council of the Soviet Union recognized this declaration of freedom.

Estonia's first year of independence was devoted to the formulation of new directions. The pace of change quickened with the introduction of a new currency, the *kroon,* in 1992. From then on, Estonia has been progressing steadily toward a democratic, prosperous society. It expects to join the European Union (EU) around 2004.

Estonia had the smallest number of Soviet troops of any of the Baltic countries, and the last Russian soldiers left in August 1994.

GOVERNMENT

The highest legislative body in Estonia is the 101-member state council (*Riigikogu*), which elects the president, the formal head of the country. In 2001, the very popular Lennart Meri was succeeded by Arnolt Ruutel. A coalition of center-right parties has been in power since 1999.

IRINA RYBACEK / Reviewed by EDWARD W. WALKER, Ph.D., Columbia University

 LATVIA

Picturesque lakes and medieval castles give the Latvian countryside a storybook appearance.

The area of present-day Latvia did not become a separate national entity until the 20th century, and even today, Latvians account for only slightly over half of the population of the country. Between 1920 and 1940, Latvia was an independent republic, profiting from the weakness of the two major powers that had traditionally competed over its territory—Russia and Germany. During World War II, Latvia was overrun by the Soviets, and then by the Germans; during the Cold War decades, it was one of the constituent republics of the Soviet Union. Together with its Baltic neighbors, Latvia moved toward independence in the late 1980s. It was recognized as an independent state in September 1991.

THE LAND

Most of Latvia is a flatland, except for low hills that rise in the Vidzeme elevation east of Riga and in the extreme southeast. About two-thirds of the country is covered with forests, meadows, pastures, and swamps. The chief river is the Daugava, which flows from Russia and Ukraine. The country also contains about 4,000 small lakes.

Latvia borders Estonia to the north, Russia to the east, Belarus to the southeast, Lithuania to the south, and the Baltic Sea to the west. The Gulf of Riga is a deep indentation that is usually icebound from December to March. The main ports on the Baltic shore are Ventspils and Liepāja.

The climate is humid, and the sky is usually cloudy—Latvia enjoys only about 30 to 40 days of sunshine a year. The January temperatures range from 28° F. (− 2° C.) on the coast to 19° F. (− 7° C.) in the east, while the mean temperature in June is 63° F. (17° C.).

THE PEOPLE

Latvians, or Letts, are the main ethnic group, but they represent only about 54 percent of the population. Other nationalities include the Russians (33 percent), Belorussians, Ukrainians, and Poles.

The Latvians are descended from the Baltic people known as Latgalls (Latgallians), who lived in the area since the early Christian era. The Letts also subsequently absorbed various other peoples, including the Kurs, Livs, Selonians, and Semigallians.

Today the Latvians, together with their neighbors the Lithuanians, are the only surviving members of the Baltic peoples, a distinct linguistic and ethnic group. In the Indo-European family of nations, the Balts are closest to the Slavs and the Germans.

Most Latvians are Lutherans, due to the historic German influence; however, religious observance was severely muted during the Communist era and is only slowly reviving. A small Roman Catholic community has also maintained itself over the years.

Citizenship. Of the three Baltic countries, Latvia contains the largest percentage of minorities. The definition of citizenship has become a problem: to whom does the new country really belong? Many argue that general human rights and freedoms are more important than nationality, but 50 years of Soviet domination have produced strong anti-Russian sentiments. Latvian is the official language of the country, even though many non-Latvian residents do not speak it. In the late 1990s, about one-third of the population did not have citizenship, but the government finally decided to simplify the rules for citizenship acquisition.

CITIES

Riga. With a population of almost 1 million, Riga, the capital of Latvia, is the largest metropolis in the entire Baltic region. The city was badly damaged in both World War I and II, and relatively few old buildings still stand. The city dates from 1158, when it was founded as a depot for merchants from Bremen. In the following century, Riga became a fortified port, and soon thereafter it joined the Hanseatic League.

Subsequently, under Polish, Swedish, and Russian control, Riga continued to be a German outpost. By the early 20th century, it was a large

FACTS AND FIGURES

OFFICIAL NAME: Republic of Latvia.

NATIONALITY: Latvian(s).

CAPITAL AND CHIEF CITY: Riga.

LOCATION: Eastern Europe. **Boundaries**—Estonia, Russia, Belarus, Lithuania, Baltic Sea.

AREA: 24,938 sq. mi. (64,589 sq. km.).

PHYSICAL FEATURES: Highest point—Gaizinkalns (1,023 ft.; 312 m.). **Lowest point**—sea level. **Chief rivers**—Daugava, Gauja, Venta, Lielupe. **Major lake**—Lubānas.

POPULATION: 2,300,000 (2002; annual growth –0.6%).

MAJOR LANGUAGES: Lettish (official), Russian, Lithuanian.

MAJOR RELIGIONS: Lutheranism, Roman Catholicism.

GOVERNMENT: Parliamentary democracy. **Head of state**—president. **Head of government**—prime minister. **Legislature**—unicameral Parliament.

ECONOMY: Chief agricultural products—grains, sugar beets, potatoes. **Industries and products**—transportation and electronics equipment, synthetic fibers, agricultural machinery. **Chief exports**—wood products, textiles, machinery. **Chief imports**—fuel, machinery and equipment, chemicals.

MONETARY UNIT: 1 Latvian lat = 100 santims.

NATIONAL HOLIDAY: November 18 (Independence Day).

A grim memorial marks the site of Salaspils, a notorious Nazi concentration camp.

industrial and trading port with some 500,000 people. During the Soviet era, Riga became one of the country's largest producers of railway engines, streetcars, minibuses, mopeds, washing machines, and tape recorders, and it was also the Soviet Union's second-most-important port after Leningrad (now St. Petersburg).

Riga is also the cultural center of Latvia, hosting many musical events, museums, and lively cafés.

Other Latvian Cities. The second-largest city is **Daugavpils**, with about 120,000 inhabitants (most of whom are Russians). **Jūrmala** has been a resort since the 19th century, but the sea is now too polluted for swimming. **Liepāja** is another important industrial center and port.

ECONOMY

The industrialization of Latvia began in the 19th century. During the Soviet period, the republic became the most industrialized part of the Soviet Union, a process that has led to serious environmental problems. About half of the energy had to be imported, but major hydroelectric stations were built on the Daugava River. A dense grid of railway lines and highways crisscrosses the country.

The major industries, centered in Riga, include the manufacture of transportation and electronics equipment, and also chemical and paper products. Dairy farming and meat production are important.

The Post-Communist Era. Latvian independence opened the country's doors to the world, and Riga's medieval streets are now lined with Western cars brought in by visiting diplomats, businessmen, and investors (many of them emigré Latvians). Yet Latvia still depends economically on Russia, and transit fees for shipping Russian oil and gas account for 60 percent of all foreign income.

In March 1992, the Latvian Supreme Council voted to return to its original owners commercial property that had been nationalized by the Soviet regime. This property consists of the almost 5,000 private businesses that were operating in Latvia in 1940, before the country was taken over by the Soviet Union.

HISTORY

When the German crusaders and traders reached the Baltic region in the 12th century A.D., they named the area around Riga Livonia (or Livland), after the Livs tribe. For the next century, the local tribes fiercely resisted efforts to introduce Christianity, but they finally succumbed. The Germans then formed the Livonian confederation, which consisted of three entities—the Teutonic Order, the archbishopric of Riga, and the free city of Riga. The local population suffered heavily: the local nobility was either vanquished or Germanized, and the peasants were enslaved.

After the period of German domination, Poles, Swedes, and Russians ruled in succession. In the early 19th century, the Russian czar Alexander I granted personal freedom to Latvian peasants, which in turn led to economic growth in the area. Young intellectuals began to formulate ideas of political self-rule, national autonomy, and even independence.

During World War I, Latvia was occupied by Germans for three years, and it lost more than one-third of its population, either through death or emigration. At the end of the war, a weakened Russia was eager to withdraw from the fighting, and it renounced its claim on the Baltic region in March 1918. Germany was soon on its knees, surrendering to the Allies in November. In 1920, after protracted fighting on Latvian soil, the country became independent, and, for the next two decades, it was a republic with a unicameral parliament. The republic's stability was undermined, however, by the rise of local Nazi and Fascist groups.

In June 1940, Latvia was invaded by the Red Army. The following month, it was incorporated into the Soviet Union. About 35,000 Latvian intellectuals were deported, mostly to Siberia. After the German invasion of the Soviet Union, Latvia became part of the German province of Ostland, which also included Estonia, Lithuania, and Belarus. A number of concentration camps were set up, the most infamous of them at Salaspils.

As the Red Army began to advance east, in pursuit of the Germans, the Baltic states were reoccupied in 1944. Some 175,000 Latvians were either killed or deported, in order to suppress the resistance to the Soviet regime, and the entire country was gradually incorporated into the Soviet Union. An intensive Russification campaign was waged for decades.

The New Beginning. Latvia became independent in September 1991. The large Russian minority, which has not yet been granted citizenship, represents an important card in Moscow's dealings with Latvia. Indeed, Russia continues to cast a shadow over Latvia, even though the last of its troops withdrew in August 1994.

Latvia's political scene has been marked by the influence of extremist groups, from the ultranationalist fascists in the People's Movement for Latvia to the Communists in the Latvian Socialist Party. The government changes very frequently—there have been nine governments during the first 10 years of independence.

GOVERNMENT

The seat of legislative power is the 100-seat unicameral parliament (Saeima), which elects the president. Since June 1999, this position has been held by Vaira Vike-Freiberga, an outspoken woman who had long lived in Canada. In 1993, the parliament renewed the country's 1933 constitution from the pre-Soviet era.

IRINA RYBACEK / Reviewed by EDWARD W. WALKER, Ph.D., Columbia University

Vytautas the Great, a major figure in Lithuanian history, built the castle above in the 15th century.

LITHUANIA

In the late 1980s, the Lithuanians, proud descendants of a great medieval power, led the three Baltic republics in their fight for liberation from Soviet overlordship. After 50 years as one of the constituent republics of the Soviet Union, Lithuania was the first to declare sovereignty, in March 1990. Full independence came in September 1991, in the wake of an abortive coup in Moscow.

The nationalist *Sajudis* movement gained international admiration for leading the country toward freedom, but it proved less able to rule effectively afterward. *Sajudis* was defeated in 1992, regained power in 1996 and, in 2000, lost again to a younger generation of politicians.

THE LAND

Present-day Lithuania is about the size of West Virginia, and its countryside consists mostly of lowlands and rolling hills. It is bordered on the north by Latvia, on the east by Belarus, on the south by Poland and the Russian enclave of Kaliningrad, and on the west by the Baltic Sea. The enclave of Kaliningrad, a highly militarized zone and the base of Russia's Baltic Fleet, is wedged between Lithuania and Poland. Although the Lithuanian government is unhappy about this Russian military presence, it has been negotiating with Moscow to establish a corridor across Lithuania for Russian military transport.

The largest river in Lithuania is the Nemunas (Neman), and there are about 3,000 lakes, mostly in the east and southeast. The climate is very humid, with most rain falling in August. In July, the warmest month, the average temperature reaches 63° F. (17° C.). The coldest month is January, with a mean temperature of 23° F. (-5° C.).

THE PEOPLE

Lithuanians represent 80 percent of the population; the remaining 20 percent consists of Russians, Poles, and Belorussians. A large Jewish minority lived in Lithuania before World War II, but it has virtually disappeared, due to Soviet deportations, German exterminations (with some apparent Lithuanian collaboration), and emigration.

Lithuanians are, together with the Latvians, the only surviving Baltic peoples. Their language contains many Slavic and German elements, but it belongs to the separate Baltic group of Indo-European languages. This group also included the language of the original Prussians, who became extinct in the Middle Ages.

Lithuanians are more vivacious and emotional than their Baltic neighbors. More than two-thirds of the people are city dwellers; a number of new urban centers, such as Alytus, Kapsukas, and Utena, were established during the Soviet period. The events of 20th-century Lithuanian history forced many people to emigrate, particularly to North America; today there are about 1 million ethnic Lithuanians in the U.S.

Religion. Most Lithuanians are Roman Catholics, in contrast to their two northern neighbors, Latvians and Estonians, who are predominantly Lutheran. This affiliation grew out of Lithuania's long relationship with Poland and out of cultural and emotional links to Central Europe.

Cultural Life. During the Soviet era, Lithuanian cultural traditions persisted despite the overwhelming presence of Russians. Many newspapers and magazines continued to be published in Lithuanian, and the awareness of Lithuanian cultural roots was quite widespread. The country's songs, fairy tales, and legends are among the oldest in Europe. Many musical events and festivals are held throughout the country, and tens of thousands participate in the national singing festivals, which are held every five years. Modern Western music has been popular for years, and there are numerous rock and jazz groups.

CITIES

Vilnius. The most colorful, vibrant, and pleasant of the three Baltic capitals, Vilnius has a population of 580,000. About 10 percent of the people are Poles. The Catholic impact on Vilnius' history is evident in its

LITHUANIA

FACTS AND FIGURES

OFFICIAL NAME: Republic of Lithuania.

NATIONALITY: Lithuanian(s).

CAPITAL: Vilnius.

LOCATION: Eastern Europe. **Boundaries**—Latvia, Belarus, Poland, Russia, Baltic Sea.

AREA: 25,173 sq. mi. (65,200 sq. km.).

PHYSICAL FEATURES: Highest point—Juozapinė (964 ft.; 294 m.), in the Ašmenos Hills. **Lowest point**—sea level. **Chief river**—Nemunas (Neman).

POPULATION: 3,500,000 (2002; annual growth –0.3%).

MAJOR LANGUAGES: Lithuanian (official), Russian, Polish.

MAJOR RELIGIONS: Roman Catholicism, Lutheranism.

GOVERNMENT: Parliamentary democracy. **Head of state**—president. **Head of government**—premier. **Legislature**—unicameral Parliament.

CHIEF CITIES: Vilnius, Kaunas, Klaipėda.

ECONOMY: Chief mineral—peat. **Chief agricultural products**—meat, milk, sugar beets. **Industries and products**—food processing, machine tools, electric motors. **Chief exports**—machinery, mineral products, textiles. **Chief imports**—machinery, minerals, chemicals.

MONETARY UNIT: 1 Lithuanian litas = 100 centas.

NATIONAL HOLIDAY: February 16 (Statehood Day).

many churches and in other buildings and monuments, including the classical palace built as the residence of Vilnius bishops, and the university founded as a Jesuit college in 1570.

Settled probably in the early 1300s by Gediminas, Vilnius flourished in the 15th century A.D., after the defeat of the Order of Teutonic Knights in 1410. In the 16th century, with a population of 25,000 to 30,000, Vilnius was one of the largest Eastern European cities. Many late-Gothic and Renaissance buildings are remnants of this era.

During World War I, the city was occupied by Germans for more than three years, and subsequent fighting reduced its population by almost one-half. In 1921, Vilnius was located within Polish borders and was an important Jewish center. After World War II broke out, the city again suffered terribly. Another German occupation resulted in a further reduction of the population and a fierce six-day battle in 1944, when the Red Army retook the city and destroyed many buildings. In the Communist era, Vilnius became a center of high-tech manufacturing industries.

Other Cities. The second-largest city is **Kaunas,** located at the juncture of the Neman and Neris rivers. Dating to the 11th century A.D., Kaunas was Lithuania's capital between the world wars, and it has served as a center of Lithuanian nationalism. **Klaipėda** (Memel in German) is the third-largest city and an old Baltic port.

ECONOMY

Lithuania was one of the more prosperous Soviet republics, with well-developed industry and relatively efficient agriculture. Mineral resources include gypsum, chalk, limestone, clay, gravel, and peat, as well as some iron ore and oil deposits. Traditional industries include food processing and the manufacture of consumer goods.

Agriculture concentrates on the production of meat and milk and the cultivation of fodder crops. Food products are exported to Russia in exchange for Russian oil.

Hardships of Independence. The economic unraveling of the Soviet Union and the disintegration of former economic structures and ties have brought countless hardships to the former Soviet republics; Lithuania is no exception. Its economic ties to Russia and other former Soviet republics remain strong. About 40 percent of Lithuanian exports go to Russia, while more than half of Lithuania's raw-material needs and electrical energy are imported from Russia. In 1995, Lithuania signed an association agreement with the European Union, but the country's admission to this organization is predicted to be far in the future.

Unfortunately, none of the governments so far has been able to push through a radical economic transformation. In the late 1990s, the country endured its most difficult time, both economically and politically. One of the reasons for the economic downturn was the Russian financial crisis. There were signs of improvement in the early 2000s, when the government finally managed to attract some significant foreign investments.

HISTORY

Lithuania was the last large European nation to accept Christianity. While the German Teutonic Order subjugated their northern neighbors, Lithuanians resisted the pressure. In the middle of the 13th century A.D., a very capable nobleman named Mindaugas created the Lithuanian state. He allowed himself to be baptized, and was subsequently confirmed as king by Pope Innocent IV. Several years later, however, he reverted to paganism: Lithuania remained a pagan country until 1387.

The most famous ruler of pre-Christian Lithuania was Gediminas, who ruled from 1315 to 1341. He fought with the Teutonic Order, and he also engaged in diplomatic dealings with European rulers and even with the pope. Gediminas invited foreign craftsmen to settle in Lithuania, and he expanded his country's territories. According to tradition, Gediminas once dreamed about a mighty iron wolf and then decided to build a city—Vilnius—that would be as impregnable as the howl of 100 wolves.

One of Gediminas' grandsons, Jogaila, accepted Latin Christianity and married the heiress of Poland, Jadwiga. This "personal union" with Poland took place in 1386. Jogaila then assumed the name Władysław and became the founder of a Polish ruling dynasty called the Jagellonians.

Shortly thereafter, Lithuania enjoyed its golden age during the reign of Vytautas the Great (1392–1430). He expanded Lithuania's territory, and in 1410, together with his uncle Jogaila, soundly defeated the Teutonic Order at the famous Battle of Grünwald (Tannenberg).

In 1569, Poland and Lithuania created a political union, and the Lithuanian aristocracy became Polonized. By the end of the 18th century, when Poland was partitioned among Russia, Austria, and Germany, most of Lithuania had already come under Russian rule.

Between the two world wars, Lithuania became independent, profiting from the weakness of Russia, but when the Soviet Union signed its nonaggression treaty with Germany in 1939, Lithuania's fate for the next 50 years was sealed. The secret protocol to the treaty, in fact, gave Lithuania to the Soviet Union, and when war broke out in September 1939, Moscow began to effectively curb Lithuania's independence. In August 1940, Lithuania was declared a constituent republic of the Soviet Union.

Independence. Together with its two Baltic neighbors, the country became a sovereign, internationally recognized state in September 1991. The excitement of the struggle for freedom gradually abated and gave way to sober concerns about building up a new economic, political, and social system. Lithuania was the first Baltic country from which the Russian troops departed (in August 1993).

The nationalist Homeland Union, formed out of the *Sajudis* movement and led by the musicologist Vytautas Landsbergis, lost in the 1992 parliamentary elections, mainly because of popular discontent with declining living standards. Several months later, Landsbergis lost the presidency to former Communist Algirdas Brazauskas. The post-Communist rule did not last long, however, because the government was not able to improve the economic situation and there were also corruption scandals. The Homeland Union Party returned to power in 1996, only to lose once more four years later, in November 2000, to a center-left coalition of younger politicians.

GOVERNMENT

The main legislative body is the 141-member parliament *(Seimas)*, which was set up by the post-Communist constitution of 1992. The president is chosen in direct elections. Valdas Adamkus, president since 1998, had lived in the United States as an émigré until Lithuania gained its independence.

IRINA RYBACEK / Reviewed by EDWARD W. WALKER, Ph.D., Columbia University

RUSSIA

With the dissolution of the Soviet Union in 1991, Russia became an independent republic. The people jubilantly adopted the tricolor flag of pre-Communist Russia.

Russia is the colossus of the Eurasian continent and the world's largest nation. This immense country, which spans more than 160 longitudinal degrees—nearly half the globe—had its origin in a small area around Moscow. It gradually grew outward until, by the early 19th century, Russia covered approximately the area of the now-defunct Soviet Union. After 1917, when the Bolshevik Revolution ended the rule of the czars, the Union of Soviet Socialist Republics, which included Russia and 14 other republics, became the first Communist-governed state.

Today Russia, or the Russian Federation, unites about 40 officially recognized nationalities and dozens of ethnic groups, organized into republics, regions, and other administrative units. Because of the weakening of central authority in Moscow and the financial and economic collapse of the late 1990s, many of these subdivisions became virtually independent. As for the 14 former Soviet republics, the Russian government still considers most of them as in its own sphere of influence, but it can no longer dictate their actions as in the Communist days.

THE LAND

To fully grasp the country's vast east-west breadth, consider the following: when it is midnight in St. Petersburg, it is 10:00 in the morning on the Bering Strait. Russia lies in both Asia and Europe, the two "conti-

FACTS AND FIGURES

OFFICIAL NAME: Russian Federation.

NATIONALITY: Russian(s).

CAPITAL: Moscow.

LOCATION: Eastern Europe and Northern Asia. **Boundaries**—Norway, Finland, Baltic Sea, Estonia, Latvia, Belarus, Ukraine, Sea of Azov, Black Sea, Georgia, Azerbaijan, Caspian Sea, Kazakhstan, China, Mongolia, North Korea, Sea of Japan, Sea of Okhotsk, Bering Sea, Arctic Ocean.

AREA: 6,592,741 sq. mi. (17,075,200 sq. km.).

PHYSICAL FEATURES: Highest point—Mt. Elbrus (18,481 ft.; 5,633 m.), in the Caucasus Range. **Lowest point**—sea level. **Chief rivers**—Pechora, Dvina, Neva, Neman, Dnieper, Don, Volga, Ob, Irtysh, Yenisei, Lena, Amur. **Major lakes**—Baikal, Ladoga, Onega.

POPULATION: 143,500,000 (2002; annual growth –0.7%).

MAJOR LANGUAGE: Russian.

MAJOR RELIGIONS: Russian Orthodoxy, Islam.

GOVERNMENT: Federation. **Head of state**—president. **Head of government**—premier. **Legislature**—bicameral Federal Assembly.

CHIEF CITIES: Moscow, St. Petersburg (formerly Leningrad), Kaliningrad, Volgograd, Novgorod, Murmansk, Archangel, Novosibirsk, Irkutsk, Vladivostok.

ECONOMY: Chief minerals—oil, coal, natural gas, manganese, lead. **Chief agricultural products**—sunflower seeds, vegetables. **Industries and products**—mining and extractive industries producing coal, oil, gas, chemicals, and metals; machine building; shipbuilding. **Chief exports**—oil, natural gas, wood and wood products. **Chief imports**—machinery and equipment, consumer goods, medicines, meat.

MONETARY UNIT: 1 ruble = 100 kopeks.

NATIONAL HOLIDAY: June 12 (Independence Day).

nents" into which geographers have traditionally divided the vast Eurasian landmass. The line dividing the two parts of Russia—European Russia and Asian Russia—follows the Ural Mountains and the Volga River. (See the sidebar on the Volga River, page 317.)

A glance at Russia's coasts illustrates an important fact about the country—its northerly location and relative isolation. In contrast, the long eastern and western coasts of North America are open to the Atlantic and Pacific oceans, making contact with other continents much simpler. Russia's longest coastline is on the Arctic seas, where the presence of ice makes navigation impossible during most of the year. Only Murmansk,

The Ural Mountains (background) form the traditional boundary between European Russia and Asiatic Russia.

whose waters are warmed by the North Atlantic Drift of the Gulf Stream, is open the year round. Other northern ports may be navigable for as little as two months a year. Along the Pacific coast, the most important Russian port is Vladivostok, but it, too, is threatened by fog and ice for much of the year. St. Petersburg (formerly Leningrad), the port closest to the centers of population and trade, is open only from May to October.

Landforms. Russia is composed mainly of an enormous lowland interrupted and fringed by mountains. The Great Russian lowland in the west is separated from the West Siberian Plain by the Urals. Moving west to east, the plain becomes the Central Siberian Plateau; the land rises even higher in the East Siberian Highlands.

The Urals, which form the major north-south mountain range, can be crossed easily at several points. The Caucasus Mountains between the Black and Caspian seas are a more formidable barrier. The snowcapped mountains contain Mount Elbrus, the highest peak in Europe as well as in all of Russia.

Climate and Vegetation. The climate of Russia is mostly continental, with extremely cold winters and rather hot summers. From north to south, the country's climate and vegetation can be divided into three broad zones—Arctic-tundra; taiga, or humid forest; and dry-fertile.

The Arctic north is subject to the most extreme cold. Winters are long and bitter, and summers are short and cool. Only hardy scrub plants and lichen grow easily, providing food for reindeer herded by the nomads. The northeastern part of this zone contains rich mineral deposits.

The taiga, a coniferous-forest region, stretches across Russia in a broad belt covering about one-half of the nation's land area. This zone, which has a fairly typical continental climate, contains one-third of the world's forestland and provides a major Russian resource—timber—from such hardy trees as spruce, pine, birch, and aspen.

Horse-drawn sleighs and dog teams are reliable means of transportation in the snowy winters of northern Russia.

Moving south to the steppe zone with its fertile soil, the climate grows somewhat milder. This zone has diminished with the end of the Soviet Union. Today most of the steppes are located within the successor republics, such as Ukraine in Europe and Kazakhstan and Uzbekistan in Central Asia.

Rivers and Lakes. Russia contains a wide and useful network of rivers, which, since the country's earliest days, have provided water links across a land that still suffers from a serious shortage of highways and railroads. Many of the rivers have now also been harnessed as a source of hydroelectric power. The most important rivers of European Russia are the Neva, Dvina, Pechora, Dnieper, Don, and Volga—the latter being Europe's longest river. Interconnecting canals have been built to improve transportation. The mightiest rivers of Asian Russia are the Ob-Irtysh system, the Yenisei, the Lena, and the Amur.

In addition to having the longest river and the highest mountain in Europe, Russia borders on the world's largest lake— the salty Caspian Sea. Lakes Ladoga and Onega in the northwest are the largest freshwater lakes in Europe, while Lake Baikal in Asian Russia is the largest in Asia.

Natural Resources. Virtually every major mineral can be found in Russia. The leading coalfields are in the Kuznetsk Basin (Kuzbas) in southern Siberia, near Cheremkhovo and west of Lake Baikal. Iron is also found in several different parts of the nation; the most important deposit lies in the Kuzbas. Russia is a major producer of oil and natural gas. The richest oil region is the Tyumen province in Siberia, just east of the Urals, but oil fields have also been found between Volgograd and the southern Urals and on Sakhalin Island off the northeast coast.

In addition, Russia has deposits of manganese, large copper reserves, and bauxite, nickel, lead, zinc, magnesium, and the rare metals gold, silver, and platinum. Two important nonmetallic minerals are also mined—apatite is used to manufacture phosphate fertilizers, and potassium salts are used in chemical production.

Russia extends eastward from Europe—all the way to the Pacific Ocean. Many European Russians have settled in the Russian Far East.

THE PEOPLE

About 82 percent of the population consists of ethnic Russians, or Great Russians. The remaining 18 percent includes approximately 100 other nationalities and smaller ethnic groups. Of these, the most numerous are The Turkic Tatars.

Many small nationalities are scattered over Siberia. The Chukchi, for example, inhabit the Chukchi Peninsula in the far northeast. Originally they were, and to some extent still are, reindeer herders leading a nomadic life and sleeping in deerskin tents called *yarangi*.

Several million Jews lived in Czarist Russia, but they were often persecuted, and many left for the United States. Under the Soviet regime, anti-Semitism persisted in more subtle ways: Jews were not harassed as Jews but as Zionists. They were assigned to live in Birobidzhan, an autonomous region in eastern Siberia, although most Jewish people continued to live in the western part of the country.

Identity Crisis. Since the dissolution of the Soviet empire, Russians have been trying to redefine their national identity. For many non-Russians, the Soviet Union was a Communist "prison of nations," but for Great Russians it was primarily an heir to a large historic empire. That vast state was at the heart of Russian national consciousness, and cities like Kiev and Odessa (in Ukraine), Baku (in Azerbaijan), and Alma-Ata (in Kazakhstan, now Almaty)—as well as whole regions such as Ukraine, Belarus, and Transcaucasia (now divided among three republics)—were thought of as Russian. With these places gone, many Russians suffered an almost personal sense of loss, but in the early 2000s, under Vladimir Putin, a new, proud Russian identity began to emerge.

Religion. One of the first acts of the Bolshevik government that came to power in 1918 was the disestablishment of the Orthodox Church. Although the 1936 Constitution of Russia guaranteed "freedom of religious worship and antireligious propaganda," the Communist Party considered religious belief to be unnecessary, and generations of students were taught that God does not exist.

The policy of *glasnost* (openness) of the late 1980s, however, made it quite clear that, despite years of suppression, religion in Russia was far from dead. The government began showing an increased tolerance for religious beliefs and actions. High Communist officials participated in the 1988 celebrations of 1,000 years of Christianity, and by 1992 more than 3,000 churches had been reopened.

The Russian Orthodox Church now holds regular services at the Kremlin, and television often features programs on various aspects of religion. When the second Russian president, Vladimir Putin, was being inaugurated in March 2000, he was blessed by Patriarch Alexei II.

Apart from the semi-official Orthodox Church, many Russian cities have become truly multi-religious. Roman Catholics and Protestants are reviving their churches, and Western evangelists draw huge crowds. The Russian old Believers, or *Raskolniki*, are active again. This dissenting church of Russian Christians, which dates to mid-17th century, has shown a remarkable resilience despite centuries-long heavy persecution. Jewish spiritual life has awakened as well. Eastern religions and sects such as Hare Krishna also attract followers throughout contemporary Russia.

Education. Before the Bolshevik Revolution of 1917, more than three-fourths of the Russian people could neither read nor write. After the revolution, schooling became available to everyone. Compulsory attendance began at the age of 7 and was to continue to at least age 17,

After years of official atheism, Russians can once again practice religion openly.

Moscow University is noted for its dramatic skyscraper campus.

although many youngsters, especially in villages, dropped out before then. Almost all preschool children were placed in day nurseries and kindergartens. Indoctrination was an integral part of Soviet education.

The post-Communist educational system is facing many problems. Money is scarce and financing of schools is suddenly uncertain. History, politics, and economics cannot be taught in the old ways, but new textbooks are few. Amid this confusion, several hundred private and religious schools opened in the 1990s, introducing extensive changes to the curriculum. Pupils of these schools study literary works by previously banned authors and engage in open discussions about all kinds of subjects. In the context of Russian history, this is an entirely unprecedented development.

The most prominent of the new centers of learning is the Russian State University for the Humanities (RSUH), a successor of the Moscow State Institute for History and Archives. This young and dynamic institution has earned a worldwide reputation for its academic excellence. It has wide international contacts and is involved in more than 100 cooperation programs with leading Western universities and educational organizations. More than 4,000 undergraduate students enroll each year, including hundreds of students from abroad. The university library has over 1.5 million books, and its multimedia center is fully equipped with computers. This is Russia looking toward the future.

Science. Nineteenth-century Russia produced such distinguished scientists as chemist Dmitry Mendeleyev (1834–1907), physiologist Ivan Pavlov (1849–1936), and a pioneer in astronautics research, Konstantin

Monuments to the Soviet space program are found throughout Russia. The monument above commemorates the flight of Sputnik I in 1957.

Tsiolkovski (1857–1935). The Communist government early on recognized the importance of science for building up the country's industry and military and emphasized mathematics and science in secondary education. Some scientific fields—most notably genetics—were suppressed because they did not conform with Communist ideology.

On October 4, 1957, the Soviet Union launched the world's first earth satellite, Sputnik I, and in 1961, it launched the first manned satellite, carrying astronaut Yuri Gagarin. These events drew worldwide attention to the achievements of Soviet science and technology, and spurred the United States to launch its space program.

After a late start in developing the atomic and hydrogen bombs, the Soviet Union became one of the world's two nuclear superpowers. Soviet scientists also made distinguished contributions in the fields of plasma physics, thermoelectricity, geophysics, and Arctic exploration. In medicine, researchers experimented with transplanting organs and tissues.

Scientific exploration has suffered in the 1990s because of lack of funds, and even the popular Russian space program has had to be curtailed. Fortunately, philanthropist George Soros has provided very generous support to many scientific and cultural programs. Initally, his aid went primarily to the central institutions, but by the end of the 1990s he had also provided increasing support to various regional institutes.

CULTURAL HERITAGE

Literature. Russia has a great literary tradition—the 19th century was an extraordinarily rich period. It began with the "golden age" of poetry from 1815 to 1830. In this short span, Russia produced not only its finest poet, but one of the giants of world literature—Aleksandr Pushkin. He was a national poet, creating a new literary language for Russia that used Russian life, folklore, and history. Pushkin's most popular work is the novel-in-verse *Eugene (Evgeni) Onegin,* which was made into an opera by the famous composer Peter Ilich Tchaikovsky.

Pushkin encouraged and influenced Nikolai Gogol (1809–52), who became the country's first truly imaginative prose writer. Gogol was born in Ukraine, but he wrote in Russian. In the novel *Dead Souls* and the play *The Inspector General,* he satirized the world of officialdom and nobility and showed sympathy for the weak and underprivileged.

In the Russian city of Saratov, a factory once used to make weapons now manufactures VCR heads.

Three prose writers of the second half of the century stand out—Ivan Turgenev, Fedor Dostoyevsky, and Leo Tolstoi. In 1852 Turgenev published *Sportsman's Sketches,* in which he portrayed the serfs as having more of a sense of humanity than their masters. Between 1855 and 1860, when the czar was preparing to abolish serfdom, Turgenev wrote several novels that expressed the reforming enthusiasm that had taken hold of Russian society. The young radicals liked his novels until he published *Fathers and Sons,* whose hero, Bazarov, they took to be an unflattering portrait of themselves, although Turgenev did catch the spirit of the intellectual youth of that period. Many called themselves Nihilists, meaning that they did not accept any authority or any principle on faith.

Fedor Dostoyevsky and Leo Tolstoi were two giants in literature whose writings and personalities could not have been more different. When he was in his 20s, Dostoyevsky (1821–81) belonged to a radical discussion group that criticized existing conditions in Russia. He was arrested and sent to Siberia for four years of hard labor. While in Siberia, he converted to the Orthodox religion, feeling that this would bring him closer to the Russian people. His most famous novels, *Crime and Punishment, The Idiot,* and *The Brothers Karamazov,* are novels of ideas— profound psychological studies with religious overtones. Leo Tolstoi (1828–1910), on the other hand, was a member of the nobility. *War and Peace* is a vast and vivid picture of how upper-class people's lives were affected by Napoleon's invasion of Russia in 1812. Another famous Tolstoi novel, *Anna Karenina,* relates the tragic consequences of a love that transgressed the moral and social laws of the late 19th century.

Music. By the middle of the 19th century, Russian music had also come into its own. European musical forms were joined to Russian musical themes, and compositions emerged that had a distinctive national flavor—such as Mikhail Glinka's opera *Russlan and Ludmilla,* and the works of Nikolay Rimsky-Korsakov and Modest Mussorgsky. Later in the century, composer Peter Tchaikovsky expressed the romantic movement in music—his compositions became quite popular throughout the world.

The Soviet Era. After the Bolshevik Revolution in 1917, many writers, composers, and artists left the country. Many of those who stayed took part in the creative experiments of the 1920s. Poets, actors, and artists often took their talents to the streets, creating public "happenings"—parades, theatricals, and poetry readings—for huge crowds.

This relative freedom came to a halt at the end of the 1920s when Stalin imposed severe controls in all areas of Soviet life. The Communist Party dictated a new outlook for literature and art called Socialist Realism. Writers were expected to glorify Communism and write glowingly about the party and its "leading role" in society, and to create positive heroes who would set a good example for Soviet citizens.

Painting was also expected to portray the Soviet people in a happy light. Abstract art was not permitted. Music was restricted as well, and some works by two leading Russian composers, Sergei Prokofiev and Dmitri Shostakovich, were not performed in those years.

By 1953 it seemed as if the creative arts had been crushed by censorship and repression. The death of Stalin, however, brought a change of climate. The period came to be known as the "Thaw," from a novel of that name by Ilya Ehrenburg, published in 1954. Ehrenburg and others began to call for more freedom of expression, but this frightened the party, and within a few years the "Thaw" ended. Many writers, however, began to publish their works in *samizdat* (underground publishing houses, where manuscripts were typed on manual typewriters) and abroad. In 1957, Boris Pasternak's now-famous novel *Doctor Zhivago* appeared in the West. The next year, Pasternak was awarded the Nobel Prize in Literature, but was forced by the government to decline it.

Much attention has also been focused on Aleksandr Solzhenitsyn, whose great talent was revealed to the public in 1962, when his short novel *One Day in the Life of Ivan Denisovich* appeared with the personal approval of Khrushchev. Reflecting Solzhenitsyn's own experience, it was the first book published in the Soviet Union to describe a prisoner's life in the forced-labor camps. In 1964, however, Solzhenitsyn came under attack by the party. In 1970, Solzhenitsyn, was awarded the Nobel Prize in Literature. *The Gulag Archipelago, 1918–1956,* which describes in detail the Stalinist prison system, appeared in Paris in 1973. It caused a tremendous uproar, and Soviet authorities forced Solzhenitsyn to emigrate. He returned to Moscow in the summer of 1994.

In the post-Stalin period, poets, especially Yevgeny Yevtushenko, Andrei Voznesensky, and Bella Akhmadulina, had a great influence on the Soviet people, particularly the younger generation. Next to poetry, the Russian people have always loved the ballet. Many cities have ballet companies, the best known being the Bolshoi Theater in Moscow. Its production of Tchaikovsky's *Swan Lake* has been seen by millions.

Post-Soviet Years. Mikhail Gorbachev's call for greater openness provoked a modest flourishing of all arts, but especially of literature, film, and theater. Books and movies dealing with subjects that were off-limits for decades began appearing. Anatoli Rybakov's *Children of the Arbat,* written in the 1960s, was published in 1988 and received much popular acclaim. The novel illuminates a short period of Stalin's rule and contains a fascinating intimate portrayal of the dictator. The movie *Repentance,* a mesmerizing allegory of Stalinism and the halfhearted de-Stalinization process, was seen by millions of Soviet citizens. Many works long forbidden by Soviet authorities (including *Doctor Zhivago*) have been published, and new talent is being cultivated in the unfamiliar atmosphere of increased tolerance. In the first post-Soviet decade, many Russians have complained that literature and the arts have lost their preeminent status, but in fact literature and the arts keep flourishing. Two leading postmodernist writers are Vladimir Sorokin and Victor Pelevin. Both Sorokin's fantastic novel *Blue Lard*, which takes place in a 21st-century Russia conquered by China, and Pelevin's *Generation P*, depicting the Russian political scene, have enjoyed a great commercial success. The film director Nikita Mikhalkov made a very popular historic movie, *The Barber from Siberia*. Two leading poets of a movement called conceptualism are D. A. Prigov and Lev Rubinshteyn.

CITIES

The Russian capital, **Moscow,** and the second-largest Russian city, **St. Petersburg** (formerly Leningrad), are discussed in separate articles following this one. Other important Russian cities include **Novgorod,** in northwest Russia, one of the oldest cities in the country; **Pskov,** known as "Novgorod's little brother"; **Kaliningrad,** formerly the German city of Königsberg, located in a small enclave squeezed between Lithuania and Poland, and the base of the Baltic Fleet; **Volgograd,** formerly known as Stalingrad, the site of one of the crucial battles of World War II; **Irkutsk,** a frontier Siberian town and the starting point for the beautiful Lake Baikal; **Novosibirsk,** a sprawling city and the headquarters of the Siberian branch of the Soviet Academy of Sciences, which was in the 1970s and

The world-famous Moscow Circus attracts thousands of people to its exciting performances.

early 1980s a breeding ground for many future "perestroichiks"; and **Vladivostok,** the easternmost port and home of the Pacific Fleet.

ECONOMY

Russia was largely an agricultural country until the late 19th century, when industrialization began, in particular in European Russia. Economic development was then interrupted by World War I and by the civil war that followed. Modern development was initiated by Stalin, whose frantic industrialization drive in the 1930s made the Soviet Union an industrial giant—with clay feet, as it turned out.

Industry. Railroad building in the late 19th century stimulated the construction of some large metalworking and machine-building factories, especially in St. Petersburg. Moscow became the center of the textile industry. After 1928, Stalin achieved a high rate of industrial growth by concentrating on the production of large quantities of iron, steel, coal, and oil—the resources required for heavy industry and for the production of weapons. Other aspects of the economy were neglected, particularly service industries and the manufacture of consumer goods. The Soviet Union thus became an economic superpower, judged by its heavy-industry output, while most of the population lived in material conditions resembling those of many undeveloped countries.

Under Stalin and his successors, the less-settled frontier regions of Central Asia and Siberia were developed. Several of the world's largest dams were built in the former Soviet Union, and the world's first nuclear-power plant was opened in 1954. By the 1980s about 40 nuclear reactors were operating in the country.

In the late 1970s, the economic backwardness of the Soviet Union had become so self-evident that no amount of political propaganda could obscure it. While the developed nations of the West began to enter the Information Age, the Soviet Union still relied on rigid planning and per-

Even in good years, Russia's farms barely produce enough grain to meet domestic needs. In bad years, as when drought conditions occur, the grain harvest falls far short of meeting the country's demands.

VOLGA RIVER

Most major European rivers flow through several countries, taking on different characteristics as they cross new borders. The Volga is Europe's longest river, but for its entire 2,293-mi. (3,690-km.) course, it never leaves Russian soil. The Volga is part of a far-flung network of waterways that connects the Caspian Sea with the Baltic, and the Black Sea with the White. Huge hydroelectric stations along the river have harnessed its waters to provide electricity and irrigation for vast areas of the Volga Basin. The Volga carries about one-half of Russia's river freight, taking food and raw materials to the industrial north and bringing heavy machinery, manufactured goods, and lumber back to the agricultural south.

vasive controls, leaving no room for initiative, inventiveness, or entrepreneurial enterprise.

Agriculture. Providing the Russian people with enough food has been a major problem under both the czars and the Communists. Three factors account for this deficiency: generally poor growing conditions; traditional absence of peasants' commitment to produce efficiently; and chronically bad agricultural infrastructure.

Although Russia is a very large country, it has relatively little fertile soil. Where the soil is at its best, there is not enough rainfall for a good harvest. Farther north, rain is plentiful, but the growing season is short. The other factor is historical: until 1861, Russian peasants were serfs (*muzhiks*), with no land of their own. In the late 19th century, a class of independent farmers began to develop, but the revolution and ensuing collectivization did away with them. The third factor has to do with the overall disorganization. During Soviet times, it was estimated that up to one-half of the harvest rotted in inappropriate storage or during transit.

Perestroika. Shortly after Mikhail Gorbachev became head of the party in 1985, he presented his plan of economic restructuring, which he called *perestroika*. Its major goal was to make individual Soviet enterprises more autonomous—to give them more freedom and more responsibility for their performance. Before, in the planned economy, all enterprises had been totally dependent on central planners, who would determine what to produce and where to sell it. Gorbachev also pushed for improved quality control, but his efforts were hampered by party bureaucrats. The Soviet Union also began to attract foreign companies, and new laws were passed that made it possible to start joint ventures.

Ultimately, *perestroika* failed: it was simply not possible to reform the Communist economic system. Gorbachev's measures destroyed the old bureaucratic command structure, but he was not able to replace it with something new. The unraveling of economic ties went hand in hand with the undermining of political authority, and so instead of improving the Soviet economy, *perestroika* led to shortages, inflation, and lower living standards. The growing popular dissatisfaction with Gorbachev's economic policies was a major factor in his dramatic downfall in 1991.

Independent Russia. Boris Yeltsin, although a Communist Party member until he was 59 years old, managed to discard the Communist ideology more thoroughly than his predecessor. In January 1992, he eliminated state price controls and hastened the privatization process. Within six months, he persuaded Western financial institutions to lend support for his economic transformation. Several of his advisers were bright young economists who advocated a "shock therapy" approach in order to quickly set up a free-market system.

Yet to overhaul the economy of such a mammoth country proved a nightmare and, throughout the 1990s, Russia lived in continual turmoil. President Yeltsin was increasingly erratic—alternately slowing down and again speeding up the reforms. In the first half of the 1990s, thousands of companies were privatized and there arose a powerful group of oligarchs, economic tycoons who not only owned large industrial enterprises, but also controlled the media and politics. Even worse, the privatization had been taken advantage of by organized crime "families," who began to run whole sectors of the economy, extorting "tribute" from individual small entrepreneurs.

Agriculture continues to be a disaster: private farmers have a difficult time receiving credit to modernize their farms, indeed, they generally face an uphill battle because of bureaucratic harassment and envy. About two-thirds of all food consumed in Russia is now imported.

In early 1998, several strikes were triggered by the failure of many enterprises to pay their employees. In August, the ruble collapsed, banks and foreign companies began to close down, the government stopped paying its foreign debt, and many upwardly mobile Russians were suddenly unemployed. The prospects looked grim indeed, and by 1999, about 10,000 Russian companies were bankrupt. This seems to have been a turning point, however. Some Western observers began to argue that the whole Russian society and even the Russian mentality had gone through deep structural changes, and that better times were coming.

True, Russia is still appallingly poor—average monthly wages at the beginning of the 21st century are about $65. Lawlessness and corruption are pervasive, and the "rules of the game" are much less clearly defined than in Western societies. There is an over-

A 250-acre greenhouse yields fresh produce all year.

The dramatic fountains draw tourists to Petrodvorets, the home of the Russian czar Peter the Great.

whelming maze of regulations so complex that nobody is even expected to obey them.

Nevertheless, there are good signs on the horizon: the ruble is stable, inflation is under control, more taxes are being collected, public finances look healthy, and most importantly, a number of Russian-run big companies are at last beginning to be managed efficiently. The economy as a whole is growing and even better growth is predicted in the years to come. President Putin has curbed the power of the oligarchs and pushed through truly revolutionary legislation: from 2002 on, Russians can now buy and sell farmland—for the first time since 1917. At the beginning of the 21st century, many are feeling cautiously optimistic about the future.

HISTORY

The history of what is now Russia began more than 1,000 years ago. By the 8th century A.D., Slavic tribes had spread out along the north-south river roads of the European Russian plain and founded trading towns, of which the two most important were Novgorod and Kiev.

Kievan Russia. Also called Kievan Rus, the first East Slavic state carried on a lively trade with Byzantium, the Eastern Roman Empire, which had its capital in Constantinople (now Istanbul). Through these contacts, Prince Vladimir of Kiev was converted to Christianity in A.D. 988. The Kievan state flourished for several centuries, but then the region was invaded by the Mongols, known in Russian sources as the Tatars.

The Tatar Rule. "No one knows for certain," says the Russian chronicle, "who they are or from where they come, or what their language is, or race, or faith, but they are called Tatars." Coming from Asia, where Genghis Khan had already built a vast empire, they sacked Kiev in A.D. 1240, and set up a headquarters on the lower Volga River. From this encampment the Tatars ruled Russia for almost 250 years.

They forced the Russian princes to pay them heavy taxes. They demanded total obedience, and any protests were harshly put down. To

"The Motherland" monument commemorates the heroic defense of Stalingrad from German invasion during World War II.

keep the Russians divided, the Tatars played one prince against another. As a result the Russian princes absorbed into their own government some of the Tatars' despotic ways of governing.

Russia Under the Czars

It was Moscow that finally overcame the Tatars. The Grand Duke Ivan III (known as the Great) ascended the throne in 1462 and completed the process of bringing all the principalities under Moscow's rule. In 43 years, he tripled Moscow's domain. By that time, Byzantium and its capital, Constantinople, had been overrun by the Turks. This caused two major events in Russia: when Ivan married the niece of the last Byzantine emperor, he concluded that Moscow was the true heir to the Byzantine Empire. He began to call himself "czar," which is Russian for Caesar. In addition the Russian Orthodox Church declared that it was no longer part of the Greek Orthodox Church. It believed that because Constantinople was in Muslim hands, Moscow had become the "third Rome," where Christianity would survive.

During the 16th century A.D., Russia continued to expand, especially down the Volga and eastward to Siberia, and settlers moved into these areas. The power of the czar increased, and the freedom of the Russian people declined. Governing in the autocratic manner of the Tatars, the czar weakened the position of the boyars (the hereditary nobility), the only group that might have opposed him. The peasants, who in theory were at liberty to move around as long as they paid their taxes, were usually in debt to their landlords, and therefore could not leave their estates. In this way, serfdom became widespread in Russia.

Ivan IV, who ruled in the second half of the 16th century, was called Ivan "the Terrible." His reign of terror decimated the boyar class and threw the country into turmoil. After Ivan's death, the Swedes and Poles took advantage of the chaos to invade the country. Finally, in 1613, an assembly of noblemen and townspeople in Nizhni Novgorod elected 16-year-old Michael Romanov as the czar. The Romanov family governed Russia for the next 300 years.

Peter the Great.   Under the first three Romanov czars, order was gradually restored in the government. The outlying areas were brought back under Moscow's control. The next Romanov, Peter the Great (who ruled from 1682 to 1725), opened Russia to European influences and made his country a major European power. From the Swedes, he wrested land on the Baltic and the Gulf of Finland and founded St. Petersburg.

He modernized the military and reorganized the government administration along Swedish lines, moving the capital from Moscow to St. Petersburg. The main burden of Peter's conquests and reforms, however, fell on the peasant-serfs. By this time, they were bound to the land by law.

Nobility and Peasants—A Widening Gap.   In the second half of the 18th century, Russian nobility entered its "golden age." European culture was fashionable in high society, and Empress Catherine the Great herself corresponded with the French philosophers Voltaire and Diderot and admired their ideas. But while in Europe these ideas helped bring about more political freedom for the people, in Russia they had no influence on life outside the aristocratic circles.

At the other extreme from the glittering life in court were Russia's 34 million peasants (who accounted for 94 percent of the total population). The majority of the peasants were serfs on noblemen's estates; the rest lived on lands belonging to the royal family.

Napoleon's invasion of Russia in 1812 brought the nation together under the leadership of Alexander I. Russian troops followed the retreating French Army and in 1813 triumphantly entered Paris. By that time, Russia had become one of the strongest nations in Europe.

In the 1820s a handful of young officers, inspired by French political ideas, concluded that the only way to end serfdom and gain political freedom in Russia was to overthrow the czar. They formed secret societies and plotted, but their revolt was quickly suppressed. Since their attempt took place in December (in 1825), they became known as the Decembrists, and their movement inspired later Russian revolutionaries.

After the Emancipation.   Serfdom was abolished after the country's defeat in the Crimean War in 1856. Alexander II became czar in 1855, and immediately implemented major changes to stop the further decline of Russian power and prestige. His Emancipation Proclamation set the serfs free in 1861. Many Russians, however, felt that this and the other reforms that followed did not go far enough in changing the situation.

Alexander II was assassinated in 1881. His son Alexander III ruled until 1894 and Nicholas II then ruled until the Bolshevik Revolution of 1917. (Alexander and Nicholas were the last two czars of Russia.) From 1904 to 1905, Russia suffered another humiliating defeat, this time in a war with Japan. Defeat came at a time when popular discontent was already at the boiling point. Workers in St. Petersburg, Moscow, and other cities went on strike, and peasants revolted. The strike spread to the railroad workers, and in October 1905 the country was brought to a standstill. Nicholas II finally sent troops to disperse the demonstrators and restore order. Hundreds of people were killed.

Despite concessions made by Nicholas in the following years, including the establishment of the Duma, a lawmaking national assembly, the czarist period was approaching its end.

The Revolutions of 1917

Toward the end of World War I, the czarist government simply collapsed from exhaustion, corruption, and lack of support. Its army had gone into battle in 1914 ill-equipped and poorly led, and suffered a series of shattering defeats by the Germans and the Austrians. As the war progressed, food grew increasingly scarce in the cities.

In 1917, two revolutions took place in Russia. The first one, the February Revolution, began on March 8 (which was February 23 on the Russian calendar then in use). It started in the wake of riots and strikes caused by shortages. Czar Nicholas II abdicated, and a provisional government was formed that declared Russia to be a republic. By this time, "soviets" (councils) of workers' and soldiers' deputies had been formed in Petrograd and in all the larger cities and towns in Russia.

The Bolshevik leader Vladimir Ilich Lenin, who had returned from exile in Switzerland in April 1917, told his followers in the soviets not to recognize the provisional government, and to demand the transfer of "all power to the soviets." By autumn the Bolsheviks had achieved a majority in both the Petrograd and Moscow soviets. Lenin decided it was the right moment to seize power. On the morning of November 7 (October 25 on the old calendar), the Bolsheviks took over the main government buildings in Petrograd (as St. Petersburg was then called). A new government was formed, with a cabinet called the Soviet of People's Commissars. Lenin was its chairman, and a fiery and brilliant young man named Leon Trotsky became commissar of foreign affairs.

The Soviet Union: 1917 to 1953

Lenin took Russia out of World War I by relinquishing large territories in the west, as agreed in the Treaty of Brest-Litovsk in March 1918. Meanwhile, however, opposition to Bolshevik rule grew among various groups of people—businessmen, landowning nobility, the Orthodox Church, and officers of the disbanded Imperial Army. They joined together to support the White Armies that fought the Communists in a savage three-year civil war that left hundreds of thousands dead. The White Armies received military help from Britain, France, the United States, and Japan; nonetheless, the Bolsheviks emerged victorious.

The country was devastated, however, and Lenin decided in 1921 to introduce the so-called New Economic Policy (NEP). Private shopkeepers reopened their doors, and peasants and small manufacturers were allowed to sell their products at market prices. By 1929, agriculture and industry were producing as much as they had on the eve of World War I.

The Early Stalin Period. Within the party, it was generally expected that Trotsky would take Lenin's place after his death in 1924, but he was pushed aside and finally exiled by his main rival, Joseph Stalin. On Stalin's orders, Trotsky was later (in 1940) assassinated in Mexico.

In 1928, Stalin launched an economic and social revolution. The government took control of the entire economy and began to draw up five-year plans for its development. The emphasis was on heavy industry. During this massive industralization drive, workers had to work long hours, often in the cold and without food. Much work was also done by prisoners, whose numbers soon reached the hundreds of thousands.

Stalin also forced the peasants to join large collective farms. The peasants rebelled, going so far as to slaughter half the country's farm animals rather than give them up. Several million peasants perished during those years, by starvation or in forced-labor camps.

Between 1936 and 1939, Stalin directed the Great Purge. Suspicious of everyone—party officials, old Bolshevik heroes, engineers, scientists, writers, high military men—Stalin had hundreds of thousands of people arrested and executed or sent to prison camps in Siberia.

World War II and the Cold War. Commemorated as "The Great Patriotic War," World War II caused approximately 20 million deaths in the Soviet Union, in fighting and by starvation. Stalin had concluded a nonaggression treaty with Nazi Germany in August 1938, but in June 1941, German armies attacked and almost reached Moscow. It took two years to stop their advance. In 1943, the Red Army began to push the Germans back, and in May 1945, Soviet soldiers entered Berlin.

The wartime alliance with the Western powers soon soured, and by the late 1940s, the Cold War had begun. Communist governments were established in Eastern European countries, Germany was divided, and an "Iron Curtain" cut Europe in two. In 1949, the United States took the initiative in forming the North Atlantic Treaty Organization (NATO) for the nations of Western Europe, Canada, the United States, Greece, and Turkey. The equivalent Eastern European group, the Warsaw Treaty Organization (Warsaw Pact), was formed in 1955 by the Soviet Union, Albania, Bulgaria, Czechoslovakia, East Germany, Hungary, and Romania.

The Post-Stalin Years

The long Stalin era ended with his death on March 6, 1953. Several men competed for succession until Nikita Khrushchev emerged as the victor. In 1964, Khrushchev was succeeded by Leonid Brezhnev.

The major event in Khrushchev's career was his denunciation of Stalin in a speech to the 20th Party Congress in 1956. Although the speech was not published in full in the Soviet Union until 1989, its contents became widely known. The revelation of Stalin's crimes shocked the Soviet people, who—despite all their suffering—regarded the dictator with respect. Suddenly they learned that he had ordered the arrests, torture, and killing of countless innocent citizens. Khrushchev opened a campaign of "de-Stalinization," which began with the elimination of Stalin's pictures and statues from public places. Most forced-labor camps were closed and political prisoners were freed. There was some easing of the strict controls, and people were able to speak out somewhat more freely.

During the 20 years of Brezhnev's rule, later dubbed as the period of "stagnation," the Soviet regime scored a number of successes abroad, but economic performance began to worsen, and dissatisfaction with the inefficient, restrictive system increased. The Soviet involvement in Afghanistan, which was in some ways comparable to the U.S. involvement in Vietnam, further undermined the legitimacy of the Communist system. Fewer and fewer believed the bombastic claims about the advantages of socialism compared to capitalism.

The Fall of the Soviet Union

The choice of Mikhail Sergeyevich Gorbachev as General Secretary of the Communist Party in 1985 marked a dramatic shift in power from the old generation of Soviet leaders to the younger generation. Soon after he took over, Gorbachev began to push for economic, political, and social reforms. One of his first campaigns was a war on alcoholism, which had become a plague to Soviet society, causing innumerable economic losses and contributing to a decline in life expectancy.

The two terms that summed up Gorbachev's policy were *glasnost* (meaning openness, intellectual liberalization, and loosening of ideological controls) and *perestroika,* or economic restructuring. Gorbachev also changed Soviet foreign policy by letting Central European countries discard their Communist rulers and by establishing friendly relations with Western powers.

The optimism felt by many Soviet citizens during the first few years of *glasnost* soon abated. Living standards went down, and new freedoms brought ethnic tensions and violent conflicts. In August 1991, hard-liners attempted to stop the disintegration of the Soviet empire, but they utterly failed. During the following months, Gorbachev was pushed aside and Boris Yeltsin became the nation's preeminent leader. The Soviet Union was formally dissolved on December 25, 1991.

The Russian Federation. The new Russia began its existence in a festive mood. Its president was the popular Boris Yeltsin, the first Russian leader ever elected by the people and the undisputed hero of August 1991. His popularity soon began to decline, however, as he had to deal with the revolutionary transformation of his huge country.

Locked in a hostile conflict with a mainly Communist parliament in October 1993, Yeltsin ordered troops to storm the parliament building. In the bloodiest event in Moscow since 1917, more than 180 people died. Another serious problem was the war in the Caucasian republic of Chechnya. In December 1994, Russian troops invaded the republic to suppress the independence movement, and the fighting lasted until 1996. By that time, more than 30,000 people had died, and thousands had become refugees. A peace treaty between Russia and Chechnya was signed in 1997.

Yeltsin's reputation was severely tarnished by this unpopular conflict. Nevertheless, in 1996, he pulled off a spectacular comeback, winning a second presidential term. In 1998, the country endured a major banking crisis, and living standards, which for many city-dwellers had been improving, suddenly plunged. Increasingly erratic, Yeltsin dismissed one prime minister after another until August 1999, when he named former KGB spy Vladimir Putin to this post. Shortly thereafter, a second war in Chechnya began,

Toppled statues of Communist heroes bear witness to many people's disdain for the Communist system.

Mikhail Gorbachev (above, with U.S. President Reagan in 1988) set in motion the events that led to the fall of the Soviet Union and the rise of Boris Yeltsin (right) to Russia's presidency.

allegedly in response to Chechen terrorism. International humanitarian organizations charged Russia with torturing prisoners and civilians, and Chechen insurgents have been accused of frequent kidnappings.

On December 31, 1999, Yeltsin announced his resignation and named Putin the acting president. This act alone testifies to the far-reaching changes in Russian affairs: Yeltsin became the first Russian leader to ever voluntarily and constitutionally relinquish power and step down.

In March 2000, Russia elected its second president, with 53 percent of the populace choosing Vladimir Putin. So far, he has gained enormous popularity within Russia, and has managed to help his fellow citizens to overcome the widespread disillusionment that was caused by the fall of the Communist system and the subsequent breakup of the Soviet Union. Russians praise him for being strong, resolute, and patriotic. In May 2001, his approval rating was about 75 percent. Nevertheless, the international community has criticized Putin for the ongoing military action in Chechnya and for the muzzling of independent media.

Following the September 2001 terrorist attacks in the United States, President Putin eagerly joined the international antiterrorist campaign, and therefore strengthened Russia's ties to the Western world. In a related development, the first talks in years between Russians and Chechens offered hope that this conflict could be solved. These hopes were shattered in October 2002, when Chechen terrorists seized a Moscow theater, taking more than 700 people hostage. Several days later, Russian troops stormed the theater, ending the siege; all the terrorists and more than 115 hostages died as a result of the operation.

Vladmimir Putin (below), who was elected to the presidency of Russia in March 2000, is faced with innumerable problems, not the least of which is the war in Chechnya, a rebellious province that is seeking its independence from Russia. Most of Grozny (left), the Chechen capital, now lies in ruins as a result of the prolonged conflict.

GOVERNMENT

According to the first post-Communist constitution, which was approved in December 1993, Russia is a federal democratic state with a strong presidency. Its official name is the Russian Federation, and it consists of 89 administrative units. These include 21 autonomous republics, 49 administrative regions (*oblast*), 1 autonomous region, 10 autonomous districts (*okrug*), 6 counties (*kraj*), and the cities of Moscow and St. Petersburg, which have special administrative status. Many of the republics and regions have become virtually independent during the 1990s. In order to reinforce central control, President Putin divsided the country into seven federal districts, which will be overseen by prefects appointed by the president.

The head of state is the president, who is popularly elected for a four-year term. He or she cannot serve more than two consecutive terms. The main legislative body is the two-chamber Federal Assembly. The upper one, the Federal Council, has 178 deputies, two from each administrative unit. The lower chamber is the 450-member State Duma.

COLETTE SHULMAN, Editor, *We The Russians*
Reviewed by EDWARD W. WALKER, Ph.D., Columbia University

A soldier patrols inside the Kremlin, a complex of churches, palaces, and government buildings.

MOSCOW

Moscow, the capital of Russia, was once called the "third Rome," after it became the center of Eastern Orthodoxy. During most of the 20th century, it was the Mecca of the Communist world. The city often struck Westerners as a dreary, uninviting place, but by the start of the 21st century it had become a buzzing metropolis, always crowded and full of contrasts—peasant women in head scarves rubbing shoulders with city dwellers in trendy Western-style clothing. The population of Moscow is about 9 million; it is the sixth largest city in the world.

The Kremlin and Red Square. The heart of Moscow is the Kremlin ("fortified palace"), from which the city originally grew. It is a large triangle enclosed by massive walls built in the 15th century. Inside are splendid cathedrals where the czars of Russia were crowned, and palaces where they lived and entertained. The palaces now function as congress halls, government offices, a museum, and a theater.

The Assumption Cathedral, with five golden domes, dates from the late 15th century. During the Communist era, it was turned into a museum. In 1989 it became a house of worship again, as the first Mass since 1918 was held there. The cathedral contains tombs of many Orthodox leaders, and also beautiful icons and murals. One of its most fascinating relics is a wooden throne made for Ivan the Terrible in 1551.

The Annunciation Cathedral houses icons by the most famous icon painter, Theophanes the Greek. He was a Byzantine artist who moved to Moscow in the late 14th century and collaborated with several other artists in decorating Moscow churches.

The tallest structure of the Kremlin is the Ivan the Great Bell Tower, one of Moscow's landmarks. The bell in the tower weighs 65 tons. The Kremlin's one modern building, completed in 1961, is the Palace of Congresses, which is used to hold large and important meetings.

On a sunny afternoon, Muscovites flock to the outdoor markets to see what the local farmers have brought into town. Coffee and other imported foods are also readily available at stores throughout the city.

Just outside the Kremlin is Red Square, or *Krasnaya Ploshchad*, which originally meant "beautiful square," but, in the 20th century, came to be translated as "Red Square." During the Communist era, this was a scene of regular massive parades that were supposed to show the might of the Communist empire. The largest Communist parades would occur on May 1 to celebrate International Labor Day, and on November 7, to celebrate the October Revolution.

The most fascinating building in Moscow, and a symbol of Russian history, is the colorful St. Basil's Cathedral at the south end of Red Square. At first sight, it looks like a fairy-tale jumble of shapes and colors, but the nine main chapels are actually arranged in a well-thought-out scheme. The cathedral was built in the mid-16th century to celebrate the defeat of the Volga Tatars by Ivan the Terrible. The newest Moscow attraction is the Cathedral of Christ the Redeemer, rebuilt at the same site where the original building—demolished on Stalin's orders—once stood.

One relic of the previous era still survives in Moscow: the Lenin mausoleum just outside the Kremlin in Red Square. People once stood in long lines to view the embalmed body of the idolized Soviet leader, everyone quiet and in awe. Visitors continue to come to the tomb, but times have changed; almost unbelievably, many Russian children no longer even know who Lenin was.

The Growth of Moscow. According to tradition, Moscow (also referred to as Muscovy) was founded in A.D. 1147 by Yuri Dolgorukii, prince of Suzdal. In 1263 it became the home of the princes of Vladimir, and soon thereafter it grew into the most important principality in Russia. By the end of the reign of Ivan III (the Great), early in the 16th century, Moscow controlled a large area stretching as far east as the Urals and as far north as the Barents Sea, in large part because of the city's strategic location.

When Peter the Great became Russian czar in 1696, he decided to bring Russia closer to Europe. He considered Moscow a symbol of the Asian backwardness of the country and so he built a new city, St.

Tourists still gather to watch the precision marching of the soldiers (above) at Lenin's Tomb, although the tomb itself is held in considerably less awe than it was during the Soviet years. American computer companies have found eager customers among young Muscovites (right), who have enthusiastically embraced the electronics age.

Petersburg, and relocated the capital there. Two centuries later, the Bolshevik revolution took place in St. Petersburg, but the Soviet rulers soon moved their capital back to Moscow. In a sense, this action symbolized the Soviet retreat from the prevailing European cultural influence.

Post-Communist Moscow. Dozens of new restaurants and cafés have appeared in Moscow since the late 1980s. Moscow's McDonald's is the largest fast-food restaurant in the world, serving tens of thousands of hamburgers every day and employing a staff of 1,200. Moscow has also become a huge construction site: old buildings are being reconstructed, ultramodern structures are going up, and roads are being repaired.

Newspapers and other media often report about the rising crime in Russian cities, but for ordinary people and tourists, the streets are comparatively safe—murders, for example, generally involve members of criminal gangs or people in higher positions who have made enemies. More frightening to the average citizen have been terrorist attacks in 1999 and 2000, probably connected with the war in Chechnya.

Most Muscovites continue to live in small, crowded quarters—often housing several families in two or three rooms—while the newly rich buy apartments in condominiums at prices higher than those in New York or London. In the early 2000s, there were clear signs of an emerging middle class that is prosperous and confident. Yet even the poorest Muscovites remain resourceful, somehow managing to eke out a living. Moscow has transformed itself from a drab metropolis with one domineering ideology to a vibrant, challenging place—the symbol of the new Russia.

IRINA RYBACEK / Reviewed by EDWARD W. WALKER, Ph.D., Columbia University

Nevski Prospekt is the most fashionable street in St. Petersburg, the Russian city formerly called Leningrad.

ST. PETERSBURG

Known as Leningrad from 1924 to 1991, this most westerly Russian city was built as a portal to Europe, and its 18th- and 19th-century architecture still gives it a European look. St. Petersburg lies at the same latitude as Alaska, and therefore receives almost 24 hours of sunlight in summer. In winter the reverse is true—streetlamps are lighted all day and their reflections glisten in the snow.

With a population of about 5 million people, St. Petersburg is a city of unusual grandeur and spaciousness. Its majestic river, the Neva, is bounded by elegant palaces and huge squares. Its main avenue, the Nevsky Prospect, is one of the most handsome and famous streets in Europe.

From the Peter and Paul Fortress that stands on an island in the Neva, a golden stiletto spire thrusts upward into the vast northern sky. This spire belongs to the Cathedral of Sts. Peter and Paul, which also boasts a splendid baroque interior. The fortress was built in 1703, and was originally intended to become part of the city's fortifications, but it was used mostly as a political prison. Its most famous inmates included the writers Dostoyevsky and Gorky, and the revolutionist, Trotsky.

The city owes its elegant style to Bartolommeo Rastrelli, an architect of Italian origin. His grandest creation, the huge Winter Palace, stretches at great length along the Neva. The palace contains 1,057 rooms and 117 staircases, and is part of the famous Hermitage Museum, which was built to house the czarist family's private art collection. Today the Hermitage displays paintings by major Western European artists, as well as large collections of Egyptian, Russian, and Oriental art.

Peter the Great and His Successors. St. Petersburg is a relatively young city. It was founded in 1703 by czar Peter the Great as a "window to Europe" and for two centuries served as the capital of Russia. Peter was a giant among the czars, both physically (standing over 6.5 ft.—or 2 m.—tall) and in what he accomplished for Russia. He traveled to Europe and upon his return set up schools, had foreign books translated, founded the first Russian newspaper, and brought technicians and craftsmen to the city to work.

Under Peter's successors, St. Petersburg became a splendid, cosmopolitan metropolis. The court of Catherine the Great, who ruled from 1762 to 1796, was a brilliant intellectual center.

St. Petersburg and Russian Literature. Literature flourished in 19th century St. Petersburg. Countless novels and stories by leading Russian authors of the 19th century were set in the city: *Crime and Punishment* by Fedor Dostoyevsky, *Anna Karenina* by Leo Nikolaevich Tolstoi, stories by Nikolai

St. Petersburg's Hermitage Museum contains one of the most extensive art collections in the world.

Gogol, Ivan Turgenev, and many others. The popular American movie based on one of the greatest Russian novels of the 20th century, *Doctor Zhivago* by Boris Pasternak, portrays the city in its prerevolutionary beauty and its revolutionary fervor.

Leningrad. The Communists celebrated the city as the birthplace of the Revolution of 1917, and renamed it Leningrad. John Reed, an American journalist who was in St. Petersburg during the revolution, wrote an eyewitness account of these events in his book *The Ten Days That Shook the World*. A movie biography of Reed, *Reds*, starring Warren Beatty, vividly portrays the revolutionary atmosphere of the city.

The Years of Terror unleashed by Stalin in the 1930s began in Leningrad, and the next decade brought another terror: the 900-day siege by Germans in World War II. The Piskarevsky Cemetery contains the mass grave of some of the 600,000 Leningraders who died at that time.

St. Petersburg Again. Even decades after the change in name, Leningrad's residents continued to refer to their city as "Piter." When the Communist ideology began to unravel, the first public suggestions about restoring the original name were made, and in late 1991, the residents decided to part with the Soviet past and voted overwhelmingly to discard "Leningrad" and to restore the historic "St. Petersburg."

When Vladimir Putin, a native of the city, was elected president of Russia in March 2000, a debate was already under way about moving the capital from Moscow to St. Petersburg again. The city is preparing for a celebration to mark its 300th anniversary, which is planned for 2003.

IRINA RYBACEK / Reviewed by EDWARD W. WALKER, Ph.D., Columbia University

St. Sophia Cathedral in Kiev is one of the Ukrainian capital's most notable structures. The church took more than 800 years to build.

UKRAINE

For centuries, Ukrainians were dominated by Poles and Russians, against whom they sometimes rebelled. In the late 1980s and early 1990s, the promise and then reality of independent Ukrainian statehood was enthusiastically celebrated in mass gatherings. The main pro-independence movement, Rukh, played an important role in those years, but gradually it faded into oblivion. In the first half of the 1990s, Ukraine went through an unprecedented economic crisis that brought it to the brink of total collapse. Leonid Kuchma, who in July 1994 won the presidency as a supporter of closer ties with Russia, has since then alternated between a pro-Russian and a pro-Western position.

Ukrainians trace their origins to the Kievan Rus, a powerful early medieval state that was the first political entity of the Eastern Slavs. After Ukraine's collapse in the 13th century A.D., the region was tossed between its neighbors to the east and the west. Most of present-day Ukraine was under Russian control from the late 18th century on, except for the northwestern section stretching between the cities of Uzhgorod and Lviv (Lvov). This area belonged to Austria-Hungary, and then, between the two world wars, it became part of Poland and Czechoslovakia.

Ukraine attracted world attention in 1986 at the time of the Chernobyl nuclear disaster. About 90 times as much radioactive material as was in the Hiroshima bomb blew into the skies just north of Kiev. Immediately after the accident, about 31 people died, and some 160,000 had to be evacuated. For several days, there was no official news on what happened; only when the radioactive cloud began to spread over Sweden did the Soviets start to supply details about the explosion and its aftermath. Cancer rates in the region continue to be high. Under international pressure, the Ukrainian government closed down the plant in December 2000.

The initial efforts by Moscow to cover up the catastrophe spurred on the reborn Ukrainian nationalism. By the time the Soviet Union collapsed, many Communist officials had become Ukrainian nationalists.

THE LAND

A little larger than France, Ukraine is now the second-largest European country after Russia. It borders on Belarus in the north, Russia in the east, the Sea of Azov and the Black Sea in the south, Moldova and Romania in the southeast, and Hungary, Slovakia, and Poland in the west. Ukraine lies on the East European Plain. Most of the country is a low-lying flatland, with an average elevation of about 575 ft. (175 m.). The only mountainous areas are the Carpathians in the west and the Crimean Mountains in the far south. Known as the "breadbasket" of the former Soviet Union, Ukraine has fertile, humus-rich soil that produced about one-quarter of all Soviet grain.

About 3 percent of the territory consists of marshlands, particularly in the north and along the estuaries of rivers. The Pripet Marshes, which extend along the River Pripet and are shared with Belarus, are the most extensive marshland in Europe. A natural reserve at Askania-Nova (just north of the Crimea), established in 1921, contains parts of the original steppe.

Rivers. Four major rivers flow through Ukraine from the north to the south. The westernmost is the Dniester (Dnister in Ukrainian), which rises in the Carpathian Mountains and in its midstream passes through Moldova before entering the Black Sea. Because the water level of the Dniester fluctuates greatly, the river is not navigable for most of its course. The Southern Bug (Boh or Buh) is entirely within Ukraine's territory, and also empties into the Black Sea. The northern Donets crosses the easternmost part of Ukraine, where it joins the River Don.

The Dnieper (Dnipro) is the third-longest European river, after the Volga and the Danube. It rises near Moscow, in Russia, and enters Ukraine north of Kiev. It is navigable for three-quarters of the year, but freezes over for about three months. Large hydroelectric stations are situated on the middle and lower reaches of the Dnieper, creating three huge reservoirs—one just north of Kiev, another one north of Kremenchug, and the largest one near Zaporozhye (Zaporizhia).

In the extreme southwest, the Danube River forms the border between Ukraine and Romania. Ukraine also contains more than 20,000 other streams and rivers, but it has very few lakes.

Climate. Generally, the western part of Ukraine has a milder climate than the eastern part, where the winters are colder and the summers hotter. Kiev has freezing temperatures during the winter months, while Odessa on the Black Sea has a pleasant Mediterranean climate, with average January temperatures of 39° F. (4° C.) and July temperatures of 75° F. (24° C.).

THE PEOPLE

Ukraine was the second-most-populous republic of the former Soviet Union. About 73 percent of the people are ethnic Ukrainians who belong to the linguistic and ethnic group of East Slavs (which also includes Russians and Belorussians). The remaining 27 percent consist of Russians, Poles, Belorussians, Bulgarians, Jews, and small numbers of other nationalities. Emigration waves during the 20th century have created a large Ukrainian diaspora, with about 2.5 million Ukrainians living in other countries. Approximately 1.5 million people of Ukrainian descent live in North America; the Ukrainian community is especially active in Canada. Thousands of Ukrainian emigrés have visited their native country in the years since the dissolution of the Soviet Union. In an odd turn of events, the local residents have often been surprised and puzzled by the fervent, strongly anti-Communist, and often intolerant nationalism of their kin from overseas.

Millions of Ukrainians continue to live in the former Soviet republics: about 4 million in Russia, and large numbers in Kazakhstan, Uzbekistan, Belorussia, and elsewhere. Because of economic problems at home, hundreds of thousands of Ukrainians also have gone to look for work in Poland, Slovakia, and the Czech Republic.

The Ukrainian language is written in the Cyrillic alphabet and is linguistically very similar to Russian and Belorussian. For centuries, Ukrainian has been overshadowed by Russian, and even now, with the newly established independence of Ukraine, Russian is widely spoken throughout the country. Ethnic minorities have so far fared quite well, and Ukrainians display little animosity toward them.

Ukraine is known for its *chernozem,* a humus-rich soil, but the farms produce much less than their counterparts in Western Europe and the United States.

Education. During the Soviet era, Russification was pervasive, and the "brain drain" of the most talented Ukrainian students to Moscow undermined a sense of Ukrainian separateness. Ukrainian intellectuals, in an effort to remedy the situation, have founded new schools that concentrate on Ukrainian history, language, and literature. The national curriculum is being established, but it is a difficult task because it is often hard to distinguish between what is Ukrainian and what is Russian. Kiev Mohyla Academy, a leading European educational institute before 1917, was reopened in 1990.

Religion. Ukraine's own Orthodox Church was forcibly absorbed by the Russian Orthodox Church in the late 17th century. Much of the population of western Ukraine, which had been part of Poland for several centuries before the Polish partitions in 1772–95, became members of the Uniate Church, also known as the Ukrainian Catholic Church, in the late 16th century. This church, which recognizes the Roman pope as leader, but in ritual follows the practices of Russian Orthodoxy, was closely tied to Ukrainian nationalism during the 19th century. Following World War II, the Uniate Church was accused of collaborating with the Nazis and was forced to merge into the Russian Orthodox Church. In 1988, the church began to surface from its underground existence, claiming between 4 million and 7 million adherents. The Ukrainian self-governing Orthodox Church has also been revived since the breakup of the Soviet Union. Roman Catholicism is practiced in scattered communities in western Ukraine. In June 2001, a visit by Pope John Paul II represented a first step toward bridging Catholicism and Orthodoxy. More than 1 million Ukrainians attended a Mass celebrated by the pope in the Greek Catholic rite.

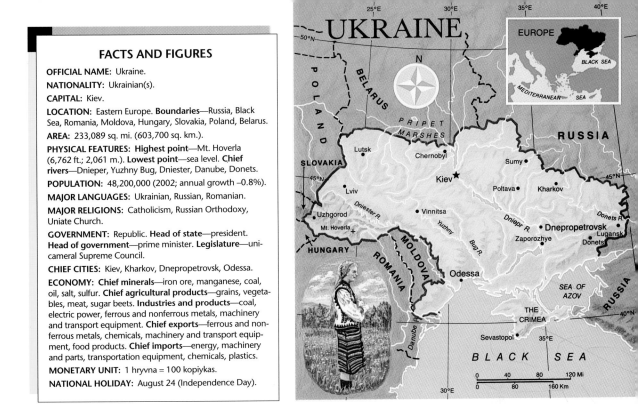

FACTS AND FIGURES

OFFICIAL NAME: Ukraine.

NATIONALITY: Ukrainian(s).

CAPITAL: Kiev.

LOCATION: Eastern Europe. **Boundaries**—Russia, Black Sea, Romania, Moldova, Hungary, Slovakia, Poland, Belarus.

AREA: 233,089 sq. mi. (603,700 sq. km.).

PHYSICAL FEATURES: Highest point—Mt. Hoverla (6,762 ft.; 2,061 m.). **Lowest point**—sea level. **Chief rivers**—Dnieper, Yuzhny Bug, Dniester, Danube, Donets.

POPULATION: 48,200,000 (2002; annual growth –0.8%).

MAJOR LANGUAGES: Ukrainian, Russian, Romanian.

MAJOR RELIGIONS: Catholicism, Russian Orthodoxy, Uniate Church.

GOVERNMENT: Republic. **Head of state**—president. **Head of government**—prime minister. **Legislature**—unicameral Supreme Council.

CHIEF CITIES: Kiev, Kharkov, Dnepropetrovsk, Odessa.

ECONOMY: Chief minerals—iron ore, manganese, coal, oil, salt, sulfur. **Chief agricultural products**—grains, vegetables, meat, sugar beets. **Industries and products**—coal, electric power, ferrous and nonferrous metals, machinery and transport equipment. **Chief exports**—ferrous and nonferrous metals, chemicals, machinery and transport equipment, food products. **Chief imports**—energy, machinery and parts, transportation equipment, chemicals, plastics.

MONETARY UNIT: 1 hryvna = 100 kopiykas.

NATIONAL HOLIDAY: August 24 (Independence Day).

Before World War II, the Jewish population of Ukraine was very large, both in its Russian part and in the northwestern region, which belonged to Poland and Czechoslovakia. Hundreds of thousands of Jews were exterminated during the war, and others have emigrated since the 1970s, when the Soviet Union permitted its Jewish citizens to leave for Israel. Many went to the United States instead. Large Jewish communities still exist in Ukraine, however, and are being revitalized.

Cultural Heritage. The Kievan period produced the earliest works of East Slavic literature, including the 10th-century *Russian Primary Chronicle,* also known as *Tale of Bygone Years* (the main source for the Kievan Rus history), and the 12th-century historical epic *Lay of Igor's Campaign.* The Mongol invasions of the 13th century extinguished cultural life for several centuries. In the 19th century, the poet-painter Taras Shevchenko was a major Ukrainian cultural figure and the creator of the modern literary Ukrainian language. Born a serf, he became a passionate advocate for the equality of all Slavic nations and a fierce Ukrainian nationalist.

Because of the symbiotic relationship between Ukraine and Russia, a number of Ukrainian-born writers and artists became part of the Russian culture; the best known among them is probably Nikolai Gogol, author of such internationally acclaimed works as *The Inspector General* and the novel *Dead Souls.*

Folk arts include wood carving, embroidery, and ceramics, all with intricate ornamentation. *Pysanky*, the art of painting beautiful patterns on Easter eggs, has been passed down from generation to generation.

Food. Ukrainian specialties include *kotleta po kievski,* a popular chicken dish named for the capital city of Kiev. It is made by rolling a flattened chicken breast around a finger of seasoned butter. The rolled chicken breast is then dipped in bread crumbs and quickly deep-fried until it reaches a golden-brown color. In the United States, this tasty dish is known everywhere as "Chicken Kiev." Another favorite and ubiquitous dish is *vareniki*, a kind of ravioli with various fillings, mostly sweet. *Holubtsi*, another favorite dish, are cabbage rolls filled mainly with rice and a small amount of ground beef. The beet-based soup called *borshch* (or borscht) is as popular in Ukraine as it is in Russia.

CITIES

Kiev. As the chronicles say, Kiev (Kyyiv in Ukrainian), the capital of Ukraine, is the place "whence the Russian lands took their beginnings." On the hillside overlooking the river is a statue of Prince Vladimir holding a large cross. In the late 10th century A.D., he introduced Christianity into Kievan Rus and later became the patron saint of Russia. The name of Kiev's main street, the Kreshchatik, is thought to come from the verb *krestit,* meaning "to christen," because Prince Vladimir christened his 12 sons in a brook that flowed through the valley where the street is now located.

Kiev is home to more than 2.8 million people and is a large industrial and cultural center. It was badly damaged during World War II, particularly during the two-year occupation by the Nazis, and many parts had to be rebuilt. Wide boulevards and parks characterize the modern city, while St. Sophia Cathedral and the Monastery of the Caves (Pecherskaya Lavra) are the two major reminders of Kiev's long history.

The Crimean peninsula is the site of many castles originally built as fortifications against the almost endless series of invaders.

THE CRIMEA

Inhabited since long before the Christian era, the peninsula of Crimea—which juts into the Black Sea and is connected with the mainland only by the narrow Perekop Isthmus—has been a crossroads for settlers, invaders, and traders of many nationalities: the Greeks, Scythians, Sarmatians, Romans, Khazars, Tatars, Venetians, Genoese, Turks, and Russians. In the civil war following the Bolshevik takeover, the Crimea was the last outpost of the anti-Bolshevik "White" resistance. During World War II, the peninsula was occupied by Germans for three years.

After the war, Stalin ordered the deportation of about 350,000 Crimean Tatars to Central Asia for their alleged collaboration with the Germans. This deportation was one of many forcible relocations of large groups of people by which Stalin terrorized the country. As early as the 1960s, the Tatars began to press for their return to the Crimea, their home since the 14th century, and by 1994, about 250,000 of them had relocated.

Since the mid-1800s, the Crimea has been a favorite recreation spot, first for imperial Russia and then for the former So-

Kiev was probably settled as early as the 6th century A.D., but it was in the 9th century that it became the cradle of the Ukrainian and Russian nations. It was a busy trade center profiting from its advantageous location along a river route; after Vladimir's acceptance of Christianity, Kiev blossomed into a splendid Byzantine city. St. Sophia Cathedral, which was built starting in the 11th century (but finished only in the 19th century), was the greatest of Kiev's 400 churches. The Monastery of the Caves was the first and the most important monastery of the Russian Orthodox Church; it was also a center for religious learning. There are a number of museums in the monastery compound, with Ukrainian handicrafts, ceramics, and beautiful icons, but several churches—including the Trinity Church and the All Saints' Church—still retain their religious functions.

Near Kiev is the infamous Babi Yar ravine, where some 100,000 Jews and other inhabitants of Kiev were brutally killed in 1941. This terrible event has been described in many books and studies, but the most vivid account is probably in A. Anatoli Kuznetsov's novel *Babi Yar,* which was first published in the former Soviet Union in a heavily censored edition in 1966. It appeared unabridged in the West in 1970.

Lviv. This center of western Ukraine has had many masters in its long history, as its different names testify. The Russian name for the city is Lvov, while the Polish name is Lwów, and the German name is Lemberg. Lviv has the architecture and atmosphere of a Central European city. It was never

viet Union. It has a Mediterranean climate, sandy beaches, and many sanatoriums and health spas. The Crimean Mountains are dotted with resorts.

Simferopol, which has a population of about 350,000, is the capital of the Crimea. **Yalta** has been a first-class resort area since the 19th century, but in recent history has become associated with the Cold War division of Europe. The February 1945 Yalta Conference of the three Allied leaders—Winston Churchill, Franklin D. Roosevelt, and Joseph Stalin—dealt with the postwar European arrangements and led to the military occupation of Germany as well as the founding of the United Nations. **Sevastopol,** one of the most important ports of the former Soviet Union, is the home base of the Black Sea Fleet.

The Crimea was part of Russia since 1783, but in 1954, Soviet leader Nikita Khrushchev decided to "give" the peninsula to the Ukrainian people to mark the 300th anniversary of the brotherly union of Russia and Ukraine. During that time, the transfer of the Crimea from the jurisdiction of one republic to another was a purely formal matter, since all decisions were made in Moscow. When the Soviet Union dissolved in December 1991, however, the Crimea became a point of friction between Ukraine and Russia. The peninsula is the base of the Black Sea Fleet, one of the largest components of the former Soviet Union's navy; it consists of approximately 230 aging ships, about 170 naval aircraft, and 48,000 sailors. After a series of negotiations, the Russian and Ukrainian governments agreed in May 1997 to divide the fleet in the ratio 82:18.

Approximately three-quarters of the population of the Crimea consider themselves to be Russians, not Ukrainians. In May 1992, the Crimean parliament voted to declare independence from Ukraine, and in January 1994, the head of a vocal pro-Russian party won the presidency of Crimea. Since then, however, Ukraine's central government in Kiev has reasserted its control over the peninsula, with tacit approval from the Kremlin. According to the 1996 constitution, Crimea retains its autonomy.

under Russian control until 1939, when the Soviet army invaded Poland. In 1941, Lviv was again taken by Germans, and almost half a million people subsequently died in its Jewish ghetto and nearby concentration camps. In 1944, the Red Army arrived and turned Lviv into a Soviet city. It remained part of the Communist empire until 1991. Today, Lviv is an important manufacturing center and a hub of Ukrainian nationalism, which has always been stronger in western Ukraine than in the eastern part.

Odessa. Odessa is not really a Ukrainian city: it has been a Russian cosmopolitan port for about 200 years. The site was controlled by the Ottoman Turks until the late 18th century, but when Russia conquered the region (during the reign of Catherine II, the Great), a new port was built and named after the ancient Greek colony Odessos. By 1880, Odessa was the second-largest Russian port, and its population included Russians, Ukrainians, Germans, Turks, Jews, and many others. The city was one of the centers of the Russian Revolution of 1905; during the Civil War of 1917–20, it was held, in quick succession, by Ukrainian nationalists, Bolsheviks, White Russians, Austrians, and French and other Allies.

Modern Odessa has more than 1 million inhabitants. It is also the principal seaport of independent Ukraine.

Other Cities. In the nation's extreme west, just 2.5 mi. (4 km.) from the Slovak border, lies the city of **Uzhgorod,** the center of Transcarpathia (also known as Ruthenia). The second-largest Ukrainian city is **Kharkov** (Kharkiv in Ukrainian, 1.6 million people), which lies close to the Russian border and is mostly Russian. Kharkov was the capital of Ukraine from 1920 to 1934. In addition to Odessa, two other Black Sea ports—**Kherson** and **Mykolayiv**—are also important shipbuilding centers.

ECONOMY

Ukraine was the second-most-important Soviet republic. Its resources include iron and manganese ores, coal, petroleum, salt, and other minerals. Ukraine was a center of steel production, coal and iron mining, and the chemical and food-processing industries. The mineral deposits are located primarily in eastern Ukraine, in the Donets basin, also known as the Donbas. It is a very Russianized part of the country. Thanks to its rich soil, Ukraine was able to supply most of the Soviet Union's grain.

The disintegration of the Communist economic system brought many hardships. One of them was hyperinflation: in 1993, the inflation rate was 10,000 percent. It went down to a mere 180 percent in 1995, and by the end of the decade there was some hope for economic revival. Yet despite massive foreign aid—from the United States and international agencies—Ukraine remains one of the poorest countries of Europe. By 2002, the situation had slightly improved, but the country continues to be plagued by corruption, and no serious economic reforms have yet been carried through. Leonid Kuchma, elected to the presidency in 1994 and again in 1999, promised to improve relations with the West, but has instead supported closer ties with Russia.

One of the most serious problems faced by Ukraine is lack of energy. About 40 percent of Ukraine's electricity is produced in nuclear plants, even though many of them are not considered safe by Western standards. The notorious Chernobyl plant was shut down in December 2000, and Western countries have promised aid and credits to enhance the safety of Ukraine's other nuclear reactors.

Yalta's balmy summers attract thousands of vacationers from Ukraine and other former Soviet republics.

HISTORY

Kievan Rus. This state originated in the 9th century, and in the 12th century split into several principalities. Its two names—Kievan Rus and Kievan Russia—reflect the controversy of its origins. Those who consider it a direct ancestor of the Moscow-centered Russian Empire prefer the designation "Kievan Russia," while those who emphasize that Kiev did not play this ancestral role use the term "Kievan Rus," because "Rus" was used by the early Kievans themselves. Most Ukrainians prefer "Kievan Rus."

According to chronicles, Slav and Finnish tribes from the area around Novgorod, south of present-day St. Petersburg, invited a Viking named Rurik, probably from Denmark, to rule their country. Rurik came with his followers—whom the Slavs called Varangians or Rus—and established his rule. Rurik's successors then founded a state around Kiev, and became the first ruling dynasty of Eastern Slavs, the Rurikids. The seventh Rurikid ruler, Prince Vladimir I, converted to Christianity in the 990s. Under his successor, Yaroslav the Wise, Kievan Rus reached its greatest glory. Learning and art were encouraged, many new churches were built, and the first codification of laws was completed.

Mongols, Turks, and Cossacks. In the 13th century, Mongols from the east overran Ukraine and created a large empire based on the Volga and known as the Golden Horde. Two centuries later the rise of the Ottoman Turks led to the downfall of the Horde. About that time, groups of marauders and adventurers formed in the Ukrainian steppes and became known as Cossacks (from the Turkic word meaning "outlaw").

Meanwhile, Poland gained control of most of the present-day Ukrainian territory. The Cossacks, however, free-spirited and independent, resisted domination, and when the Polish monarchs decided to subjugate them, they rose in a rebellion led by Bogdan Khmelnitsky in 1648. The Cossacks maintained their independence until the late 18th century.

Russia and the Soviet Union. By the late 18th century, most of modern-day Ukraine was part of the Russian Empire, and it remained under Russian rule for the next 200 years. Ukrainian nationalism developed during the 19th century, only to be repeatedly suppressed. A non-Communist Ukrainian People's Republic briefly existed from late 1917 to early 1918, but was then overwhelmed by Soviet forces.

The official closing-down ceremony for the Chernobyl nuclear-power plant was a nationally televised event

In the 1930s, millions of Ukrainian peasants starved to death in a violent collectivization campaign and the ensuing famine. Countless others were deported to Siberian labor camps. When Hitler attacked the Soviet Union in 1941, many Ukrainians at first welcomed the invaders, hoping that the Germans would liberate them from Soviet Communist rule. This sympathy soon evaporated, however, and Ukraine endured heavy losses, both in material destruction and in human lives.

Today, Ukraine is still living with the aftermath of the Chernobyl nuclear disaster of 1986. Although the immediate number of casualties was not very high, the increased rate of cancer in the area is undoubtedly linked to radiation, which affected about 7 million people. Scientists argue that it will take decades before a full evaluation of the catastrophe can be made.

Independent Ukraine. In the mid-1990s, less than half of the population supported Ukrainian independence. The western part of the country is more nationalist, while the east continues to lean toward Russia. President Kuchma has tried to balance these attitudes, staying friendly with Russia while also cultivating the West.

By early 2001, Ukraine was in the midst of a severe political crisis, sparked by the mysterious death of a journalist critical of the government. Following a series of antigovernment demonstrations, a pro-Western prime minister was forced to resign. Strong indications suggest that Ukraine is turning back to Russia, although Communists made up only 15 percent of the national legislature following the 2002 elections.

GOVERNMENT

In July 1996, the parliament ratified a new post-Communist constitution, with a strong presidency. The 450-member Ukrainian parliament plays a marginal role in political decision-making. The parliamentary elections in April 2002 brought a slight victory to reformist parties.

IRINA RYBACEK / Reviewed by EDWARD W. WALKER, Ph.D., Columbia University

BELARUS

Minsk, the capital of Belarus, has been completely rebuilt since its destruction during World War II.

Between 1922 and 1991, Belarus was part of the Soviet Union, as one of its constituent republics. It was generally known as Belorussia or Byelorussia; in some older sources, the region was also occasionally referred to as White Ruthenia. The western third of the present territory of Belarus belonged to Poland from 1920 to 1939.

During the final years of the Soviet empire, Belarus was a bastion of conservative Communism. In contrast to Ukrainians, Belorussians have never had a strong sense of national separateness from the Russians, and the country thus gained independence almost against its will. Yet in the first years after the demise of the Soviet Union, there was a certain sense of excitement. The new political leaders abolished censorship and struck down the prohibition to engage in private enterprise; several political parties were formed; and independent newspapers and journals began to carry uncensored news from around the world.

Then, in 1994, Belarus took a retrogressive turn when in its first free elections ever, the voters chose for president Alexandr Lukashenko, a 40-year-old former chairman of an agricultural cooperative. In his electoral campaign, he captivated the audiences by promising to tackle the post-Communist corruption and to free the country from the dominance of the old Communist bosses. It did not take long, however, before Lukashenko began to behave as a supreme boss himself.

And thus, in 2002, with Yugoslavia's former president and dictator Slobodan Milošević facing a trial at the International Tribunal at The Hague, Belarus is the only remaining European dictatorship. The economy is in disarray, and disregard for human rights is reportedly widespread. Lukashenko has repeatedly flaunted basic democratic procedures, bringing the country into international isolation.

THE LAND

Belarus is a landlocked country in Eastern Europe, bordering on Poland in the west, Lithuania and Latvia in the northwest, Russia in the north and east, and Ukraine in the south. The country is generally flat; more than half of the republic lies at elevations of 660 ft. (200 m.) or less. Several low ridges are scattered in the center of the republic and in the north.

Belarus has more than 20,000 streams and more than 10,000 lakes. The largest river is the Dnieper, which flows through the western part of the country. Its main tributary, the Pripyat, forms the axis of the Pripyat (or Pripet) Marshes, the most extensive marshland in Europe, with rich peat deposits. Another of the Dnieper's tributaries is Berezina (Byarezina in Belorussian). In 1812, a four-day battle at the banks of the Berezina between Russian troops and Napoleon's retreating army signaled the end of the French emperor's Russian campaign.

About one-third of Belarus is covered with forests. On the border with Poland lies the Belavezhskaya Pushcha, a huge natural reserve that contains a unique large remnant of virgin European forest. This area is administered jointly with neighboring Poland. Dozens of species of birds and mammals live in the reserve, including the only surviving herd of European bison.

Belarus has a humid and relatively mild continental climate, with an average July temperature of 64° F. (18° C.). Although the average January temperature is 21° F. (–6° C.), there are many days when the thermometer stays above the freezing point.

THE PEOPLE

About 80 percent of the country's inhabitants are Belorussians, which means "White Russians." The name apparently derives from the color of the traditional clothing. Belarus' minorities include Russians, Poles, and Ukrainians. The Jewish community is very small, about 1 percent of the population; before World War II, Jews accounted for about 10 percent of all inhabitants. Most of the ethnic Belorussians live in the countryside, while the minorities are scattered throughout the cities.

Belorussians belong to the ethnic and linguistic group of Eastern Slavs, which also includes Russians and Ukrainians. Their very similar languages are all written in the Cyrillic alphabet. Until recently, most people in Belarus spoke only Russian, and even today, about one-quarter of the population cannot speak or write Belorussian.

FACTS AND FIGURES

OFFICIAL NAME: Republic of Belarus.

NATIONALITY: Belorussian(s).

CAPITAL: Minsk.

LOCATION: Eastern Europe. **Boundaries**—Poland, Lithuania, Latvia, Russia, Ukraine.

AREA: 80,154 sq. mi. (207,600 sq. km.).

PHYSICAL FEATURES: Highest point—Dzerzhinskaya Mountain (1,135 ft.; 346 m.). **Lowest point**—Nyoman River (295 ft.; 90 m.). **Chief rivers**—Dnieper, Pripyat.

POPULATION: 9,900,000 (2002; annual growth –0.5%).

MAJOR LANGUAGES: Belorussian, Russian.

MAJOR RELIGIONS: Russian Orthodoxy, Roman Catholicism.

GOVERNMENT: Republic. **Head of state**—president. **Head of government**—prime minister. **Legislature**—bicameral Parliament.

CHIEF CITIES: Minsk, Brest, Gomel, Mogilev, Vitebsk.

ECONOMY: Chief minerals—oil, natural gas, peat. **Chief agricultural products**—grains, potatoes, vegetables. **Industries and products**—tractors, metal-cutting machine tools. **Chief exports**—machinery and transport equipment, chemicals. **Chief imports**—fuel, natural gas.

MONETARY UNIT: 1 Belarusian ruble = 100 kapejik.

NATIONAL HOLIDAY: July 3 (Independence Day).

Belorussian completely disappeared as a literary language between the 17th and 19th centuries, and in its modern form was standardized only after 1918. There was a revival of Belorussian literature during the 1920s, but later the Soviet regime promoted the use of Russian. The most important contemporary author in the language is historical novelist Vasil Byka, who writes primarily about the experiences of World War II.

The largest religious denomination is Russian Orthodoxy, but there are also more than 1 million Roman Catholics and still smaller minorities of Protestants, Jews, and Muslims.

The capital of Belarus is **Minsk,** which was almost completely destroyed during World War II. It has since been rebuilt, and is now a busy industrial metropolis of nearly 1.7 million people. A few old buildings have been renovated, particularly the 17th-century Orthodox cathedral, but most of the city is new, with wide streets and many parks. Today, Minsk is also the capital of the Commonwealth of Independent States, the loose confederation that replaced the Soviet Union in 1996.

Close to Minsk lies the infamous Kuropaty Forest, which made headlines in the late 1980s when mass graves of thousands of executed "enemies of the people" were discovered there. These people were the victims of the "Great Terror" unleashed by Stalin in the late 1930s.

ECONOMY

Of all the Soviet republics, Belarus suffered the greatest destruction during World War II. After the war, the economy was completely rebuilt, and Minsk, Gomel (Homel), and Mogilev (Mahilyov) became industrial centers. Transport equipment, machinery, and flax were the main products.

Southeastern Belarus was damaged by the 1986 nuclear disaster near the Ukrainian city of Chernobyl. About one-fifth of the country's soil was contaminated and thousands of farm animals had to be killed.

The Independent Belarus. Although the government has repeatedly promised economic reforms, little has been done. Privatization has been stopped, and corruption is rampant. In the late 1990s, the country was in the midst of an economic crisis, made even worse by the financial collapse of Russia. President Aleksandr Lukashenko, however, blamed the problems on a "Western campaign against the Belorussian currency."

Lukashenko has advocated a closer union with Russia for a number of years, hoping that it would boost the sagging economy of the country. A union treaty signed in 1997 envisions an eventual complete unification of Belarus with Russia.

HISTORY

The region of present-day Belarus was settled by Slavic tribes in the 6th century A.D., and several towns—including Polotsk, Turov, Minsk, and Brest—became centers of small principalities. From the 14th through the 16th centuries, the area was controlled by Lithuania; it was at that time that the distinct Belorussian ethnic community was formed.

In the late 18th century A.D., Belarus became part of Russia. Some industrialization occurred in the following century, but overall the region remained underdeveloped. This in turn led to emigration, mostly to the United States and Canada, but also to Siberia.

During World War I and immediately thereafter, Belarus was a battlefield, first between the Russian and German armies, and then between the

Belorussians have held protests in Prague (above) and else-where to call attention to repression in their homeland.

Soviets and the Poles. In January 1919, a Bolshevik Belorussian Soviet Socialist Republic was proclaimed, but the subsequent war with Poland led to the loss of its western third. The Treaty of Riga signed in March 1921 divided Belarus between the Soviet Union and Poland.

Shortly after the German attack on Poland in early September 1939 that opened World War II, Soviet armies entered Poland from the east and occupied the region that they had lost in 1921. The Germans came again in June 1941, swarming over Belarus in the first days of the attack on the Soviet Union. About 200 concentration camps were set up in the region, and one-fourth of the population died during the war.

Since the independence of Belarus in 1991, the country's leaders have continued to cling to the old Communist ideals and to court the government in the Kremlin. The winner of the July 1994 presidential elections in Belarus was Aleksandr Lukashenko, who has become increasingly dictatorial. In what observers claim to be a clearly fraudulent election, Lukashenko won a second five-year term in 2001.

In comparison with the old Communist regimes, however, there is a little bit more maneuvering space for independent opinion and opposition groups. In the early 2000s, there existed nine opposition parties, about 500 nongovernmental organizations, and some independent media; all are harassed and therefore operate somewhat secretly. Some of Lukashenko's critics have mysteriously disappeared, but there have also been antigovernment demonstrations that the police tolerated—especially in 2000 and 2001—and numerous contacts continue with journalists and politicians from abroad.

Belarus was one of the four Soviet republics with nuclear weapons on its soil. Although the president halted their removal in 1995, declaring that if NATO was enlarged towards the east, nuclear missiles would remain in Belarus, they were subsequently withdrawn.

GOVERNMENT

A new constitution was adopted by Belarus in March 1994. Amendments approved in a referendum in 1996 greatly increased presidential powers. The bicameral parliament, on the other hand, has been rendered quite powerless.

IRINA RYBACEK / Reviewed by EDWARD W. WALKER, Ph.D., Columbia University

MOLDOVA

Moldova's hilly land and moderate climate favor the cultivation of grapes and tobacco.

An heir of the medieval principality of Moldavia, the present-day Moldova is one of the successor states of the former Soviet Union. Before 1918, the region was part of Russia; then, until 1940, it was part of Romania. After World War II, Moldova reverted to the Soviet Union as one of its constituent republics—the second-smallest in area, but with the highest population density. In late 1991, Moldova became independent.

The initial post-independence years looked promising, but within a decade, Moldova turned from one of the more prosperous Soviet republics into one of the poorest countries in Europe, as well as the former Soviet Union. For most Moldovans, democracy has come to mean corruption, crime, and a sharp decline in living standards. These factors have some citizens yearning for the bygone days of the Communist era.

THE LAND

Moldova, a landlocked country, borders Romania on the west and Ukraine on the north, south, and east. Most of its territory is low-lying hilly land, with deep valleys and steep forested slopes. The climate is moderately continental, with mild winters and pleasant autumns. Rainfall is irregular; long dry periods are common, especially in the south.

Moldova lies between two large rivers, the Prut in the west, which forms the border with Romania, and the Dniester in the east. The latter originates in Ukraine and is navigable for most of its course through Moldova. The Prut joins the Danube a few miles after it leaves Moldovan territory in the south. The Trans-Dniester region was attached to Moldova after World War II, although it historically belonged to Ukraine.

THE PEOPLE

About two-thirds of the population consists of Moldovans; the remaining third is composed mostly of Ukrainians and Russians. Only minute differences in accent and vocabulary distinguish the Moldovan language from Romanian. It is a Romance language, derived from Latin. During the Soviet era, Moldovan was written in Cyrillic, but the Latin script was reintroduced in 1989.

There is a small minority of Turkic people known as Gagauz, who number about 150,000 and live mostly around Komrat in the southern region of the country. In 1994, the Gagauz were granted autonomy and their language gained official status.

Way of Life. Folk dancing and music are popular in Moldova, and several orchestras and groups (such as the Doina Choir and Zhok Folk Dance) have become internationally known. One orchestra, called Fluierash, uses rare ancient instruments, including a type of bagpipe and an ancient clarinet. As in other Eastern European countries, however, Western music is becoming increasingly popular with young people.

Education. In the late 19th century, most of the gentry was Russified, and many of the peasants were illiterate. During the interwar period, when Moldova formed part of Romania, only one institution of higher education existed in the country—a teacher-training college. Despite the ideological brainwashing of the Soviet era, Moldova made significant educational progress, particularly in technical fields. A large percentage of Soviet scientists were Moldovan by origin.

Cities. The capital of the republic is **Chişinău** (formerly known as Kishinev), a modern city of about 750,000. Moldova's second-largest city is **Tiraspol,** an industrial center. The city of **Bendery,** founded in the 15th century by Genoese traders, is a center of industry and a military base.

ECONOMY

After World War II, plants producing tractors, building materials, and textiles were constructed, but the leading industry was food processing. During the Soviet era, Moldova supplied about one-fifth of all the wine and one-third of all the tobacco consumed in the country. There were also many high-tech plants serving space and submarine programs.

During the 1990s, the economic situation went downhill, and the Russian financial crisis of 1998 further compounded the country's predicament. Subsistence farming and wine sales are now the mainstays of the economy, but most rural people are destitute.

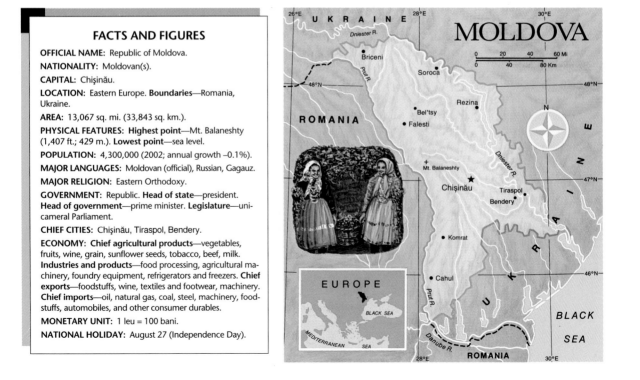

FACTS AND FIGURES

OFFICIAL NAME: Republic of Moldova.

NATIONALITY: Moldovan(s).

CAPITAL: Chişinău.

LOCATION: Eastern Europe. **Boundaries**—Romania, Ukraine.

AREA: 13,067 sq. mi. (33,843 sq. km.).

PHYSICAL FEATURES: Highest point—Mt. Balaneshty (1,407 ft.; 429 m.). **Lowest point**—sea level.

POPULATION: 4,300,000 (2002; annual growth –0.1%).

MAJOR LANGUAGES: Moldovan (official), Russian, Gagauz.

MAJOR RELIGION: Eastern Orthodoxy.

GOVERNMENT: Republic. **Head of state**—president. **Head of government**—prime minister. **Legislature**—unicameral Parliament.

CHIEF CITIES: Chişinău, Tiraspol, Bendery.

ECONOMY: Chief agricultural products—vegetables, fruits, wine, grain, sunflower seeds, tobacco, beef, milk. **Industries and products**—food processing, agricultural machinery, foundry equipment, refrigerators and freezers. **Chief exports**—foodstuffs, wine, textiles and footwear, machinery. **Chief imports**—oil, natural gas, coal, steel, machinery, foodstuffs, automobiles, and other consumer durables.

MONETARY UNIT: 1 leu = 100 bani.

NATIONAL HOLIDAY: August 27 (Independence Day).

HISTORY

Moldova, formerly called Moldavia, lies within the region of ancient Scythia and Dacia. After the 14th century, Moldova was known as Bessarabia, probably after the medieval Vlach dynasty of Bassarab. The historical Bessarabia also included the area between present-day Moldova and the Black Sea.

Russia played an important role in Moldavia's history starting in the early 18th century, during the reign of Peter I (the Great). A century later, the Treaty of Bucharest sealed the Russian ascendancy. Throughout much of the 19th century, Moldavia had a certain degree of local autonomy, but Russification was pervasive. Moldavian nationalism began to appear in the late 19th century.

During the civil war that followed the Bolshevik takeover, Moldavian nationalists succeeded in shaking off Russian rule, and Bessarabia became part of Romania. The region was economically neglected, however, and did not become integrated into Romania proper. The former Soviet Union never relinquished its claim over the area, and, in August 1940, it invaded Bessarabia and set up the Moldavian Soviet Socialist Republic. A year later, the region was reoccupied by Romania, Germany's ally, but in 1944, the Russians again took control. The peace treaty of February 1947 between the Soviet Union and Romania confirmed the new borders.

Moldavia Becomes Moldova. In 1990, Moldavian nationalists renamed the republic Moldova and declared its sovereignty. Full independence came in late 1991. In the early period of the new statehood, Moldova's reunification with Romania was often discussed, but the radical anticommunist nationalists who imagined a union with their Romanian kin were rejected by the majority of the population. In a March 1994 referendum, 95 percent voted for Moldovan independence.

Mircea Snegur, a former Communist official who adopted a moderate nationalist platform, was elected president in December 1991, and was then reelected in 1994. In 1998 and 1999, a center-right government was briefly in power, but it ultimately collapsed. In early 2001, the Communists were voted back into power, and President Vladimir Voronin—himself an ethnic Russian—promised to bring Moldova toward a much-closer union with Russia. His government tried to make Russian a mandatory language to be taught in schools, but in spring 2002, huge two-month-long demonstrations forced the authorities to forego this plan.

Trans-Dniester Republic. In late 1990, the predominantly Ukrainian and Russian population of the left bank of the Dniester proclaimed an autonomous Trans-Dniester Republic. This important region contains about 40 percent of the country's industry. After months of tension, fighting erupted in March 1992. By July, when a peacekeeping agreement was signed, some 700 people had been killed, and 50,000 had become refugees. Although a treaty calling for the withdrawal of 15,000 Russian troops was concluded in October 1994, Russian soldiers remained in Moldova in 2002. The region's final status has not yet been decided.

GOVERNMENT

According to the new post-Communist constitution, adopted in July 1994, Moldova is a "presidential parliamentary republic." The legislative power is vested in a 104-member unicameral Parliament.

IRINA RYBACEK / Reviewed by EDWARD W. WALKER, Ph.D., Columbia University

ILLUSTRATION CREDITS

The following list credits, according to page, the sources of illustration used in volume 4 of LANDS AND PEOPLES. The credits are listed illustration by illustration—top to bottom, left to right. Where necessary, the name of the photographer or artist has been listed with the source, the two separated by a dash. If two or more illustrations appear on the same page, their credits are separated by semicolons.

1 © Chip & Rosa Maria de la Cueva Peterson
3 © Ian Yeomans/Woodfin Camp & Assoc.
6 © Harry Griffiths/Photo Researchers
7 © E. Preau/Sygma
8 © Yoshiaki Matsuda/FPG Int.
9 Herbert Fristedt
10 © Chip & Rosa Maria de la Cueva Peterson
13 Multi-Media Photography, Inc.
14 Multi-Media Photography, Inc.
15 Carlsberg Breweries
17 Multi-Media Photography, Inc.
18 © Weinberg-Clark/The Image Bank; Susan Heimann
19 Ernst Z. Rothkopf
21 S. E. Hedin
23 Norwegian Embassy Information Service
24 Norwegian Embassy Information Service
27 Mulvey-Crump Associates, Inc.
29 E. C. Johnson—Leo deWys Inc.
30 © J. Messerschmidt/Leo deWys Inc.
31 © Steve Vidler/Leo deWys Inc.
32 © J. Messerschmidt/Leo deWys Inc.
33 Multi-Media Photography, Inc.
35 Mulvey-Crump Associates, Inc.
36 Art Resource; Floyd Norgaard—Lenstour Photo Service
38 Henry I. Kurtz
42 © M. Desjardins/Photo Researchers
43 © Swedish Tourist Board, New York
44 Jerry Frank
45 Marvin Newman/Multi-Media Photography, Inc.
46 © J. Braennhage/Leo deWys Inc.
47 Herbest Fristedt
49 S. E. Hedin
51 Pete Turner
52 Multi-Media Photography, Inc.
53 I. Holmasen/Ostman Agency
54 © Jim Pickerell/Black Star
56 © Mike Yamashita/Woodfin Camp
59 © F. Gohier/Photo Researchers
60 © Jim Pickerel/Black Star; Sven Samelius/Ostman Agency
61 Multi-Media Photography, Inc.; Kay Honkanen/Ostman Agency
62 © Pete Turner
63 © Floyd Norgaard/Lenstour Photo Service
65 © Robert Frerck/Click, Chicago
66 © Robert Frerck/Odyssey Productions
67 V. Lefteroff/Leo deWys Inc.
69 Douglas Lyttle
70 © Michael Howard/Leo deWys Inc.
73 © Robert Frerck/Odyssey Productions
74 Jerry Frank
76 J. Blatter/F. & N. Schwitter Library
79 © Victor Englebert
82 Dick Huffman/Monkmeyer Press Photo Service
83 Victor Englebert
84 © Steve Vidler/Leo deWys Inc.
85 © Joachim Messerschmidt/Leo deWys Inc.
87 © Robert Frerck/Odyssey Productions
88 © Robert Frerck/Odyssey Productions
90 © Mike Busselle/Leo deWys Inc.
91 © Sipa Pool-Vladimir Sichov/Sipa
93 Charles Shapp; © Nik Wheeler/Black Star
95 © Robert Frerck/The Stock Market
96 © Robert Frerck/The Stock Market
96 Alan Band Associates
97 Jerry Frank
99 The Metropolitan Museum of Art, Bequest of Mrs. H. O. Havemeyer, 1929. H. O. Havemeyer Collection
100 Hans Hanau/Rapho Guillumette Pictures; The Metropolitan Museum of Art, Bequest

of Mrs. H. O. Havemeyer, 1929. H. O. Havemeyer Collection
101 Art Resource
102 Alan Band Associates
103 Katherine Young
104 Virginia Carleton/Art Resource
105 © Robert Frerck/Odyssey Productions
106 © J. Pavlovsky/Sygma
107 © Robert Frerck/Odyssey Productions
108 © Robert Frerck/The Stock Market
109 © Robert Frerck/The Stock Market
111 © Robert Frerck/Odyssey Productions
112 © Robert Frerck/Odyssey Productions
114 Fritz Henle/Photo Researchers
117 © Steve Vidler/Leo deWys Inc.
119 Archivo Mateu
120 Archivo Mateu; Duchscherer/Monkmeyer Press Photo Service
123 Mulvey-Crump Associates, Inc.
124 © Steve Vidler/Leo deWys Inc.
126 © Leo deWys Inc.
127 Diversified Map Company
128 © Lael Morgan/Click-Chicago
129 © Arthur Hustwitt/Leo deWys Inc.
130 Bettina Cirone
131 Renzo Cantagalli
132 Renzo Cantagalli
133 Grolier Photo Library
135 Renzo Cantagalli
137 © Cotton Coulson/Woodfin Camp & Assoc.
139 Renzo Cantagalli
140 © John G. Ross/Photo Researchers
141 © Alfred Tessi/The Image Bank
142 Art Resource
143 Alan Shayne/Photo Researchers
144 © Randy Wells/The Stock Market
145 © Giorgio Ricatto/Shostal/Superstock
146 Douglas Lyttle
147 Susan Heimann
148 © Monkmeyer Press Photo Service
149 F. & N. Schwitter Library
150 Herbert Fristedt
151 © Roberto Koch, Contrasto from Picture Group
152 © Piergiorgio Sclarandis/Black Star
155 Grolier Photo Library
157 Charles Shapp
159 Herbert Fristedt
161 Charles Shapp
163 Gianni Tortoli/Photo Researchers
164 Mulvey-Crump Associates, Inc.
166 © D. Brogioni/Picture Group
168 © Shostal/Superstock
169 © M. Courtney-Clarke/Photo Researchers
171 © Cotton Coulson/Woodfin Camp & Assoc.
172 © Robert Frerck/Woodfin Camp & Assoc.
173 © J. Messerschmidt/Bruce Colemen Inc.
174 A. Earle Harrington
176 F. & N. Schwitter Library
177 © Stefano Rellandini/Reuters/TimePix
178 © Dan Budnik/Woodfin Camp & Associates
179 © Dave Bartruff/Danita Delimont, Agent
180 © Allesandro Bianchi/AP/Wide World Photos; © Ben Mangor/SuperStock
181 Andrew Medichini/AP/Wide World Photos
182 © D. Rawson/Photo Researchers
185 © Art Resource
186 Linda Bartlett
187 © Grolier, Inc.
189 © Chuck O'Rear/Woodfin Camp & Assoc.
190 © Comstock
191 © Harry S. Zolindakis
192 Michael A. Vaccaro
193 © Susan McCartney/Photo Researchers
194 © Klaus D. Francke/The Stock Market

196 G. Tomisch/Photo Researchers
197 Stern/Monkmeyer Press Photo Service
198 Art Resource
199 © Michael Howard/Leo deWys Inc.
200 © Harry S. Zolindakis
201 © Steve Vidler/Leo deWys Inc.
202 Art Resource
203 © Harry S. Zolindakis
204 © Harry S. Zolindakis
207 Harrison Forman
208 © Ray Manley/Shostal/Superstock
209 FPG/Benachi
210 © Harry S. Zolindakis
211 © Harry S. Zolindakis
212 © Chris Niedenthal/Black Star
213 © Momatiuk/Eastcott/Woodfin Camp & Assoc.
216 © Susan McCartney/Photo Researchers
217 © Wendy Chan/The Image Bank
218 © Chuck Fishman/Woodfin Camp & Assoc.
219 © Piotr Malecki/Gamma Liaison
221 S. E. Hedin
223 © Philppot/Sygma
224 © Libor Hajsky/CTK Photo
227 © Saskia Bergerova/CTK Photo
228 © Michal Krumphanzl/CTK Photo
230 AP/Wide World Photos
231 © Chip Hires/Gamma-Liaison
232 © Jana Misauerova/CTK Photo
233 © Chip Hires/Gamma-Liaison
236 S. E. Hedin/Ostman Agency
237 S. E. Hedin/Ostman Agency
238 S. E. Hedin/Ostman Agency
241 © Bill Weems/Woodfin Camp & Assoc.
243 © Albert Moldavy/Eriako Associates
244 Art Resource
246 © Bill Weems/Woodfin Camp & Assoc.
248 © Shostal/Superstock
249 © Editura Ştiinţifică şl Enciclopedică
250 © Editura Ştiinţifică şl Enciclopedică
253 © Shepard Sherbell/SABA
254 © Dorigney/Rea/SABA
258 © Kurt Scholz/Superstock
259 © Margot Granitsas
260 © Adam Woolfitt/Woodfin Camp & Assoc.
262 Bulgarian Tourist Office
263 © Kurt Scholz/Superstock
264 © Adam Woolfitt/Woodfin Camp & Assoc.
266 © David Burnett/Leo deWys Inc.
267 © Margot Granitsas/Photo Researchers
268 © Harry Redl/Black Star
269 © Paolo Koch/Photo Researchers
273 © François Lehr/Sipa
274 © Alon Reininger/Woodfin Camp & Assoc.
277 © Porterfield-Chickering/Photo Researchers
278 © Stanislav Zbynek/CTK Photo
281 © Peternek/SABA
282 © Horvat/SABA
285 © Robert Frerck/Odyssey Productions
288 © Laurent Van Der Stockt/Gamma-Liaison
291 © Voja Miladinovic/Sipa Press
293 © Jim & Mary Whitmer
295 © Ints Kalnin/Woodfin Camp & Assoc.
297 © Janis Miglavs
299 © Sovfoto
301 © Amanda Merullo/Stock Boston
305 © David Berkwitz/Sipa
307 © Wolfgang Kaehler
308 © Nicolas Vannier/Gamma-Liaison; Inge Morath/Magnum Photos
309 © Jacek Palkiewicz/Gamma-Liaison
310 © Sichov/Sipa
311 S. E. Hedin/Ostman Agency
312 Editorial Photocolor Archives, N.Y.
313 © Frank Siteman/Stock, Boston
315 © Miro Vintoniv/Stock, Boston

HOW TO USE THE INDEX

In this index, the headings of all entries are in boldface type. Headings which are titles of articles are in all capital letters. The headings, including those of more than one word, are alphabetized letter by letter, as in a dictionary.

> **NEW ENGLAND**
> **Newfoundland**
> **Northeast Passage**
> **NORTHERN IRELAND**
> **Northmen**

Names of persons are listed under the surname, followed by the first name. When there are two or more persons with the same surname, the names are listed alphabetically according to the first name.

> **Smith, Adam**
> **Smith, Ian Douglas**
> **Smith, Joseph**

Rulers of the same name are listed alphabetically by country. Roman numerals are listed numerically under each individual country.

> **Charles I** (king of England)
> **Charles II** (king of England)
> **Charles VII** (king of France)
> **Charles V** (Holy Roman emperor)
> **Charles II** (king of Spain)
> **Charles IV** (king of Spain)

Names of mountains and lakes are inverted.

> **Chad, Lake**
> **Erie, Lake**
> **Everest, Mount**
> **McKinley, Mount**

But when "Mount," "Lake," or "Fort" is used in the name of a place or town, it is entered directly.

> **Fort Smith** (Arkansas)
> **Fort Worth** (Texas)
> **Lake Placid** (resort town, New York)
> **Mount Desert Isle** (Maine)

Inverted headings are alphabetized up to the comma. If the headings are identical up to the comma, alphabetization is determined by the word or words following the comma.

> **Paris, Treaty of**
> **Paris Commune**
> **Victoria, Lake**
> **Victoria Falls**

Mac and Mc are entered as Mac and Mc, and are listed in their alphabetical positions.

> **Mackenzie, Sir Alexander**
> **MacMahon, Patrice de**
> **Mboya, Tom**
> **McKinley, Mount**

In place names, "St." is interfiled with "Saint."

> **St. George** (Bermuda)
> **Saint Lawrence, Gulf of**
> **St. Louis** (Missouri)

Names of saints are entered under the personal name when the saint is better known by that name; otherwise they are entered under the surname.

> **Paul, Saint**
> **Xavier, Saint Francis**

Life dates are given for personal names when needed to differentiate between two persons of the same name.

> **Augustine, Saint** (died 604; 1st archbishop of Canterbury)
> **Augustine, Saint** (354-430; church father)

Matter in parentheses is disregarded in alphabetizing, except when used to distinguish identical headings.

> **New Amsterdam** (Dutch settlement in America, now New York City)
> **New Amsterdam** (Guyana)
> **Pearl Harbor**
> **Pearl River** (Mississippi)
> **Pearl (ZHU) River** (China)

Cross-references are of two kinds, See and See also. Both refer to Index entries.

See references are from an alternative heading of a subject to the ones under which the subject is indexed.

> **American Indians** see Indians of Central and South America; Indians of North America
> **Bolshevik Revolution** see Russian Revolution and Civil War

See also references refer to headings under which additional or related matter can be found.

> **Antilles**
> see also Greater Antilles; Lesser Antilles
> **CANADA**
> see also names of provinces, territories, cities

• • • D • • •

• • • O • • •

• • • T • • •

• • • U • • •